The Directory of

Scottish Government

●

2010

D0994180

ISBN 978-1-905332-26-7   ISSN 1465-4776
©2010 Carlton Publishing and Printing Ltd. All Rights Reserved.

Carlton Publishing and Printing Ltd
Maple House, Maple View, Steeds Lane
Kingsnorth, Kent, TN26 1NQ
$G_{7} IF T$
Tel: (01923) 800801 *Fax:* (01923) 800802
E-mail: info@carlton-group.co.uk
Web: www.carlton-group.co.uk

CONTENTS

CONTENTS

INTRODUCTION

This is the eleventh edition of The Directory of Scottish Government. The Directory is a consumer's guide to the many individuals and bodies that contribute to the governance of Scotland, including MSPs, MPs, MEPs, executive agencies, public bodies, health bodies and local authorities.

The Directory of Scottish Government reflects the same priorities – accessibility of content and clarity in presentation – as its companion works. These companion works are: *The Directory of Westminster & Whitehall, The Directory of Executive Agencies & Public Bodies – "Quangos" and The Directory of Northern Ireland Government.*

We are most grateful to all those who have supplied the information – responsibilities, names, CVs, office addresses, telephone, fax numbers, E-mail addresses and web sites etc – that are contained within this publication.

I should also like to thank those involved in researching and producing this book, for making it as accurate and up-to-date as possible. Their wider reward lies in the contribution this book makes to the openness and accessibility of government.

Imogen Carlton

(Editor)

CIVIL SOCIETY / VOLUNTARY SECTOR

✦ SCOTTISH CHURCHES PARLIAMENTARY OFFICE

at the Scottish Storytelling Centre
43-45 High Street
Edinburgh, EH1 1SR
   Tel: (0131) 558 8137
   E-mail: graham@actsparl.org
   Web: www.actsparl.org
Contact: Graham Blount
Position: Parliamentary Officer

Churches are active in every kind of community in Scotland, in ways ranging from personal caring and support, to a wide variety of local and national projects. They have a strong commitment to building on that experience, through tough thinking and faithful reflection. The SCPO exists to help the churches engage, on that basis, with the Scottish Parliament and Executive, through updates and briefings and by bringing people together for dialogue.

CONSTITUTIONAL AFFAIRS

✦ ELECTORAL REFORM SOCIETY

6 Chancel Street
London SE1 0UU
   Tel: (020) 7928 1622
   Fax: (020) 7401 7789
   E-mail: ers@electoral-reform.org.uk
   Web: www.electoral-reform.org.uk
Contact: Ken Ritchie
Position: Chief Executive

The Society campaigns for the strengthening of our democracy, particularly through electoral systems which increase voter choice, provide representation to all significant opinions and ensure the accountability of elected representatives. It also provides information and educational services on electoral issues. The Electoral Reform Society has supported 'Fairshare', the Scottish cross-party campaign for the use of the Single Transferable Vote (STV) electoral system and in 2007 opened an office in Edinburgh to promote understanding of the system.

The Society has two subsidiaries: Electoral Reform Services (020 8365 8909) which conducts and advises on ballots and market research, and Electoral Reform International Services (020 7620 3794) which provides electoral assistance in Africa, Asia, Latin America and eastern Europe. The Society's associated charity, the McDougall Trust, produces the journal 'Representation'.

Scottish Parliament

SCOTTISH PARLIAMENT

INTRODUCTORY NOTE

Functions and Powers

The Scottish Parliament has the power to legislate on devolved matters in Scotland. In addition to public legislation, it can also pass private legislation in devolved areas. The Scottish Executive is accountable to the Scottish Parliament (in a way similar to that in which the UK Government is accountable to the UK Parliament).

The Parliament also oversees the operation of Scottish public bodies and of other public bodies in so far as they relate to devolved matters.

The Scottish Parliament has its own committees on a range of matters.

The Scottish Parliament has the power to vary the standard rate of income tax set by the UK Parliament. It can increase or decrease the standard rate by up to 3p. Liability to payment will be determined by residency. Under present arrangements, dividend and savings income would not be affected.

All matters not specifically reserved to the UK Parliament and Government are devolved. Devolved areas include various aspects of policy relating to agriculture, fisheries and food; the arts; economic development; education and training; the environment; health; home affairs and the law; housing; local government; social work; sport; and transport. (For a fuller list of devolved responsibilities see pp9-10 below).

There are certain matters which are, however, reserved to the UK Parliament and Government. These relate principally to defence, foreign affairs, central economic and fiscal policies, social security, border controls and immigration. (For a fuller list of reserved responsibilities, see pp10-12 below).

The Parliament assumed full legislative powers on 1st July 1999, and first met on 12th May 1999.

Scottish Parliamentary Elections

The Parliament has 129 members. 73 members of the Scottish Parliament (MSPs) are elected on a 'first past-the-post' basis to represent individual constituencies. A further 56 additional members are elected on a "topping-up" basis, seven from each of eight regions.

In Scottish Parliamentary elections, each elector can cast two votes – one for a constituency representative and one for a political party or for a candidate standing as an individual. The regional seats are allocated on the basis of the total party votes for each region; - but taking account of the number of constituency seats won by parties in the region. In effect, this is a "topping-up" process to give an overall result in terms of seats which reflects more closely the votes cast for parties.

SCOTTISH PARLIAMENT

Entitlement to 'additional member' seats is calculated initially by dividing the number of votes for each party by the number of constituency seats won in the region, plus one. The party with the highest total is then allocated the first seat. The process then continues, including any additional member seats already won in the calculation, until all seven seats have been allocated. The individuals are chosen according to their position on their respective party lists (but excluding any who have already been elected on a constituency basis).

The first elections were held on Thursday 6th May 1999; the second on 1st May 2003. The third elections were held on Thursday 3rd May 2007.

Meetings of the Parliament
The Parliament meets in the new parliament building at the bottom of the Royal Mile, opposite Holyrood Palace, Edinburgh. The Committees meet in the Parliament's Committee Chambers in the same building, which has been in use since September 2004.

The Parliament tends to meet on Wednesday afternoons and all day on Thursdays.

The main body of the Parliament does not meet when Committees of the Parliament are sitting: – usually on Tuesday and Wednesday mornings. There are also weeks when the Parliament is in recess and does not meet.

CONTACTING MSPs AND THE PARLIAMENT

The address of the Scottish Parliament is:

Scottish Parliament, Edinburgh, EH99 1SP
Tel: (0131) 348 5000 or (0845) 278 1999 *(Local Rate)*
Fax: (0131) 348 5601
E-mail: firstname.surname.msp@scottish.parliament.uk
Web: www.scottish.parliament.uk

Note: The Public Information Service of the Parliament is at the same address and telephone; but the email address is: sp.info@scottish.parliament.uk

SCOTTISH PARLIAMENT

DEVOLVED MATTERS

All matters not specifically reserved to the UK Parliament and Government are regarded as devolved to the Scottish Parliament and Executive. These include the following:

Agriculture
Including implementation of measures under the Common Agricultural Policy; domestic agriculture (including crofting, animal and plant welfare); food standards; forestry; fisheries (including implementation of measures under the Common Fisheries Policy, domestic fisheries and aquaculture).

Economic Development
Including enterprise companies; financial assistance to industry (subject to UK guidelines and consultation); inward investment; promotion of trade and exports; promotion of tourism.

Education and Training
Including pre-school and school education; school inspection; the supply, training and conditions of service of teachers; further and higher education (including policy, funding and student support); science and research funding (except for UK Research Councils); training policy and lifelong learning; vocational qualifications; careers advice and guidance.

Environment
Including environmental protection; air, land and water pollution; water supplies and sewerage; promotion of sustainable development (within international commitments agreed by the UK); natural heritage and countryside issues; built heritage, (including historic buildings/monuments); flood prevention, coastal protection and reservoir safety.

Health
Including overall responsibility for the NHS in Scotland and for public and mental health; education and training of health professionals; terms and conditions of NHS staff and GPs.

Home Affairs and the Law
Including the criminal justice and prosecution system; the civil and criminal courts; tribunals concerned with devolved matters; criminal law and procedure (except for offences created in statute law relating to reserved matters, including drugs and firearms); civil law (except in relation to reserved matters); electoral law in relation to local government elections; judicial appointments (except for the Lord President of the Court of Session and the Lord Justice Clerk, which are Crown appointments made on the advice of the Prime Minister following nominations from the Scottish Executive); legal aid; the parole system; prisons and treatment of offenders; police and fire services (including fire safety); civil defence and emergency planning; liquor licensing; protection of animals; functions under international agreements in devolved areas (e.g child abduction, reciprocal enforcement of maintainance orders).

Devolved Matters (Continued)

Housing and Local Government
Including policy and framework for Scottish local government; local finance and domestic/non-domestic taxation; housing issues and policy (including Communities Scotland); area regeneration (including designation of enterprise zones); land-use planning and building control.

Social Work
Including the Children's Hearings system and voluntary sector issues.

Sport and the Arts
Including the Scottish Sports Council and various national bodies relating to the arts, libraries museum and galleries in Scotland; also support for the Gaelic language.

Transport
Passenger and road transport, including the Scottish road network, road safety; policy on buses; concessionary fares; cycling; taxis and minicabs; disability and transport (non-technical aspects); some rail grant powers; Strathclyde PTE; consultation arrangements in public transport; "appropriate" powers relating to air and sea transport (covering ports, harbours, piers, freight shipping and ferry services, Highland and Island airports, other planning and environmental issues relating to airports); inland waterways.

Other Matters
Including statistics, public registers and records.

RESERVED MATTERS

Certain matters are restricted to the UK Parliament and Government, for which they continue to be responsible. These include, in particular:

UK Constitutional Matters
Including the Crown, UK Parliament, electoral law (except local government), civil service, honours and awards.

Defence and National Security
Including the armed forces, security services, treason, provisions for dealing with terrorism and subversion.

Foreign Policy
Including conclusion of European Union and international agreements in reserved and devolved areas; also international development issues.

Reserved Matters (Continued)

Border Controls and Protection
Including designation of UK land and maritime borders and fisheries limits, immigration and nationality, extradition; also criminal law relating to drugs and firearms.

Economic, Fiscal and Trade Matters
Overall economic policy, including macro-economic, monetary and fiscal affairs (except for tax varying and local taxation powers); granting of UK tax concessions; the currency; common markets for UK goods and services, including company law, corporate insolvency and intellectual property; regulation of financial institutions; competition policy (but with rights for representation of Scottish interests); international trade policy (including export credit guarantees); consumer protection; also regulation of energy supply industries, telecommunications, pharmaceutical prices, weights, and measures, and other standards.

Employment Legislation
Including industrial relations, equal opportunities, health and safety, and the employment service.

Equality Legislation
Covering racial, gender and disability discrimination.

Social Security
Including benefits, contributions, child support, occupational and personal pension regulation

Transport Safety and Regulation
Including regulation of aviation, shipping, marine and air safety; aspects of rail safety and regulation (including accident prevention and investigation); also some aspects of road traffic regulation (including driver and vehicle licensing and testing, road haulage, vehicle standards and general speed limits).

Certain matters relating to Culture/Media
Including regulatory framework for broadcasting and film classification and distribution of videos; licensing of theatres and cinemas; gambling (including the National Lottery); some cultural property matters.

Certain matters relating to Health
Including abortion, human fertilisation and embryology, genetics, xenotransplantation and vivisection; also control/safety of medicines and reciprocal health agreements.

SCOTTISH PARLIAMENT

Reserved Matters (Continued)

Regulation of Certain Professions
Including medical, dental nursing and other health professions; also vets, architects, auditors, estates agents, insolvency practitioners, insurance intermediaries; additionally matters relating to the Civil Service Commissioners, UK Senior Salaries Review Body, and primary legislation in respect of public service pensions.

Other Matters
Including UK Research Councils, nuclear safety, the Ordnance Survey and data protection.

Joint Ministerial Committee
A Joint Ministerial Committee comprising representatives of the UK Government and the devolved administrations, (including the Scottish Executive) discusses matters of common interest, including those where there may be an overlap of responsibilities.

There are also a number of concordats – non statutory agreements – on certain matters between the UK Government and the devolved administrations.

COMPOSITION OF THE PARLIAMENT

The composition of the Parliament is:

Party	Constituency MSPs	Regional MSPs	Total MSPs
Conservative	3	13	16
Green	-	2	2
Labour	37	9	46
Liberal Democrat	11	5	16
SNP	21	26	47
Independent (Margo MacDonald)	-	1	1
Presiding Officer (Alex Fergusson)	1	-	1
Totals	**74**	**55**	**129**

Note: The above figures include Alex Fergusson MSP who stood as a Conservative but who, as Presiding Officer, renounces party political allegiance while holding that post. The Deputy Presiding Officers participate and vote fully in the Parliament when not in the chair.

✦ WEST LOTHIAN DRUG AND ALCOHOL SERVICE
43 Adelaide Street, Craigshill, Livingston, EH54 5HQ
Tel: (01506) 430225
Fax: (01506) 441939
E mail: enquiries@wldas.org

Contact:
Margot Ferguson – *General Manager*

The West Lothian Drug and Alcohol Service is a voluntary organisation, which has an excellent reputation for preventative and caring services in drugs, alcohol, tobacco, HIV/AIDS and sexual health, including:

* Training and consultation for professional workers, students and commercial sector
* Education for young people and wider community
* Counselling and Support for individuals and their families
* Information and Health Promotion materials
* Employment, Training and Education Opportunities for Drug Misusers
* Dedicated Counselling for Young People
* Smoking Cessation Services

Notes: (i) For directly elected constituency members, the name of the constituency is given alongside their name, with the size of majority shown below. For additional members, the name of the region is given, with the count on which they were elected shown below.

(ii) The following abbreviations for political parties are used:
Scot Cons – Scottish Conservative Party
Scot Grn - Scottish Green Party
Scot Lab – Scottish Labour Party
Scot Lib Dem – Scottish Liberal Democrat Party
SNP – Scottish National Party
(iii) Offices Held refers to offices in the Scottish Parliament or Executive.
(iv) To contact the Scottish Parliament telephone (0131) 348 5000

Adam, Brian MSP . . . . Aberdeen North
SNP . . . . Majority 3,749 over Labour
Born . . . . 10th June 1948 in Newmill, Banffshire
Educated . . . . Keith Grammar School; Aberdeen University
Elected . . . . 2003 MSP for Aberdeen North (previously, 1999 - 2003, MSP for North East Scotland Region)
Constituency Office . . . . . . 825-827 Great Northern Road, Aberdeen, AB24 2BR
Tel: (01224) 789457 Fax: (01224) 695397
E-mail: brian.adam.msp@scottish.parliament.uk
Political Career . . . . 1988 - 99 SNP Group Leader, Aberdeen City Council
1999 - 2001 SNP Deputy Whip and
SNP Deputy Business Manager
2001 - 04 SNP Deputy Spokesman on
Education and Lifelong Learning
2004 - 07 Convener, Standards and Public
Appointments Committee
2005 - 07 SNP Deputy Spokesman on Tourism
2007 - SNP Chief Whip
Professional Career . . . . . . 1970 - 73 Section Leader, QA Laboratory, Glaxo, Montrose
1973 - 88 Biochemist/Senior Biochemist,
Aberdeen City Hospital
1988 - 99 Senior/Principal Biochemist,
Aberdeen Royal Infirmary

Aitken, Bill MSP . . . . .Glasgow Region
Scot Cns. . . . . List
Born . . . . 15th April 1947, Glasgow
Educated . . . . Allan Glen's School, Glasgow;
  Glasgow College of Technology
Elected . . . . 1999 MSP for Glasgow Region
Parliamentary Office . . . . . Tel: (0131) 348 5641 Fax: (0131) 348 5655
  Mobile: 07977 579262
  E-mail: bill.aitken.msp@scottish.parliament.uk
  Secretary – Mrs Sandra Robinson
  E-mail: sandra.robinson@scottish.parliament.uk
Regional Office . . . . .570 Mosspark Boulevard, Glasgow, G52 1SD
  Tel: (0141) 810 5743 Fax: (0141) 810 5987
Political Career . . . . .1975 - 77 Chairman, Scottish Young Conservatives
  1976 - 99 Councillor, Glasgow City Council
    (Convener of Licensing 1977 - 80;
    Leader of Opposition 1980 - 84, 1992 - 96)
  1999 - 2001 Conservative Spokesman on Social Justice
  1999 - 2003 Conservative Deputy Whip and Deputy
    Business Manager
  2001 - 03 Deputy Convener, Justice II Committee
  2001 - 03 Conservative Deputy Spokesman on
    Justice and Home Affairs
  2003 - 07 Conservative Chief Whip and Parliamentary
    Business Manager
  2007 - Conservative Shadow Cabinet Secretary for Justice
  2007 - Convener, Justice Committee
Professional Career . . . . . .Insurance Underwriter
Language Spoken . . . . . . .French
Parliamentary Interests . . .Finance; Home Affairs; Local Government; Justice
Leisure Interests . . . . .Football; Foreign Travel; Reading; Walking

Alexander, Wendy MSP. . . Paisley North
Scot Lab. . . . . Majority 5,113 over SNP
Born . . . . 27th June 1963 in Glasgow
Educated . . . . Park Mains High School;
Erskine and Pearson College, Canada;
Glasgow University; Warwick University;
INSEAD, France
Elected . . . . 1999 MSP for Paisley North
Parliamentary Office . . . . . Tel: (0131) 348 5852 Fax: (0131) 348 6949
E-mail: wendy.alexander.msp@scottish.parliament.uk
Constituency Office . . . . . . Abbey Mill Business Centre, Mile End, 12 Seedhill Road,
Paisley, PA1 1JS
Tel: (0141) 560 1025 Fax: (0141) 560 1026
PA – Ms Lorraine McFarlane
E-mail: lorraine.mcfarlane@scottish.parliament.uk
Secretary – Mrs Lorraine Haxton
Political Career . . . . .1999 - 2000 Minister for Communities
2000 - 01 Minister for Enterprise and Lifelong Learning
2001 - 02 Minister for Enterprise Transport and
Lifelong Learning
2007 Labour Shadow Cabinet Secretary for
Finance and Sustainable Growth
2007 - 08 Leader, Labour Party Scottish Parliament
Professional Career . . . . . .1987 - 88 Editor, LEDIS
1988 - 92 Research Officer, Scottish Labour Party
1994 - 97 Management Consultant,
Booz Allen and Hamilton
1997 - 99 Special Adviser to Secretary of State
for Scotland
Trade Union . . . . .Unite
Languages Spoken . . . . . . .French
Parliamentary Interests . . .Scotland's Economic Future; Women in Politics
Leisure Interests . . . . .Ornithology; Scotland's Islands; Swimming; Theatre
Published Books . . . . .1987: First Ladies of Medicine
2003: Chasing the Tartan Tiger
2005: New Wealth for Old Nations
2005: Donald Dewar: Scotland's First Minister

Allan, Alasdair MSP . . . . . Western Isles
SNP . . . . Majority 687 over Labour
Date of Birth . . . . 6th May 1971
Educated . . . . Aberdeen University
Elected . . . . 2007 MSP for Western Isles
Parliamentary Office . . . . . Tel: (0131) 348 6744 Fax: (0131) 348 6746
E-mail: alasdair.allan.msp@scottish.parliament.uk
Web: www.alasdairallanmsp.com
Parliamentary Assistant – Mr Alan Masterston
Tel: (0131) 348 6745
E-mail: alan.masterston@scottish.parliament.uk
Constituency Office . . . . . . 31 Bayhead, Stornoway, HS1 2DU
Tel: (01851) 702272 Fax: (01851) 701767
Office Manager – Mr Kenny MacLeod
E-mail: kenny.macleod@scottish.parliament.uk
Constituency Assistant *(Ulst and Barra)* –
Mr Bryan MacPherson
Tel: (01870) 602287
E-mail: bryan.macpherson@scottish.parliament.uk
Political Career . . . . 2003 - 06 National Secretary, SNP
2008 - Deputy Convener, Local Government and
Communities Committee
Professional Career . . . . . . Senior Media Relations Officer, Church of Scotland
Freelance Journalist
Self-employed, Alasdair Allan Enterprises
Trade Union . . . . NUJ
Languages Spoken . . . . Gaelic; Scots
Parliamentary Interests . . . Independence; Minority Languages
Leisure Interests . . . . Back District Gaelic Choir

Baillie, Jackie MSP . . . . . . Dumbarton
Scot Lab. . . . . Majority 1,611 over SNP
Born . . . . 15th January 1964 in Hong Kong
Educated . . . . St Anne's School, Windermere;
                        Cumbernauld College; Strathclyde University
Elected . . . . 1999 MSP for Dumbarton
Parliamentary Office . . . . . Tel: (0131) 348 5905 Fax: (0131) 348 5986
                        E-mail: jackie.bailie.msp@scottish.parliament.uk
Constituency Office . . . . . .125 College Street, Dumbarton, G82 1NH
                        Tel: (01389) 734214 Fax: (01389) 761498
                        Web: www.dumbarton-labour.org.uk
                        Parliamentary Assistants – Ms Anne McBride
                                       Mr Christopher McGilchrist
                                        Ms Fiona Mitchell
                    E-mails: anne.mcbride@scottish.parliament.uk
                            christopher.mcgilchrist@scottish.parliament.uk
                            fiona.mitchell@scottish.parliament.uk
Political Career . . . . .1999 - 2000 Deputy Minister for Communities
                        2000 - 01 Minister for Social Justice
                        2007 - 08 Convener, European and External Relations
                            Committee, Scottish Parliament
                        2008 - Deputy Convener, Finance Committee
Professional Career . . . . . .1986 - 87 Administrative Assistant, Ruchill
                        Unemployed Workers' Centre
                        1987 - 90 Co-ordinator, Gorbals Unemployed
                        Worker's Centre
                        1990 - 96 Resource Centre Manager,
                        Strathkelvin District Council
                        1996 - 99 Community Economic Development
                        Manager, East Dunbartonshire Council
Trade Unions . . . . .UNISON; Unite
Parliamentary Interests . . .Cross Party Groups on Learning Disability and Tackling
                        Debt; Housing and Homelessness; Social Justice;
                        Voluntary Sector
Directorships Held . . . . . . .Strathleven Regeneration Company *(non-executive)*

Baker, Claire MSP . . . . Mid Scotland and Fife Region
Scot Lab. . . . . List
Born . . . . 4th March 1971 in Fife
Educated. . . . . Beath High School, Cowdenbeath;
Edinburgh University; Glasgow University
Elected . . . . .2007 MSP for Mid Scotland and Fife Region
Parliamentary Office . . . . .Tel: (0131) 348 6759 Fax: (0131) 348 6761
E-mail: claire.baker.msp@scottish.parliament.uk
Regional Office . . . . .219 Wellesley Road, Methil, Fife, KY8 3BN
Tel: (01333) 300974 Fax: (01333) 300413
Political Career . . . . .2008 - Labour Spokesman on Further and
Higher Education
Professional Career . . . . . .2005 - 07 Policy Manager, Scottish Council for
Voluntary Organisations
Trade Union . . . . .Unite

Baker, Richard MSP . . . . . North East Scotland Region
Scot Lab . . . . List
Born. . . . . 29th May 1974 in Edinburgh
Educated. . . . . St Bees School, Cumbria; Aberdeen University
Elected . . . . .2003 MSP for North East Scotland Region
Parliamentary Offices . . . .Tel: (0131) 348 5916 Fax: (0131) 348 5979
E-mail: richard.baker.msp@scottish.parliament.uk
Researcher – Mr Gordon Aikman
E-mail: gordon.aikman@scottish.parliament.uk
Regional Office . . . . .68 Rosemount Place, Aberdeen, AB25 2XJ
Tel: (01224) 641171 Fax: (01224) 641104
Office Manager – Ms Margaret Slessor
E-mail: margaret.slessor2@scottish.parliament.uk
Political Career . . . . .2007 - 08 Labour Spokesman on Higher Education
and Student Funding
2008 Labour Chief Whip
2008 - Labour Shadow Justice Cabinet Secretary
Professional Career . . . . . .1998 - 2000 President, National Union of
Students, Scotland
2000 - 02 Press Officer, Help the Aged
2002 - 03 Research Officer, Labour MSPs
Trade Union . . . . .Unite
Leisure Interests . . . . .Acting; Choral Singing; Football

Boyack, Sarah MSP . . . . . . Edinburgh Central
Scot Lab . . . . Majority 1,193 over Liberal Democrats
Born . . . . 16th May 1961 in Glasgow
Educated . . . . Royal High School, Edinburgh;
      Glasgow University; Heriot-Watt University
Elected . . . . 1999 MSP for Edinburgh Central
Parliamentary Office . . . . . Tel: (0131) 348 5751 Fax: (0131) 348 6829
      E-mail: sarah.boyack.msp@scottish.parliament.uk
      Web: www.sarahboyack.net
Constituency Office . . . . . . 22A Rutland Square, Edinburgh, EH1 2BB
      Tel: (0131) 476 2539 Fax: (0131) 656 0368
Political Career . . . . .1999 - 2000 Minister for Transport and
      Environment
      2003 - 07 Convener, Environment and Rural
      Development Committee
      2000 - 01 Minister for Transport and Planning
      2007 - 08 Labour Shadow Minister for the Environment
      2008 - Labour Shadow Cabinet Secretary for
      Rural Affairs and Environment
Professional Career . . . . . .1986 - 88 Planning Assistant, Brent London Borough
      Council
      1988 - 92 Senior Planning Office,
      Central Regional Council, Stirling
      1992 - 99 Lecturer in Planning, Edinburgh
      College of Art
Trade Union . . . . .Educational Institute of Scotland
Professional Association . . .University Lecturers Association

Brankin, Rhona MSP . . . . . Midlothian
Scot Lab . . . . Majority 1,702 over SNP
Born . . . . 19th January 1950 in Glasgow
Educated . . . . Jordanhill College School, Glasgow; Aberdeen University;
Northern College; Moray House, Edinburgh
Elected . . . . 1999 MSP for Midlothian
Parliamentary Office . . . . . Tel: (0131) 348 5838 Fax: (0131) 348 5988
E-mail: rhona.brankin.msp@scottish.parliament.uk
Constituency Office . . . . . . PO Box 11, 95 High Street, Dalkeith,
Midlothian, EH22 1AX
Tel: (0131) 654 1585 Fax: (0131) 654 1586
Political Career . . . . 1995 - 96 Chair, Scottish Labour Party
1996 - 98 Member, Scottish Constitutional Convention
1999 - 2000 Deputy Minister for Culture and Sport
2000 - 01 Deputy Minister for Rural Development
2004 - 05 Deputy Minister for Health and
Community Care
2005 - 07 Deputy Minister for Environment and
Rural Development
2007 Minister for Communities
2007 - Labour Shadow Education and
Lifelong Learning Cabinet Secretary
Professional Career . . . . . . 1975 - 77 Teacher, Dingwall Primary School
1983 - 94 Learning Support Teacher at
Invergordon, then Alness Academy and
Inverness High School
1994 - 99 Lecturer in Special Educational Needs,
Northern College, Dundee
Languages Spoken . . . . French
Parliamentary Interests . . . Arts; Education; Architecture and Built Environment; Sport
Leisure Interests . . . . Golf; Theatre; Outdoor Pursuits

Brocklebank, Edward MSP Mid Scotland and Fife Region
Scot Cons . . . . List
Born . . . . 24th September 1942 in St Andrews
Educated . . . . Madras College, St Andrews
Elected . . . . 2003 MSP for Mid Scotland and Fife Region
Parliamentary Office . . . . . Tel: (0131) 348 5610 Fax: (0131) 348 6484
E-mail: ted.brocklebank.msp@scottish.parliament.uk
Web: www.conservativemsps.com
Parliamentary Aide – Mr Dominic Heslop
Tel: (0131) 348 5643
E-mail: dominic.heslop@scottish.parliament.uk
Press Officer – Mr Richard Forgan
Tel: (0131) 348 5619
E-mail: richard.forgan@scottish.parliament.uk
Regional Office . . . . Volunteer House, 69-73 Crossgate, Cupar,
Fife, KY15 5AS
Tel: (01334) 659200
Political Career . . . . 2003 - 05 Conservative Spokesman on Fisheries
2005 - 07 Conservative Spokesman on Rural
Development and Fisheries
2007 - Conservative Shadow Minister for Europe,
External Affairs and Culture
Professional Career . . . . . . 1960 - 1963 DC Thomson, Dundee
1963 - 1965 Freelance Journalist
1965 - 1970 Journalist, Scottish TV
1970 - 1976 GTV Reporter
1977 - 1985 GTV Head of News and Current Affairs
1985 - 1995 GTV Head of Documentaries and Features
1995 - 2003 Managing Director, Greyfriars
Productions Ltd
Trade Union . . . . NUJ
Languages Spoken . . . . French
Parliamentary Interests . . . Rural Affairs; Environment; Broadcasting; Scottish
Language and Culture
Leisure Interests . . . . Ornithology; Golf; Writing; Painting; Rugby

Brown, Gavin MSP . . . . . . Lothians Region
Scot Cons . . . . List
Born . . . . 4th June 1975
Elected . . . . 2007 MSP for Lothians Region
Parliamentary Office . . . . . Tel: (0131) 348 6931 Fax: (0131) 348 5935
    E-mail: gavin.brown.msp@scottish.parliament.uk
    Web: www.gavinbrown.org
    PA – Ms Aris Wilson
Regional Office . . . . 13 Mentone Gardens, Edinburgh, EH9 2DJ
    Tel: (0131) 662 8577
Political Career . . . . 2007 - Conservative Spokesman on Energy, Enterprise and
    Tourism
Professional Career . . . . . . Lawyer
Parliamentary Interests . . . Police; Environment; Hospitals
Leisure Interests . . . . Debating; Tae Kwon-Do
Professional Associations . . Chamber of Commerce; Institute of Directors
Directorship . . . . Speak With Impact Ltd *(Founder and Managing Director)*

Brown, Keith MSP . . . . . Ochil
SNP . . . . Majority 490 over Lab
Born . . . . 20th December 1961
Educated . . . . Tynecastle High School, Edinburgh;
    University of Dundee;
    Prince Edward Institute, Ontario
Elected . . . . 2007 MSP for Ochil
Parliamentary Office. . . . . Tel: (0131) 348 6335 Fax: (0131) 348 6336
    E-mail: keith.brown.msp@scottish.parliament.uk
    Web: www.keithbrownmsp.com
Constituency Office. . . . . . 80 Mill Street, Alloa, FK10 1DY
    Tel: (01259) 219333
    Constituency Manager – Mrs Ellen Forson
    E-mail: ellen.forson@scottish.parliament.uk
Political Career. . . . . 2007 - 08 Convener, Standards, Procedures and Public
    Appointments Committee
    2009 - Minister for Schools and Skills

Brown, Robert MSP .... Glasgow Region
Scot Lib Dem .... List
Born .... 25th December 1947 in Newcastle-upon-Tyne
Educated .... The Gordon Schools, Huntly, Aberdeenshire;
                         University of Aberdeen
Elected .... 1999 MSP for Glasgow Region
Parliamentary Office.... Tel: (0131) 348 5792 Fax: (0131) 244 6487
                         E-mail: robert.brown.msp@scottish.parliament.uk
                         Web: www.robertbrownmsp.org.uk
Regional Office .... 9 Newton Terrace, Glasgow, G3 7PJ
                         Tel: (0141) 572 5000
                         Political Assistant – Miss Mairi Rough
                         E-mail: mairi.rough@scottish.parliament.uk
Political Career. .... 1977 - 92 Councillor and Liberal Democrat
                         Group Leader, Glasgow District Council
                         1995 - 2001 Vice-Chairman, Scottish Liberal
                         Democrat Policy Committee
                         2001 - Convener, Scottish Liberal Democrat Policy Committee
                         1999 - 2003 Liberal Democrat Spokesman
                         on Social Justice and Housing
                         1999 - 2005 Member, Scottish Parliament Corporate Body
                         2003 - 05 Convener, Education Committee
                         2003 - 05 Liberal Democrat Spokesman on
                         Education and Young People
                         2005 - 07 Deputy Minister for Education and Young People
                         2007 - 08 Liberal Democrat Business Manager
                         2008 - Liberal Democrat Shadow Justice Secretary
Professional Career ..... 1969 - 72 Legal Assistant, Edmonds and Ledingham, Aberdeen
                         1972 - 74 Procurator Fiscal Depute, Dumbarton
                         1974 - 2005 Assistant, then Partner,
                         Ross Harper and Murphy (solicitors)
Professional Association. . Law Society of Scotland
Parliamentary Interests . . Education; Housing; Human Rights; Transport;
                         Voluntary Sector
Leisure Interests .... History
Published Books .... 1983 - The Law of the School *(contributor)*

Brownlee, Derek MSP . . . . South of Scotland Region
Scot Cons . . . . List
Born . . . . 10th August 1974 in Strathaven
Educated . . . . Selkirk High School; Aberdeen University
Elected . . . . 2005 for South Scotland *(replacement from List)*
Parliamentary Office . . . . . Tel: (0131) 348 5635 Fax: (0131) 348 5932
E-mail: derek.brownlee.msp@scottish.parliament.uk
Personal Assistant – Ms Gillian Gillies
Tel: (0131) 348 5638
Press Officer – Mr Craig Wilson
Tel: (0131) 348 5633
Regional Office . . . . 131-132 Drumlanrig Street, Thornhill, DG3 5LP
Tel: (01848) 331815 Fax: (01848) 331630
Personal Assistant – Ms Gillian Walker
Political Career . . . . 2005 Conservative Spokesman on Finance, Local
Government and Public Services
2005 - 08 Conservative Spokesman on Finance
2008 - Conservative Finance and Sustainable
Growth Shadow Cabinet Secretary
Professional Career . . . . . . 1999 - Chartered Accountant
Professional Association . . . Institute of Chartered Accountants of Scotland

Butler, Bill MSP . . . . Glasgow Anniesland
Scot Lab . . . . Majority 4,306 over SNP
Born . . . . 30th March 1956 in Glasgow
Educated . . . . St Mungo's Academy, Glasgow; Stirling University;
Notre Dame College of Education, Bearsden
Elected . . . . 1999 for Glasgow Anniesland
Parliamentary Office . . . . . E-mail: bill.butler.msp@scottish.parliament.uk
Constituency Office . . . . . . 129 Dalsetter Avenue, Glasgow, G15 8SZ
Tel: (0141) 944 9441 Fax: (0141) 944 9442
E-mail: billbutlermsp@gmail.com
Web: www.billbutler.wordpress.com
Political Career . . . . 1987 - 2001 Councillor, Glasgow City Council
2005 - 07 Deputy Convener, Standards and Public
Appointments Committee
2005 - Deputy Convener, Justice Committee
Professional Career . . . . . . 1980 - 2000 Teacher of English
Trade Union . . . . Educational Institute of Scotland; GMB
Leisure Interests . . . . Film; Theatre; Football (Partick Thistle FC)

Campbell, Aileen MSP . . . . South of Scotland Region
SNP . . . . List
Born . . . . 18th May 1980 in Perth
Educated . . . . Perth Academy; University of Glasgow
Elected . . . . 2007 MSP for South of Scotland Region
Parliamentary Office . . . . . Tel: (0131) 348 6707   Fax: (0131) 348 6709
                              E-mail: aileen.campbell.msp@scottish.parliament.uk
                              Web: www.aileencampbell.com
                              Political Adviser – Mr Patrick Grady
                              E-mail: patrick.grady@scottish.parliament.uk
                              Parliamentary Assistant – Mr Andrew Gear
                              E-mail: andrew.gear@scottish.parliament.uk
Regional Office . . . . Tel: (0845) 602 6076
                              Office Manager – Mrs Gloria Mitchell
                              E-mail: gloria.mitchell@scottish.parliament.uk
Political Career . . . . 2005 - 06 Parliamentary Assistant to Nicola Sturgeon MSP
                              2006 - 07 Parliamentary Assistant to Shona Robison MSP
Professional Career . . . . . . 2003 - 05 Copy Assistant, then (from 2005) Editor,
                              Keystone
                              2005 Editorial Assistant, Scottish Standard
Parliamentary Interests . . . International Development; Children and Young People;
                              Human Rights; Tibet; Scots Language; Racial Equality
Leisure Interests . . . . Reading; Films; Music; Football (St Johnstone FC)

Carlaw, Jackson MSP . . . . West of Scotland Region
Scot Cons . . . . List
Born . . . . 12th April 1959 in Glasgow
Educated . . . . Glasgow Academy
Elected . . . . 2007 MSP for West of Scotland Region
Parliamentary Office . . . . . Tel: (0131) 348 6800 Fax: (0131) 348 6803
                              E-mail: jackson.carlaw.msp@scottish.parliament.uk
                              Adviser – Mr Alistair Haw
                              Secretary – Ms Sandra Robinson
Political Career . . . . 2007 – Conservative Spokesman on Public Health
Professional Career . . . . . . 1977 - 2002 Scottish Motor Retail Industry
                              2002 - 07 Consultant
Leisure Interests . . . . Walking; Reading; Travel; Arts Generally

Chisholm, Malcolm MSP . . Edinburgh North and Leith
Scot Lab. . . . . Majority 2,444 over Lib Dem
Born . . . . 7th March 1949 in Edinburgh
Educated . . . . George Watson's College; Edinburgh University
Elected. . . . . 1999 MSP for Edinburgh North and Leith
Parliamentary Office . . . . . Tel: (0131) 348 5908 Fax: (0131) 348 5974
                                   E-mail: malcolm.chisholm.msp@scottish.parliament.uk
                                   Web: www.malcolmchisholm.org.uk
Constituency Office . . . . . .5 Croall Place, Leith Walk, Edinburgh, EH7 4LT
                                   Tel: (0131) 558 8358 Fax: (0131) 557 6781
Political Career . . . . .1992 - 2001 MP for Edinburgh Leith, then
                                   (from 1997) Edinburgh North and Leith
                                   1995 - 96 Opposition Whip, House of Commons
                                   1996 - 97 Opposition Spokesman on Scottish
                                   Affairs, House of Commons
                                   1997 - 99 Parliamentary Secretary, Scottish Office
                                   2000 - 02 Deputy Minister for Health and
                                   Community Care
                                   2001 - 04 Minister for Health and Community Care
                                   2004 - 07 Minister for Communities
Professional Career . . . . . .English Teacher
Trade Unions . . . . .UNISON; Educational Institute of Scotland
Leisure Interests . . . . Cinema; Hill Climbing; Reading; Swimming

Coffey, Willie MSP. . . . . . . Kilmarnock and Loudon
SNP . . . . Majority 1,342 over Labour
Born . . . . 24th May 1958
Elected . . . . .2007 MSP for Kilmarnock and Loudon
Parliamentary Office . . . . .Tel: (0131) 348 6514 Fax: (0131) 348 6517
                                   E-mail: willie.coffey.msp@scottish.parliament.uk
Constituency Office . . . . . .1 Willock Street, Kilmarnock, KA1 4HE
                                   Tel: (01563) 537300
Political Career . . . . .Councillor, East Ayrshire Council

Constance, Angela MSP. . . Livingston
SNP . . . . Majority 870 over Labour
Born . . . . 15th July 1970 in Broxburn
Educated . . . . Glasgow University; Stirling University
Elected . . . . 2007 MSP for Livingston
Parliamentary Office . . . . . Tel: (0131) 348 6750 Fax: (0131) 348 6752
        E-mail: angela.constance.msp@
        scottish.parliament.uk
        Web: www.angelaconstancemsp.org
        Parliamentary Assistant – Mrs Norma Lazizi
        Tel: (0131) 348 6768
        E-mail: norma.lazizi@scottish.parliament.uk
Constituency Office . . . . . . Unit 5, Ochil House, Owen Square,
        Livingston, EH54 6PW
        Tel: (01506) 460403 Fax: (01506) 462044
        Personal Assistant – Mrs Ann Margaret Watson
        E-mail: annmargaret.watson@scottish.parliament.uk
        Administration Assistant – Mrs Mary Knox
        E-mail: mary.knox@scottish.parliament.uk
Political Career . . . . 1997 - 2007 Councillor, West Lothian Council
Professional Career . . . . . . 2001 - 07 Social Worker/Mental Health Officer,
        South Lanarkshire Council
Professional Career . . . . . . All Matters Concerning Livingston
Leisure Career . . . . My Son; Jogging

Craigie, Cathie MSP . . . . Cumbernauld and Kilsyth
Scot Lab . . . . Majority 2,079 over SNP
Born. . . . . 14th April 1954 in Stirling
Educated . . . . Kilsyth Academy
Elected . . . . 1999 MSP for Cumbernauld and Kilsyth
Parliamentary Office . . . Tel: (0131) 348 5756 Fax: (0131) 348 5977
        E-mail: cathie.cragie.msp@scottish.parliament.uk
Constituency Office. . . . . 6 Market Square, Kilsyth, Glasgow, G65 0AZ
        Tel: (01236) 825372 Fax: (01236) 820556
        Parliamentary Assistant – Mr Frank McNally
        Secretary/Caseworker – Ms Margaret McCulloch
Political Career . . . . 1984 - 96 Councillor, Cumbernauld and
        Kilsyth District Council (Leader 1994 - 96)
        1996 - 99 Councillor, North Lanarkshire Council
        (Chair, Environmental Services)
Parliamentary Interests. . Education; Health; Housing; Mortgage Rights;
        Social Inclusion

Crawford, Bruce MSP Stirling
SNP . . . . Majority 620 over Labour
Born. . . . . 16th February 1955 in Perth
Educated . . . . Kinross and Perth High School
Elected . . . . 2007 MSP for Stirling (1999 - 2007
        MSP for Mid Scotland and Fife Region)
Parliamentary Office . . . Tel: (0131) 348 5687 Fax: (0131) 348 5708
        E-mail: bruce.crawford.msp@scottish.parliament.uk
        Web: www.brucecrawfordmsp.net
Constituency Office. . . . . Unit 111, Stirling Enterprise Park, John Player Building,
        Stirling, FK7 7RP
        Tel: (01786) 471899 Fax: (01786) 471853
        Constituency Manager – Miss Eilidh MacKechnie
        E-mail: eilidh.mackechnie@scottish.parliament.uk
        Communications Manager – Cllr Steven Paterson
        E-mail: steven.paterson@scottish.parliament.uk
Political Career . . . . 1988 - 96 Councillor, Perth and Kinross District Council
        1995 - 2001 Councillor, Perth and Kinross Council
        (Leader 1995 - 99)
        1999 - 2007 MSP for Mid Scotland and Fife Region
        1999 - 2000 Chief Whip, SNP
        2000 - 01 SNP Spokesman on Transport and the Environment
        2001 - 03 SNP Spokesman on Environment and Energy
        2003 - 04 SNP Business Manager and Chief Whip
        2004 - 07 SNP Business Convener
        2005 - 06 Deputy Convener, Local Government
        and Transport Committee
        2007 - Minister for Parliamentary Business
Professional Career. . . . . 1975 - 99 Civil Servant, Scottish Office
        1996 - 99 Board Member: Scottish Enterprise
        Tayside, Perthshire Tourist Board, Perth College
        1996 - 99 Chairman, Perth and Kinross Recreational
        Facilities Ltd
        1996 - 99 Board Member Perth College
        1996 - 99 Board Member Perthshire Tourist Board
        1998 - 2000 Chairman, Kinross-shire Partnership Ltd
Parliamentary Interests. . Enterprise; Europe; Local Government; Tourism;
        Transport
Leisure Interests . . . . Football; Golf

Cunningham, Roseanna MSP Perth
SNP . . . . Majority 2,495 over Conservative
Born . . . . 27th July 1951 in Glasgow
Educated . . . . University of Western Australia; Edinburgh University;
                     Aberdeen University
Elected . . . . 1999 MSP for Perth
Parliamentary Office . . . . .Tel: (0131) 348 5697 Fax: (0131) 348 5952
                     E-mail: roseanna.cunningham.msp@scottish.parliament.uk
                     Web: www.roseannacunningham.org
                     Parliamentary Researcher – Mrs Sheena Cleland
                     Tel: (0131) 348 6087
                     E-mail: sheena.cleland@scottish.parliament.uk
                     Press Officer – Mr Calum Smith
                     Mobile: 07841 922681
                     E-mail: calum.smith@scottish.parliament.uk
                     Constituency Assistant
Constituency Office . . . . . .9 York Place, Perth, PH2 8EP
                     Tel: (01738) 639598 Fax: (01738) 587637
                     E-mail: rcmp.perth@snp.org
                     Constituency Assistant – Mr Alistair Cassidy
                     E-mail: alistair.cassidy@scottish.parliament.uk
Political Career . . . . .1995 - 2001 MP for Perth and Kinross,
                       then (1997) for Perth
                     1999 - 2000 Convener, Justice and Home
                       Affairs Committee, Scottish Parliament
                     1999 - 2003 SNP Shadow Minister for Justice
                     2000 - 04 Deputy Leader, SNP
                     2003 - 04 SNP Shadow Minister for Environment
                       and Rural Affairs, Culture and Sport
                     2004 - 07 Convener, Health Committee
                     2007 - 09 Convener, Rural Affairs and Environment
                       Committee
                     2009 - Minister for the Environment
Professional Career . . . . . .1983 - 89 Solicitor, Dumbarton District Council,
                       then Glasgow District Council
                     1989 - 90 Solicitor, Ross Harper and Murphy
                     1990 - Advocate
Professional Association . . .Faculty of Advocates
Parliamentary Interests . . .Culture and Sport; Environment; Equality; Justice;
                     Land Reform; Rural Affairs;
Leisure Interests . . . . .Cinema; Hill Walking; Reading; Traditional Music

Curran, Margaret MSP . . . Glasgow Baillieston
Scot Lab . . . . Majority 3,934 over SNP
Born . . . . 24th November 1958 in Glasgow
Educated . . . . Glasgow University; Dundee College
Elected . . . . .1999 MSP for Glasgow Baillieston
Parliamentary Office . . . . .Tel: (0131) 348 5892
                                          E-mail: margaret.curran.msp@scottish.parliament.uk
Constituency Office . . . . . .Westwood Business Centre, 69 Aberdalgie Road,
                                          Glasgow, G34 9HJ
                                          Tel: (0141) 771 4844 Fax: (0141) 771 4877
                                          Scottish Parliamentary Officer – Ms Rachel McGee
                                          E-mail: rachel.mcgee@scottish.parliament.uk
                                          Parliamentary Research and Communications
                                             Assistant – Ms Lucy Richmond
                                          E-mail: lucy.richmond@scottish.parliament.uk
Political Career . . . . .1979 - 80 Chair, Scottish Labour Students
                                          1994 - 99 Convener, Scottish Women's Caucus
                                          1999 - 2000 Convener, Social Inclusion, Housing
                                             and Voluntary Sector Committee
                                          2000 - 01 Deputy Minister for Social Justice;
                                             Deputy Minister, Scottish Parliamentary Bureau
                                          2001 - 03 Minister for Social Justice
                                          2003 - 04 Minister for Communities
                                          2004 - 07 Minister for Parliamentary Business
                                          2008 - Labour Shadow Policy Development
                                             Cabinet Secretary
Professional Career . . . . . .1982 - 83 Welfare Rights Officer
                                          1983 - 89 Community Worker
                                          1989 - 99 Lecturer, University of Strathclyde
Trade Union . . . . .Unite; Communication Workers Union
Parliamentary Interests . . .Housing; Regeneration, Social Inclusion;
                                          Women's Issues; Anti Social Behaviour;
                                          Crime and Justice. Economic Policy
Leisure Interests . . . . .Cinema; Reading; Theatre

Don, Nigel MSP . . . . North East Scotland Region
SNP . . . . List
Born . . . . 16th April 1954
Educated . . . . King's College School; Pembroke College, Cambridge;
                          University of London
Elected . . . . 2007 MSP for North East Scotland Region
Parliamentary Office . . . . . Tel: (0131) 348 5996 Fax: (0131) 348 6998
                          E-mail: nigel.don.msp@scottish.parliament.uk
Regional Office . . . . 825-827 Great Northern Road, Aberdeen, AB24 2BR
                          Tel: (01224) 663316 Fax: (01224) 695397
Political Career . . . . 1979 - 80 Chair, Scottish Labour Students
                          Councillor, Dundee City Council
Professional Career . . . . . . Chemical Engineer, Unilever
                          Self-employed Musician/Performer/Teacher/
                          Arranger/Composer
Trade Union . . . . Musicians' Union
Professional Association . . . Performing Right Society
Parliamentary Interests . . . Law; Energy; Nutrition and Weight Management;
                          Environment; Culture
Leisure Interesets . . . . Sport; Music

Doris, Bob MSP . . . . Glasgow Region
SNP . . . . List
Born . . . . 11th May 1973 in the Vale of Leven
Educated . . . . St Andrew's College, Bearsden; Glasgow University
Elected . . . . 2007 MSP for Glasgow Region
Parliamentary Office . . . . . Tel: (0131) 348 6547 Fax: (0131) 348 6549
                          E-mail: bob.doris.msp@scottish.parliament.uk
                          Web: www.bobdoris.org
Regional Office . . . . Room 329, Baltic Chambers, 50 Wellington Street,
                          Glasgow, G2 6HJ
                          Tel: (0141) 202 0675 Fax: (011) 202 0676
Professional Career . . . . . . 1995 - 2006 Teacher of History and Modern Studies
Trade Unions . . . . Educational Institute of Scotland
Parliamentary Interests . . . Championing Scottish Independence; Kinship Care;
                          Good Quality Affordable and Social Rented Housing;
                          Job Creation and Anti-Poverty Initiatives; Community Safety
Leisure Interests . . . . Football; Pool; Good Food

Eadie, Helen MSP . . . . Dunfermline East
Scot Lab . . . . Majority 3,993 over SNP
Born . . . . 7th March 1947 in Stenhousemuir
Educated . . . . .Larbert High School; Falkirk Technical College;
London School of Economics
Elected . . . . .1999 MSP for Dunfermline East
Parliamentary Office . . . . .Tel: (0131) 348 5749 Fax: (0131) 348 6948
E-mail: helen.eadie.msp@scottish.parliament.uk
Web: www.heleneadie.com
Constituency Office . . . . . . 25 Church Street, Inverkeithing, Fife, KY11 1 LG
Tel: (01383) 412856 Fax: (01383) 412855
Web: www.scottishlabour.org.uk/dunfermlineeast1
Parliamentary Aides – Miss Eleanor Casson
Miss Ann Nilsen
E-mails eleanor.casson@scottish.parliament.uk
ann.nilsen@scottish.parliament.uk
Researcher *(Part Time)* – Mr Robert Eadie
E-mail: robert.eadie@scottish.parliament.uk
Political Career . . . . .1970 - 76 Parliamentary Assistant to Harry Ewing MP
and Alex Eadie MP, House of Commons
1986 - 98 Member, Fife Regional Council
(Deputy Leader 1992 - 96)
2000 - 03 Deputy Convener, Public Petitions Committee
Professional Career . . . . . .1976 - 84 Equal Opportunities and Political Officer, GMB
1984 - 86 Manager West Fife Enterprise
Trade Union . . . . .GMB
Subject Interests . . . . .Co-operative Development; Enterprise; Environment;
Europe; Health; Natural Heritage; Transport
Leisure Interests . . . . .Apple Mac Computers; Reading; Swimming;
Travel (Particularly Bulgaria)

Ewing, Fergus MSP . . . . . . Inverness East, Nairn and Lochaber
SNP . . . . Majority 5,471 over Liberal Democrat
Born . . . . 20th September 1957 in Glasgow
Educated . . . . Loretto School, Edinburgh; Glasgow University
Elected . . . . 1999 MSP for Inverness East, Nairn and Lochaber
Parliamentary Office . . . . . Tel: (0131) 348 5732 Fax: (0131) 348 5716
E-mail: fergus.ewing.msp@scottish.parliament.uk
Web: www.fergusewing.com
Parliamentary Assistant – Ms Rebecca Dixon
E-mail: rebecca.dixon@scottish.parliament.uk
Constituency Office . . . . . . Highland Railhouse, Station Square,
Inverness, IV1 1LE
Tel: (01463) 713004 Fax: (01463) 710194
Office Manager – Mr Norman Will
E-mail: norman.will@scottish.parliament.uk
Secretary – Mrs Rosie MacInnes
E-mail: rosie.macinnes@scottish.parliament.uk
Political Career . . . . 1992 - Member, SNP National Executive
Committee and National Council
1999 - 2000 SNP Spokesman on Highlands and
Islands, Tourism and Small Businesses
2000 - 03 Deputy Convener, Rural Development
Committee
2003 - 04 SNP Spokesman on Finance and
Public Services
2003 - 05 Deputy Convener, Finance Committee
2004 - 07 SNP Spokesman on Transport, Tourism
and Telecoms
2005 - 07 Deputy Convener, Local Government
and Transport Committee
2007 - Minister for Community Safety
Professional Career . . . . . . 1981 - 85 Solicitor, (Leslie Wolfson & Co)
1985 - 2001 Solicitor (Partner, Ewing & Co)
Professional Association . . . Law Society of Scotland
Parliamentary Interests . . . Finance; Public Services
Leisure Interests . . . . Hill Walking; Jazz Piano; Reading; Running

Fabiani, Linda MSP . . . . . . Central Scotland Region
SNP . . . . List
Born . . . . 14th December 1956 in Glasgow
Educated . . . . Hyndland School, Glasgow;
        Napier University, Edinburgh; Glasgow University
Elected . . . . 1999 MSP for Central Scotland Region
Parliamentary Office . . . . . Tel: (0131) 348 5699 Fax: (0131) 348 6473
        E-mail: linda.fabiani.msp@scottish.parliament.uk
        Web: www.linda-fabiani.co.uk
        Researcher – Mr Calum Cashley
        Tel: (0131) 348 5698
        E-mail: calum.cashley@scottish.parliament.uk
        Assistant – Ms Morag Dunbar
        Tel: (0131) 348 5698
        E-mail: morag.dunbar@scottish.parliament.uk
Regional Office . . . . Suite 3.3, The Dalziel Building, 7 Scott Street,
        Motherwell, ML1 1PN
        Tel: (01698) 265925 Fax: (01698) 269033
        Assistant – Mr David McAnsh
        E-mail: david.mcansh@scottish.parliament.uk
Political Career . . . . 2001 - 03 SNP Deputy Spokesman on Social Justice,
        Housing and Urban Regeneration
        2003 - 04 SNP Deputy Business Manager and Whip
        2004 - 05 Deputy Shadow Minister for Social Justice
        2006 - 07 Convener, European and External
        Relations Committee
        2007 - 09 Minister for Europe External Affairs
        and Culture
Professional Career . . . . . . 1982 - 94 Housing Association Administrator
        and Manager
        1994 - 99 Director, East Kilbride and District
        Housing Association
Trade Union . . . . Unite
Professional Association . . . Chartered Institute of Housing of Scotland
Parliamentary Interests . . . Foreign Affairs; Housing; Human Rights;
        Social Justice
Leisure Interests . . . . Culture; Music; Reading

Ferguson, Patricia MSP . . . Glasgow Maryhill
Scot Lab . . . . Majority 2,310 over SNP
Born . . . . 24th September 1958 in Glasgow
Educated . . . . Garnethill Convent Secondary School, Glasgow;
                                 Glasgow College of Technology
Elected . . . . .1999 MSP for Glasgow Maryhill
Parliamentary Office . . . . .Tel: (0131) 348 5317 Fax: (0131) 348 5925
                                 E-mail: patricia.ferguson.msp@scottish.parliament.uk
Constituency Office . . . . . .154 Raeberry Street, Glasgow, G20 6EA
                                 Tel: (0141) 946 1300 Fax: (0141) 946 1412
                                 Web: www.patriciaferguson.labour.co.uk
                                 Parliamentary Assistant – Mr Christopher Kelly
                                 Administrative Assistants – Ms Susan Johnston
                                            Mrs Isobel Tait
Political Career . . . . .1999 - 2001 Deputy Presiding Officer
                                 2001 - 04 Minister for Parliamentary Business
                                 2004 - 07 Minister for Tourism, Culture and Sport
Professional Career . . . . . .1978 - 90 Health Service Administrator
                                 1990 - 94 Administrator, Scottish Trades Union Congress
                                 1994 - 96 Scottish Labour Party Organiser
                                 1996 - 99 Scottish Officer, The Scottish Labour Party
Trade Union . . . . .GMB/Apex
Parliamentary Interests . . .Education; Health; Housing; The Arts; Sport
Leisure Interests . . . . .Hill Walking; Music; Football (Partick Thistle FC);
                                 Reading; Theatre; Travel

MEMBERS OF THE SCOTTISH PARLIAMENT

Fergusson, Alex MSP . . . . . Galloway and Upper Nithsdale
Presiding Officer . . . . Majority 3,333 over SNP *(Elected as Conservative)*
Born . . . . 8th April 1949 in Leswalt
Educated . . . . Eton College; West of Scotland Agricultural College
Elected . . . . 2003 MSP for Galloway and Upper Nithsdale (previously,
1999 - 2003, MSP for South of Scotland Region)
Parliamentary Office . . . . . Tel: (0131) 348 5636 Fax: (0131) 348 5932
Mobile: 07767 212191
E-mail: alex.fergusson.msp@scottish.parliament.uk
Web: www.alexfergusson.org.uk
Secretary – Mrs Gillian Gillies
Tel: (0131) 348 5638
E-mail: gillian.gillies@scottish.parliament.uk
Constituency Office . . . . . . 132 Drumlanrig Street, Thornhill, Dumfriesshire, DG3 5LP
Tel: (01848) 331725 Fax: (01848) 331630
Secretary – Miss Susan Kerr
E-mail: susan.kerr@scottish.parliament.uk
Researcher – Mrs Gillian Dykes
E-mail: gillian.dykes@scottish.parliament.uk
Political Career . . . . 1999 - 2001 Deputy Conservative Spokesman on
Rural Affairs
2001 - 03 Conservative Spokesman on Rural Affairs
2001 - 03 Convener, Rural Development Committee
2003 - 07 Conservative Spokesman on Agriculture
and Forestry
2007 - Presiding Officer, Scottish Parliament
Professional Career . . . . . . 1969 - 71 Farm Management Consultant
1971 - 99 Farmer
Professional Association . . . Scottish Rural Property and Business Association Ltd
(SRPBA
Parliamentary Interests . . . Rural Affairs
Leisure Interests . . . . Folk Music; Rugby; Walking

Finnie, Ross MSP . . . . West of Scotland Region
Scot Lib Dem . . . . List
Born . . . . 11th February 1947 in Greenock
Educated . . . . Greenock Academy
Elected . . . . 1999 MSP for West of Scotland Region
Parliamentary Office . . . . . Tel: (0131) 348 5784 Fax: (0131) 348 5966
E-mail: ross.finnie.msp@scottish.parliament.uk
Web: www.rossfinniemsp.org.uk
Personal Assistant – Ms Karen Galbraith
E-mail: karen.galbraith@scottish.parliament.uk
Regional Office . . . . 54 Kelly Street, Greenock, PA16 8TR
Tel: (01475) 805020 Fax: (01475) 805021
Staff – Ms Karen Galbraith
E-mail: karen.galbraith@scottish.parliament.uk
Researcher – Mr Paul Mullan
E-mail: paul.mullan@scottish.parliament.uk
Political Career . . . . 1977 - 99 Councillor, Inverclyde Council
1982 - 86 Chairman, Scottish Liberal Party
1999 - 2007 Minister for Environment and
  Rural Development
2007 - Liberal Democrat Shadow Health Secretary
2008 - Deputy Convener, Health and Sport Committee
Professional Career . . . . . . 1970 - 73 Audit Assistant Arthur Anderson
  & Co., Glasgow
1973 - 78 Corporate Finance Manager,
  Corporate Finance James Findlay Bank Ltd (Glasgow)
1978 - 86 Director, Corporate Finance
1986 - 91 Local Director, Glasgow Corporate
  Finance Singer & Friedlander Ltd
1991 - 99 Chartered Accountant Ross Finnie & Co
  (Chartered Accountant & Corporate Finance Advisers)
1992 - 99 Non-Executive Director, Boko Holdings Ltd
  Mico Ltd; Systems Reliability Scotland Ltd

MEMBERS OF THE SCOTTISH PARLIAMENT

FitzPatrick, Joe MSP . . . . . Dundee West
SNP . . . . Majority 1,946 over Labour
Born . . . . .1st April 1967 in Dundee
Educated . . . . .Whitefield High School; Inverness College;
Abertay University
Elected . . . . .2007 MSP for Dundee West
Parliamentary Office . . . . .Tel: (0131) 348 6273 Fax: (0131) 348 6275
E-mail: parliament@joe.fitzpatrick.net
Web: www.joefitzpatrick.net
Staff – Mr Neil Guy
E-mail: neil.guy@scottish.parliament.uk
Constituency Office . . . . . .8 Old Glamis Road, Dundee, DD3 8HP
Tel: (01382) 623200 Fax: (01382) 903205
E-mail: dundee@joefitzpatrick.net
Staff – Mr Stewart Hunter
E-mail: stewart.hunter@scottish.parliament.uk
Professional Career . . . . . .Forestry Commission
Former Assistant to Shona Robison and Stewart Hosie

Foulkes, Rt Hon Lord [George] MSP Lothians Region
Scot Lab. . . . . List
Born . . . . .21st January 1942 in Oswestry
Educated . . . . .Keith Grammar School, Banffshire;
Haberdashers' Aske's School;
Edinburgh University
Elected . . . . .2007 MSP for Lothians Region
Parliamentary Office . . . . .Tel: (0131) 348 6827 Fax: (0131) 348 6829
E-mail: george.foulkes.msp@scottish.parliament.uk
Web: www.georgefoulkesmsp.com
Staff – Ms Kezia Dudgale
Ms Alice Ednie
Ms Claire McIntosh
Political Career . . . . .1979 - 83 MP for South Ayrshire
1983 - 2005 MP for Carrick, Cumnock and Doon Valley
1984 - 92 Opposition Spokesman on Foreign and
Commonwealth Affairs, House of Commons
1992 - 93 Opposition Spokesman on Defence,
House of Commons
1994 - 97 Opposition Spokesman on Overseas Development,
House of Commons
1997 - 2001 Parliamentary Secretary, Department for
International Development
2001 - 02 Minister of State, Scotland Office
2005 - Life Peer
Professional Career . . . . . .1970 - 73 Director, Enterprise Youth
1973 - 79 Director, Age Concern Scotland
Trade Union . . . . .GMB
Parliamentary Interests . . .International Development; Education
Leisure Interests . . . . .Football (Heart of Midlothian FC)

Fraser, Murdo MSP . . . . . . Mid Scotland and Fife
Scot Cons . . . . List
Born . . . . 5th September 1965 in Inverness
Educated . . . . Inverness Royal Academy; Aberdeen University
Elected . . . . 2001 MSP Mid Scotland and Fife *(Replaced Nick Johnston)*
Parliamentary Office . . . . . Tel: (0131) 348 5293 Fax: (0131) 348 5934
   E-mail: murdo.fraser.msp@scottish.parliament.uk
   Media Contact – Sam McMillan
   E-mail: samuel.mcmillan@scottish.parliament.uk
Regional Office . . . . Control Tower, Perth Airport, Scone, PH2 6PL
   Tel: (01738) 553990 Fax: (01738) 553967
   Personal Assistant – Mrs Oksana Last
   E-mail: oksana.last@scottish.parliament.uk
   Researcher – Ms Caroline Shiers
   E-mail: caroline.shiers@scottish.parliament.uk
Political Career . . . . 1989 - 91 Chairman, Scottish Young Conservatives
   1998 - 99 Scottish Conservative Spokesman on
      Land Reform
   2001 - 03 Conservative Deputy Spokesman on
      Education, Culture and Sport
   2003 - 05 Conservative Spokesman on Enterprise
      and Lifelong Learning
   2005 - Deputy Leader, Scottish Conservatives, and
      Conservative Shadow Cabinet Secretary on
      Education and Lifelong Education
   2008 - Deputy Convener, Public Audit Committee
Professional Career . . . . . . Solicitor
Professional Association . . . Law Society of Scotland
Leisure Interests . . . . Football; Scottish History; Walking

Gibson, Kenneth MSP . . . . Cunninghame North
SNP . . . . Majority 48 over Labour
Born . . . . 8th September 1961 in Paisley
Educated . . . . Bellahouston Academy; Stirling University
Elected . . . . 2007 MSP for Cunninghame North
Parliamentary Office . . . . . Tel: (0131) 348 6536 Fax: (0131) 348 6539
   E-mail: kenneth.gibson.msp@scottish.parliament.uk
   Web: www.kennethgibson.co.uk
Constituency Office . . . . . . 15 Main Street, Dairy, KA24 5DL
   Tel: (01294) 833687 Fax: (01294) 835662
Political Career . . . . 1992 - 96 Councillor, Glasgow District Council
   1995 - 99 Councillor, Glasgow City Council
   1999 - 2003 MSP for Glasgow Region
   2007 - 08 Deputy Convener, Local Government
      and Communities Committee
   2008 - Deputy Convener, Education, Lifelong Learning and
      Culture Committee
Parliamentary Interests . . . Education; Local Government
Leisure Interests . . . . Cinema; Theatre, Swimming; Classical History

Gibson, Rob MSP . . . . Highlands and Islands Region
SNP . . . . List
Born . . . . 10th October 1945 in Glasgow
Educated . . . . The High School of Glasgow; Dundee University;
Dundee College of Education
Elected . . . . 2003 MSP for Highlands and Islands Region
Parliamentary Office . . . . . Tel: (0131) 348 5726 Fax: (0131) 348 5943
E-mail: rob.gibson.msp@scottish.parliament.uk
Web: www.robgibsonmsp.blogspot.com
Parliamentary Assistants – Ms Haley St Dennis
Mr Owen Thompson
E-mails: haley.stdennis@scottish.parliament.uk
owen.thompson@scottish.parliament.uk
Regional Office . . . . 4 Grant Street, Wick, Caithness, KW1 5AY
Tel: (01955) 605016 Fax: (01955) 604963
Constituency Assistants – Mr Niall MacDonald
Mrs Gail Ross
E-mails: niall.macdonald@scottish.parliament.uk
gail.ross@scottish.parliament.uk
Political Career . . . . Former Councillor, Ross and Cromarty District Council
2005 - 07 SNP Deputy Spokesman on Environment
2007 - 08 Deputy Convener, Education, Lifelong Learning
and Culture Committee
2008 - Deputy Convener, Economy, Energy and
Tourism Committee
Professional Career . . . . . . 1973 - 77 Teacher (Modern Studies, Geography) and
Assistant Principal Teacher of Guidance,
Invergordon Academy
1977 - 95 Principal Teacher of Guidance,
Alness Academy
Trade Union . . . . Musicians' Union
Languages Spoken . . . . French; Scots
Parliamentary Interests . . .Environment; Rural Affairs; Scots and Gaelic Languages
Leisure Interests . . . . .Hill Walking; Organic Gardening; Traditional Music
Published Books . . . . .1983/2006: The Highland Clearance Trail
2003: Plaids and Bandanas

Gillon, Karen MSP. . . . . . . Clydesdale
Scot Lab. . . . . Majority 2,893 over SNP
Born. . . . . 18th August 1967 in Edinburgh
Educated. . . . . Jedburgh Grammar School; Birmingham University
Elected . . . . 1999 MSP for Clydesdale *(previously Karen Turnbull)*
Parliamentary Office . . . . . Tel: (0131) 348 5823 Fax: (0131) 348 6485
E-mail: karen.gillon.msp@scottish.parliament.uk
Web: www.karengillon.co.uk
Researcher – Mr Murray Cheek
Tel: (0131) 348 5000
E-mail: murray.cheek@scottish.parliament.uk
Constituency Office . . . . . .7 Wellgate, Lanark, M11 9DS
Tel: (01555) 660526 Fax: (01555) 660528
Office Manager – Mrs Mary Austin
E-mail: mary.austin@scottish.parliament.uk
Political Career . . . . .1995 - 97 Member, STUC General Council
1996 - 99 Chair, UNISON Scotland
Political Committee
1997 - Member, Scottish Labour Party Executive
1997 - 99 Personal Assistant to Rt Hon Helen Liddell MP,
House of Commons
2001 - 03 Convener, Education, Culture and Sport
Committee
2003 - 07 Deputy Convener, Procedures Committee
2008 - Labour Spokesman on Rural Development,
Economy and Skills
Professional Career . . . . . .1991 - 95 Project Worker, Blantyre,
1994 - 97 Community Education Worker,
North Lanarkshire Council
Trade Union . . . . .UNISON
Parliamentary Interests . . .Corporate Homicide; Education; Malawi; Public Health;
Rural Issues; Sport
Leisure Interests . . . . .Cooking; Flower Arranging; Music; Reading; Sport

Glen, Marlyn MSP . . . . North East Scotland Region
Scot Lab. . . . . List
Born. . . . . 30th September 1951 in Dundee
Educated . . . . Kirkton High School; St Andrews University;
Open University
Elected . . . . 2003 MSP for North East Scotland Region
Parliamentary Office . . . . . E-mail: marlyn.glen.msp@scottish.parliament.uk
Web: www.marlynglen.org.uk
Staff – Mr Alan Cowan
Regional Office . . . . The Factory Skatepark, 15 Balunie Drive,
Dundee, DD4 8PS
Tel: (01382) 509509 Fax: (01382) 509709
Office Manager – Ms Ina Paton
E-mail: ina.paton@scottish.parliament.uk
Staff – Mr Joe Handy
Ms Ann Russell
Political Career . . . . Councillor, Dundee District Council
2009 - Deputy Convener, Equal Opportunities
Committee
Professional Career . . . . . . From 1974 Teacher
Trade Union . . . . Educational Institute of Scotland
Parliamentary Interests . . . Equalities; Nuclear Disarmament; Social Justice;
Environment

Godman, Trish MSP . . . . . West Renfrewshire
Scot Lab. . . . . Majority 2,178 over Conservative
Born. . . . . 31st October 1939 in Glasgow
Educated. . . . . St Gerard's Senior Secondary School;
Jordanhill College
Elected . . . . 1999 MSP for West Renfrewshire
Parliamentary Office . . . . . Tel: (0131) 348 5837 Fax: (0131) 348 6460
E-mail: trish.godman.msp@scottish.parliament.uk
Constituency Office . . . . . . Renfrew House, Cottage 27, Quarrier's Village,
Bridge of Weir, PA11 3SX
Tel: (01505) 615337 Fax: (01505) 690717
Political Career . . . . Councillor, Glasgow City Council
1999 - 2003 Convener, Local Government Committee
2003 - Deputy Presiding Officer
Professional Career . . . . . . 1979 - 89 Social Worker
Trade Union . . . . Unite
Parliamentary Interests . . . Community Care, Drug Misuse; Health;
Local Government
Leisure Interests . . . . Allotment; Cinema; Dancing; Music; Reading

Goldie, Annabel MSP. . . . . West of Scotland Region
Scot Cons . . . . List
Born . . . . 27th February 1950 in Glasgow
Educated . . . . .Greenock Academy; Strathclyde University
Elected . . . . .1999 MSP for West of Scotland Region
Parliamentary Office . . . . .Tel: (0131) 348 5662 Fax: (0131) 348 5937
                             E-mail: annabel.goldie.msp@scottish.parliament.uk
                             Head of Leader's Office - Mrs Patricia Clark
                             Tel: (0131) 348 5618
                             E-mail: patricia.clark@scottish.parliament.uk
                             PA - Ms Gillian Cameron
                             Tel: (0131) 348 5663
                             E-mail: gillian.cameron@scottish.parliament.uk
                             Researcher - Ms Grace Shipley
                             Tel: (0131) 348 5645
                             E-mail: grace.shipley@scottish.parliament.uk
Regional Office . . . . .10 Shuttle Street, Paisley, PA1 1YD
                             Tel: (0141) 887 6161 Fax: (0141) 889 0023
Political Career . . . . .1997 Chairman, Scottish Conservative Party
                             1998 - Deputy Leader, Scottish Conservative Party
                             2001 - 03 Deputy Leader and Conservative Spokesman
                                on Enterprise and Lifelong Learning
                             1999 - 2005 Conservative Deputy Leader,
                              Scottish Parliament
                             2003 - 05 Conservative Spokesman on
                              Justice and Home Affairs
                             2003 - 06 Convener, Justice II Committee
                             2005 - Leader, Scottish Conservatives
Professional Career . . . . . .1974 - 2006 Solicitor
                             1978 - 2006 Partner in Law Firm
Languages Spoken . . . . . . .French
Leisure Interests . . . . .Bird Watching; Gardening; Reading; Cycling
Directorship . . . . .Prince's Scottish Youth Business Trust *(unpaid)*

Gordon, Charlie MSP .... Glasgow Cathcart
Scot Lab.............. Majority 2,189 over SNP
Born .... 28th October 1951 in Glasgow
Educated .... Langside College
Elected .... 2005 MSP for Glasgow Cathcart
Parliamentary Office ..... Tel: (0141) 632 8645
E-mail: charlie.gordon.msp@scottish.parliament.uk
Web: www.charliegordonmsp.com
Parliamentary Assistant – Mr Stuart Donaldson
Constituency Office ...... Lesser Hampden, Somerville Drive, Mount Florida,
Glasgow, GA2 9BA
Tel & Fax: (0141) 632 8645
Web: www.votecharliegordon.com
Political Career .... 1987 - 96 Councillor, Strathclyde Regional Council
1995 - 2005 Councillor, Glasgow City Council
(Leader 1999 - 2005)
Professional Career ...... 1975 - 93 Railwayman
Trade Union .... GMB
Parliamentary Interests ... Transport; Tourism; Skills; Jobs
Leisure Interests .... Reading; Conversation; Football
Directorship Held .... Hampden Park Ltd (non-executive)

Grahame, Christine MSP . South of Scotland Region
SNP .... List
Born .... 9th September 1944 in Burton-on-Trent
Educated .... Boroughmuir Secondary School, Edinburgh;
Edinburgh University
Elected .... 1999 MSP for South of Scotland Region
(previously Christine Creech)
Parliamentary Office ..... Tel: (0131) 348 5729 Fax: (0131) 348 5954
E-mail: christine.grahame.msp@scottish.parliament.uk
Web: www.christinegrahame.com
Parliamentary Press Officer - Mr Mark Hirst
E-mail: mark.hirst@scottish.parliament.uk
Regional Office .... 69 Bank Street, Galashiels, TD1 1EL
Tel: (01896) 759575 Fax: (01896) 754765
E-mail: parliament@christinegrahame.com
Parliamentary Assistant – Mrs Janine Herd
Political Career .... 2000 - 01 SNP Spokesman on Social Security
2004 - SNP Spokesman on Social Justice
2007 - Convener, Health and Sport Committee
Professional Career ...... Secondary School Teacher and Solicitor
Professional Association ... Law Society of Scotland
Parliamentary Interests ... Health; Justice
Leisure Interests .... Gardening

Grant, Rhoda MSP . . . . . . Highlands and Islands Region
Scot Lab . . . . List
Born . . . . .26th June 1963 in Stornoway
Educated . . . . .Plockton High School; Open University
Elected . . . . .2007 MSP for Highlands Region
Parliamentary Office . . . . .Tel: (0131) 348 5766 Fax: (0131) 348 5767
E-mail: rhoda.grant.msp@scottish.parliament.uk
Web: www.rhodagrant.org.uk
Parliamentary Assistant – Mr Richard Welsh
E-mail: richard.welsh@scottish.parliament.uk
Regional Office . . . . .Queensgate Business Centre, 1-3 Fraser Street,
Inverness, IV1 1DW
Tel: (01463) 716299 Fax: (01463) 716572
Political Career . . . . .1999 - 2003 MSP for Highlands and Islands Region
2008 - Labour Whip
Professional Career . . . . . .1987 - 93 Administrator, Highlands Regional Council
1993 - 99 Administrator, UNISON
Trade Union . . . . .UNISON
Leisure Interests . . . . .Swimming

Gray, Iain MSP . . . . East Lothian
Scot Lab . . . . Majority 2,448 over SNP
Born . . . . .7th June 1957 in Edinburgh
Educated . . . . .Inverness Royal Academy; Edinburgh University;
Moray House College
Elected . . . . .2007 MSP for East Lothian
Parliamentary Office . . . . .Tel: (0131) 348 5839 Fax: (0131) 348 6359
E-mail: iain.gray.msp@scottish.parliament.uk
Constituency Office . . . . . .65 High Street, Tranent, EH33 1LN
Tel: (01875) 616610
Political Career . . . . .1999 - 2003 MSP for Edinburgh Pentlands
1999 - 2000 Deputy Minister for Community Care
2000 - 01 Deputy Minister for Justice
2001 - 02 Minister for Social Justice
2002 - 03 Minister for Enterprise, Transport and
Lifelong Learning
2007 - 08 Labour Shadow Minister for Enterprise, Trade
and Tourism
2008 - Labour Leader, Scottish Parliament
Professional Career . . . . . .1978 - 86 Physics Teacher
1986 - 99 Campaigns Manager, Oxfam in Scotland
Trade Union . . . . .Unite
Language Spoken . . . . . . .Portuguese
Leisure Interests . . . . .Football; Reading; Fitness Training; Bonsai;
Hill Walking

Harper, Robin MSP . . . . . . Lothians Region
Scot Grn . . . . List
Born . . . . .4th August 1940 in Thurso, Caithness
Educated . . . . .St Marylebone Grammar School;
                       Elgin Academy; Aberdeen University;
                       Edinburgh University
Elected . . . . .1999 MSP for Lothians Region
Parliamentary Office . . . . .Tel: (0131) 348 6421 Fax: (0131) 348 5972
                       E-mail: robin.harper.msp@scottish.parliament.uk
                       Web: www.robinharper.wordpress.com
                       PA – Ms Sally Cowburn
                       E-mail: sally.cowburn@scottish.parliament.uk
Political Career . . . . .1995 - 98 Council Convener, Scottish Green Party
                       2003 - Co-Convener Green Group, and Green Party
                          Spokesman on Education, Young People and Sport
Professional Career . . . . . .1962 - 68 Teacher (Glasgow, then Fife)
                       1968 - 70 Education Officer, Kenya
                       1970 - 99 Teacher (Fife, then Midlothian and Edinburgh)
                       2000 - 03 Rector, Edinburgh University
                       2005 - 08 Elected Rector, Aberdeen University
Trade Unions . . . . .Equity; Educational Institute of Scotland
Language Spoken . . . . . . .French
Parliamentary Interests . . .Environment; Marine Affairs; Mental Health;
                       Urban Planning; Education
Leisure Interests . . . . .Lowland, Hill and Forest Walking; Music; Trees
Directorships Held . . . . . . .Scottish Lime Centre *(unpaid)*;
                       Sounds of the Future Company *(unpaid)*;
                       Theatre Workshop, Edinburgh *(unpaid)*

Harvie, Christopher MSP Mid Scotland and Fife Region
SNP . . . . List
Born . . . . 21st September 1944 in Motherwell
Educated . . . . .Kelso High School; Royal High School, Edinburgh;
                   Edinburgh University
Elected . . . . .2007 MSP for Mid Scotland and Fife Region
Parliamentary Office . . . . .Tel: (0131) 348 6765   Fax: (0131) 348 6767
                   E-mail: christopher.harvie.msp@scottish.parliament.uk
                   Researcher – Ms Christine Frasch
                   Tel: (0131) 348 6766
                   E-mail: christine.frasch@scottish.parliament.uk
Regional Office . . . . .53 Kirk Wynd, Kirkcaldy, KY1 1EH
                   Tel: (01592) 200349
                   Assistant – Mr David Torrance
                   E-mail: david.torrance@scottish.parliament.uk
Professional Career . . . . . .1968 - 69 History Tutorial Assistant, Edinburgh
                   University
                   1969 - 80 Lecturer, Senior Lecturer, then Acting Head
                   of History, Open University
                   1980 - 2007 Professor of British and Irish Studies,
                   University of Tübingen
Languages Spoken . . . . . . .German; French
Parliamentary Interests . . .Economics; Transport; Planning
Leisure Interests . . . . .Walking; Painting; Music
Directorships Held . . . . . . .Scottish Association for Public Transport (Hon President);
                   Scottish Review of Books
Published Books . . . . .1970; 1981: Industrialisation and Culture, 1832 - 1914
                   (editor)
                   1976: The Lights of Liberalism
                   1977; 1994; 2004: Scotland and Nationalism: Scottish
                   Society and Politics
                   1981; 1987; 1998; 2000: No Gods and Precious Few
                   Heroes
                   1985: Britain Today: The Economy (joint author)
                   1985; 1992: Britain Today: Politics and Society
                   (joint author)
                   1989: Forward! Scottish Labour from 1888 to the Present
                   (editor)
                   1991: The Centre of Things: Political Fiction in Britain
                   from Disraeli to the Present
                   1992: Cultural Weapons: Scotland and Survival in a New
                   Europe
                   1993: The Rise of Regional Europe
                   1995: Fool's Gold: The Story of North Sea Oil
                   1999: Travelling Scot
                   2000: The Road to Home Rule (joint author)
                   2001: Deep-Fried Hillman Imp: Scotland's Transport
                   2002: Scotland: A Short History
                   2004: Mending Scotland: Essays in Regional Economics
                   2008: A Floating Commonwealth: Politics, Culture and
                   Technology on Britain's Atlantic Coast, 1860 - 1930
                   2010: Broonland

Harvie, Patrick MSP . . . . . Glasgow Region
Scot Grn. . . . . List
Born . . . . 18th March 1973 in Vale of Leven, Dunbartonshire
Educated. . . . . Dumbarton Academy,
                              Manchester Metropolitan University
Elected . . . . 2003 MSP for Glasgow Region
Parliamentary Office . . . . . Tel: (0131) 348 6363 Fax: (0131) 348 6375
                              E-mail: patrick.harvie.msp@scottish.parliament.uk
                              Web: www.patrickharviemsp.com
Regional Office . . . . Suite 4/2, 52 St Enoch Square, Glasgow, G1 4AA
                              Tel & Fax: (0141) 248 3850
Political Career . . . . 2004 - Convener, Transport, Infrastructure and
                              Climate Committee
Professional Career . . . . . . 1997 - 2003 Development Worker, Promoting Health and
                              Challenging Exclusion (PHACE Scotland)
Parliamentary Interests . . . Citizenship; Ecological Issues; Equality; Food Culture;
                              Global Justice Issues; Media & Technology;
                              Sexual Health; Urban Environment
Leisure Interests. . . . . Cinema; Food & Drink
Directorships . . . . Gala Scotland Ltd

Henry, Hugh MSP . . . . Paisley South
Scot Lab. . . . . Majority 4,230 over SNP
Born . . . . 12th February 1952 in Glasgow
Educated. . . . . St Mirin's Academy, Paisley; Glasgow University;
                              Jordanhill College of Education
Elected . . . . 1999 MSP for Paisley South
Parliamentary Office . . . . . Tel: (0131) 348 5929 Fax: (0131) 348 5950
                              E-mail: hugh.henry.msp@scottish.parliament.uk
Constituency Office . . . . . . St James Business Centre, Linwood Road, Paisley, PA3 3AT
                              Tel: (0141) 848 7361
Political Career . . . . 1984 - 96 Councillor, Renfrew District Council
                              1995 - 99 Leader, Renfrewshire Council
                              2001 - 02 Deputy Minister for Health and
                              Community Care
                              2002 - 07 Deputy Minister for Justice
                              2007 - Convener, Public Audit Committee
Professional Career . . . . . . 1973 - 75 Accountant, IBM UK Ltd
                              1976 - 79 Teacher, Education Department,
                              Strathclyde Regional Council
                              1979 - 84 Senior Welfare Rights Officer, Strathclyde
                              Regional Council
                              1993 - 96 Community Care Manager, Community
                              Enterprise, Strathclyde

Hepburn, Jamie MSP. . . . . Central Scotland Region
SNP . . . . List
Born . . . . .21st May 1979 in Glasgow
Educated . . . . .Hyndland Secondary, Glasgow; Glasgow University
Elected . . . . .2007 MSP for Central Scotland Region
Parliamentary Office . . . . .Tel: (0131) 348 6574 Fax: (0131) 348 6575
E-mail: jamie.hepburn.ms@scottish.parliament.uk
Web: www.jamiehepburn.org
Parliamentary Assistant – Mr Patrick Grady
E-mail: patrick.grady@scottish.parliament.uk
Regional Office . . . . .Suite 3.3, The Dalziel Building, 7 Scott Street,
Motherwell, ML1 1PN
Tel: (01698) 337303 Fax: (01698) 269033
Staff – Mr Neil McCallum
E-mail: neil.mccallum@scottish.parliament.uk
Professional Career . . . . . .2001 - 02 Front of House Assistant, Glasgow
Citizen's Theatre
2002 Data Processor, Scottish Power
2002 - 07 Research Assistant to Alex Neil MSP
Trade Union . . . . .NUJ
Parliamentary Interests . . .European and External Affairs
Leisure Interests . . . . .Football; Reading (History and Biographies)

Hume, Jim MSP. . . . . South of Scotland Region
Scot Lib Dem . . . . List
Born . . . . .4th November 1962 in Peebles
Educated . . . . .Selkirk Secondary;
East Scotland College of Agriculture;
Edinburgh University
Elected . . . . .2007 MSP for South of Scotland Region
Parliamentary Office . . . . .Tel: (0131) 348 6702 Fax: (0131) 348 6705
Mobile: 07825 522771
E-mail: jim.hume.msp@scottish.parliament.uk
Web: www.jimhumemsp.com
Parliamentary Assistant – Ms Fiona Milne
Tel: (0131) 348 6703
E-mail: fiona.milne@scottish.parliament.uk
Research Assistant – Ms Charlotte Raw
Tel: (0131) 348 6704
E-mail: charlotte.raw@scottish.parliament.uk
Regional Assistant – Mrs Marjorie McCreadie
Political Career . . . . .2007 - Councillor, Scottish Borders Council
2007 - Liberal Democrat Deputy Spokesman on the
Environment, Rural Development and Energy
Professional Career . . . . . .1988 - Partner, John Hume and Sons
2004 - 06; 2007 Director, National Farmers Union of
Scotland
Trade Union . . . . .National Farmers Union of Scotland
Professional Association . . .Chartered Institute for Marketing
Parliamentary Interests . . .Environment; Rural Affairs
Leisure Interests . . . . .Gardening; Amateur Radio; Motorcycling
Published Books . . . . .1998: Shepherds (joint author)

Hyslop, Fiona MSP . . . . . . Lothians Region
SNP . . . . List
Born . . . . 1st August 1964 in Ayr
Educated . . . . Ayr Academy; Glasgow University;
Scottish College of Textiles
Elected . . . . 1999 MSP for Lothians Region
Office Held . . . . 2007 - Cabinet Secretary for Education and
Lifelong Learning
Parliamentary Office . . . . . Tel: (0131) 348 5921
E-mail: fiona.hyslop.msp@scottish.parliament.uk
Web: www.fionahyslop.com
Parliamentary Assistant – Miss Jennifer Adam
E-mail: jennifer.adam@scottish.parliament.uk
Regional Office . . . . 59 West Main Street, Whitburn, West Lothian, EH47 0QD
Tel: (01501) 749941
Office Manager – Mrs Mary Dickson
E-mail: mary.dickson@scottish.parliament.uk
Political Career . . . . 1999 - 2001 SNP Spokesman on Social Justice and Housing
2001 - 03 SNP Spokesman on Parliament
Government Strategy
2003 - 07 SNP Spokesman on Education
and Lifelong Learning
2007 - Cabinet Secretary for Education and Lifelong
Learning
Professional Career . . . . . . 1986 - 99 Marketing Manager, Standard Life
Parliamentary Interests . . . Children; Education; Life-Long Learning
Leisure Interests . . . . Cinema; Swimming

Ingram, Adam MSP . . . . . . South of Scotland Region
SNP . . . . List
Born . . . . 1st May 1951 in Kilmarnock
Educated . . . . Kilmarnock Academy; Glasgow University;
Paisley College
Elected . . . . 1999 MSP for South of Scotland Region
Parliamentary Office . . . . . Tel: (0131) 348 5733 Fax: (0131) 348 5563
E-mail: adam.ingram.msp@scottish.parliament.uk
Regional Office . . . . 45 Dalblair Road, Ayr, KA7 1UF
Tel: (01292) 290611 Fax: (01292) 290629
Political Career . . . . 1994 - 99 SNP Vice-Convener for Organisations
2005 - 07 SNP Deputy Spokesman on Children
and Early Education
2007 - Minister for Children and Early Years
Professional Career . . . . . . 1971 - 76 Manager, A. H. Ingram, Family Firm of Bakers
1985 - 86 Senior Economic Assistant, Manpower
Service Commission
1987 - 88 Researcher and Lecturer, Paisley College
1989 - 91 Development Options Ltd
1991 - 95 EES Consultants Ltd
1995 - 99 Freelance Economic Consultant
Leisure Interests . . . . Cricket; Football; Golf

Jamieson, Cathy MSP . . . . Carrick, Cumnock and Doon Valley
Scot Lab . . . . Majority 3,986 over SNP
Born . . . . 3rd November 1956 in Kilmarnock
Educated . . . . James Hamilton Academy, Kilmarnock;
Glasgow School of Art; Glasgow University;
Goldsmiths College, London; Caledonian University
Elected . . . . 1999 MSP for Carrick, Cumnock and Doon Valley
Parliamentary Office . . . . . Tel: (0131) 348 5776 Fax: (0131) 348 5968
E-mail: cathy.jamieson.msp@scottish.parliament.uk
Web: www.cathyjamiesonmsp.co.uk
Constituency Office . . . . . . Cumnock Community College, Caponacre Industrial Estate,
Cumnock, KA18 1SH
Tel: (0845) 458 1800 Fax: (0845) 458 1801
Political Career . . . . 1996 - 99 Member, Labour Party Scottish Executive
1997 - 99 Member, Labour Party National Executive
2001 - 03 Minister for Education and Young People
2001 - 03 Deputy Convener, European Committee
2001 - 07 Deputy Labour Leader, Scottish Parliament
2003 - 07 Minister for Justice
2008 - Labour Health and Wellbeing Shadow Cabinet
Secretary
Professional Career . . . . . . 1983 - 86 Social Worker
1986 - 92 Community Intermediate Treatment
Worker/Senior Intermediate Treatment Officer,
Strathclyde Regional Council
1992 - 99 Principal Officer, Who Cares? Scotland
Trade Union . . . . Unite
Parliamentary Interests . . . Children and Young People; Social Inclusion;
Social Services; Social Economy; Transport; Environment
Leisure Interests . . . . Art; Ayrshire History; Football (Kilmarnock FC);
Photography

Johnstone, Alex MSP . . . . . North East Scotland Region
Scot Cons . . . . List
Born . . . . 31st July 1961 in Stonehaven
Educated . . . . Mackie Academy, Stonehaven
Elected . . . . 1999 MSP for North East Scotland Region
Parliamentary Office . . . . . Tel: (0131) 348 5647 Fax: (0131) 348 5656
E-mail: alexander.johnstone.msp@scottish.parliament.uk
Web: www.alexjohnstone.msp.org.uk
PA – Ms Lindsey Walls
Tel: (0131) 348 5651
E-mail: lindsey.walls@scottish.parliament.uk
Regional Office . . . . 265a High Street, Arbroath, DD11 1EE
Tel: (01241) 430467 Fax: (01241) 430476
Political Career . . . . 1999 - 2001 Conservative Spokesman on Rural
Development Committee
1999 - 2001 Convener, Rural Affairs Committee
2001 - 03 Conservative Chief Whip and
Business Manager
2003 - 07 Conservative Spokesman on Environment
2007 - Conservative Shadow Minister for Transport,
Infrastructure and Climate Change
Professional Career . . . . . . 1980 - Dairy and Arable Farmer
Trade Union . . . . National Farmers Union of Scotland
Professional Association . . . Scottish Rural Property and Business Association
Parliamentary Interests . . . Economy; Industry; Rural Affairs; Transport
Leisure Interests . . . . Information Technology

Kelly, James MSP . . . . Glasgow Rutherglen
Scot Lab . . . . Majority 4,378 over SNP
Born . . . . 23rd October 1963 in Glasgow
Educated . . . . Trinity High School, Cambuslang;
Glasgow College of Technology
Elected . . . . 2007 MSP for Glasgow Rutherglen
Parliamentary Office . . . . . Tel: (0131) 348 6510 Fax: (0131) 348 6513
E-mail: james.kelly.msp@scottish.parliament.uk
Web: www.jameskellymsp.com
Constituency Office . . . . . . 51 Stonelaw Road, Rutherglen,
South Lanarkshire, G73 3TN
Tel: (0141) 647 0707 Fax: (0141) 643 1491
Staff – Ms Alexa Kelly
Political Career . . . . 2008 - Labour Whip
Professional Career . . . . . . 1985 - 88 Analyst Programmer, Argyll and
Clyde Health Board
1988 - 2004 Analyst/Programmer/Computer Auditor;
Finance Officer/Settlements Analyst Scottish Power
2004 - 07 Business Analyst, SAIC
Trade Union . . . . Unite
Parliamentary Interests . . . Finance; Health
Leisure Interests . . . . Golf; Football; Running Half Marathons

Kerr, Andy MSP . . . . East Kilbride
Scot Lab. . . . . Majority 1,972 over SNP
Born . . . . 17th March 1962 in East Kilbride
Educated. . . . . Claremont High School, East Kilbride;
         Glasgow College of Technology
Elected . . . . 1999 MSP for East Kilbride
Parliamentary Office . . . . .Tel: (0131) 348 5903 Fax: (0131) 348 5930
         E-mail: andy.kerr.msp@scottish.parliament.uk
         Web: www.andykerrmsp.co.uk
Constituency Office . . . . . .The Civic Centre, Andrew Street,
         East Kilbride, G74 1AB
         Tel: (01355) 806223 Fax: (01355) 806343
         Casework Manager – Mr Gordon Craig
         E-mail: gordon.craig@scottish.parliament.uk
         Secretary – Mrs Patricia Chambers
         E-mail: patricia.chambers@scottish.parliament.uk
Political Career . . . . .1999 - 2001 Convener, Transport and Environment
         Committee
         2001 - 04 Minister for Finance and Public Services
         2004 - 07 Minister for Health and Community Care
         2007 Labour Spokesman for Health
         2007 - 08 Labour Shadow Cabinet Secretary for
         Public Services
         2008 - Labour Finance and Sustainable Growth
         Shadow Cabinet Secretary
Professional Career . . . . . .1987 - 90 Research Officer, Strathkelvin District Council
         1990 - 93 Managing Director, Achieving Quality
         (Consultancy)
         1993 - 99 Strategy and Development Manager, Land
         Services, Glasgow City Council
Trade Union . . . . .UNISON
Parliamentary Interests . . .Environment; Local Government; Transport;
         Health and Wellbeing
Leisure Interests . . . . .Family; Football; Reading; Running

Kidd, Bill MSP . . . . Glasgow Region
SNP . . . . List
Born . . . . 24th July 1956 in Partick, Glasgow
Educated. . . . . Hyndland Secondary School
Elected . . . . 2007 MSP for Glasgow Region
Parliamentary Office . . . . .Tel: (0131) 348 6591 Fax; (0131) 348 5945
         E-mail: bill.kidd.msp@scottish.parliament.uk
Regional Office . . . . .Room 330, 3rd Floor, Baltic Chambers,
         50 Wellington Street, Glasgow, G2 6HJ
         Tel: (0141) 202 0677
Political Career . . . . .2007 - Councillor, Glasgow City Council
         2007 - SNP Deputy Whip
Parliamentary Interests . . . Eradication of Poverty; Job Creation; Housing Policy;
         Nuclear Power and Weapons - Non-Proliferation and
         Abolition

Lamont, Johann MSP . . . . Glasgow Pollok
Scot Lab. . . . . Majority 4,393 over SNP
Born. . . . . 11th July 1957 in Glasgow
Educated. . . . . Woodside Secondary School; Jordanhill College;
                                   Glasgow University; Strathclyde University
Elected . . . . .1999 MSP for Glasgow Pollok
Parliamentary Office . . . . .Tel: (0131) 348 5847
                                   E-mail: johann.lamont.msp@scottish.parliament.uk
                                   Web: www.johannlamont.blogspot.com
Constituency Office . . . . . .Unit 8, The Wedge, 1066 Barrhead Road,
                                   Glasgow, G53 5AB
                                   Tel: (0141) 270 1890 Fax: (0141) 270 1891
                                   PA – Ms Celine Lauter
                                   E-mail: celine.lauter@scottish.parliament.uk
Political Career . . . . .1993 -94 Chair, Scottish Labour Party
                                   2001 - 03 Convener, Social Justice Committee
                                   2003 - 04 Convener, Communities Committee
                                   2004 - 06 Deputy Minister for Communities
                                   2006 - 07 Deputy Minister for Justice
                                   2007 - 08 Labour Spokesman for Communities and Sport
                                   2008 - Labour Deputy Leader with special responsibility
                                      for Equalities
Professional Career . . . . . .1979 - 99 Teacher (Principal Teacher, Education
                                   Support at Castlemilk High, 1991 - 99)
Trade Union . . . . .Unite
Professional Association . . .Educational Institute of Scotland
Parliamentary Interests . . .Children's Rights; Poverty; Social Inclusion;
                                   Women's Rights
Leisure Interests . . . . .Family; Football; Running

Lamont, John MSP . . . . . .Roxburgh and Berwickshire
Scot Cons . . . . Majority 1,985 over Liberal Democrat
Born . . . . .15th April 1976 in Irvine
Educated . . . . .Kilwinning Academy; Glasgow University
Elected . . . . .2007 MSP for Roxburgh and Berwickshire
Parliamentary Office . . . . .Tel: (0131) 348 6533 Fax: (0131) 348 6534
                                   E-mail: john.lamont.msp@scottish.parliament.uk
                                   Web: www.john2win.com
                                   Parliamentary Adviser – Mr Ben Rose
Constituency Office . . . . . .25 High Street, Hawick, Roxburghshire, TD9 9BU
                                   Tel: (01450) 375948 Fax: (01450) 379613
                                   Caseworkers – Mrs Claire Balderston
                                                 Mrs Debbie Whalley
Political Career . . . . .2007 - Conservative Shadow Minister for Community Safety
Professional Career . . . . . .2000 - 07 Solicitor
Professional Association . . .Law Society of England and Wales
Leisure Interests . . . . .Travel; Cooking; Theatre; Running

Livingstone, Marilyn MSP Kirkcaldy
Scot Lab . . . . Majority 2,622 over SNP
Born . . . . 30th September 1952 in Kirkcaldy
Educated . . . . Viewforth Secondary School; Fife College
Elected . . . . 1999 MSP for Kirkcaldy
Parliamentary Office . . . . . Tel: (0131) 348 5744 Fax: (0131) 348 6944
                                    E-mail: marilyn.livingstone.msp@scottish.parliament.uk
                                    Web: www.marilynlivingstonemsp.org.uk
Constituency Office . . . . . . 3 East Fergus Place, Kirkcaldy, KY1 1XT
                                    Tel: (01592) 564114 Fax: (01592) 561085
                                    PA - Ms Christine Flynn
                                    E-mail: christine.flynn@scottish.parliament.uk
Political Career . . . . 1991 - 95 Councillor, Kirkcaldy District Council
                                    1995 - 99 Councillor, Fife Council
                                    2003 - 07 Ministerial Parliamentary Aide
                                       to the First Minister
                                    2007 - Deputy Convener, Standards, Procedures and Public
                                       Appointments Committee
Professional Career . . . . . . 1982 - 99 Head, Business School, Fife College
Trade Unions . . . . UNISON; Educational Institute of Scotland
Parliamentary Interests . . . Disability Issues; Enterprise; Equal Opportunity Issues;
                                    Lifelong Learning
Leisure Interests . . . . Environment; Hillwalking

Lochhead, Richard MSP . . Moray
SNP . . . . Majority 7,924 over Conservative
Born . . . . 24th May 1969 in Paisley
Educated . . . . Williamson High School, Glasgow; Stirling University
Elected . . . . 1999 - 2006 MSP for North East Scotland Region
                     2006 MSP for Moray (By-election)
Parliamentary Office . . . . .Tel: (0131) 348 5713 Fax: (0131) 348 5737
                     E-mail: richard.lochhead.msp@scottish.parliament.uk
                     Parliamentary Officer – Ms Catriona Murray
                     E-mail: catriona.murray@scottish.parliament.uk
                     Parliamentary Assistant – Mr Marc Macrae
                     E-mail: marc.macrae@scottish.parliament.uk
Constituency Office . . . . . .9 Wards Road, Elgin, Moray, IV30 1NL
                     Tel: (01343) 551111 Fax: (01343) 556355
Political Career . . . . .1994 - 98 Manager for Alex Salmond MP
                     1999 - 2000 SNP Spokesman on Fisheries and
                       Water Industry
                     2001 - 03 SNP Deputy Spokesman on Parliament and
                       Government Strategy
                     2003 - 04 SNP Spokesman on Rural Development
                       and Environment
                     2000 - 04 SNP Deputy Spokesman on Environment
                       and Rural Affairs (with special responsibility for fisheries)
                     2003 - 04 Convener, European and External
                       Relations Committee
                     2004 - 07 SNP Spokesman on Environment Rural Affairs,
                       Energy and Fisheries
                     2007 - Cabinet Secretary for Rural Affairs, and the
                       Environment
Professional Career . . . . . . 1987 - 89 Trainee, South of Scotland Electricity Board
                     1998 - 99 Economic Development Officer,
                       Dundee City Council
Trade Union . . . . .UNISON
Parliamentary Interests . . .Drugs; Economic Development; Energy; Environment;
                     Film Industry; Fishing; Rural Affairs
Leisure Interests . . . . .Cinema; Cycling; Music; Reading; Travel; Arts

MacAskill, Kenny MSP . . . Edinburgh East and Musselburgh
SNP . . . . Majority 1,382 over Labour
Born . . . . 28th April 1958 in Edinburgh
Educated . . . . Linlithgow Academy; Edinburgh University
Elected . . . . 2007 MSP for Edinburgh East and Musselburgh
        (1999 - 2007 MSP for Lothians Region)
Parliamentary Office . . . . . Tel: (0131) 348 5012 Fax: (0131) 348 5563
        E-mail: kenny.macaskill.msp@scottish.parliament.uk
        Web: www.kenny-macaskill.co.uk
        Personal Assistant – Mrs Karen Newton
        E-mail: karen.newton@scottish.parliament.uk
Constituency Office . . . . . . 16A Willowbrae Road, Edinburgh, EH8 7DB
        Tel & Fax: (0131) 661 9546
        Office Manager – Mrs Karen Newton
        E-mail: karen.newton@scottish.parliament.uk
        Constituency Assistant – Ms Laura McGravie
        Tel: (0131) 348 6982
        E-mail: laura.mcgravie@scottish.parliament.uk
Political Career . . . . 1999 - 2007 MSP for Lothians Region
        1999 - 2000 SNP Spokesman on Transport and
        the Environment
        2000 - 01 SNP Spokesman on Enterprise and
        Lifelong Learning
        1999 - 2003 Convener, Sub-ordinate Legislation
        Committee
        2002 - 04 SNP Spokesman on Tourism, Transport
        and Telecommunications
        2003 - 05 Deputy Convener, Audit Committee
        2004 - 07 SNP Spokesman on Justice
        2007 - SNP Cabinet Secretary for Justice
Professional Career . . . . . . Solicitor (Senior Partner from 2000)
Parliamentary Interests . . . Justice Issues
Leisure Interests . . . . Football; Keeping Fit; Reading; Sport
Published Books . . . . 2004: Building a Nation - Post Devolution
        Nationalism in Scotland
        2006: Global Scots - Voices from Afar (joint author)
        2006: Wherever the Saltire Flies (joint author)

Macdonald, Lewis MSP . . . Aberdeen Central
Scot Lab. . . . . Majority 382 over SNP
Born. . . . . 1st January 1957 in Stornoway
Educated. . . . . Inverurie Academy; Aberdeen University
Elected . . . . 1999 MSP for Aberdeen Central
Parliamentary Office . . . . . Tel: (0131) 348 5915 Fax: (0131) 348 5958
Mobile: 07770 646792
E-mail: lewis.macdonald.msp@scottish.parliament.uk
Web: www.lewismacdonaldmsp.com
Constituency Office . . . . . . 70 Rosemount Place, Aberdeen, AB25 2XJ
Tel: (01224) 646333 Fax: (01224) 645450
Constituency Assistant – Ms Rachel Duncan
E-mail: rachel.duncan@scottish.parliament.uk
Constituency Officer – Mr David Groundwater
E-mail: david.groundwater@scottish.parliament.uk
Political Career . . . . 1987 -92 Researcher to Frank Doran MP
1993 - 97 Researcher to Tom Clarke MP
2000 - 01 Convener, Holyrood Progress Group
(Parliamentary Building)
2001 - 02 Deputy Minister for Transport and Planning
2002 - 03 Deputy Minister for Enterprise, Transport
and Lifelong Learning
2003 - 04 Deputy Minister for Enterprise and
Lifelong Learning
2004 - 05 Deputy Minister for Environment and
Rural Development
2005 - 07 Deputy Minister for Health and
Community Care
2007 - 08 Labour Shadow Minister for Public Health
2008 - Labour Spokesman on Energy, Enterprise and
Tourism
Professional Career . . . . . . 1992 - 93 History Lecturer, Aberdeen University
Trade Union . . . . Unite
Parliamentary Interests . . . Energy; Media; Gaelic; Education; Transport; Health;
Sport; Environment; Lifelong Learning
Leisure Interests . . . . Patron; Aberdeen Football Club Supporters Trust;
Sport; Hill Walking; History

MacDonald, Margo MSP . . Lothians Region
Independent. . . . . List
Born . . . . .19th April 1943 in Hamilton
Educated . . . . .Hamilton Academy; Dunfermline College
Elected . . . . .2003 MSP for Lothians Region (previously,
           1999 - 2003, SNP MSP for Lothians Region)
Parliamentary Office . . . . .Tel: (0131) 348 5714 Fax: (0131) 348 6271
           E-mail: margo.macdonald.msp@scottish.parliament.uk
           Web: www.margomacdonald.org
           Parliamentary Assistant/Researcher – Mr Peter Warren
           E-mail: peter.warren@scottish.parliament.uk
           Secretary – Mrs Mary Blackford
           Tel: (0131) 348 5724
           E-mail: mary.blackford@scottish.parliament.uk
Political Career . . . . .1973 - 74 MP for Govan
           1974 - 79 Deputy Leader, SNP
Professional Career . . . . . .1963 - 65 Teacher
           1978 - 81 Director, Shelter
           1981 - 91 Broadcaster, Editor and Reporter
           Freelance Journalist
Leisure Interests . . . . .Country Music; Hibernian Football Club

Macintosh, Ken MSP . . . . . Eastwood
Scot Lab. . . . . Majority 891 over Conservative
Born. . . . . 15th January 1962 in Inverness
Educated. . . . . Royal High School, Edinburgh;
           Edinburgh University
Elected . . . . .1999 MSP for Eastwood
Parliamentary Office . . . . .Tel: (0131) 348 5897 Fax: (0131) 348 5983
           E-mail: ken.macintosh.msp@scottish.parliament.uk
           Web: www.kenmacintoshmsp.co.uk
Constituency Office . . . . . .2 Stewart Drive, Clarkston, East Renfrewshire, G76 7EZ
           Tel: (0141) 621 2080 Fax: (0141) 621 2082
           Office Manager – Mrs Marion Anderson
           E-mail: marion.anderson@scottish.parliament.uk
Political Career . . . . .2001 - 03 Deputy Convener, Procedures Committee
           2003 - 05 Deputy Convener, Standards Committee
           2006 - 07 Deputy Convener, Subordinate Legislation
            Committee
           2007 - Labour Shadow Minister for Schools and Skills
Professional Career . . . . . .1987 - 99 Journalist, BBC News and Current Affairs
Parliamentary Interests . . .Culture; Education; Finance; Sport
Leisure Interests . . . . .Football; Golf; Music; Reading; Tennis

Martin, Paul MSP . . . . Glasgow Springburn
Scot Lab . . . . Majority 5,095 over SNP
Born . . . . .17th March 1967 in Springburn, Glasgow
Educated . . . . .All Saints Secondary School, Glasgow;
                                Barmulloch College, Glasgow
Elected . . . . .1999 Member, Scottish Parliament for
                                Glasgow Springburn
Parliamentary Office . . . . .Tel: (0131) 348 5844
                                E-mail: paul.martin.msp@scottish.parliament.uk
                                Web: www.paulmartinmsp.org.uk
Constituency Office . . . . . .604 Alexandra Parade, Glasgow, G31 3BS
                                Tel: (0141) 564 1364
                                Secretary – Mrs Irene Hayes
Political Career . . . . .1993 - 99 Councillor, Glasgow City Council
                                2008 - Labour Spokesman on Community Safety
Trade Union . . . . .AEEU
Parliamentary Interests . . .Crime; Housing; Police; Youth
Leisure Interests . . . . .Football; Golf; Reading; Walking

Marwick, Tricia MSP . . . .Central Fife
SNP . . . . .Majority 1,166 over Labour
Born . . . . .5th November 1953 in Cowdenbeath, Fife
Elected . . . . .2007 - MSP for Central Fife (1999 - 2007
                                MSP for Mid Scotland and Fife Region)
Parliamentary Office . . . . .Tel: (0131) 348 5680 Fax: (0131) 348 5944
                                E-mail: tricia.marwick.msp@scottish.parliament.uk
                                Web: www.tricia.marwick.com
                                Personal Assistant - Ms Karen Newton
                                Tel: (0131) 348 5012
                                E-mail: karen.newton@scottish.parliament.uk
Constituency Office . . . . . .10 Commercial Street, Markinch, Fife, KY7 6DE
                                Tel & Fax: (01592) 764815
                                Staff – Mr Robbie McGregor
Political Career . . . . .1999 - 2007 MSP for Mid Scotland and Fife Region
                                1999 - 2000 SNP Deputy Business Manager
                                2000 - 01 SNP Business Manager
                                2001 - 03 Deputy Convener, Standards Committee
                                2001 - 03 SNP Business Manager and Spokeswoman
                                on Local Government
                                2003 - 04 Convener, Standards Committee
                                2005 - 07 SNP Spokesperson on Housing
Professional Career . . . . . .1992 - 99 Public Affairs Officer, Shelter (Scotland)
Parliamentary Interests . . .Housing; Social Exclusion
Leisure Interests . . . . .Reading

Mather, Jim MSP. . . . . . . Argyll and Bute
SNP . . . . Majority 815 over Liberal Democrat
Born . . . . 6th March 1947 in Lochwinnoch
Educated. . . . . Paisley Grammar School; Greenock High School;
Glasgow University
Elected . . . . 2007 - MSP for Argyll and Bute (2003 - 07
MSP for Highlands and Islands Region
Parliamentary Office . . . . .Tel: (0131) 348 5700
E-mail: jim.mather.msp@scottish.parliament.uk
Constituency Office . . . . . .31 Combie Street, Oban, PA34 4HS
Tel: (01631) 571359 Fax: (01631) 571360
Web: www.argyll-snp.com
Political Career . . . . .2000 - 04 Treasurer, SNP
2003 - 07 MSP for Highlands and Islands Region
2003 - 07 SNP Spokesman on Enterprise
2007 - Minister for Enterprise, Energy
and Tourism
Professional Career . . . . . .1970 - 73 Accountant, Chivas Brothers Ltd
1973 - 83 Marketing Manager, IBM UK Ltd
1983 - 96 Director, Computers for Business
(Scotland) Ltd
1997 - 99 Director, Startech Partners Ltd

Matheson, Michael MSP . . Falkirk West
SNP . . . . Majority 776 over Labour
Born . . . . 8th September 1970 in Glasgow
Educated . . . . .John Bosco Secondary School, Glasgow;
Queen Margaret College; Open University
Elected . . . . .2007 MSP for Falkirk West (1999 - 2007
MSP for Central Scotland Region)
Parliamentary Office . . . . .Tel: (0131) 348 5671 Fax: (0131) 348 6474
E-mail: michael.matheson.msp@scottish.parliament.uk
Constituency Office . . . . . .15A East Bridge Street, Falkirk, FK1 1YB
Tel: (01324) 629271 Fax: (01324) 635576
Secretary – Mr Andrew MacLadden
Admin Assistant – Mrs Irene Coleman
Political Career . . . . .1999 - 2007 MSP for Central Scotland Region
1999 - 2004 SNP Deputy Spokesman on Justice
2004 - 06 SNP Spokesman on Culture and Sport
2009 - Deputy Convener, European and External Relations
Committee
Professional Career . . . . . .1991 - 99 Community Occupational Therapist
Professional Association . . .Council for the Professions Supplementary to Medicine
Parliamentary Interests . . .Community Care; Equality Issues; Health;
Public Health; Mountain Rescue
Leisure Interests . . . . .Mountaineering; Travel

Maxwell, Stewart MSP. . . . West of Scotland Region
SNP . . . . List
Born . . . . 24th December 1963 in Glasgow
Educated. . . . . King's Park Secondary School;
Glasgow College of Technology
Elected . . . . 2003 MSP for West of Scotland Region
Parliamentary Office . . . . . Tel: (0131) 348 5669
E-mail: stewart.maxwell.msp@ scottish.parliament.uk
Web: www.stewartmaxwellmsp.com
Regional Office . . . . .Unit 27, Sir James Clark Building, Abbey Mill Business
Centre, Seedhill Road, Paisley, PA1 1TJ
Tel: (0141) 887 2607
Constituency Assistants – Mr Fraser Brown
Mr Sean Lafferty
Political Career . . . . .2003 - 04 Deputy Convener, Justice I Committee
2004 - 06 Shadow Deputy Minister for Health
2006 - 07 Shadow Minister for Sport, Culture
and Media
2007 - 09 Minister for Communities and Sport
Professional Career . . . . . .1986 - 88, 1991 - 92 Wilmax Ltd (Wholesale Meat
Family Business)
1988 - 91 Admin Officer, Scottish Training Foundation
1993 - 94 Industrial Training Manager, Strathclyde
Fire Brigade
1994 - 2000 Senior Admin Officer, Strathclyde
Fire Brigade
2000 - 03 Management Information System Project
Manager, Strathclyde Fire Brigade

McArthur, Liam MSP . . . . Orkney
Scot Lib Dem . . . . Majority 2,476 over SNP
Born . . . . .8th August 1967 in Edinburgh
Educated . . . . .Sanday and Kirkwall Grammar, Orkney;
Edinburgh University
Parliamentary Office . . . . .Tel: (0131) 348 5815 Fax: (0131) 348 5807
E-mail: liam.mcarthur.msp@scottish.parliament.uk
Web: www.liammcarthurmsp.org.uk
Constituency Office . . . . . .31 Broad Street, Kirkwall, KW15 1DH
Tel: (01856) 876541 Fax: (01856) 876162
Political Career . . . . .2008 - Liberal Democrat Shadow Environment,
Rural Development and Energy Secretary
Professional Career . . . . . .1993 - 2002 Political Consultant, Brussels and London
2002 - 05 Special Adviser to Deputy First Minister
2005 - 07 Political Consultant
Languages Spoken . . . . . . .French; Spanish
Parliamentary Interests . . .Scottish Economy; Renewable Energy; Tourism;
Agriculture; Fishing
Leisure Interests . . . . .Sport (particularly Football); Music; Historic Buildings;
Family
Directorship . . . . .Hearts and Balls (Rugby Injury Charity)

McAveety, Frank MSP. . . . Glasgow Shettleston
Scot Lab. . . . . Majority 2,881 over SNP
Born . . . . .27th July 1962 in Glasgow
Educated . . . . .All Saints Secondary School, Glasgow;
                         Strathclyde University;
                         St Andrews College of Education
Elected . . . . .1999 MSP for Glasgow Shettleston
Parliamentary Office . . . . .Tel: (0131) 348 5906 Fax: (0131) 348 5987
                         E-mail: frank.mcaveety.msp@scottish.parliament.uk
                         Web: www.frankmcaveetymsp.org
Constituency Office . . . . . .1346 Shettleston Road, Glasgow, G32 9AT
                         Tel: (0141) 764 0175 Fax: (0141) 764 0876
                         Constituency Assistant – Mr Alex Glass
Political Career . . . . .1988 - 95 Councillor, Glasgow District Council
                         1995 - 99 Councillor, Glasgow City Council
                           (Leader 1997-99)
                         1995 - 97 Convener of Arts and Culture,
                           City of Glasgow
                         1999 - 2000 Deputy Minister for Local Government
                         2002 - 03 Deputy Minister for Health and
                           Community Care
                         2003 - 04 Minister for Tourism, Culture and Sport
                         2007 - Convener, Public Petitions Committee
                         2008 - Labour Spokesman on Sport
Professional Career . . . . . .1984 - 94 Secondary School History and
                         English Teacher, Glasgow
                         1994 - 99 Secondary School History and
                         English Teacher, Renfrewshire
Trade Unions . . . . .Unite; Educational Institute of Scotland
Parliamentary Interests . . .Culture; Housing; Local Government; Sport
Leisure Interests . . . . .Music; Reading; Sport; Writing

McCabe, Tom MSP . . . . . . Hamilton South
Scot Lab. . . . . Majority 3,652 over SNP
Born. . . . . 28th April 1954 in Hamilton
Educated . . . . St Martin's Secondary School, Hamilton;
Bell College of Technology
Elected . . . . 1999 MSP for Hamilton South
Parliamentary Office . . . . . Tel: (0131) 348 5830 Fax: (0131) 348 5125
E-mail: tom.mccabe.msp@scottish.parliament.uk
Web: www.tommccabe.co.uk
Researcher – Miss Gemma Climson
E-mail: gemma.climson@scottish.parliament.uk
Constituency Office . . . . . . 23 Beckford Street, Hamilton, ML3 0BT
Tel: (01698) 454018 Fax: (01698) 454222
Personal Assistant – Ms Kathleen Ferguson
E-mail: kathleen.ferguson@scottish.parliament.uk
Political Career . . . . 1988 - 96 Councillor, Hamilton District
Council (Leader, 1992 - 96)
1996 - 99 Leader, South Lanarkshire Council
1999 - 2001 Minister for Parliament
1999 - 2001 Labour, Business Manager;
Member, Scottish Parliamentary Bureau
2003 - 04 Deputy Minister for Health and
Community Care
2004 - 07 Minister for Finance and Public
Services
Professional Career . . . . . . 1974 - 93 Hoover plc
1993 - 98 Welfare Rights Officer
Trade Union . . . . Unite
Parliamentary Interests . . . Healthcare; Social Work; Economic Development
Leisure Interests . . . . Reading; Walking; Exercise; Golf; Travelling; Cinema

McConnell, Rt Hon Jack MSP Motherwell and Wishaw
Scot Lab. . . . . Majority 5,938 over SNP
Born. . . . . 30th June 1960 in Irvine
Educated. . . . . Arran High School; Stirling University
Elected . . . . 1999 MSP for Motherwell and Wishaw
Parliamentary Office . . . . . Tel: (0131) 348 5831 Fax: (0131) 348 6833
E-mail: jack.mcconnell.msp@scottish.parliament.uk
Web: www.jackmcconnell.org
Researcher – Mr Greg Black
Tel: (0131) 348 8531
E-mail: greg.black@scottish.parliament.uk
Head of Office – Ms Susan Dalgety
Tel: (0131) 348 5848
E-mail: susan.dalgety@scottish.parliament.uk
Constituency Office . . . . . . 265 Main Street, Wishaw, Lanarkshire, ML2 7NE
Tel: (01698) 303040 Fax: (01698) 303060
Assistant – Mrs Linda Shevlin
Political Career . . . . 1984 - 93 Councillor, Stirling District Council
(Leader 1990 - 92)
1992 - 98 General Secretary, Scottish Labour Party
1999 - 2000 Minister for Finance
2000 - 01 Minister for Education, Europe and
External Affairs
2001 - 07 First Minister of Scotland
2007 Labour Leader, Scottish Parliament
Professional Career . . . . . . 1983 - 92 Mathematics Teacher, Alloa
Trade Union . . . . Community; GMB
Leisure Interests . . . . Golf; Music

McGrigor, Jamie MSP. . . . Highlands and Islands Region
Scot Cons . . . . List
Born . . . . 19th October 1949 in London
Educated . . . . Cladich School, Argyll; Eton College
Elected . . . . 1999 MSP for Highlands and Islands
Parliamentary Office . . . . . Tel: (0131) 348 5648 Fax: (0131) 348 5656
Mobile: 07788 900998
E-mail: jamie.mcgrigor.msp@scottish.parliament.uk
Web: www.jamiemcgrigormsp.com
Assistant – Mr Douglas Pattullo
Tel: (0131) 348 5616
E-mail: douglas.pattullo@scottish.parliament.uk
Assistant – Miss Anna Ptaszynski
Tel: (0131) 348 5673
E-mail: anna.ptaszynski@scottish.parliament.uk
Regional Office . . . . 61 Chalmers Street, Ardrishaig, Argyll, PA30 8DX
Tel: (01546) 606586 Fax: (01546) 605387
E-mail: abscua@btconnect.com
Staff – Mrs Pauline Houston
Tel: (01546) 603811
E-mail: paulinehouston@hotmail.com
Political Career . . . . 2003 - 07 Conservative Spokesman on Tourism,
Culture and Sport
2007 - Conservative Spokesman on Communities
and Sport
Professional Career . . . . . . 1968 - 69 Manager, Furniture Shipping Business
1969 - 71 Shipping Agent
1972 - 74 Stockbroker
1975 - 79 Fish Farmer
1977 - Hill Farmer (Sheep and Cattle)
Parliamentary Interests . . . Fisheries; Rural Development; Housing
Leisure Interests . . . . Fishing; Literature; Music

McInnes, Alison MSP. . . . . North East Scotland Region
Scot Lib Dem . . . . List
Born . . . . 17th July 1957 in Ayrshire
Educated. . . . . Irvine Royal Academy;
McLaren High School, Callander;
Glasgow University
Elected . . . . 2007 MSP for North East Scotland Region
Parliamentary Office . . . . .Tel: (0131) 348 5463 Fax: (0131) 348 5465
E-mail: alison.mcinnes.msp@scottish.parliament.uk
Web: www.alisonmcinnes.co.uk
Regional Office . . . . .67 High Street, Inverurie, Aberdeenshire, AB51 3QJ
Tel: (01467) 628706
Political Career . . . . .1992 - 95 Councillor, Gordon District Council
1995 - 2007 Councillor, Aberdeenshire Council
2008 - Liberal Democrat Shadow Transport,
Local Government and Climate Change Secretary
Professional Career . . . . . .1999 - 2005 Board Member, East Areas Board of
Scottish Natural Heritage
1999 - 2007 Non-Executive Director, Scottish
Enterprise Grampian
Parliamentary Interests . . .Climate Change; Visual Impairment. Epilepsy;
Oil and Gas
Leisure Interests . . . . .Architecture; the Arts; Gardening; Cooking
Directorship Held . . . . . . .Callisto Productions Ltd

McKee, Ian MBE MSP . . . . . Lothians Region
SNP . . . . .List
Born . . . . .2nd April 1940 in South Shields
Educated . . . . .Fettes College; Edinburgh University
Elected . . . . .2007 MSP for Lothians Region
Parliamentary Office . . . . .Tel: (0131) 348 6815 Fax: (0131) 348 6818
E-mail: ian.mckee.msp@scottish.parliament.uk
Web: www.ianmckee.org
Office Manager – Mrs Loraine Henderson
Tel: (0131) 348 6816
E-mail: loraine.henderson@scottish.parliament.uk
Parliamentary Assistant – Mr Tony Giugliano
Tel: (0131) 348 6817
E-mail: tony.giugliano@scottish.parliament.uk
Political Career . . . . .2009 - Deputy Convener, Subordinate Legislation
Committee
Professional Career . . . . . .1966 - 71 Medical Officer, RAF
1971 - 2006 GP, Edinburgh
1979 - 2002 Managing Director, Hermiston
Publications Ltd
Parliamentary Interests . . .Health; Culture; Debt Relief
Leisure Interests . . . . .Hill Walking; Theatre; Football

McKelvie, Christina MSP . Central Scotland Region
SNP . . . . List
Born . . . . 4th March 1968 in Glasgow
Educated . . . . St Leonards Secondary School;
Aniesland College; Cardonald College;
Nautical College; St Andrews University
Elected . . . . 2007 MSP for Central Scotland Region
Parliamentary Office . . . . . Tel: (0131) 348 6680 Fax: (0131) 348 6683
E-mail: christina.mckelvie.msp@scottish.parliament.uk
Web: www.christinamckelviemsp.org
Staff – Mr Calum Cashley
Regional Office . . . . Suite 3.3, Dalziel Building, 7 Scott Street,
Motherwell, ML1 1PN
Tel: (01698) 337302 Fax: (01698) 269033
Constituency Assistant – Ms Martha McAllister
E-mail: martha.mcallister@scottish.parliament.uk
Professional Career . . . . . . Social Services
Trade Union . . . . UNISON

McLaughlin, Anne MSP . . Glasgow Region
SNP . . . . List
Born . . . . 8th March 1966 in Greenock
Educated . . . . Port Glasgow High School;
Royal Scottish Academy of Music and Drama;
Glasgow University
Elected . . . . 2009 MSP for Glasgow Region *(replaced Bashir Ahmed)*
Parliamentary Office . . . . . Tel: (0131) 348 6543 Fax: (0131) 348 3545
E-mail: anne.mclaughlin.msp@scottish.parliament.uk
Web: www.annemclaughlinmsp.com
Constituency Office . . . . . . Room 332, Baltic Chambers, 50 Wellington Street,
Glasgow, G2 6HJ
Tel: (0141) 202 0681 Fax: (0141) 202 0682
Staff *(part time)* – Ms Janet Connor
Mr Michael Dixon
Ms Esther Sassaman
Leisure Interests . . . . Cinema; Reading; Music

McLetchie, David MSP . . . Edinburgh Pentlands
Scot Cons . . . . Majority 4,525 over Labour
Born . . . . 6th August 1952 in Edinburgh
Educated . . . . George Heriots School, Edinburgh;
                     Edinburgh University
Elected . . . . 2003 MSP for Edinburgh Pentlands (previously,
                     1999 - 2003, MSP for Lothians Region)
Parliamentary Office . . . . . Tel: (0131) 348 5659 Fax: (0131) 348 5935
                     E-mail: david.mcletchie.msp@scottish.parliament.uk
                     Web: www david4pentlands.com
                     PA – Ms Ann Menzies
                     E-mail: ann.menzies@scottish.parliament.uk
                     Researcher/Caseworker – Mr Martin Donald
                     Tel: (0131) 348 5957
                     E-mail: martin.donald@scottish.parliament.uk
Constituency Office . . . . . . 20 Spylaw Street, Edinburgh, EH13 0JX
                     Tel: (0131) 441 7782
                     Researcher/Caseworker – Mr Martin Donald
Political Career . . . . 1994 - 97 President, Scottish Conservative and
                     Unionist Association
                     1997 - 98 Vice Chairman, Scottish Conservative and
                     Unionist Party
                     1999 - 2005 Leader, Scottish Conservative MSPs
                     2007 - Conservative Chief Whip and
                     Business Manager
Professional Career . . . . . . 1976 - 2005 Solicitor then Partner, Tods Murray WS,
                     Edinburgh
Professional Association . . . Law Society of Scotland
Parliamentary Interests . . . Constitutional Affairs; Education; Law Reform; Tax
Leisure Interests . . . . Crime Fiction; Football; Golf; Music

McMahon, Michael MSP . . Hamilton North and Bellshill
Scot Lab . . . . Majority 4,865 over SNP
Born . . . . 18th September 1961 in Lanark
Educated . . . . Our Lady's High School, Motherwell;
                     Glasgow Caledonian University
Elected . . . . 1999 MSP for Hamilton North and Bellshill
Parliamentary Office . . . . . Tel: (0131) 348 5828 Fax: (0131) 348 5993
                     E-mail: michael.mcmahon.msp@scottish.parliament.uk
Constituency Office . . . . . . 188 Main Street, Bellshill, ML4 1AE
                     Tel: (01698) 304501 Fax: (01698) 300223
                     Caseworker - Ms Yvonne Smith
                     Tel: (01698) 304503
Political Career . . . . 2003 - 07 Convener, Public Petitions Committee
                     2007 - 08 Labour Chief Whip
                     2008 - Labour Parliamentary Business Manager
Professional Career . . . . . . 1977 - 92 Welder, Terex Equipment Ltd, Motherwell
                     1996 - Political Researcher
Trade Union . . . . GMB
Published Books . . . . 2006: Celtic Minded 2

McMillan, Stuart MSP ...... West of Scotland Region
SNP .... List
Born .... 6th May 1972 in Barrow-in-Furness
Educated. .... Port Glasgow High School;
                        Central College of Commerce, Glasgow;
                        University of Abertay Dundee
Elected .... 2007 MSP for West of Scotland Region
Parliamentary Office ..... Tel: (0141) 889 9519 Fax: (0141) 889 4693
                        E-mail: stuart.mcmillan.msp@scottish.parliament.uk
                        Web: stuart-mcmillan.net
                        Parliamentary Assistant – Ms Kirsty Boyle
                        Tel: (0131) 348 6810
                        E-mail: kirsty.boyle@scottish.parliament.uk
Regional Office .... Unit 27, Sir James Clarke Building, Seedhill,
                        Paisley, PA1 1TJ
                        Tel: (0141) 889 9519 Fax: (0141) 889 4693
                        Office Co-ordinator – Mr Iain Fraser
                        E-mail: iain.fraser@scottish.parliament.uk
                        Parliamentary Assistant – Mr Niall Sommerville
                        E-mail: niall.sommerville@scottish.parliament.uk
Professional Career ...... 1998 - 2000 Supply Analyst, IBM UK Ltd
                        2000 - 03 Researcher, SNP Whips Office,
                           House of Commons
                        2003 - 07 Office Manager, Bruce McFee MSP
Parliamentary Interests ... Economy; Energy; Tourism; Marine Tourism;
                        Boating
Leisure Interests .... Football; Bagpipes

McNeill, Duncan MSP ... Greenock and Inverclyde
Scot Lab .... Majority 3,024 over SNP
Born .... 7th September 1950 in Greenock
Parliamentary Offices ... Tel: (0131) 348 5912 Fax: (0131) 348 5991
                        E-mail: duncan.mcneil.msp@scottish.parliament.uk
                        Web: www.duncanmcneil.com
Constituency Office ..... The Parliamentary Office, 20 Union Street,
                        Greenock, PA16 8JL
                        Tel: (01475) 791820 Fax: (01475) 791821
                        PA - Alison McKenzie
Political Career .... 1993 - 2003 Labour Group Whip
                        2001 - 07 Member, Scottish Parliament Corporate Body
                        2007 - Convener, Local Government and
                           Communities Committee
Professional Career ..... Shipyard Worker
                        Trade Union Organiser (GMB)
Trade Union .... GMB
Leisure Interest .... Golf

McNeill, Pauline MSP . . .Glasgow Kelvin
Scot Lab . . . . .Majority 1,207 over SNP
Born . . . . .12th September 1962 in Paisley
Educated . . . . .Our Ladies High School, Cumbernauld;
Strathclyde University;
Glasgow College of Building and Printing
Elected . . . . .1999 MSP for Glasgow Kelvin
Parliamentary Office . . . .Tel: (0131) 348 5909 Fax: (0131) 348 6486
E-mail: pauline.mcneill.msp@scottish.parliament.uk
Web: www.paulinemcneill.org.uk
Constituency Office . . . . .1274 Argyle Street, Glasgow, G3 8AA
Tel: (0141) 589 7120 Fax: (0141) 589 7122
Constituency Organiser - Ms Alexis Mosson
Researcher – Ms Nicola Dowds
Caseworker – Mr Martin McElroy
Political Career . . . . .2001 - 03 Convener, Justice II Committee
1999 - 2003 Vice-Chair, Scottish Parliament
Labour Group
2003 - 07 Convener, Justice I Committee
2007 - Labour Shadow Minister for Children and Early Years
2007 - 08 Labour Shadow Spokesman on Justice
2008 - Labour Shadow Europe, External Affairs and
Culture Secretary
Professional Career . . . . .Graphic Designer
1986 - 88 President, Scottish NUS
1988 - 99 Regional Organiser, GMB
Trade Union . . . . .GMB
Parliamentary Interests . .E-commerce; Education; Health; Justice;
Music Industry; Planning Law; Affordable Housing;
Public Transport; Household Recycling;
Hospital Services
Leisure Interests . . . . .Guitar Playing; Music; Singing
Directorships Held . . . . . .Board Member, Routes out of Prostitution
Board Member, Patrick Music and Community
Arts Initiative
Social Inclusion Partnership

McNulty, Des MSP....... Clydebank and Milngavie
Scot Lab.............. Majority 3,179 over SNP
Born................. 28th July 1952 in Stockport
Educated.............. St Bede's, Manchester; York University;
Glasgow University
Elected .... 1999 MSP for Clydebank and Milngavie
Parliamentary Office .....Tel: (0131) 348 5918 Fax: (0131) 348 5978
E-mail: des.mcnulty.msp@scottish.parliament.uk
Researcher – Ms Katie Ewart
Tel: (0131) 348 5919
E-mail: katie.ewart@scottish.parliament.uk
Constituency Office ......Clydebank Central Library, Dunbarton Road,
Clydebank, G81 1XH
Tel & Fax: (0141) 952 7711
E-mail: des.direct@scottish.parliament.uk
Parliamentary Officer – Ms Lesley Whyte
E-mail: lesley.whyte@scottish.parliament.uk
Administrator – Ms Jackie Brockett
Political Career ....1990 - 96 Councillor, Strathclyde Region
1995 - 99 Councillor, Glasgow City Council
1999 - 2001 Member, Scottish Parliament
Corporate Body
2001 - 07 Convener, Finance Committee
2007 - Labour Spokesman on Transport,
Infrastructure and Climate Change
Professional Career ......Formerly Head of Sociology, then Head of Strategic
Planning, Glasgow University
1996 - 99 Chairman, Glasgow Healthy City
Partnership
1998 - 99 Member, Greater Glasgow Health Board
Trade Union ....GMB; Educational Institute of Scotland
Parliamentary Interests ...Health; Education; Environment; Housing;
Local Government
Leisure Interests ....Music; Theatre; Design and Architecture
Directorships ....Clydebank Rebuilt
Tron Theatre
Wise Group

Milne, Dr Nanette MSP . . . North East Scotland Region
Scot Cons . . . . List
Born . . . . 27th April 1942 in Aberdeen
Educated . . . . Aberdeen High School for Girls;
                              Aberdeen University
Elected . . . . 2003 MSP for North East Region
Parliamentary Office . . . . . Tel: (0131) 348 5651 Fax: (0131) 348 6480
                              E-mail: nanette.milne.msp@scottish.parliament.uk
                              Web: www.nanettemilne.co.uk
                              Researcher – Mr Miles Briggs
                              Tel: (0131) 348 5884
                              E-mail: miles.briggs@scottish.parliament.uk
Regional Office . . . . 265a High Street, Arbroath, DD11 1EE
                              Tel: (01241) 430467
Political Career . . . . 1988 - 99 Councillor, Aberdeen City Council
                              2003 - 05 Conservative Deputy Spokesman on
                                 Health and Community Care
                              2005 - 07 Conservative Spokesman on Health
                              2007 - Conservative Shadow Minister for the Environment
Professional Career . . . . . . 1969 - 73 Anaesthetics Registrar, Aberdeen Hospitals
                              1978 - 92 Part-time research work in Oncology,
                                 Aberdeen Hospitals
Professional Association . . . Aberdeen Medico Chirurgical Society
Parliamentary Interests . . . Health; Environment; Rural Affairs
Leisure Interests . . . . Cooking; Entertaining; Gardening; Golf; Skiing; Walking

Mitchell, Margaret MSP . . Central Scotland Region
Scot Cons . . . . List
Born . . . . 15th November 1952 in Coatbridge
Educated . . . . Coatbridge High School; Jordanhill College;
Strathclyde University; Open University;
Hamilton Teacher Training College
Elected . . . . 2003 MSP for Central Scotland Region
Parliamentary Office . . . . . Tel: (0131) 348 5639 Fax: (0131) 348 6483
E-mail: margaret.mitchell.msp@scottish.parliament.uk
Web: www.margaretmitchellmsp.org
PA – Ms Norma Summers
E-mail: norma.summers@scottish.parliament.uk
Regional Office . . . . .104 Cadzow Street, Hamilton, ML3 6HP
Tel: (01698) 282815 Fax: (01698) 281533
Staff – Ms Liz McLean
E-mail: liz.mclean@scottish.parliament.uk
Political Career . . . . .1988 - 95 Councillor, Hamilton District Council
(Leader, Conservative Group)
1999 - 2003 Special Adviser to David McLetchie MSP
and Lord James Douglas-Hamilton MSP
2003 - 05 Conservative Deputy Spokesman on
Justice and Home Affairs
2005 - 07 Conservative Spokesman on Justice
2007 - Convener, Equal Opportunities Committee
Professional Career . . . . . .1974 - 90 Teacher, Strathclyde Regional Council
1990 - Justice of the Peace
1992 - 95 Non Executive Director, Hairmyres and
Stonehouse NHS Trust
Trade Union . . . . .Educational Institute of Scotland
Professional Association . . .General Teaching Council
Language Spoken . . . . . . .French
Parliamentary Interests . . .Local Government; Health; Justice; Education
Leisure Interests . . . . .Photography; Cycling; Music; Golf

Morgan, Alasdair MSP . . . South of Scotland Region
SNP . . . . List
Born . . . . 21st April 1945 in Aberfeldy, Perthshire
Educated . . . . Breadalbane Academy, Aberfeldy;
Glasgow University; Open University
Elected . . . . 2003 MSP for South of Scotland (previously,
1999 - 03, MSP for Galloway and
Upper Nithsdale)
Parliamentary Office . . . . . Tel: (0845) 241 3098
E-mail: alasdair.morgan.msp@scottish.parliament.uk
Web: www.amorgan.org.uk
Parliamentary Assistants – Mr Robert Davidson
Mr Doug Snell
Political Career . . . . 1983 - 90 National Treasurer, SNP
1990 - 91 Senior Vice Convener, SNP
1992 - 97 National Secretary, SNP
1997 - 2001 MP for Galloway and Upper Nithsdale
1997 - 2003 Vice-President, SNP
1999 - 2000 Shadow Minister for Rural Affairs
2000 Convener, Justice Committee 1
2000 - 01 Convener, Home Affairs Committee
2001 - 03 SNP Spokesman on Finance
2003 - 04 Convener, Enterprise and Culture Committee
2004 - 05 SNP Spokesman on Finance
2003 - 05 Convener, SNP Scottish Parliamentary Group
2005 - 07 SNP Chief Whip and Business Manager
2007 - 08 Deputy Presiding Officer
2007 - Convener, Scottish Parliamentary Pensions
Scheme Committee
2009 – Convener, Trustees, Scottish Parliamentary
Pension Scheme
Professional Career . . . . . . 1971 - 74 Teacher
1974 - 86 IT Programmer/Systems Analyst
1986 - 97 IT Manager/Consultant
Languages Spoken . . . . French
Parliamentary Interests . . . Rural Affairs; Transport
Leisure Interests . . . . Hill Walking

Mulligan, Mary MSP . . . . . Linlithgow
Scot Lab. . . . . Majority 1,150 over SNP
Born . . . . .12th February 1960 in Liverpool
Educated . . . . .Notre Dame High School, Liverpool;
University of Manchester
Elected . . . . .1999 MSP for Linlithgow
Parliamentary Office . . . . .Tel: (0131) 348 5779 Fax: (0131) 348 5768
E-mail: mary.mulligan.msp@scottish.parliament.uk
Constituency Office . . . . . .19 South Bridge Street, Bathgate,
West Lothian, EH48 1TU
Tel: (01506) 636555 Fax: (01506) 634978
Constituency Assistant – Mr John McGinty
Political Career . . . . .1988 - 99 Councillor, Edinburgh City Council
1999 - 2000 Convener, Education, Culture and
Sport Committee, Scottish Parliament
2001 - 03 Deputy Minister for Health and
Community Care
2003 - 04 Deputy Minister for Communities
2008 - Labour Spokesman on Housing and Communities
Professional Career . . . . . .1981 - 82 Assistant Staff Manager, BHS plc
1982 - 86 Assistant Manager, Edinburgh
Woollen Mill Ltd
Trade Union . . . . .USDAW
Parliamentary Interests . . .Education; Equality; Local Government
Leisure Interests . . . . .Cinema; Family; Reading; Theatre

Munro, John Farquhar MSP Ross, Skye and Inverness West
Scot Lib Dem. . . . . Majority 3,486 over SNP
Born. . . . . 26th August 1934 in Aultnachruinne, Wester Ross
Educated . . . . .Plockton High School; Merchant Marine College
Elected . . . . .1999 MSP for Ross, Skye and Inverness West
Parliamentary Office . . . . .Tel: (0131) 348 5790 Fax: (0131) 348 5963
E-mail: john.munro.msp@scottish.parliament.uk
Parliamentary Researcher – Mr Jamie Paterson
Constituency Office . . . . . . 5 MacGregor's Court, Dingwall, IV15 9HS
Tel: (01349) 865460
Web: www.highlandlibdems.org.uk
Secretary – Mrs Jackie Garner
Political Career . . . . .1974 - 95 Councillor, Skye and Lochalsh District Council
(Convener 1984 - 95)
1995 - 99 Councillor, Highland Council
(Chair, Transport Services Committee)
1999 - Liberal Democrat Spokesman on Gaelic Language
and the Highlands and Islands
2008 - Deputy Convener, Public Petitions Committee
Professional Career . . . . . .1951 - 61 Merchant Marine Service
1961 - 75 Construction Industry (Plant Fitter, then Manager)
1975 - 93 Heavy Haulage, Civil Engineering and
Quarrying Contractor
1971 - 97 Crofter
Languages Spoken . . . . . . .Gaelic
Leisure Interests . . . . .Fishing; Sailing

Murray, Dr Elaine MSP. . . Dumfries
Scot Lab. . . . . Majority 2,839 over Conservative
Born. . . . . 22nd December 1954 in Hitchin, Hertfordshire
Educated. . . . . Edinburgh University; Cambridge University
Elected . . . . 1999 MSP for Dumfries
Parliamentary Office . . . . . Tel: (0131) 348 5826 Fax: (0131) 348 5834
                               E-mail: elaine.murray.msp@scottish.parliament.co.uk
                               Web: www.elainemurray.scottishparliament.co.uk
Constituency Office . . . . . . 5 Friars Vennel, Dumfries, DG1 2RQ
                               Tel: (01387) 279205 Fax: (01387) 279206
                               Researcher – Dr Jeff Leaver
                               E-mail: jeffrey.leaver@scottish.parliament.co.uk
                               Secretary – Mrs Fiona Rae
                               E-mail: fiona.rae@scottish.parliament.co.uk
                               Admin Assistant – Ms Joanne Duffy
                               E-mail: joanne.duffy@scottish.parliament.co.uk
Political Career . . . . 1990 - 93 Assistant to Alex Smith MEP
                               1994 - 96 Councillor, Strathclyde Regional Council
                               1995 - 99 Councillor, South Ayrshire Council
                               2001 - 03 Deputy Minister for Tourism,
                                   Culture and Sport
                               2007 - 08 Deputy Convener, Finance Committee
                               2007 - 08 Labour Shadow Minister for Enterprise
                               2008 - Labour Spokesman on Environment
Professional Career . . . . . . 1979 - 82 Research Fellow, Cambridge University
                               1982 - 84 Research Fellow, Royal Free Hospital
                               1984 - 87 Senior Scientific Officer, National Institute
                                   of Food Research
                               1992 - 99 Associate Lecturer, Open University
Trade Unions . . . . AUT; Unite
Parliamentary Interests . . . Education; Finance; Rural Issues; Enterprise; Energy;
                               Science and Technology
Leisure Interests . . . . Family, Gardening; Horse Ownership; Keep Fit; Music;
                               Pets; Reading; Cooking

Neil, Alex MSP . . . . Central Scotland Region
SNP . . . . List
Born. . . . . 22nd August 1951 in Irvine
Educated . . . . Ayr Academy; Dundee University
Elected . . . . 1999 MSP for Central Scotland Region
Parliamentary Office. . . . . Tel: (0131) 348 5703
E-mail: alex.neil.msp@scottish.parliament.uk
Web: www.alexneilmsp.net
Parliamentary Researcher – Mr Neil Gray
Tel: (0131) 348 5702
E-mail: neil.gray@scottish.parliament.uk
Secretary – Ms Isabella Neil
E-mail: isabella.neil@scottish.parliament.uk
Political Career. . . . . 1974 - 76 Research Officer, Labour Party (Scotland)
1976 - 79 Secretary, (Independent) Scottish Labour Party
1999 - 2000 SNP Spokesman on Social Services
2000 - 03 Convener, Enterprise and Lifelong
Learning Committee
2004 - 07 Convener, Enterprise and Culture Committee
2007 - 09 Deputy Convener, European and External
Relations Committee
2009 - Minister for Housing and Communities
Professional Career . . . . . 1979 - 1983 Marketing Manager, Digital Equipment
Corporation
1987 - 89 Executive Director, Prince's Scottish Youth
Business Trust (PSYBT)
1987 - 93 Chairman Network, Scotland Ltd
1987 - 99 Economic Consultant
Leisure Interests . . . . Books; Travel

O'Donnell, Hugh MSP. . . Central Scotland Region
Scot Lib Dem. . . . . List
Born. . . . . 1st May 1952 in Glasgow
Educated . . . . Queen Margaret University, Edinburgh
Elected . . . . 2007 MSP for Central Scotland Region
Parliamentary Office. . . . . Tel: (0131) 348 5796 Fax: (0131) 348 5963
E-mail: hugh.odonnell.msp@scottish.parliament.uk
Researcher – Mr Michael Nisbet
Personal Aide - Ms Doreen Nisbet
Tel: (0131) 348 5795
E-mail: doreen.nisbet@scottish.parliament.uk
Regional Office . . . . PO Box 29452, Glasgow, G67 9BQ
Tel: (0845) 600 9580
Political Career. . . . . 2008 - Liberal Democrat Deputy Spokesman on
Education and Young People
Professional Career . . . . . 1972 - 85 Retail Manager
1985 - 90 Property Manager
1990 - 97 Lecturer
1999 - 2007 Political Researcher
Parliamentary Interests . . Equality Issues; Minority Community Issues
Leisure Interests . . . . Historical Reading; Ti Chi

Oldfather, Irene MSP .... Cunninghame South
Scot Lab.............. Majority 2,168 over SNP
Born................ 6th August 1955 in Glasgow
Educated............. Irvine Royal Academy; Strathclyde University
Elected .... 1999 MSP for Cunninghame South
Parliamentary Office ..... Tel: (0131) 348 5769 Fax: (0131) 348 5778
E-mail: irene.oldfather.msp@scottish.parliament.uk
Constituency Office ...... Sovereign House, Academy Road, Irvine, KA12 8RL
Tel: (01294) 313078 Fax: (01294) 313605
Secretary – Mrs Karen Cunningham
Political Career .... 1995 Councillor, North Ayrshire Council
1998 - 2002 Alternate Member, European Union
   Committee of the Regions
2002 - Member, European Union Committee
   of the Regions
2001 - 03 Convener, European Committee
2003 - 05 Deputy Convener, European Committee
2008 - Convener, European and External Relations
   Committee
Professional Career ...... Journalist
Lecturer, Paisley University
Trade Union .... NUJ; Unite
Languages Spoken .... French
Parliamentary Interests ... European Enlargement; Tobacco Control
Leisure Interests .... Ballet; Family; Music; Reading

Park, John MSP . . . . Mid Scotland and Fife Region
Scot Lab . . . . List
Born . . . . 14th September 1973 in Dunfermline
Elected . . . . 2007 MSP for Mid Scotland and Fife Region
Parliamentary Office . . . . . Tel: (0131) 348 6753
                                     E-mail: john.park.msp@scottish.parliament.uk
                                     Web: www.johnparkmsp.org
                                     Parliamentary Assistant – Ms Pamela McTavish
                                     Press and Campaigns Officer – Ms Jenny Duncan
                                     Tel: (0131) 348 6742
                                     E-mail: jennie.duncan@scottish.parliament.uk
                                     Parliamentary Researcher – Ms Eilidh Macdonald
                                     Tel: (0131) 348 6754
                                     E-mail: eilidh.macdonald@scottish.parliament.uk
Regional Office . . . . 219 Wellesley Road, Methil, Fife, KY8 3BN
                                     Tel: (01333) 300974 Fax: (01333) 300413
                                     Parliamentary Assistant – Ms Lesley McEwan
Political Career . . . . 2008 - Labour Shadow Economy and Skills Minister
Professional Career . . . . . . 1989 - 98 Electrical Fitter, Rosyth Dockyard
                                     1998 - 2001 Trade Union Convener, Rosyth Dockyard
                                     2001 - 03 Research Officer, then National Industrial
                                        Campaigns Officer Unite
                                     2003 - 04 Head of Employee Relations, Babcock
                                        Naval Services
                                     2004 - 07 Assistant Secretary, STUC
Trade Union . . . . Unite
Parliamentary Interests . . . Business/Industrial Issues; Skills; Energy; Housing;
                                     Industrial Relations; Sport
Leisure Interests . . . . Football; Walking; Music and Film

Paterson, Gil MSP . . . . West of Scotland Region
SNP . . . . List
Born . . . . 11th November 1942 in Glasgow
Educated . . . . Possilpark Secondary School, Glasgow;
                                     Queen Margaret University, Edinburgh
Elected . . . . 2007 MSP for West of Scotland Region
Parliamentary Office . . . . . Tel: (0131) 348 6812 Fax: (0131) 348 6814
                                     E-mail: gil.paterson.msp@scottish.parliament.uk
                                     Web: gilmsp.weebly.com
Political Career . . . . 1997 - 2003 MSP for Central Scotland Region
                                     2007 - 09 Deputy Convener, Subordinate Legislation
                                        Committee
                                     2007 - Convener, Standards, Procedures and Public
                                        Appointments Committee
Professional Career . . . . . . 1973 - 99 Part Owner, Gils Motor Factors
Leisure Interests . . . . Reading; Climbing; Skiing; Snowboarding

Peacock, Peter MSP . . . . . . Highlands and Islands Region
Scot Lab. . . . . List
Born . . . . .27th February 1952 in Edinburgh
Educated . . . . .Hawick High School; Jordanhill College of Education
Elected . . . . .1999 MSP for Highlands and Islands Region
Parliamentary Office . . . . .Tel: (0131) 348 5766 Fax: (0131) 348 5767
E-mail: peter.peacock.msp@scottish.parliament.uk
Web: www.peterpeacock.org.uk
Parliamentary Assistant – Mr Richard Welsh
E-mail: richard.welsh@scottish.parliament.uk
Regional Office . . . . .PO Box 5717, Inverness, IV1 1YT
Tel: (01463) 716299 Fax: (01463) 716572
Political Career . . . . .1986 - 96 Councillor, Highland Regional Council
(Vice-Convener 1990 - 96)
1995 - 99 Leader/Convener, Highland Council
1999 - 2000 Deputy Minister for Children and
Education
2000 - 03 Deputy Minister for Finance and
Public Services
2003 - 06 Minister for Education and Young People
2008 - Deputy Convener, Scottish Parliamentary
Pensions Scheme Committee
Professional Career . . . . . .1973 - 75 Community Education Officer, Orkney
County Council
1975 - 87 Area Officer and Central Policy Adviser,
Scottish Association of Citizens Advice Bureau
1991 - 94 Chairman, Scottish Library and
Information Council
Trade Union . . . . .Unison
Parliamentary Interests . . .Rural Affairs; Environment
Leisure Interests . . . . .Bird Watching; Cooking

Peattie, Cathy MSP . . . . . . Falkirk East
Scot Lab. . . . . Majority 1,872 over SNP
Born. . . . . 24th November 1951 in Bridge of Allan
Educated. . . . . Moray Secondary School, Grangemouth
Elected . . . . .1999 MSP for Falkirk East
Parliamentary Office . . . . .Tel: (0131) 348 5746 Fax: (0131) 348 5750
E-mail: cathy.peattie.msp@scottish.parliament.uk
Web: www.cathypeattiemsp.org.uk
Researcher – Mr Dave Smith
Tel: (0131) 348 5747
Constituency Office . . . . . .Room 9, 5 Kerse Road, Grangemouth, FK3 8HQ
Tel: (01324) 666026 Fax: (01324) 473951
E-mail: mail@cathypeattiemsp.org.uk
Administrators – Ms Kate Irvine
Mr John Tennant
Political Career . . . . .2001 - 03 Deputy Convener, Education, Culture
and Sport Committee
2003 - 07 Convener, Equal Opportunities Committee
2007 - Deputy Convener, Transport, Infrastructure
and Climate Change Committee
Professional Career . . . . . .1980 - 86 Field Worker and Training Officer,
Scottish Pre-School Playgroup Association
1986 - 90 Development Worker, Volunteer
Network, Falkirk
1990 - 91 Community Development Worker,
Langlees Community Flat, Falkirk
1991 - 93 Manager, Community Outreach
1993 - 99 Director, Falkirk Voluntary Action
Resource Centre
Trade Unions . . . . .UNISON; Unite
Parliamentary Interests . . .Culture; Education; Equal Opportunities; Voluntary Sector
Leisure Interests . . . . .Reading; Music; Grandchildren

Pringle, Mike MSP....... Edinburgh South
Scot Lib Dem.......... Majority 1,929 over Labour
Born................ 25th December 1945 in Northern Rhodesia (now Zambia)
Educated.............. Edinburgh Academy
Elected ....2003 MSP for Edinburgh South
Parliamentary Office .....Tel: (0131) 348 5788 Fax: (0131) 348 6489
E-mail: mike.pringle.msp@scottish.parliament.uk
Web: www.mikepringlemsp.com
Parliamentary Assistant - Ms Rosemary Macdonald
E-mail: rosemary.macdonald@scottish.parliament.uk
Researcher/Constituency Organiser - Dr Conor Snowden
E-mail: conor.snowden@scottish.parliament.uk
Constituency Office ......4 Grange Road, Edinburgh, EH9 1UH
Tel: (0131) 477 3748
Staff – Mr Rory Edwards
Political Career ....1992 - 2003 Councillor, Edinburgh City Council
1994 - 96 Councillor, Lothian Regional Council
2003 - 07 Liberal Democrat Deputy Spokesman on Justice
2007 - 08 Liberal Democrat Spokesman for
Community Safety
2008 - Liberal Democrat Deputy Spokesman on Justice
Professional Career ......1966 - 72 Bank Official, Royal Bank of Scotland
1974 - 89 Chairman, TMM Ltd
Parliamentary Interests ...Justice
Leisure Interests ....Cinema; Football; People; Wine Collecting

Purvis, Jeremy MSP ..... Tweeddale, Ettrick and Lauderdale
Scot Lib Dem.......... Majority 598 over SNP
Born ....15th January 1974 in Berwick-upon-Tweed
Educated ....Berwick-upon-Tweed High School; London University
Elected ....2003 MSP for Tweeddale, Ettrick and Lauderdale
Parliamentary Office .....Tel: (0131) 348 5801 Fax: (0131) 348 6488
E-mail: jeremy.purvis.msp@scottish.parliament.uk
Web: www.jeremypurvis.org
Constituency Office ......11 Island Street, Galashiels, TD1 1NZ
Tel: (01896) 663656 Fax: (01896) 663655
Political Career ....1993 - 98 Research/Parliamentary/Personal Assistant
2003 - 05 Liberal Democrat Spokesman on Finance
2005 - 07 Liberal Democrat Spokesman on Justice
2007 - 08 Liberal Democrat Shadow Cabinet Secretary for
Education and Lifelong Learning
2008 - Liberal Democrat Shadow Economy and
Finance Secretary
Professional Career ......1998 - 2001 Staff Member, Parliamentary Affairs
Company
2001 - 03 Director, McEwan Purvis (Strategic
Communications, Consultancy)
Parliamentary Interests ...Culture; Economy; Europe; Rural Development
Leisure Interests ....Classic Cars; Painting; Reading

Robison, Shona MSP . . . . . Dundee East
SNP . . . . Majority 4,524 over Labour
Born . . . . .26th May 1966 in Redcar
Educated . . . . .Alva Academy; Glasgow University;
                  Jordanhill College
Elected . . . . .2003 MSP for Dundee East (previously,
                  1999 - 2003, MSP for North East Scotland Region)
Parliamentary Office . . . . .Tel: (0131) 348 5707 Fax: (0131) 348 5562
                  E-mail: shona.robison.msp@scottish.parliament.uk
                  Web: www.shonarobinson.com
Constituency Office . . . . . .8 Old Glamis Road, Dundee, DD3 8HP
                  Tel: (01382) 623200 Fax: (01382) 903205
                  E-mail: shona@dundeesnp.org
                  Constituency Worker – Ms Anya Lawrence
                  Tel: (01382) 903201
                  E-mail: anya@dundeesnp.org
                  Researcher – Mr Willie Sawers
                  Tel: (01382) 903204
                  E-mail: willie@dundeesnp.org
Political Career . . . . .1995 - 2004 Member, SNP National Executive Committee
                  1999 - 2003 Secretary, SNP Parliamentary Group
                  1999 - 2003 Deputy Shadow Minister for Health
                  2004 - 07 SNP Shadow Minister for Health
                  2007 - Minister for Public Health and Sport
Professional Career . . . . . .1990 - 99 SNP Community Worker and Home Care
                  Organiser, Glasgow City Council
Parliamentary Interests . . .Community Care; Equal Opportunities
Leisure Interests . . . . .Spending Time with Daughter; Hill Walking; Cooking

Rumbles, Michael MSP . . .West Aberdeenshire and Kincardine
Scot Lib Dem . . . . .Majority 5,170 over SNP
Born . . . . .10th June 1956 in South Shields
Educated . . . . .Sunderland Polytechnic;
                  Royal Military Academy, Sandhurst;
                  University of Wales, Aberystwyth
Elected . . . . .1999 MSP for West Aberdeenshire and Kincardine
Parliamentary Office . . . . .Tel: (0131) 348 5798 Fax: (0131) 348 6463
                  E-mail: mike.rumbles.msp@scottish.parliament.uk
Constituency Office . . . . . .6 Dee Street, Banchory, Aberdeenshire, AB31 5ST
                  Tel: (01330) 820268
Political Career . . . . .1999 - 2001 Liberal Democrat Spokesman on
                    Rural Affairs
                  1999 - 2003 Convener, Standards Committee
                  2003 - 05 Liberal Democrat Spokesman on Health
                  2008 - Liberal Democrat Parliamentary Business Manager
                  and Chief Whip
Professional Career . . . . . .1979 - 94 Army Officer
                  1995 - 99 Team Leader in Business Management,
                  Aberdeen College
Parliamentary Interests . . .Further and Higher Education
Leisure Interests . . . . .Family; Hill Walking

Russell, Mike MSP . . . . South of Scotland Region
SNP . . . . List
Born . . . . .9th August 1953 in Bromley, Kent
Educated . . . . .Marr College, Troon; Edinburgh University
Elected . . . . .2007 MSP for South of Scotland Region
(Previously 1999 - 2004 MSP for South of Scotland
Region)
Parliamentary Office . . . . .Tel: (0131) 348 6326 Fax: (0131) 348 6689
E-mail: michael.russell.msp@scottish.parliament.uk
Web: www.mikerussellsnp.net
Private Secretary – Mr Darren Dickson
Tel: (0131) 348 6960
Diary Secretary – Ms Carol-Ann Miller
Tel: (0131) 348 5885
Adviser – Mr Michael Russell-Aileen Orr
Mobile: 07980 0661546
Regional Office . . . . .Tel: (0131) 244 7716/1653
Regional Office Manager – Mr Mark Maclachlan
Political Career . . . . .1994 - 99 Chief Executive and Campaign Director, SNP
2003 - Shadow Minister for Children and Education
2003 - SNP Spokesman on Culture, Broadcasting
and Gaelic
2007 - 09 Minister for the Environment
2009 - Minister for Culture, External Affairs and the
Constitution
Professional Career . . . . . .Television Producer and Director
Author

Salmond, Rt Hon Alex MP MSP   Gordon
SNP . . . . .Majority 2,062 over Liberal Democrat
Born . . . . .31st December 1954 in Linlithgow
Educated . . . . .Linlithgow Academy; St Andrews University
Elected . . . . .2007 MSP for Gordon
Parliamentary Office . . . . .E-mail: alex.salmond.msp@scottish.parliament.uk
Constituency Office . . . . . .84 North Street, Inverurie, Aberdeenshire, AB51 4QX
Tel: (01467) 670070 Fax: (01779) 474460
Web: www.snp.org
Office Manager – Ms Hannah Bardell
E-mail: hannah.bordell@scottish.parliament.uk
Political Career . . . . .1987 - MP for Banff and Buchan
1987 - 90 Deputy Leader, SNP
1990 - 2000 Leader, SNP
1999 - 2001 MSP for Banff and Buchan
2007 - First Minister, Scotland
Professional Career . . . . . .1978 - 80 Assistant Economist, Department of Agriculture
and Fisheries, Scotland
1980 - 82 Assistant Economist, Royal Bank of Scotland
1982 - 84 Oil Economist, Royal Bank of Scotland
1984 - 87 Oil and Bank Economist, Royal Bank of Scotland

Scanlon, Mary MSP . . . . . . Highlands and Islands Region
Scot Cons . . . . List
Born . . . . .25th May 1947 in Dundee
Educated . . . . Craigo Secondary School, Montrose;
Dundee University
Elected . . . . .1999 MSP for Highlands and Islands Region
Parliamentary Office . . . . .Tel: (0131) 348 5460 Fax: (0131) 348 6673
Mobile: 07775 830480
E-mail: mary.scanlon.msp@scottish.parliament.uk
Web: www.maryscanlonmsp.com
Personal Assistant – Mrs Aileen Weurman
Tel: (0131) 348 5461
E-mail: aileen.weurman@scottish.parliament.uk
Regional Office . . . . 14A Ardross Street, Inverness, IV3 5NS
Tel: (01463) 241004 Fax: (01463) 241164
Press Officer – Ms Lindsay McCallum
E-mail: lindsay.mccallum@scottish.parliament.uk
Parliamentary Aide – Mr Douglas Ross
Tel: (01343) 547436
E-mail: douglas.ross@scottish.parliament.uk
Political Career . . . . .1999 - MSP for Highlands and Islands Region
1999 - 2003 Conservative Spokesman on Health,
Scottish Parliament
2003 - 06 Conservative Spokesman for Communities,
Scottish Parliament
2007 - Conservative Shadow Cabinet Secretary for
Health and Wellbeing
Professional Career . . . . . .1962 - 72 Administrative/Secretarial Post
(BT; BRS; Civil Service)
1983 - 99 Lecturer. Economics/Business Management
Professional Association . . .Institute of Professional Development
Parliamentary Interests . . .Health and Wellbeing
Leisure Interests . . . . .Hill Walking; Swimming

Scott, John MSP. . . . . . Ayr
Scot Cons. . . . . Majority 3,906 over Labour
Born . . . . 7th June 1951 in Girvan
Educated. . . . . George Watson's College, Edinburgh;
                Edinburgh University
Elected . . . . 2003 MSP for Ayr (previously, 2000 MSP for Ayr
                (By-election)
Parliamentary Office. . Tel: (0131) 348 5664 Fax: (0131) 348 5617
                E-mail: john.scott.msp@scottish.parliament.uk
Constituency Office . . . 17 Wellington Square, Ayr, KA7 1EZ
                Tel: (01292) 286251 Fax: (01292) 280480
Political Career . . . . . . 2001 - 03 Conservative Spokesman on Environment
                2003 - 07 Member, Scottish Parliament Corporate Body
                2003 - 07 Deputy Convener, Public Petitions Committee
                2007 - Deputy Convener, Rural Affairs and Environment
                  Committee
                2008 - Conservative Rural Affairs and Environment Secretary
Professional Career . . . 1973 - Farmer, W Scott & Son
                1993 - 99 Convener, NFU Scotland Hill Farming Committee
                1994 - 96 President, Ayrshire Executive, National Farmers Union
                1999 Founder, Ayrshire Farmers Market
                2001 - 05 Chairman, Scottish Association of Farmers' Markets
Trade Union . . . . NFU
Leisure Interests. . . . . . Bridge; Curling; Geology; Rugby

Scott, Tavish MSP . . . . Shetland
Scot Lib Dem. . . . . . . Majority 4,909 over SNP
Born . . . . 6th May 1966 in Inverness
Educated. . . . . Anderson High School, Lerwick;
                Napier College, Edinburgh
Elected . . . . 1999 MSP for Shetland
Parliamentary Office. . Tel: (0131) 348 5815 Fax: (0131) 348 5807
                E-mail: tavish.scott.msp@scottish.parliament.uk
                Web: www.tavishscott.com
Constituency Office . . . 171 Commercial Street, Lerwick, ZE1 0HX
                Tel: (01595) 690044 Fax: (01595) 690055
                E-mail: tscott@supanet.com
Political Career . . . . . . 1989 - 91 Researcher to Jim Wallace MP
                1990 - 92 Press Officer, Scottish Liberal Democrats
                1994 - 99 Councillor, Shetlands Islands Council
                1999 - 2000 Liberal Democrat Spokesman
                  on Transport and the Environment
                2000 - 01 Deputy Minister for Parliament
                2001 - 03 Liberal Democrat Spokesman on
                  Enterprise and Lifelong Learning
                2003 - 05 Deputy Minister for Finance, Public
                  Services and Parliamentary Business
                2005 - 07 Minister for Transport
                2007 - 08 Convener, Economy, Energy and Tourism Committee
                2008 - Leader, Scottish Liberal Democrats
Professional Career . . . 1992 - 99 Farmer
                1997 - 99 Director, Shetlands Islands Tourism
Trade Union . . . . NFUS (Associate)
Leisure Interests   Football; Golf; Cinema

Simpson, Dr Richard MSP   Mid Scotland and Fife Region
Scot Lab . . . . List
Born . . . . .22nd October 1942 in Edinburgh
Educated . . . . .Perth Academy; Trinity College, Glenalmond;
Edinburgh University
Elected . . . . .2007 MSP for Mid Scotland and Fife Region
Parliamentary Office . . . . .Tel: (0131) 348 6756 Fax: (0131) 348 6758
E-mail: richard.simpson.msp@scottish.parliament.uk
Web: www.richardsimpsonmsp.com
Regional Office . . . . .22 Viewfield Street, Stirling, FK8 1UA
Tel: (01786) 446515 Fax: (01786) 446513
Political Career . . . . .1999 - 2003 MSP for Ochil
2008 - Labour Spokesman on Health
Professional Career . . . . . .1970 - 99 GP and Psychiatrist
1970 - 2007 Consultant Psychiatrist, NHS Lothian
1982 - Medical Adviser on Adoption and Fostering,
Stirling, Clackmannanshire and Falkirk Authorities
1987 - Research Fellow, then Hon Professor in
Psychology, Stirling University
Professional Associations . .Royal College of General Practitioners;
Royal College of Psychiatrists (Fellow)
British Medical Association
Parliamentary Interests . . .Health Issues
Leisure Interests . . . . .Rugby; Golf; Opera; Classical Music

Smith, Elaine MSP . . . . Coatbridge and Chryston
Scot Lab. . . . . Majority 4,510 over SNP
Born . . . . .7th May 1963 in Coatbridge
Educated . . . . .St Patrick's High School, Coatbridge;
Glasgow College;
St Andrew's Teacher Training College
Elected . . . . .1999 MSP for Coatbridge and Chryston
Parliamentary Office . . . . .Tel: (0131) 348 5824 Fax: (0131) 348 5834
E-mail: elaine.smith.msp@scottish.parliament.uk
Web: www.elaine-smith.co.uk
Research Assistant – Ms Joanne Smith
Constituency Office . . . . . . Unit 65, Fountain Business Centre, Coatbridge,
Lanarkshire, ML3 3AA
Tel: (01236) 449122 Fax: (01236) 449137
Caseworker – Mrs Lesley Dobbin
E-mail: lesley.dobbin@scottish.parliament.uk
Political Career . . . . .2008 - 09 Deputy Convener, Equal Opportunities
Committee
Professional Career . . . . . .Secondary School Teacher
Local Government Office
Trade Union . . . . .Unite
Professional Association. . . General Teaching Council
Parliamentary Interests . . .Children; Employment; Equal Opportunities;
Trade Unions; Voluntary Sector; Health
Leisure Interests . . . . .Bowling; Family; Reading; Swimming

Smith, Elizabeth MSP. . . . Mid Scotland and Fife Region
Scot Cons . . . . List
Born . . . . 27th February 1960
Educated . . . . George Watson's College; Edinburgh University
Elected. . . . . 2007 MSP for Mid Scotland and Fife Region
Parliamentary Office . . . . Tel: (0131) 348 6762 Fax: (0131) 348 6764
E-mail: elizabeth.smith.msp@scottish.parliament.uk
Regional Office . . . . 100A Main Street, Methven, Perth, PH1 3QP
Tel: (01738) 842892 Fax: (01738) 842893
E-mail: perth@scottishtories.com
Web: www.elizabeth4perth.com
Political Career . . . . 1997 - 2005 Political Adviser to Sir Malcolm Rifkind MP
2007 - Conservative Shadow Minister for Children,
Schools and Skills
Professional Career . . . . . 1983 - 97 Teacher, George Watson's College, Edinburgh
Leisure Interests . . . . Cricket; Hill Walking; Travel; Photography;
Classical Music; Cooking; Writing
Published Books . . . . 2003: Outdoor Adventures (joint author)
2006: History of George Watson's Ladies' College

Smith, Iain MSP . . . . North East Fife
Scot Lib Dem . . . . Majority 5,016 over Conservative
Born . . . . 1st May 1960 in Gateside, Fife
Educated . . . . Bell Baxter High School, Cupar;
                                     Newcastle-upon-Tyne University
Elected . . . . 1999 MSP for North East Fife
Parliamentary Office . . . . Tel: (0131) 348 5817 Fax: (0131) 348 5962
                                     E-mail: iain.smith.msp@scottish.parliament.uk
                                     Web: www.iainsmith.org
                                     Parliamentary Assistant – Mr Thomas Clement
Constituency Office . . . . . 16 Millgate, Cupar, Fife, KY15 5EG
                                     Tel: (01334) 656361 Fax: (01334) 654045
                                     E-mail: is@iainsmith.org
                                     Constituency Assistant – Mr Adam Stachura
                                     Constituency Caseworker – Ms Jane Ann Liston
Political Career . . . . 1982 - 96 Councillor, Fife Regional Council
                                       (Leader, Liberal Democrat Group, 1986 - 96)
                                     1995 - 99 Councillor, Fife Council (Leader,
                                       Liberal Democrat Group)
                                     1999 - 2000 Deputy Minister for Parliament
                                       and Liberal Democrat Business Manager
                                     1999 - 2000 Member, Scottish Parliamentary Bureau
                                     2000 - 04 Liberal Democrat Spokesman on Local Government
                                     2003 - 05 Convener, Procedures Committee
                                     2003 - 05 Liberal Democrat Spokesman on Local
                                       Government and Transport
                                     2005 - 07 Liberal Democrat Spokesman on Education
                                     2005 - 07 Convener, Education Committee
                                     2007 - Liberal Democrat Shadow Minister for Europe,
                                       External Affairs and Culture
                                     2007 - 08 Convener, Liberal Democrat Group
                                     2008 - Liberal Democrat Shadow Culture, Europe and
                                       External Relations Secretary
                                     2008 - Convener, Economy, Energy and Tourism Committee
Professional Career . . . . . 1982 - 85 Advice Worker/Centre Manager,
                                       Bonnethill Advice Centre, Dundee
                                     1987 - 99 Constituency Agent to Menzies Campbell MP
                                       and North East Fife Liberal Democrats
Parliamentary Interests . . Constitutional Affairs; Education
Leisure Interests . . . . Cinema; Reading; Sport (Football and Cricket); Travel

Smith, Margaret MSP . . . . Edinburgh West
Scot Lib Dem . . . . Majority 5,886 over SNP
Born . . . . .18th February 1961 in Edinburgh
Educated . . . . .Broughton High School, Edinburgh;
Edinburgh University
Elected . . . . .1999 MSP for Edinburgh West
Parliamentary Office . . . . .Tel: (0131) 348 5785 Fax: (0131) 348 5965
E-mail: margaret.smith.msp@scottish.parliament.uk
Web: www.margaretsmithmsp.com
Parliamentary Researcher – Ms Sarah Atherton
Tel: (0131) 348 5786
E-mail: sarah.atherton@scottish.parliament.uk
Constituency Office . . . . . .3 Drum Brae Avenue, Edinburgh, EH12 8TE
Tel: (0131) 317 7292 Fax: (0131) 317 7306
Political Career . . . . .1995 - 99 Councillor, Edinburgh City Council
1999 - 2003 Convener, Health and Community
Care Committee
2001 - 03 Liberal Democrat Spokesman on Health
and Community Care
2003 - 04 Deputy Convener, Equal Opportunities
Committee
2003 - 05 Liberal Democrat Spokesman on Justice
2003 - 05 Liberal Democratic Spokesman on Local
Government and Transport
2005 - 07 Liberal Democrat Chief Whip
2007 - 08 Liberal Democrat Spokesman on Justice
2008 - Liberal Democrat Shadow Education and
Young People Secretary
Professional Career . . . . . .Freelance Journalist
Parliamentary Interests . . .Justice; Health
Leisure Interests . . . . .Golf; Reading; Travel

Somerville, Shirley-Anne MSP   Lothians Region
SNP . . . . List
Born . . . . 2nd September 1974 in Kirkcaldy
Educated . . . . Kirkcaldy High School; University of Stirling;
                                         University of Strathclyde
Elected . . . . .2007 MSP for Lothians Region
                                         (replaced Stefan Tymkewycz from SNP list)
Parliamentary Office . . . . .Tel: (0131) 348 6823 Fax: (0131) 348 6825
                                         E-mail: shirley-anne.somerville.msp@scottish.parliament.uk
                                         Web: www.shirleyannesomerville.org
                                         Parliamentary Assistant – Miss Ria Donaldson
                                         E-mail: ria.donaldson@scottish.parliament.uk
Constituency Office . . . . . .59 West Main Street, Whitburn, EH47 0QD
                                         Tel: (01501) 749941
Professional Career . . . . . .1999 - 2001 Parliamentary Researcher,
                                         Duncan Hamilton MSP
                                         2001 - 04 Policy and Public Affairs Officer, Chartered
                                         Institute of Housing
                                         2004 - 07 Media and Campaigns Officer, Royal College
                                         of Nursing

Stephen, Nicol MSP . . . . . . Aberdeen South
Scot Lib Dem . . . . Majority 2,732 over SNP
Born . . . . 23rd March 1960 in Aberdeen
Educated . . . . .Robert Gordon's College, Aberdeen;
                                         Aberdeen University; Edinburgh University
Elected . . . . .1999 MSP for Aberdeen South
Parliamentary Office . . . . .E-mail: nicol.stephen.msp@scottish.parliament.uk
Constituency Office . . . . . .173 Crown Street, Aberdeen, AB11 6JA
                                         Tel: (01224) 252728 Fax: (01224) 590926
                                         Constituency Manager – Mr Ian Mollison
                                         E-mail: ian.mollison@scottish.parliament.uk
                                         Constituency Assistant – Mr John Sleigh
                                         E-mail: john.sleigh@scottish.parliament.uk
Political Career . . . . .1982 - 92 Councillor, Grampian Regional Council
                                         (Chairman, Economic Development and
                                         Planning 1986 -91)
                                         1991 - 92 MP for Kincardine and Deeside
                                         1999 - 2000 Deputy Minister for Enterprise and
                                         Lifelong Learning
                                         2000 - 03 Deputy Minister for Education, and
                                         Young People
                                         2003 - 05 Minister for Transport
                                         2005 - 07 Deputy First Minister, and Minister for
                                         Enterprise and Lifelong Learning
                                         2005 - 08 Leader, Scottish Liberal Democrats
Professional Career . . . . . .Solicitor and Notary Public
Leisure Interests . . . . .Golf

Stevenson, Stewart MSP . . Banff and Buchan
SNP . . . . Majority 10,530 over Conservative
Born . . . . 15th October 1946 in Cupar, Fife
Educated. . . . . Bell Baxter School, Cupar, Fife; Aberdeen University
Elected . . . . 2001 MSP for Banff and Buchan (By-election)
Parliamentary Office . . . . .Tel: (0131) 348 5894
E-mail: msp@stewartstevenson.net
Web: www.stewartsevenson.net
Parliamentary Assistant – Mr Neil Dunsire
Constituency Office 17 Maiden Street, Peterhead, AB42 1EE
Tel: (01779) 470444 Fax: (01779) 474460
Constituency Manager – Mr Stephen Smith
Political Career . . . . .2003 - 04 SNP Deputy Spokesman on Health and
Social Justice
2005 - 07 Deputy Convener, Justice 1 Committee
2005 - 07 SNP Deputy Spokesman on Justice
2007 - Minister for Transport, Infrastructure and
Climate Change
Professional Career . . . . . .1969 - 99 Information Technology, Bank of Scotland
(latterly Director)
Trade Union . . . . .UNIFI
Parliamentary Interests . . .Job Creation; Prisons; Rural Affairs
Leisure Interests . . . . .Photography; Reading; Writing

Stewart, David MSP. . . . . . Highlands and Islands Region
Scot Lab. . . . . List
Born . . . . .5th May 1956 in Inverness
Educated . . . . .Inverness High School; Paisley College;
Stirling University; Open University Business School
Elected . . . . .2007 MSP for Highlands Region
Parliamentary Office . . . . .Tel: (0131) 348 6831 Fax: (0131) 348 6833
E-mail: david.stewart.msp@scottish.parliament.uk
Web: www.davidstewart.org.uk
Parliamentary Assistant – Mr Richard Welsh
Tel: (0131) 348 5766
E-mail: richard.welsh@scottish.parliament.uk
Regional Office . . . . .PO Box 5717, Inverness, IV1 1YT
Tel: (01463) 716299 Fax: (01463) 716572
Political Career . . . . .1997 - 2005 MP for Inverness East, Nairn and
Lochaber
2007 - Labour Chief Whip
Professional Career . . . . . .1981 - 87 Social Worker, Dumfries, then Dingwall
1987 - 97 Area Team Manager, Inverness
2005 - 07 Assistant Director for Rural Affairs, Scottish
Council for Voluntary Organisations
Trade Union . . . . .UNISON
Parliamentary Interests . . .Rural Affairs; Health; Energy; Aviation;
Voluntary Sector

Stone, Jamie MSP . . . . Caithness, Sutherland and Easter Ross
Scot Lib Dem . . . . Majority 2,323 over SNP
Born . . . . 16th June 1954 in Edinburgh
Educated . . . . Tain Royal Academy; Gordonstoun School;
St Andrews University
Elected . . . . 1999 MSP for Caithness, Sutherland and Easter Ross
Parliamentary Office . . . . . Tel: (0131) 348 5790 Fax: (0131) 348 5807
E-mail: jamie.stone.msp@scottish.parliament.uk
Researcher – Mr Jamie Paterson
Constituency Office . . . . . . 26 Tower Street, Tain, IV19 1DY
Tel: (01862) 892726 Fax: (01862) 893698
Web: www.highlandslibdems.org.uk
Personal Assistant – Mrs Heather Macmillan
Political Career . . . . 1983 - 84 Chairman, Tain Community Council
1986 - 96 Councillor, Ross and Cromarty District Council
1989 - 95 Member, Scottish Constitutional Convention
1995 - 99 Councillor, Highland Council
1999 - 2000 Liberal Democrat Spokesman on Education
and Children
2000 - Liberal Democrat Member of the Hollyrood
Progress Group
2001 - 03 Liberal Democrat Spokesman on Equal
Opportunities and Fisheries
2003 - 04 Liberal Democrat Spokesman on Enterprise,
Lifelong Learning and Tourism
2004 - 07 Convener, Scottish Parliament Business Exchange
2003 - 07 Liberal Democrat Spokesman on Enterprise and
Lifelong Learning
2007 - Convener, Subordinate Legislation Committee
2008 - Liberal Democrat Deputy Spokesman on Health
Professional Career . . . . . . 1981 - 84 Site Administrator, Bechtel Great Britain Ltd
1984 - 86 Manager, Odfjell Drilling (UK) Ltd
1986 - 94 Director, Highland Fine Cheeses Ltd
1994 - 99 Director, Various Other Companies
1990 - Freelance Newspaper Writer
Trade Union . . . . GMB
Professional Association . . . Trading Standards Institute
Parliamentary Interests . . . Enterprise; Lifelong Learning; Tourism
Leisure Interests . . . . Butterflies; Fungi; Gardening; Golf; Music; Reading
Directorships Held . . . . Grey Coast Theatre Ltd *(unpaid)*
Highland Fine Celtic Foods Ltd *(unpaid)*

Sturgeon, Nicola MSP . . . Glasgow Govan
SNP . . . . Majority 744 over Labour
Born . . . . 1970 in Irvine, Ayrshire
Educated . . . . Greenwood Academy, Irvine; Glasgow University
Elected . . . . 2007 MSP for Glasgow Govan (1999 - 2007
                               MSP for Glasgow Region
Parliamentary Office . . . . Tel: (0131) 348 5695
                               E-mail: nicola.sturgeon.msp@scottish.parliament.uk
Constituency Office . . . . . 213 Paisley Road West, Glasgow, G51 1NE
                               Tel: (0141) 427 4590 Fax: (0141) 427 0650
                               Parliamentary and Constituency Assistant –
                                Ms Mhairi Hunter
                               E-mail: mhairi.hunter@scottish.parliament.uk
                               Constituency Assistant – Mr Michael Dixon
                               E-maill: michael.dixon@scottish.parliament.uk
Political Career . . . . 1999 - 2000 SNP Spokesman on Children and Education
                               2000 - 03 SNP Spokesman on Health and Community Care
                               2003 - 04 SNP Spokesman on Justice and European Affairs
                               2004 - 07 SNP Deputy Leader and SNP Leader in the
                               Scottish Parliament
                               2007 - Deputy First Minister and Cabinet Secretary for
                               Health and Wellbeing
Professional Career . . . . . 1993 - 95 Trainee Solicitor, McClure Naismith, Glasgow
                               1995 - 97 Solicitor, Bell & Craig, Stirling
                               1997 - 99 Solicitor, Drumchapel Law and Money Advice Centre
Parliamentary Interests . . Equality; Health Issues; Shipbuilding
Leisure Interests . . . . Reading; Theatre

Swinney, John MSP . . . . . North Tayside
SNP . . . . Majority 7,584 over Conservative
Born . . . . 13th April 1964 in Edinburgh
Educated . . . . Forrester High School, Edinburgh; Edinburgh University
Elected . . . . 1999 MSP for North Tayside
Parliamentary Office . . . . Tel: (0131) 348 5717 Fax: (0131) 348 5946
                               E-mail: john.swinney.msp@scottish.parliament.uk
                               Web: www.johnswinneymsp.com
                               PA – Ms Cath Steven
Constituency Office . . . . . 35 Perth Street, Blairgowrie, Perthshire, PH10 6DL
                               Tel: (01250) 876576 Fax: (01250) 876991
                               Office Manager – Miss Elaine Wylie
                               Constituency Assistant – Mr Stephen Carter
Political Career . . . . 1986 - 92 National Secretary, SNP
                               1997 - 2001 MP for North Tayside
                               1998 - 2000 SNP Deputy Leader and Spokesman
                                  on Enterprise and Lifelong Learning
                               1999 - 2000 Convener, Enterprise and Lifelong
                                  Learning Committee
                               2000 - 04 Leader, SNP
                               2004 - 05 Convener, European and External
                                  Relations Committee
                               2005 - 07 SNP Spokesman on Finance and Public Services
                               2005 - 07 Deputy Convener, Finance Committee
                               2007 - Cabinet Secretary for Finance and Sustainable Growth
Professional Career . . . . . 1986 - 87 Research Officer, Scottish Coal Project
                               1987 - 92 Senior Development Manager, Business Options
                               1992 - 97 Strategic Planning Principal, Scottish Amicable
Parliamentary Interests . . Enterprise; Higher and Further Education
Leisure Interests . . . . Cycling; Hill Walking

Thompson, David MSP . . . Highlands and Islands Region
SNP . . . . List
Born . . . . 20th September 1949 in Lossiemouth
Educated. . . . . Lossiemouth High School; Inverness College
Elected . . . . 2007 MSP for Highlands Region
Parliamentary Office . . . . . Tel: (0131) 348 5325 Fax: (0131) 348 5327
E-mail: dave.thompson.msp@scottish.parliament.uk
Web: www.davethompsonmsp.org
Parliamentary Assistant – Ms Haley St Dennis
E-mail: haley.stdennis@scottish.parliament.uk
Regional Office . . . . Thorfin House, Bridgend Business Park, Dingwall,
Ross-shire, IV15 9SL
Tel: (01349) 864701 Fax: (01349) 866327
Parliamentary Manager– Mr Andrew Ferguson
E-mail: andrew.ferguson@scottish.parliament.uk
Parliamentary Assistant – Mr Gerry Burke
E-mail: gerry.burke@scottish.parliament.uk
Professional Career . . . . . . 1965 - 67 Apprentice Mechanic, Avery Scales
1967 - 95 Trading Standards Officer, Banff, Moray
and Nairn County Council; Ross and Cromarty
County Council; Comhairle nan Eilean Siar;
Highland Regional Council
1995 - 2001 Director of Protective Services,
Highland Council
Trade Union . . . . GMB
Professional Association . . .Trading Standards Institute
Languages Spoken . . . . Gaelic; Scots
Leisure Interests . . . . .DIY, Hillwalking, Golf

Tolson, Jim MSP . . . . Dunfermline West
Scot Lib Dem . . . . Majority 476 over Labour
Born . . . . 26th May 1965 in Kirkcaldy
Educated. . . . . Napier University; Lauder College
Elected . . . . .2007 MSP for Dunfermline West
Parliamentary Office . . . . .Tel: (0131) 348 6337 Fax: (0131) 348 6339
E-mail: jim.tolson.msp@scottish.parliament.uk
Web: www.jimtolson.com
Constituency Office . . . . . .2nd Floor, 1 High Street, Dunfermline, KY12 7DL
Tel: (01383) 841700 Fax: (01383) 841793
Political Career . . . . .1992 - 96 Councillor, Dunfermline District Council
1995 - 2007 Councillor, Fife District Council
2007 - 08 Liberal Democrat Shadow Minister for
Communities and Sport
2008 - Liberal Democrat Deputy Spokesman on
Local Government and Transport
Professional Career . . . . . .1981 - 2000 Fitter/Turner
2003 - 07 Sales Advisor
Parliamentary Interests . . .Housing; Health; Planning; Transport
Leisure Interests . . . . .Gardening; Travel; Motoring

Watt, Maureen MSP . . . . . North East Scotland
SNP . . . . List
Born . . . . 23rd June 1951 in Banffshire
Educated. . . . . Keith Grammar School;
                              Strathclyde University; Birmingham University
Elected . . . . , ... 2006 MSP for North East Scotland
Parliamentary Office . . . . . Tel: (0131) 348 6675 Tel: (0131) 348 6676
                              E-mail: maureen.watt.msp@scottish.parliament.uk
                              Parliamentary Assistant – Mr Neil Dunsire
                              E-mail: neil.dunsire@scottish.parliament.uk
Regional Office . . . . .825-827 Great Northern Road, Aberdeen, AB24 2BR
                              Tel: (01224) 697182 Fax: (01224) 695397
                              Parliamentary Assistants – Ms Jennifer Gibson
                                            Mr Callum McCaig
                              E-mails: jennifer.gibson@scottish.parliament.uk
                                        callum.mccaig@scottish.parliament.uk
Political Career . . . . .2006 - 07 MSP for North East Scotland
                                    (replaced Margaret Ewing from SNP list)
                              2007 - 09 Minister for Schools and Skills
                              2009 - Convener, Rural Affairs and Environment
                              Committee
Professional Career . . . . . .1974 - 76 Teacher, Comprehensive School, Reading
                              1977 - 91 Human Resources, Deutag Drilling
                              1999 - 2006 Assessor, Office of the Commissioner
                              for Public Appointments in Scotland
Language Spoken . . . . German
Parliamentary Interests . . . Scottish Independence; Education; Health;
                              Rural Affairs
Leisure Interests. . . . . Yoga; Pilates; Gardening

Welsh, Andrew MSP . . . . . Angus
SNP . . . . Majority 8,243 over Conservative
Born . . . . 19th April 1944 in Glasgow
Educated. . . . . Govan High School; Glasgow University
Elected . . . . .1999 MSP for Angus
Parliamentary Offices . . . .Tel: (0131) 348 5690 Fax: (0131) 348 5677
                Mobile: 07774 294778
                E-mail: andrew.welsh.msp@scottish.parliament.uk
Constituency Office . . . . . .31 Market Place, Arbroath, Angus, DD11 1HR
                Tel: (01241) 439369 Fax:(01241) 871561
                Agent – Mrs Sandra Thomson
                E-mail: sandra.thomson@scottish.parliament.uk
Political Career . . . . .1974 Councillor, Stirling District Council
                1974 - 79 MP for South Angus
                1977 - 79 SNP Whip, House of Commons
                1984 - 87 Provost, Angus District Council
                1987 - 2001 MP for Angus East, then
                  (from 1997) Angus
                1987 - 99 SNP Chief Whip, House of Commons
                1999 - Member Scottish Commission for
                  Public Audit
                1999 - 2003 Convener, Audit Committee
                1999 - 2004 Member, Corporate Body,
                  Scottish Parliament
                2003 - 04 Deputy Convener, Local
                  Government and Transport Committee
                2004 - 07 Deputy Convener, Audit Committee
                2007 - Convener, Finance Committee
Professional Career . . . . . .1962 - 66 Bank Clerk, National Commercial
                Bank of Scotland
                1972 - 74 Teacher, Stirling
                1979 - 83 Lecturer in Public Administration, Dundee
                  College of Commerce
                1983 - 87 Senior Lecturer in Public Administration
                  and Business Studies, Angus College
Trade Union . . . . .Educational Institute of Scotland
Languages Spoken . . . . . . .French; Chinese
Parliamentary Interests . . .Education; Housing; Local Government
Leisure Interests . . . . .Languages; Music

White, Sandra MSP . . . . . . Glasgow Region
SNP . . . . List
Born . . . . 17th August 1951 in Govan, Glasgow
Educated . . . . .Garthamlock Secondary School; Glasgow College;
                    Cardonald College
Elected . . . . .1999 MSP for Glasgow Region
Parliamentary Office . . . . .Tel: (0131) 348 5688 Fax: (0131) 348 5945
                    E-mail: sandra.white@scottish.parliament.uk
                    Web: www.sandra-white.org
Regional Office . . . . .Room 331, 3rd Floor, Baltic Chambers,
                    50 Wellington Street, Glasgow, G2 6HJ
                    Tel: (0141) 202 0679
                    Assistant – Ms Jacqueline Mills
                    E-mail: jacqueline.mills@scottish.parliament.uk
Political Career . . . . .2001 - 04 SNP Group Whip
                    2005 - 07 SNP Deputy Spokesman on Social Justice
Professional Career . . . . . .Former Press Officer, William Wallace Society
Parliamentary Interests . . .Deaf Issues; Housing; Local Government; Social Services;
                    Sports and Leisure; Transport
Leisure Interests . . . . .Meeting People; Reading; Walking

Whitefield, Karen MSP . . . Airdie and Shotts
Scot Lab. . . . . Majority 1,446 over SNP
Born . . . . 8th January 1970 in Bellshill, Lanarkshire
Educated . . . . .Calderhead High School, Shotts;
                    Glasgow Caledonian University
Elected . . . . .1999 MSP for Airdie and Shotts
Parliamentary Office . . . . .Tel: (0131) 348 5832 Fax: (0131) 348 5993
                    E-mail: karen.whitefield.msp@scottish.parliament.uk
                    Web: www.karenwhitefield.com
                    Parliamentary Assistant – Mr David Fagan
                    E-mail: david.fagan@scottish.parliament.uk
                    Research Assistant – Ms Cara Hilton
                    E-mail: cara.hilton@scottish.parliament.uk
Constituency Office . . . . . .3 Sandvale Place, Shotts, North Lanarkshire, ML7 5EF
                    Tel: (01501) 822200 Fax: (01501) 823650
                    Constituency Assistant – Mrs Marion Kirk
Political Career . . . . .1992 - 99 Personal Assistant to Rachel Squire MP
                    2003 - 05 Deputy Convener, Justice II Committee
                    2004 - 07 Convener, Communities Committee
                    2007 - Convener, Education, Life Long
                      Learning and Culture Committee
                    2008 - Labour Spokesman on Children and Early Years
Professional Career . . . . . .1992 Civil Servant, Benefits Agency
Trade Unions . . . . .Unite; USDAW
Parliamentary Interests . . .Education (particularly Early Years); Carers;
                    Voluntary Sector; Transport, Housing
Leisure Interests . . . . .Gardening; Cinema; Reading; Travel
Directorships Held . . . . . . .Petersburn Development Trust *(unpaid)*

Whitton, David MSP . . . . . Strathkelvin and Bearsden
Scot Lab . . . . Majority 3,388 over SNP
Born . . . . 22nd April 1952 in Forfar
Educated . . . . .Morgan Academy, Dundee
Elected . . . . .2007 MSP for Strathkelvin and Bearsden
Parliamentary Office . . . . .Tel: (0131) 348 6747 Fax: (0131) 348 6749
                              E-mail: david.whitton.msp@scottish.parliament.uk
Constituency Office . . . . . .78 Townhead, Kirkintilloch, C66 1NZ
                              Tel & Fax: (0141) 777 9299
                              Staff – Mr Manjinder Shergill
                              E-mail: manjinder.shergill@scottish.parliament.uk
Political Career . . . . .1998 - 99 Special Adviser, Secretary of State
                              for Scotland
                              1999 - 2000 Special Adviser, First Minister Scottish
                              Parliament
                              2008 - Labour Deputy Shadow Spokesman for Finance
Professional Career . . . . . .1970 - 86 Journalist, Various National Newspapers
                              1986 - 96 Various Posts, Scottish TV
                              1996 - 98 Director, Media House
                              2000 - 07 Managing Director, Whitton PR Ltd
Trade Union . . . . .NUJ
Parliamentary Interests . . .Economy; Transport; Sport; Trade Unions;
                              Social Justice Policy; Finance; Housing; Crime;
                              Anti-Social Behaviour
Leisure Interests . . . . .Golf; Grandchildren

Wilson, Dr Bill MSP . . . . . . West of Scotland Region
SNP . . . . List
Born . . . . 11th December 1963 in Paisley
Educated . . . . .Glasgow University; Aberdeen University;
                             Queen's University, Belfast
Elected . . . . .2007 MSP for West of Scotland Region
Parliamentary Office . . . . .Tel: (0131) 348 6805 Fax: (0131) 348 6806
                             E-mail: bill.wilson.msp@scottish.parliament.uk
                             Web: www.billwilsonmsp.org
                             Researcher/Office Manager – Dr Robert Eric Swanepoel
                             E-mail: eric.swanepoel@scottish.parliament.uk
Regional Office . . . . .Unit 27, Sir James Clark Building,
                             Abbey Mill Business Centre, Seedhill, Paisley, PA1 1TJ
                             Tel: (0141) 840 2772 Fax: (0141) 889 4693
                             Constituency Agent/Office Managers –
                               Ms Lisa Cameron
                               Mr David McCartney
                               E-mails: lisa.cameron@scottish.parliament.uk
                                      david.mccartney@scottish.parliament.uk
Professional Career . . . . . .1989 - 99 Academic Researcher, Queen's University,
                             Belfast, Ulster University, Glasgow University
                             2001 - 02 Computing Officer, Glasgow Caledonian
                             University
                             2002 - 05 Computer Programmer, Prudential, then
                             Standard Life
                             2005 - 07 Statistician, Scottish Funding Council
Language Spoken . . . . . . .Scots
Parliamentary Interests . . .Environment; Scots Language; Drug and Rehabilitation;
                             Health and Safety; Corporate Crime; Poverty;
                             Human Rights and Civil Liberties
Leisure Interests . . . . .Hill Walking; Reading
Books Published . . . . .2007: Is There a Scottish Road to Socialism? *(contributor)*

Wilson, John MSP . . . . Central Scotland Region
SNP . . . . List
Born . . . . 28th November 1956 in Falkirk
Educated. . . . . Camelon High School, Falkirk;
Coatbridge College; Glasgow University
Elected . . . . .2007 MSP for Central Scotland Region
Parliamentary Office . . . . .Tel: (0131) 348 6684 Fax: (0131) 348 6686
E-mail: john.wilson.msp@scottish.parliament.uk
Web: www.johnwilsonmsp.com
Parliamentary Officer – Mr Paul Welsh
Tel: (0131) 348 6685
E-mail: paul.welsh@scottish.parliament.uk
Parliamentary Assistant – Miss Lesley Boyle
E-mail: lesley.boyle@scottish.parliament.uk
Regional Office . . . . Suite 3.3, The Dalziel Building, 7 Scott Street,
Motherwell, ML1 1PN
Tel: (01698) 337304 Fax: (01698) 269033
Parliamentary Assistant – Ms Clare Adamson
E-mail: clare.adamson@scottish.parliament.uk
Political Career . . . . .1980 - 82 Councillor, Falkirk Council
2007 - 09 Councillor, North Lanarkshire Council
Professional Career . . . . . . 2001 - 07 Director, Scottish Low Pay Unit
Trade Union . . . . .Unite
Parliamentary Interests . . .Justice; Housing; Effective Community
Empowerment and Democratic Renewal
Leisure Interests . . . . .Archery; Gardening

Note: *The following abbreviations are used herein:*

Scot Cons . . . . *Scottish Conservative and Unionist Party*
Ind . . . . *Independent*
Scot Lab . . . . *Scottish Labour Party*
Lib Dem . . . . *Scottish Liberal Democrat Party*
Scot Grn . . . . *Scottish Green Party*
SNP . . . . *Scottish National Party*

Constituency MSPs

A

Aberdeen Central. . . . . Macdonald, Lewis . . . . Scot Lab
Aberdeen North. . . . . Adam, Brian . . . . SNP
Aberdeen South. . . . . Stephen, Nicol . . . . Scot Lib Dem
Aberdeenshire, West and
    Kincardine . . . . Rumbles, Mike. . . . . Scot Lib Dem
Airdire and Shotts . . . . Whitefield, Karen . . . . Scot Lab
Angus. . . . . Welsh, Andrew . . . . SNP
Argyll and Bute . . . . Mather, Jim . . . . SNP
Ayr. Scott, John . . . . Scot Cons

B

Banff and Buchan . . . . Stevenson, Stewart . . . . SNP

C

Caithness, Sutherland and
    Easter Ross . . . . Stone, Jamie . . . . Scot Lib Dem
Carrick, Cumnock and
    Doon Valley . . . . Jamieson, Cathy . . . . Scot Lab
Clydebank and Milngavie . . McNulty, Des. . . . . Scot Lab
Clydesdale . . . . Gillon, Karen . . . . Scot Lab
Coatbridge and Chryston . . Smith, Elaine . . . . Scot Lab
Cumbernauld and Kilsyth . . Craigie, Cathie . . . . Scot Lab
Cunninghame North . . . . . . Gibson, Kenneth. . . . . SNP
Cunninghame South . . . . . . Oldfather, Irene . . . . Scot Lab

D

Dumbarton	Baillie, Jackie	Scot Lab
Dumfries	Murray, Dr Elaine	Scot Lab
Dundee East	Robison, Shona	SNP
Dundee West	FitzPatrick, Joe	SNP
Dunfermline East	Eadie, Helen	Scot Lab
Dunfermline West	Tolson, Jim	Scot Lib Dem

E

East Kilbride	Kerr, Andy	Scot Lab
East Lothian	Gray, Iain	Scot Lab
Eastwood	Macintosh, Ken	Scot Lab
Edinburgh Central	Boyack, Sarah	Scot Lab
Edinburgh East and Musselburgh	MacAskill, Ken	SNP
Edinburgh North and Leith	Chisholm, Malcolm	Scot Lab
Edinburgh Pentlands	McLetchie, David	Scot Cons
Edinburgh South	Pringle, Mike	Scot Lib Dem
Edinburgh West	Smith, Margaret	Scot Lib Dem

F

Falkirk East	Peattie, Cathy	Scot Lab
Falkirk West	Matheson, Mike	SNP
Fife Central	Marwick, Tricia	SNP
Fife, North East	Smith, Iain	Scot Lib Dem

G

Galloway and Upper Nithsdale	Fergusson, Alex	Ind
Glasgow Anniesland	Butler, Bill	Scot Lab
Glasgow Baillieston	Curran, Margaret	Scot Lab
Glasgow Cathcart	Gordon, Charlie	Scot Lab
Glasgow Govan	Sturgeon, Nicola	SNP
Glasgow Kelvin	McNeill, Pauline	Scot Lab
Glasgow Maryhill	Ferguson, Patricia	Scot Lab
Glasgow Pollok	Lamont, Johann	Scot Lab
Glasgow Rutherglen	Kelly, James	Scot Lab

Glasgow Shettleston . . . . . . McAveety, Frank . . . . Scot Lab
Glasgow Springburn . . . . . . Martin, Paul . . . . Scot Lab
Gordon . . . . Salmond, Rt Hon Alex . . . . SNP
Greenock and Inverclyde. . . McNeil, Duncan. . . . . Scot Lab

H

Hamilton North and
　　　Bellshill . . . . McMahon, Michael . . . . Scot Lab
Hamilton South . . . . McCabe, Tom . . . . Scot Lab

I

Inverness East, Nairn and
　　　Lochaber. . . . . Ewing, Fergus . . . . SNP

K

Kilmarnock and Loudoun . . Coffey, Willie. . . . . SNP
Kirkcaldy . . . . Livingstone, Marilyn . . . . Scot Lab

L

Linlithgow . . . . Mulligan, Mary. . . . . Scot Lab
Livingston . . . . Constance, Angela. . . . . SNP

M

Midlothian . . . . Brankin, Rhona. . . . . Scot Lab
Moray . . . . Lochhead, Richard . . . . SNP
Motherwell and Wishaw . . . McConnell, Rt Hon Jack . . . . Scot Lab

N

North Tayside . . . . Swinney, John . . . . SNP

O

Ochil . . . . Brown, Keith. . . . . SNP
Orkney. . . . . McArthur, Liam. . . . . Scot Lib Dem

P

Paisley North . . . . Alexander, Wendy . . . . Scot Lab
Paisley South . . . . Henry, Hugh . . . . Scot Lab
Perth . . . . Cunningham, Roseanna . . . . SNP

R

Renfrewshire, West . . . . Godman, Trish . . . . Scot Lab
Ross, Skye and Inverness
   West . . . . Munro, John Farquhar . . . . Scot Lib Dem
Roxburgh and
      Berwickshire . . . . Lamont, John . . . . Scot Cons

S

Shetland . . . . Scott, Tavish . . . . Scot Lib Dem
Stirling . . . . Crawford, Bruce . . . . SNP
Strathkelvin and Bearsden . . Whitton, David . . . . Scot Lab

T

Tweeddale, Ettrick and
      Lauderdale . . . . Purvis, Jeremy . . . . Scot Lib Dem

W

Western Isles . . . . Allan, Alasdair . . . . SNP

Regional MSPs

Central Scotland	Fabiani, Linda	SNP
	Hepburn, Jamie	SNP
	McKelvie, Christina	SNP
	Mitchell, Margaret	Scot Cons
	Neil, Alex	SNP
	O'Donnell, Hugh	Lib Dem
	Wilson, John	SNP
Glasgow	Aitken, Bill	Scot Cons
	Brown, Robert	Scot Lib Dem
	Doris, Bob	SNP
	Harvie, Patrick	Scot Grn
	Kidd, Bill	SNP
	Anne McLaughlin	SNP
	White, Sandra	SNP
Highlands and Islands	Gibson, Rob	SNP
	Grant, Rhoda	Scot Lab
	McGrigor, Jamie	Scot Cons
	Peacock, Peter	Scot Lab
	Scanlon, Mary	Scot Cons
	Stewart, David	Scot Lab
	Thompson, David	SNP
Lothians	Brown, Gavin	Scot Cons
	Foulkes, Lord [George]	Scot Lab
	Harper, Robin	Scot Grn
	Hyslop, Fiona	SNP
	MacDonald, Margo	Ind
	McKee, Ian	SNP
	Somerville, Shirley-Anne	SNP

Mid Scotland and Fife . . . . . Baker, Claire . . . . Scot Lab
Brocklebank, Ted . . . . Scot Cons
Fraser, Murdo. . . . . Scot Cons
Harvie, Christopher. . . . . SNP
Park, John . . . . Scot Lab
Simpson, Dr Richard . . . . Scot Lab
Smith, Elizabeth . . . . Scot Cons

North East Scotland . . . . . . Baker, Richard . . . . Scot Lab
Don, Nigel. . . . . SNP
Glen, Marlyn . . . . Scot Lab
Johnstone, Alex. . . . . Scot Cons
McInnes, Alison . . . . Lib Dem
Milne, Nanette . . . . Scot Cons
Watt, Maureen . . . . SNP

South of Scotland . . . . Brownlee, Derek. . . . . Scot Cons
Campbell, Aileen. . . . . SNP
Grahame, Christine. . . . . SNP
Hume, Jim . . . . Lib Dem
Ingram, Adam . . . . SNP
Morgan, Alasdair. . . . . SNP
Russell, Michael . . . . SNP

West of Scotland . . . . Carlaw, Jackson . . . . Scot Cons
Finnie, Ross . . . . Scot Lib Dem
Goldie, Annabel . . . . Scot Cons
Maxwell, Stewart. . . . . SNP
McMillan, Stuart. . . . . SNP
Paterson, Gil . . . . SNP
Wilson, Dr Bill . . . . SNP

SCOTTISH PARLIAMENT CONSTITUENCIES
COVERED BY REGION

Central Scotland . . . . Airdrie and Shotts
Coatbridge and Chryston
Cumbernauld and Kilsyth
East Kilbride
Falkirk East
Falkirk West
Hamilton North and Bellshill
Hamilton South
Kilmarnock and Loudoun
Motherwell and Wishaw

Glasgow. . . . . Glasgow Anniesland
Glasgow Ballieston
Glasgow Cathcart
Glasgow Govan
Glasgow Kelvin
Glasgow Maryhill
Glasgow Pollok
Glasgow Rutherglen
Glasgow Shettleston
Glasgow Springburn

Highlands and Islands. . . . . Argyll and Bute
Caithness, Sutherland and Easter Ross
Inverness East, Nairn and Lochaber
Moray
Orkney
Ross, Skye and Inverness West
Shetland
Western Isles

Lothians . . . . Edinburgh Central
Edinburgh East and Musselburgh
Edinburgh North and Leith
Edinburgh Pentlands
Edinburgh South
Edinburgh West
Linlithgow
Livingston
Midlothian

SCOTTISH PARLIAMENT CONSTITUENCIES
COVERED BY REGION

Mid Scotland and Fife. . . . . Dunfermline East
Dunfermline West
Fife Central
Fife North East
Kirkcaldy
Ochil
Perth
Stirling
Tayside North

North East Scotland . . . . Aberdeen Central
Aberdeen North
Aberdeen South
Aberdeenshire West and Kincardine
Angus
Banff and Buchan
Dundee East
Dundee West
Gordon

South of Scotland . . . . Ayr
Carrick, Cumnock and Doon Valley
Clydesdale
Cunninghame South
Dumfries
East Lothian
Galloway and Upper Nithsdale
Roxburgh and Berwickshire
Tweeddale, Ettrick and Lauderdale

West of Scotland . . . . Clydebank and Milngavie
Cunninghame North
Dumbarton
Eastwood
Greenock and Inverclyde
Paisley North
Paisley South
Strathkelvin and Bearsden
West Renfrewshire

Scottish Conservative

Aitken, Bill. . . . . Glasgow Region
Brocklebank, Ted . . . . Mid Scotland and Fife Region
Brown, Gavin . . . . Lothians Region
Brownlee, Derek. . . . . South of Scotland Region
Carlaw, Jackson . . . . West of Scotland Region
Fraser, Murdo. . . . . Mid Scotland and Fife Region
Goldie, Annabel. . . . . West of Scotland Region
Johnstone, Alex. . . . . North East Scotland Region
Lamont, John . . . . Roxburgh and Berwickshire
McGrigor Jamie. . . . . Highlands and Islands Region
McLetchie, David . . . . Edinburgh Pentlands
Milne, Nanette . . . . North East Scotland Region
Mitchell, Margaret . . . . Central Scotland Region
Scanlon, Mary . . . . Highlands and Islands Region
Scott, John. . . . . Ayr
Smith, Elizabeth . . . . Mid Scotland and Fife Region

Scottish Green

Harper, Robin. . . . . Lothians Region
Harvie, Patrick. . . . . Glasgow Region

Scottish Labour

Alexander, Wendy. . . . . Paisley North
Baillie, Jackie. . . . . Dumbarton
Baker, Claire . . . . Mid Scotland and Fife Region
Baker, Richard . . . . North East Scotland Region
Boyack, Sarah . . . . Edinburgh Central
Brankin, Rhona . . . . Midlothian
Butler, Bill. . . . . Glasgow Anniesland
Chisholm, Malcolm. . . . . Edinburgh North and Leith
Craigie, Cathie. . . . . Cumbernauld and Kilsyth
Curran, Margaret. . . . . Glasgow Baillieston
Eadie, Helen . . . . Dunfermline East
Ferguson, Patricia . . . . Glasgow Maryhill
Foulkes, Lord [George]. . . . . Lothians Region
Gillon, Karen . . . . Clydesdale
Glen, Marlyn . . . . North East Scotland Region
Godman, Trish . . . . West Renfrewshire

Scottish Labour Party (Continued)

Gordon, Charlie . . . . Glasgow Cathcart
Grant, Rhoda. . . . . Highlands and Islands Region
Gray, Iain . . . . East Lothian
Henry, Hugh . . . . Paisley South
Jamieson, Cathy. . . . . Carrick, Cumnock and Doon Valley
Kelly, James . . . . Glasgow Rutherglen
Kerr, Andy. . . . . East Kilbride
Lamont, Johann . . . . Glasgow Pollok
Livingstone, Marilyn . . . . Kirkcaldy
Macdonald, Lewis. . . . . Aberdeen Central
Macintosh, Ken . . . . Eastwood
Martin, Paul. . . . . Glasgow Springburn
McAveety, Frank . . . . Glasgow Shettleston
McCabe, Tom. . . . . Hamilton South
McConnell, Rt Hon Jack . . . . Motherwell and Wishaw
McMahon, Michael. . . . . Hamilton North and Bellshill
McNeil, Duncan . . . . Greenock and Inverclyde
McNeill, Pauline . . . . Glasgow Kelvin
McNulty, Des. . . . . Clydebank and Milngavie
Mulligan, Mary . . . . Linlithgow
Murray, Dr Elaine . . . . Dumfries
Oldfather, Irene . . . . Cunninghame South
Park, John . . . . Mid Scotland and Fife Region
Peacock, Peter . . . . Highlands and Islands Region
Peattie, Cathy. . . . . Falkirk East
Simpson, Dr Richard . . . . Mid Scotland and Fife Region
Smith, Elaine. . . . . Coatbridge and Chryston
Stewart, David. . . . . Highlands and Islands Region
Whitefield, Karen . . . . Airdie and Shotts
Whitton, David . . . . Strathkelvin and Bearsden

Scottish Liberal Democrat

Brown, Robert. . . . . Glasgow Region
Finnie, Ross. . . . . West of Scotland Region
Hume, Jim . . . . South of Scotland Region
McArthur, Liam . . . . Orkney
McInnes, Alison. . . . . North East of Scotland Region
Munro, John Farquhar. . . . . Ross, Skye and Inverness West
O'Donnell, Hugh . . . . Central Scotland Region
Pringle, Mike . . . . Edinburgh South

Scottish Liberal Democrat Party (Continued)

Purvis, Jeremy . . . . Tweeddale, Ettrick & Lauderdale
Rumbles, Michael . . . . West Aberdeenshire and Kincardine
Scott, Tavish . . . . Shetland
Smith, Iain . . . . North East Fife
Smith, Margaret . . . . Edinburgh West
Stephen, Nicol . . . . Aberdeen South
Stone, Jamie . . . . Caithness, Sutherland and Easter Ross
Tolson, Jim . . . . Dunfermline West

Scottish National Party – SNP

Adam, Brian . . . . Aberdeen North
Allan, Alasdair . . . . Western Isles
Brown, Keith . . . . Ochil
Campbell, Aileen . . . . South of Scotland Region
Coffey, Willie . . . . Kilmarnock and Loudon
Constance, Angela . . . . Livingston
Crawford, Bruce . . . . Stirling
Cunningham, Roseanna . . . . Perth
Don, Nigel . . . . North East Scotland Region
Doris, Bob . . . . Glasgow Region
Ewing, Fergus . . . . Inverness East, Nairn and Lochaber
Fabiani, Linda . . . . Central Scotland Region
FitzPatrick, Joe . . . . Dundee West
Gibson, Kenneth . . . . Cunninghame North
Gibson, Rob . . . . Highland and Islands Region
Grahame, Christine . . . . South of Scotland Region
Harvie, Christopher . . . . Mid Scotland and Fife Region
Hepburn, Jamie . . . . Central Scotland Region
Hyslop, Fiona . . . . Lothians Region
Ingram, Adam . . . . South of Scotland Region
Kidd, Bill . . . . Glasgow Region
Lochhead, Richard . . . . Moray
MacAskill, Kenny . . . . Edinburgh East and Musselburgh
Marwick, Tricia . . . . Central Fife
Mather, Jim . . . . Argyll and Bute
Matheson, Michael . . . . Falkirk West
Maxwell, Stewart . . . . West of Scotland Region
McKee, Ian . . . . Lothians Region
McKelvie, Christina . . . . Central Scotland Region
McLaughlin, Anne . . . . Glasgow Region
McMillan, Stuart . . . . West of Scotland Region
Morgan, Alasdair . . . . South of Scotland Region

SNP (Continued)

Neil, Alex . . . . Central Scotland Region
Paterson, Gil . . . . West of Scotland Region
Robison, Shona. . . . . Dundee East
Russell, Michael . . . . South of Scotland Region
Salmond, Rt Hon Alex MP . . . . Gordon
Somerville, Shirley-Anne. . . . . Lothians Region
Stevenson, Stewart . . . . Banff and Buchan
Sturgeon, Nicola . . . . Glasgow Govan
Swinney, John . . . . North Tayside
Thompson, Dave. . . . . Highlands and Islands Region
Watt, Maureen . . . . North East Scotland Region
Welsh, Andrew . . . . Angus
White, Sandra . . . . Glasgow Region
Wilson, Dr Bill. . . . . West of Scotland Region
Wilson, John. . . . . Central Scotland Region

Independent

MacDonald, Margot . . . . Lothians Region

Presiding Officer

Fergusson, Alex . . . . Galloway and Upper Nithsdale

Scottish Conservative Party
83 Princes Street
Edinburgh, EH2 2ER
Tel: (0131) 247 6890 Fax: (0131) 247 6891
E-mail: info@scottishconservatives.com
Web: www.scottishconservatives.com

Chairman . . . . Mr Andrew Fulton

Head of Media . . . . Mr Ramsay Jones

Scottish Green Party
Thorn House, 5 Rose Street
Edinburgh, EH2 2PR
Tel: (0870) 077 2207
E-mail: office@scottishgreens.org.uk
Web: www.scottishgreens.org.uk

Co-Convenors . . . . Cllr Alison Johnstone
Mr Robin Harper MSP

Campaign Director and
Press Officer . . . . Mr James McKenzie

Scottish Labour Party
John Smith House
145 West Regent Street
Glasgow, G2 4RE
Tel: (0141) 572 6900 Fax: (0141) 572 2566
E-mail: scotland@new.labour.org.uk
Web: www.scottishlabour.org.uk

General Secretary . . . . Mr Colin Smyth

Head of Press . . . . Mr Rami O'Kasha

Scottish Liberal Democrat Party
4 Clifton Terrace
Edinburgh, EH12 5DR
Tel: (0131) 337 2314 Fax: (0131) 337 3566
E-mail: administration@scotlibdems.org.uk
Web: www.scotlibdems.org.uk

Party Convener . . . . Ms Audrey Findlay

Chief Executive . . . . Mr Martin Hayman

Press Officer. . . . . Ms Jenny Stanning

Scottish National Party
107 McDonald Road
Edinburgh, EH7 4NW
Tel: (0131) 525 8900 Fax: (0131) 525 8901
E-mail: snp.hq@snp.org
Web: www.snp.org

National Secretary . . . . Dr Duncan Ross

Chief Executive . . . . Mr Peter Murrell

First Minister . . . . Rt Hon Alex Salmond MSP

Cabinet Secretaries
Deputy First Minister and
    Cabinet Secretary for Health
    and Wellbeing . . . . Nicola Sturgeon MSP
Education and Lifelong Learning . . Fiona Hyslop MSP
Finance and Sustainable Growth . . John Swinney MSP
Justice . . . . Kenny MacAskill MSP
Rural Affairs and the Environment . Richard Lochhead MSP

Ministers
Children and Early Years . . . . Adam Ingram MSP
Community Safety . . . . Fergus Ewing MSP
Culture, External Affairs and
    the Constitution . . . . Michael Russell MSP
Enterprise, Energy and Tourism . . . Jim Mather MSP
Environment . . . . Roseanna Cunningham MSP
Housing and Communities . . . . Alex Neil MSP
Parliamentary Business . . . . Bruce Crawford MSP
Public Health and Sport . . . . Shona Robison MSP
Schools and Skills . . . . Keith Brown MSP
Transport, Infrastructure and
    Climate Change . . . . Stewart Stevenson MSP

Law Officers
Lord Advocate . . . . Rt Hon Elish Angiolini QC
Solicitor General . . . . Frank Mulholland QC

SCOTTISH PARLIAMENT –
SCOTTISH CONSERVATIVE SPOKESMEN

Leader . . . . Annabel Goldie MSP

Cabinet Shadow Secretaries
Deputy Leader and Education and
    Lifelong Learning . . . . Murdo Fraser MSP

Finance and Sustainable Growth . . . . Derek Brownlee MSP

Health and Wellbeing . . . . Mary Scanlon MSP

Justice . . . . Bill Aitken MSP

Rural Affairs and the Environment . . . . John Scott MSP

Chief Whip and Business Manager . . . . David McLetchie MSP

Shadow Ministers
Children, Schools and Skills . . . . Elizabeth Smith MSP

Communities and Sport . . . . Jamie McGrigor MSP

Community Safety . . . . John Lamont MSP

Energy, Enterprise and Tourism . . . . Gavin Brown MSP

Environment . . . . Nanette Milne MSP

Europe, External Affairs and Culture . . . . Ted Brocklebank MSP

Public Health . . . . Jackson Carlaw MSP

Transport, Infrastructure and
    Climate Change . . . . Alex Johnstone MSP

SCOTTISH PARLIAMENT – LABOUR SPOKESMEN

Leader . . . . Iain Grey MSP

Deputy Leader . . . . Johann Lamont MSP

Cabinet Shadow Secretaries
Education and Lifelong Learning . . . . Rhona Brankin MSP

Europe, External Affairs and Culture . . . . Pauline McNeill MSP

Finance and Sustainable Growth . . . . Andy Kerr MSP

Health and Wellbeing . . . . Cathy Jamieson MSP

Justice . . . . Richard Baker MSP

Rural Affairs and Environment . . . . Sarah Boyack MSP

Policy Development . . . . Margaret Curran MSP

Shadow Ministers
Economy and Skills . . . . John Park MSP

Education
   Children and Early Years . . . . Karen Whitefield MSP
   Further and Higher Education . . . . Claire Baker MSP
   Schools . . . . Ken McIntosh MSP

Finance and Sustainable Growth . . . . David Whitton MSP

Environment
   Energy, Enterprise and Tourism . . . . Lewis Macdonald MSP
   Environment . . . . Elaine Murray MSP
   Rural Development, Economy and Skills . . . . . Karen Gillon MSP
   Transport, Infrastructure and Climate
     Change . . . . Des McNulty MSP

Health
   Housing and Communities . . . . Mary Mulligan MSP
   Public Health . . . . Richard Simpson MSP
   Sport . . . . Frank McAveety MSP

Justice
   Community Safety . . . . Paul Martin MSP

Parliamentary Business Manager . . . . Michael McMahon MSP

Chief Whip . . . . David Stewart MSP
   Whips . . . . Rhoda Grant MSP
                                      James Kelly MSP

SCOTTISH PARLIAMENT – SCOTTISH LIBERAL DEMOCRAT MINISTERS AND SPOKESMEN

Leader . . . . Tavish Scott MSP

Shadow Secretaries

Culture, Europe and External
Relations . . . . Iain Smith MSP
Economy and Finance . . . . Jeremy Purvis MSP
Education and Young People . . . . . . Margaret Smith MSP
Environment, Rural
Development and Energy . . . . . . Liam McArthur
Gaelic Language . . . . John Farquhar Munro MSP
Health . . . . Ross Finnie MSP
Justice . . . . Robert Brown MSP
Local Government and
Transport . . . . Alison McInnes MSP
Parliamentary Business Manager
and Chief Whip . . . . Mike Rumbles MSP

Spokesmen

Local Government and
Transport . . . . Jim Tolson MSP
Education and Young People . . . . . . Hugh O'Donnell MSP
Environment, Rural Development
and Energy . . . . Liam McArthur MSP
Justice . . . . Mike Pringle MSP
Health . . . . Jamie Stone MSP

SCOTTISH GREEN PARTY

Co-Convener . . . . Patrick Harvie MSP

The Scottish Parliament
Edinburgh, EH99 1SP
Tel: (0131) 348 5000 Fax: (0131) 348 5601
E-mail: sp.info@scottish.parliament.uk *(Public Information)*

Presiding Officer

E-mail: presiding.officer@scottish.parliament.uk

Presiding Officer. . . . . Alex Fergusson MSP

Deputy Presiding Officers. . . . . Trish Godman MSP
Alasdair Morgan MSP

Scottish Commission for Public Audit

Convener. . . . . Angela Constance MSP

Members . . . . Robert Brown MSP
Derek Brownlee MSP
Lord [George] Foulkes MSP
Hugh Henry MSP

Scottish Parliament Corporate Body

Presiding Officer. . . . . Alex Fergusson MSP

Members . . . . Tom McCabe MSP
Alex Johnstone MSP
Trishia Marwick MSP
Mike Pringle MSP

Secretariat . . . . Tel: (0131) 348 6222 / 5307

Parliamentary Bureau

Presiding Officer . . . . Alex Fergusson MSP

Secretariat . . . . Tel: (0131) 348 5192

Parliamentary Staff

Clerk and Chief Executive . . . . Mr Paul Grice
Head of Office to the Clerk/Chief Executive . . . Ms Alli Williams
Office of the Presiding Officer . . . . Ms Jane McEwan

Assistant Clerks/Chief Executive . . . . Mr Stewart Gilfillan
Mr Ian Leitch
Mr Bill Thomson

Solicitor to the Scottish Parliament . . . . Ms Lynda Towers

Allowances Office . . . . Ms Jackie Giulianotti

Broadcasting . . . . Ms Ruth Connelly

Business Information Technology, Head . . . . . . Mr Alan Balharrie

Chamber Office . . . . Mr Ken Hughes

Committee Office . . . . Ms Elizabeth Watson

Corporate Publications . . . . Ms Tori Spratt

**Education and Community
     Partnerships** . . . . Ms Rosemary Everett

Events and Exhibitions . . . . Mr Roy Devon

Facilities Management, Head . . . . Mr Jerry Headley

Finance . . . . Ms Lisbeth Craig

Financial Resources . . . . Mr Derek Croll

Human Resources, Head . . . . Mr Colin Chisholm

Information Centre . . . . Ms Henrietta Hales

Media Relations . . . . Ms Annette McCann

Office Holder Services and Allowances . . . . Mr Huw Williams

Official Report . . . . Ms Henrietta Hales

Procurement . . . . Ms Lynn Garvie

Public Affairs, Head . . . . Ms Michelle Hegarty

Public Information Service . . . . Ms Linda Orton

Research, Information and
  Reporting, Head . . . . Ms Henrietta Hales

Security Office . . . . Mr Bill Anderson

Visitor and Outreach Services . . . . Mr Gordon Stewart

OFFICE OF THE SCOTTISH PARLIAMENTARY COUNSEL

Office of the Scottish Parliamentary Counsel
Victoria Quay, Edinburgh, EH6 6QQ
Tel: (0131) 244 0520
E-mail: ospc@scotland.gsi.gov.uk

First Scottish Parliamentary Counsel . Mr Colin Wilson . . . . . . Tel: (0131) 244 1670
Scottish Legislative Counsel. . . . . Mr Stuart Foubister . . . Tel: (0131) 244 0540
Scottish Parliamentary Counsel . . . . . Mr Andy Beattie . . . . . . Tel: (0131) 244 1665
                                          Mr Willie Ferrie . . . . . . Tel: (0131) 244 1663
Depute Scottish Parliamentary
  Counsel . . . . Ms Diane Barbirou . . . . Tel: (0131) 244 1669
                                          Mr Andy Beattie . . . . . . Tel: (0131) 244 1665
                                          Mr Willie Ferrie . . . . . . Tel: (0131) 244 1663
                                          Mr Alex Gordon . . . . . . Tel: (0131) 244 1668
                                          Mr Neil Taylor . . . . Tel: (0131) 244 1696
                                          Mr Ian Young . . . . Tel: (0131) 244 7393

Notes: (i) Committees usually meet weekly or fortnightly mainly on Tuesday and Wednesday mornings in the Parliament's Committee Rooms in the Scottish Parliament, Edinburgh, EH99 1SP.
(ii) Members listed are the full members of each committee

Economy, Energy and Tourism Committee

Convener . . . . Iain Smith

Deputy Convener . . . . Rob Gibson

Members . . . . Wendy Alexander
Gavin Brown
Christopher Harvie
Marilyn Livingstone
Lewis Macdonald
Stuart McMillan

Clerk . . . . Mr Stephen Imrie
Tel: (0131) 348 5214

Education, Lifelong Learning and Culture Committee

Convener . . . . Karen Whitefield

Deputy Convener . . . . Kenneth Gibson

Members . . . . Claire Baker
Aileen Campbell
Ken Macintosh
Christina McKelvie
Elizabeth Smith
Margaret Smith

Clerk . . . . Mr Eugene Windsor
Tel: (0131) 348 5238

Equal Opportunities Committee

Convener . . . . Margaret Mitchell

Deputy Convener . . . . Marlyn Glen

Members . . . . Malcolm Chisholm
Willie Coffey
Bill Kidd
Hugh O'Donnell
Elaine Smith
Bill Wilson

Clerk . . . . Mr Terry Shevlin
Tel: (0131) 348 5216

European and External Relations Committee

Convener . . . . Irene Oldfather

Deputy Convener . . . . Michael Matheson

Members . . . . Ted Brocklebank
Patricia Ferguson
Charles Gordon
Jamie Hepburn
Jim Hume
Sandra White

Clerks . . . . Ms Lynn Tullis
Mr Simon Watkins
Tel: (0131) 348 5232

Finance Committee

Convener . . . . Andrew Welsh

Deputy Convener . . . . Jackie Baillie

Members . . . . Derek Brownlee
Linda Fabiani
Joe FitzPatrick
James Kelly
Jeremy Purvis
David Whitton

Clerk . . . . Mr James Johnston
Tel: (0131) 348 5451

Health and Sport Committee

Convener . . . . Christine Grahame

Deputy Convener . . . . Ross Finnie

Members . . . . Helen Eadie
Rhoda Grant
Michael Matheson
Ian McKee
Mary Scanlon
Dr Richard Simpson

Clerk . . . . Mr Callum Thomson
Tel: (0131) 348 5410

Justice Committee

Convener . . . . Bill Aitken

Deputy Convener . . . . Bill Butler

Members . . . . Robert Brown
Angela Constance
Cathie Craigie
Nigel Don
Paul Martin
Stewart Maxwell

Clerk . . . . Mr Andrew Mylne
Tel: (0131) 348 5047

Local Government and Communities Committee

Convener . . . . Duncan McNeil

Deputy Convener . . . . Alasdair Allan

Members . . . . Bob Doris
Patricia Ferguson
David McLetchie
Mary Mulligan
John Tolson
John Wilson

Clerk . . . . Ms Susan Duffy
Tel: (0131) 348 5223

Public Audit Committee

Convener . . . . Hugh Henry

Deputy Convener . . . . Murdo Fraser

Members . . . . Willie Coffey
Cathie Craigie
Lord [George] Foulkes
Bill Kidd
Anne McLaughlin
Nicol Stephen

Clerk . . . . Ms Tracey White
Tel: (0131) 348 5236

Public Petitions Committee

Convener . . . . Frank McAveety

Deputy Convener . . . . John Farquhar Munro

Members . . . . Bill Butler
Nigel Don
Marlyn Glen
Anne McLaughlin
Robin Harper
Nanette Milne
John Wilson

Clerk . . . . Mr Fergus Cochrane
Tel: (0131) 348 5982

Rural Affairs and Environment Committee

Convener . . . . Maureen Watt

Deputy Convener . . . . John Scott

Members . . . . Karen Gillon
Liam McArthur
Alasdair Morgan
Elaine Murray
Peter Peacock
Bill Wilson

Clerk . . . . Mr Peter McGrath
Tel: (0131) 348 5242

Standards, Procedures and Public Appointments Committee

Convener . . . . Gil Paterson

Deputy Convener . . . . Marilyn Livingstone

Members . . . . Robert Brown
Aileen Campbell
Nanette Milne
Peter Peacock
Dave Thompson

Clerks . . . . Ms Gillian Boxendine
Ms Alison Walker
Tel: (0131) 348 5183/5177

Subordinate Legislation Committee

Convener . . . . Jamie Stone

Deputy Convener . . . . Ian McKee

Members . . . . Jackson Carlaw
Margaret Curran
Bob Doris
Helen Eadie
Rhoda Grant

Clerk . . . . Mr Douglas Wards
Tel: (0131) 348 5175

Transport, Infrastructure and Climate Change Committee

Convener . . . . Patrick Harvie

Deputy Convener . . . . Cathy Peattie

Members . . . . Rob Gibson
Marlyn Glen
Charlie Gordon
Alex Johnstone
Alison McInnes
Shirley-Anne Somerville

Clerk . . . . Mr Steve Farrell
Tel: (0131) 348 5882

Scottish Government

Office of the First Minister
St Andrew's House, Regent Road
Edinburgh, EH1 3DG
Tel: (0131) 244 5218 Fax: (0131) 244 6915
E-mail: firstminister@scotland.gsi.gov.uk
Web: www.scotland.gov.uk

First Minister . . . . .Rt Hon Alex Salmond MP MSP
Principal Private Secretary (PPS) . .Mrs Karen Watt . . . . .Tel: (0131) 244 5218
Personal Assistant to PPS . . . . . .Mr Michael Birrell . . . . . .Tel: (0131) 244 5213

Deputy First Minister and Cabinet Secretary
for Health and Wellbeing . . . . . . .Ms Nicola Sturgeon MSP
Private Secretary . . . . Ms Beth Elliot . . . . Tel: (0131) 244 4017
Diary Secretary . . . . Ms Hazel Stewart . . . . . Tel: (0131) 244 2135

Minister for Culture, External
Affairs and the Constitution . . . . . .Michael Russell MSP
Private Secretary . . . . Mr Darren Dickson. . . . Tel: (0131) 244 7716
Diary/Correspondence Secretary . . . . Ms Carol-Ann Miller. . . Tel: (0131) 244 1434

Minister for Parliamentary
Business . . . . .Bruce Crawford MSP
Private Secretary . . . . Ms Gill Glass. . . . . Tel: (0131) 244 5593
Diary Secretary . . . . Mr Scott McLear. . . . . . Tel: (0131) 244 5568

Communications
Director, Communications . . . . . . .Ms Sarah Davidson . . . .Tel: (0131) 244 0162
Marketing and New Media . . . . . .Mr Roger Williams . . . .Tel: (0131) 244 2706
News, Head . . . . .Mr Andrew Baird . . . . . .Tel: (0131) 244 5086
Corporate Communications . . . . . .Mr David Hamilton . . . .Tel: (0131) 244 2045

Constitution, Law and Courts
Director, Constitution, Law
and Courts . . . . .Mr Ken Thomson . . . . .Tel: (0131) 244 2131
Constitutional and Parliamentary
Secretariat . . . . .Ms Elspeth Macdonald .Tel: (0131) 244 5205

Corporate Analytical Services
Office of the Chief Economic
Adviser .Mr Gary Gillespie . . . . .Tel: (0131) 244 1453
Office of the Chief Researcher/
Social Researcher . . . . .Ms Diana Wilkinson . . .Tel: (0131) 244 1832
Office of the Chief Statistician . . . .Mr Rob Wishart . . . . . . .Tel: (0131) 244 0302

Office of the First Minister (Continued)

Culture, External Affairs and Tourism
Director, Culture, External Affairs
and Tourism . . . . Ms Deborah Smith . . . .Tel: (0131) 244 5504
Culture and Gaelic . . . . Ms Wendy Wilkinson . .Tel: (0131) 244 0341
International . . . . .Ms Lisa Bird . . . . .Tel: (0131) 244 7702

Finance and Corporate Services
Director-General, Finance and
Corporate Services . . . . .Ms Stella Manzie . . . . . .Tel: (0131) 244 3938
Facilities and Estates Services . . . . .Mr James Hynd . . . . . . .Tel: (0131) 244 4261

Strategy and Analytical Services
Head of Strategy . . . . .Mr Douglas Greig . . . . .Tel: (0131) 244 2806

Strategy and Ministerial Support
Director, Strategy and Ministerial
Support .Ms Angiolina Foster . . . .Tel: (0131) 244 6916
Cabinet Secretariat . . . . .Ms Elinor Mitchell . . . . .Tel: (0131) 244 3223
External Support . . . . .Mr Tim Barraclough . . .Tel: (0131) 244 3242
Performance Division . . . . .Ms Trudy Sharp . . . . . .Tel: (0131) 244 3072

Children and Early Years
Victoria Quay, Edinburgh, EH6 6QQ
E-mail: ministerforchildrenandearlyyears@scotland.gsi.gov.uk

Minister . . . . Adam Ingram MSP
Private Secretary . . . . Mr Grant Moncur . . . . . Tel: (0131) 244 1469
Diary/Correspondence Secretary . . . . Ms Amanda Harding. . . Tel: (0131) 244 7851

Community Safety
St Andrew's House, Regent Road, Edinburgh, EH1 3DG
E-mail: cabinetsecretaryforcommunitysafety@scotland.gsi.gov.uk

Cabinet Secretary . . . . Fergus Ewing MSP
Private Secretary . . . . Ms Karen McKeown. . . Tel: (0131) 244 4579
Diary Secretary . . . . Mr Christopher
Inverarity . . . . Tel: (0131) 244 7981

Culture, External Affairs and the Constitution
Victoria Quay, Edinburgh, EH6 6QQ
E-mail: ministerforcultureexternalaffairsandthe constitution@scotland.gsi.gov.uk

Minister . . . . Michael Russell MSP
Private Secretary . . . . Mr Darren Dickson . . . . Tel: (0131) 244 7716
Diary/Correspondence Secretary . . . . Ms Carol-Ann Miller. . . Tel: (0131) 244 1434

Education and Lifelong Learning
St Andrew's House, Regent Road, Edinburgh, EH1 3DG
E-mail: cabinetsecretaryforeducationandlifelonglearning@scotland.gsi.gov.uk

Cabinet Secretary . . . . Fiona Hyslop MSP
Private Secretary . . . . Mr Brian Taylor . . . . . . Tel: (0131) 244 1556
Diary Secretary . . . . Ms Caroline Miller . . . . Tel: (0131) 244 1434

Enterprise, Energy and Tourism
6th Floor, Meridian Court, 5 Cadogan Street, Glasgow, G2 7AT
E-mail: ministerforenergyenterpriseandtourism@scotland.gsi.gov.uk

Minister . . . . Jim Mather MSP
Private Secretary . . . . Ms Shauna Cranney . . . Tel: (0131) 348 5580
Diary Secretary . . . . Mr Elliott Crosbie . . . . . Tel: (0131) 348 5700

OFFICES OF MINISTERS OF THE SCOTTISH GOVERNMENT

Environment

Victoria Quay, Edinburgh, EH6 6QQ
E-mail: ministerforenvironment@scotland.gsi.gov.uk

Minister . . . . Roseanna Cunningham MSP
Private Secretary . . . . Ms Becky Lucas . . . . . . Tel: (0131) 244 4425
Diary Secretary . . . . Ms Gemma Davis . . . . . Tel: (0131) 244 4426

Finance and Sustainable Growth

St Andrew's House, Regent Road, Edinburgh, EH1 3DG
E-mail: cabinetsecretaryforfinanceandsustainablegrowth@scotland.gsi.gov.uk

Cabinet Secretary . . . . John Swinney MSP
Private Secretary . . . . Mr John Nicholson . . . . Tel: (0131) 244 5227
Diary Secretary . . . . Ms Morag Ogilvie . . . . . Tel: (0131) 244 1509

Health and Wellbeing

St Andrew's House, Regent Road, Edinburgh, EH1 3DG
E-mail: cabinetsecretaryforhealthandwellbeing@scotland.gsi.gov.uk

Cabinet Secretary . . . . Nicola Sturgeon MSP
Private Secretary . . . . Ms Beth Elliot . . . . Tel: (0131) 244 4017
Diary Secretary . . . . Ms Hazel Stewart . . . . . Tel: (0131) 244 2135

Housing and Communities

Victoria Quay, Edinburgh, EH6 6QQ
E-mail: ministerforcommunitiesandsport@scotland.gsi.gov.uk

Minister . . . . Alex Neil MSP
Private Secretary . . . . Ms Laura Hitchings. . . . Tel: (0131) 244 5539
Diary Secretary . . . . Mr Gareth Hall . . . . Tel: (0131) 244 7981

Justice

St Andrew's House, Regent Road, Edinburgh, EH1 3DG
E-mail: cabinetsecretaryforjustice@scotland.gsi.gov.uk

Cabinet Secretary . . . . Kenny MacAskill MSP
Private Secretary . . . . Ms Linda Hamilton . . . . Tel: (0131) 244 5147
Diary Secretary . . . . Ms Lorraine Whigham . Tel: (0131) 244 5143

Parliamentary Business
T4.21, The Scottish Parliament, Edinburgh, EH99 1SP
E-mail: ministerforparliamentarybusiness@scotland.gsi.gov.uk

Minister . . . . Bruce Crawford MSP
Private Secretary . . . . Ms Gill Glass . . . . Tel: (0131) 348 5593
Diary Secretary . . . . Mr Scott McLear. . . . . . Tel: (0131) 348 5568

Public Health and Sport
Room 1E.10, St Andrew's House, Regent Road, Edinburgh, EH1 3DG
E-mail: ministerforpublichealth@scotland.gsi.gov.uk

Minister . . . . Shona Robison MSP
Private Secretary . . . . Mr Peter Creevy . . . . . . Tel: (0131) 244 2186
Diary Secretary . . . . Ms Fern Morris . . . . Tel: (0131) 244 5131

Rural Affairs and the Environment
Room 1N.08, St Andrew's House, Regent Road, Edinburgh, EH1 3DG
E-mail: cabinetsecretaryforruralaffairsandtheenvironment@scotland.gsi.gov.uk

Cabinet Secretary . . . . Richard Lochhead MSP
Private Secretary . . . . Ms Lea Mann . . . . Tel: (0131) 244 4456
Diary Secretary . . . . Mr Martyn McDonald . Tel: (0131) 244 4450

Schools and Skills
Victoria Quay, Edinburgh, EH6 6QQ
E-mail: ministerforschoolsandskills@scotland.gsi.gov.uk

Minister . . . . Keith Brown MSP
Private Secretary . . . . Ms Gemma Park . . . . . . Tel: (0131) 244 7821
Diary/Correspondence Secretary . . . . Mr Dominique Barlow . Tel: (0131) 244 5538

Transport, Infrastructure and Climate Change
Victoria Quay, Edinburgh, EH6 6QQ
E-mail: ministerfortransportinfrastructureandsustainablegrowth@scotland.gsi.gov.uk

Minister . . . . Stewart Stevenson MSP
Private Secretary . . . . Ms Jessica Tattersall . . . Tel: (0131) 244 5027
Diary Secretary . . . . Ms Melissa Waugh . . . . Tel: (0131) 244 7005

Scottish Ministers' Parliamentary Clerks
George IV Building, Edinburgh, RH99 1SP

Parliamentary Clerk . . . . Ms Lesley Swan . . . . Tel: (0131) 348 5000

Office of the Permanent Secretary
St Andrew's House, Regent Road
Edinburgh, EH1 3DG
Tel: (0131) 556 8400
E-mail: firstminister@scotland.gsi.gov.uk
Web: www.scotland.gov.uk

Permanent Secretary . . . . Sir John Elvidge. . . . . . . Tel: (0131) 244 5065

Strategic Board

Permanent Secretary . . . . Sir John Elvidge. . . . . . . Tel: (0131) 244 5065
Director-General Economy and
   Chief Economic Adviser . . . . Dr Andrew Goudie . . . . Tel: (0131) 244 7937
Director-General Education. . . . . Mr Leslie Evans . . . . . . Tel: (0131) 242 5700
Director-General Environment . . . . . Mr Paul Gray . . . . Tel: (0300) 244 1057
Director-General Finance and
   and Corporate Services . . . . Ms Stella Manzie CBES. . Tel: (0131) 244 4932
Director-General Health and
   Chief Executive NHS Scotland. . . Dr Kevin Woods . . . . . . Tel: (0131) 244 2410
Director-General Justice and
   Communities . . . . Mr Robert Gordon CB. . . Tel: (0131) 244 2122

Non-Executive Directors
Professor William Bound
Mr David Fisher
Ms Heather Logan

Education and Lifelong Learning

Cabinet Secretary for Education
and Lifelong Learning . . . . Fiona Hyslop MSP

Minister for Children and
Early Years. . . . . Adam Ingram MSP

Minister for Schools and Skills . . . . . Keith Brown MSP

Chief Scientific Adviser . . . . Ms Anne Glover . . . . . . Tel: (0131) 244 2663

Director General Education . . . . Ms Leslie Evans . . . . . . Tel: (0300) 244 1387

Children, Young People and Social Care
Director, Children, Young People
and Social Care . . . . Ms Sarah Smith. . . . . . . Tel: (0131) 244 0859
Care and Justice . . . . Ms Olivia McLeod . . . . Tel: (0131) 244 3727
Organisations and Quality . . . . Mr Shane Rankin. . . . . . Tel: (0131) 244 0979
Positive Futures . . . . Ms Val Cox . . . . Tel: (0131) 244 0963
Preventative Services for Children,
Young People and Families. . . . . Ms Claire Monaghan. . . Tel: (0131) 244 7640
Workforce and Capacity Issues . . . Ms Shirley Laing . . . . . . Tel: (0131) 244 7648

Education Analytical Services . . . . . . Mr John Ireland . . . . Tel: (0131) 244 0890

Lifelong Learning
Director, Lifelong Learning . . . . . . Mr Andrew Scott. . . . . . Tel: (0141) 242 0206
Determined to Succeed . . . . Mr Michael Cross . . . . . Tel: (0141) 242 0107
Employability and Skills . . . . Mr Hugh McAloon . . . . Tel: (0141) 242 0131
Further and Adult Education . . . . . Mr Michael Cross . . . . . Tel: (0141) 242 0231
Higher Education and Learner
Support. . . . . Mr Stephen Kerr . . . . . . Tel: (0141) 242 0171

Schools
Director, Schools . . . . Mr Colin Maclean . . . . . Tel: (0131) 244 7108
Curriculum. . . . . Ms Jackie Brock . . . . Tel: (0131) 244 0983
Schools . . . . Mr Colin Reeves . . . . . . Tel: (0131) 244 7870
Support for Learning . . . . Mr Mike Gibson . . . . . . Tel: (0131) 244 0909
Teachers. . . . . Mr Donald Henderson . Tel: (0131) 244 0954
Qualifications Assessment and
Skills . . . . Ms Alison Coull. . . . . . . Tel: (0131) 244 0399

Finance and Sustainable Growth

Cabinet Secretary for Finance
and Sustainable Growth . . . . Mr John Swinney MSP

Minister for Enterprise, Energy
and Tourism . . . . Mr Jim Mather MSP

Minister for Transport, Infrastructure
and Climate Change . . . . Mr Stewart Stevenson MSP

Director General Economy
and Chief Economic Adviser . . . . . Dr Andrew Goudie . . . . Tel: (0131) 244 7937

Climate Change
Director, Climate Change and
Water Industry . . . . Mr John Mason . . . . Tel: (0131) 244 0779
Climate Change . . . . Mr Philip Wright . . . . . . Tel: (0131) 244 0193
Water Industry . . . . Mr Bob Irvine . . . . Tel: (0131) 244 0246

Economic Strategy Directorate . . . . . Ms Fiona Robertson . . . Tel: (0131) 244 2269

Finance
Director, Finance . . . . Ms Alyson Stafford . . . . Tel: (0131) 244 7286
Deputy Directors, Finance . . . . . . Mr Alistair Brown . . . . . Tel: (0131) 244 7282
Mr David Reid . . . . Tel: (0131) 244 7428

Planning
Chief Planner . . . . Mr Jim Mackinnon . . . . Tel: (0131) 244 0770
National Planning Framework,
Planning Policy and South . . . . . Dr Graeme Purves . . . . Tel: (0131) 244 7533
Planning Delivery, Planning
Policy and North . . . . Mr John McNairney . . . Tel: (0131) 244 7528
Planning Modernisation and
Co-ordination . . . . Mr Roddy MacDonald . Tel: (0131) 244 7082

Planning and Environment Appeals
Chief Reporter . . . . Mrs Lindsey Nicoll . . . . Tel: (01324) 696 400
Deputy Chief Reporters . . . . Mr Mike Culshaw . . . . . Tel: (01324) 696 472
Ms Oonagh Gill . . . . . . Tel: (01324) 696 441

Finance and Sustainable Growth (Continued)

Public Service Reform

Director, Public Service Reform . . Mr John Ewing . . . . Tel: (0131) 244 7964
Efficiency and Transformational
Government . . . . Mr Craig Russell . . . . . . Tel: (0131) 244 7086
Local Government. . . . . Mr David Henderson . . Tel: (0131) 244 7018
Public Service Delivery . . . . *Vacant* . . . . Tel: (0131) 244 5514
Third Sector . . . . Ms Christine Carlin . . . Tel: (0131) 244 1568

Chief Scientific Adviser . . . . Ms Anne Glover . . . . . . Tel: (0131) 244 2663

Scottish Development International

Scottish Development
International, Chief Executive . . Ms Lena Wilson . . . . . . Tel: 00 1 617 621 3034

Transport

Head, Transport, ... Dr Jonathan Price . . . . . Tel: (0131) 244 0629
Aviation, Ports, Freight and Canals Mr Alastair Wilson . . . . Tel: (0131) 244 7187
Bus, Freight and Roads . . . . Mr Donald Carmichael . Tel: (0131) 244 0146
Ferries . . . . Mr Graham Laidlaw . . . Tel: (0131) 244 0843
Strategy, Transport . . . . Ms Janet Egdell . . . . Tel: (0131) 244 7269

Health and Wellbeing

**Cabinet Secretary for Health
and Wellbeing** . . . . Ms Nicola Sturgeon MSP

**Minister for Housing and
Communities** . . . . Mr Stewart Maxwell MSP

Minister for Public Health . . . . Mrs Shona Robison MSP

**Director-General Health and Chief
Executive NHS Scotland** . . . . Dr Kevin Woods . . . . . . Tel: (0131) 244 2410

e-Health
Director, e-Health . . . . Mr Derek Feeley . . . . . . Tel: (0131) 244 1727
e-Health Architecture and
Design . . . . Mr Eddie Turnbull . . . . Tel: (0131) 244 2405
e-Health Change and Benefits
(Acting) . . . . Mr Alistair Bishops . . . . Mob: 07748 623286
e-Health Programme, Director . . . Mr Paul Rhodes . . . . . . Tel: (0131) 244 3577
e-Health Programme . . . . Ms Lesly Donovan . . . . Tel: (0131) 244 2539
e-Health Strategy . . . . Mr Alan Hyslop . . . . . . Tel: (0131) 244 2366

Equalities, Social Inclusion and Sport
Director, Equalities, Social
Inclusion and Sport . . . . Mrs Elizabeth Hunter . . Tel: (0131) 244 7108
Equality Unit . . . . Ms Yvonne Strachan . . . Tel: (0131) 244 5197
Social Inclusion . . . . Ms Frances Wood . . . . . Tel: (0131) 244 5120
Sport and Games Legacy . . . . Ms Katherine Vincent . . Tel: (0131) 244 1604

Health Delivery
Director , Health Delivery . . . . Mr John Connaghan . . . Tel: (0131) 244 3480
Deputy Director, Delivery
Performance Management
Team . . . . *Vacant* . . . . Tel: (0131) 244 1772
Access Support Team . . . . Mr Mike Lyon . . . . Tel: (0131) 244 4150
Improvement and Support Team . Mr Stephen Gallagher . . Tel: (0131) 244 5219

Health Finance
Director, Health Finance . . . . Mr John Matheson . . . . Tel: (0131) 244 3464
Health Analytical Services . . . . Ms Angela Campbell . . . Tel: (0131) 244 2534
Health Finance . . . . Ms Jane Davidson . . . . . Tel: (0131) 244 3561
Property and Capital Planning . . . Mr Mike Baxter . . . . Tel: (0131) 244 2082

Health Workforce
Director, Health Workforce . . . . . . Dr Ingrid Clayden . . . . . Tel: (0131) 244 1826
Workforce Employment and
Retention . . . . Mrs Jacqui Jones . . . . . . Tel: (0131) 244 2493
Workforce Planning and
Development . . . . Mr John Nicholls . . . . . . Tel: (0131) 244 2858
Workforce Projects and
Consultancy . . . . Mr John Cowie . . . . Tel: (0131) 244 3024

Health and Wellbeing (Continued)

Healthcare Policy and Strategy

Director, Healthcare Policy
and Strategy . . . . Mr Derek Feeley . . . . . . Tel: (0131) 244 1727
Child and Maternal Health . . . . . . Mr John Froggatt . . . . . Tel: (0131) 244 6926
Healthcare Planning . . . . Ms Jill Vickerman . . . . . Tel: (0131) 244 3244
Patients and Quality . . . . Mr Andrew Macleod. . . Tel: (0131) 244 5079

Housing and Regeneration

Director, Housing and
Regeneration . . . . Mr Mike Foulis . . . . Tel: (0131) 244 0768
Communities Analytical Services . Mr Dominic Munro . . . Tel: (0131) 244 7287
Housing Access and Support . . . . Ms Shona Stephen . . . . Tel: (0131) 244 1530
Housing Markets and Supply . . . . Miss Rachel Gwyon . . . Tel: (0131) 244 5511
Regeneration . . . . Ms Diane McLafferty . . Tel: (0131) 244 0697
Social Housing. . . . . Mr Aidan Grisewood . . Tel: (0131) 244 5591

Medical Officer and Public Health

Chief Medical Officer . . . . Dr Harry Burns. . . . . . . Tel: (0131) 244 2264
Deputy Chief Medical Officers . . . Dr Aileen Keel . . . . Tel: (0131) 244 2799
Chief Scientist . . . . Professor Sir John Savill Tel: (0131) 244 2769
Director, Chief Scientist's Office. . Ms Alison Spaull. . . . . . Tel: (0131) 244 2320
Health Improvement Strategy . . . . Ms Kay Barton . . . . Tel: (0131) 244 2894
Public Health and Substance
Misuse . . . . Mr Mike Palmer . . . . . . Tel: (0131) 244 2448

Nursing Officer

Chief Nursing Officer . . . . Ms Roz Muir. . . . . Tel: (0131) 244 2310
Deputy Chief Nursing Officer . . . *Vacant* . . . . Tel: (0131) 244 2310
Chief Health Professions Officer. . Ms Jacqui Lunday. . . . . Tel: (0131) 244 2311
Policy and Business Support
Units. . . . . Miss Uriel Jamieson . . . Tel: (0131) 244 2471

Primary and Community Care

Director, Primary and
Community Care . . . . Mr Graeme Dickson . . . Tel: (0131) 244 3210
Adult Care and Support -
Change Team. . . . . Mrs Jean Maclellan . . . . Tel: (0131) 244 2091
Chief Dental Officer . . . . Ms Margie Taylor. . . . . Tel: (0131) 244 2302
Chief Pharmaceutical Officer . . . . Mr Bill Scott . . . . Tel: (0131) 244 2518
Community Care. . . . . Mr Adam Rennie . . . . . Tel: (0131) 244 1835
Mental Health . . . . Mr Geoff Huggins . . . . Tel: (0131) 244 3749
Partnership Improvement and
Outcomes. . . . . Mr Mike Martin . . . . . . Tel: (0131) 244 3991
Primary Care . . . . Mr Frank Strang . . . . . . Tel: (0131) 244 2305
Scrutiny Bodies Project . . . . Mr Shane Rankin . . . . . Tel: (0131) 244 0979
Shifting the Balance of Care . . . . . Ms Kathleen Bessos . . . Tel: (0131) 244 2242

SCOTTISH GOVERNMENT

Justice

Cabinet Secretary for Justice . . . . Mr Kenny MacAskill MSP

Minister for Community Safety . . . . . Mr Fergus Ewing MSP

Director-General Justice and
Communities . . . . Mr Robert Gordon CB . . . Tel: (0131) 244 2120

Constitution, Law and Courts Directorate
Director, Constitution, Law
and Courts . . . . Mr Ken Thomson . . . . . Tel: (0131) 244 2131
Civil Law Division . . . . Mr Richard Dennis . . . . Tel: (0131) 244 2698
Constitutional and Parliamentary
Secretariat . . . . Ms Jan Marshall . . . . . . Tel: (0131) 244 0570
Legal System Division . . . . Mr Colin McKay . . . . . Tel: (0131) 244 2698
Mental Health Tribunal for
Scotland . . . . Mr Colin McKay . . . . . Tel: (0131) 244 4820
National Conversation,
Referendum and Elections
Division . . . . Mr David Rogers . . . . . Tel: (0131) 244 5210

Criminal Justice
Director, Criminal Justice . . . . Ms Bridget Campbell . . Tel: (0131) 244 8491
Community Justice Services . . . . . Ms Wilma Dickson . . . . Tel: (0131) 244 5434
Criminal Law and Licensing . . . . . Dr George Burgess . . . . Tel: (0131) 244 3537
Criminal Procedure . . . . Ms Roma Menlowe . . . . Tel: (0131) 244 4348
Offender Management Strategy . . Ms Jane Richardson . . . Tel: (0131) 244 8528
Victims, Witnesses, Parole and
Life Sentence Review . . . . Ms Patricia Scotland . . . Tel: (0131) 244 5652

Police and Community Safety
Director, Police and Community
Safety . . . . Mr Kenneth Hogg . . . . . Tel: (0131) 244 2127
Drugs and Community Safety . . . . Mr Alan Johnston . . . . . Tel: (0131) 244 4918
Justice Analytical Services . . . . . . Professor James
Sheffield . . . . Tel: (0131) 244 5604
Police Division . . . . Mr Christie Smith . . . . . Tel: (0131) 244 3251
Scottish Resilience . . . . Mr Ian Walford . . . . Tel: (0131) 244 3992

Inspectorates
HM Chief Inspector Prisons . . . . . Brigadier Hugh
Monro CBE . . . . Tel: (0131) 244 8482
HM Chief Inspector of
Constabulary . . . . Mr Bill Skelly . . . . Tel: (0131) 244 5606
Head of the Scottish Fire and

Rural Affairs and the Environment

Cabinet Secretary for Rural Affairs
and the Environment. . . . . Mr Richard Lochhead MSP

Minister for Environment . . . . Ms Roseanna Cunningham MSP

Director-General Environment . . . . . Mr Paul Gray . . . . Tel: (0131) 244 6021

Environmental Quality
Director, Environmental
   Quality . . . . Mr John Mason. . . . . . . Tel: (0131) 244 0779
Drinking Water Quality . . . . Mr Colin McLaren . . . . Tel: (0131) 244 0186
Waste and Pollution Reduction. . . Ms Kim Fellows . . . . . . Tel: (0131) 244 0235
Water, Air, Soils and Flooding . . . Mr Bob Irvine . . . . Tel: (0131) 244 0246

Greener Scotland
Head of Greener Scotland. . . . . . . Mr Tom Davy. . . . . Tel: (0131) 244 0050

Marine
Director, Marine . . . . Mr Mike Neilson. . . . . . Tel: (0131) 244 6034
Aquaculture, Freshwater
   Fisheries and Licensing Policy. . Ms Heather Jones . . . . . Tel: (0131) 244 6220
Head, Compliance. . . . . Mr Paul Du Vivier . . . . Tel: (0131) 244 6059
Head, Planning and Policy . . . . . . Ms Linda Rosborough . Tel: (0131) 244 6944
Head, Performance . . . . Mr Willie Cowan. . . . . . Tel: (0131) 244 6265
Head, Science . . . . Mr Robin Cook. . . . . . . Tel: (01224) 295 393
Sea Fisheries Policy. . . . . Mr David Brew . . . . Tel: (0131) 244 6430

Rural
Director, Rural . . . . Mr Peter Russell . . . . . . Tel: (0131) 244 6032
Agriculture and Rural
   Development . . . . Mr David Barnes. . . . . . Tel: (0131) 244 6363
Animal Health and Welfare. . . . . . Ms Colette Backwell . . . Tel: (0131) 244 6401
Food and Drink. . . . . Mr David Thomson . . . Tel: (0131) 244 4406
Landscapes and Habitats. . . . . Mr Ian Hooper . . . . Tel: (0131) 244 6416
Rural Communities . . . . Mr Bruce Beveridge . . . Tel: (0131) 244 6190
Veterinary . . . . Mr Simon Hall . . . . Tel: (0131) 244 6275

Rural Affairs and the Environment (Continued)

**Rural and Environment Research
and Analysis**
Director, Rural and Environment
  Research and Analysis . . . . Professor Maggie Gill . . Tel: (0131) 244 6042
Research and Science Division . . . Mr Ron Stagg . . . . Tel: (0131) 244 7144
Rural and Environment
  Analytical Services . . . . Ms Rebekah
                                        Widdowfield. . . . . Tel: (0131) 244 6128

Rural Payments and Inspections
Director, Rural Payments and
  Inspection. . . . . Ms Valerie MacNiven . . Tel: (0131) 244 6029
Head, IT . . . . Mr Rab Fleming . . . . . . Tel: (0131) 244 8037
Chief Agricultural Officer . . . . Mr Drew Sloan . . . . Tel: (0131) 244 5905
CAP Payments . . . . Ms Gillian Tucker. . . . . Tel: (0131) 244 6319
Scottish Agricultural Science. . . . . Mr Gordon MacHeay . . Tel: (0131) 244 8843

Crown Office and Procurator Fiscal Service

25 Chambers Street, Edinburgh, EH1 1LA

Tel: (0131) 226 2626 Fax: (0131) 226 6910 / 4069

Web: www.crownoffice.gov.uk

Lord Advocate for Scotland . . . . Rt Hon Elish Angiolini QC
Private Secretary . . . . Mr David Stewart
Legal Secretary . . . . Mr Colin Troup . . . . . . Tel: (0844) 561 3739

Solicitor-General for Scotland . . . . . Mr Frank Mulholland
Private Secretary . . . . Mr Kevin Fulton

Crown Agent for Scotland and
 Chief Executive . . . . Mr Norman McFadyen Tel: (0844) 561 2000

Deputy Crown Agent for Scotland . . . . . Mr John Dunn

Deputy Chief Executive of Crown
  Office and Procurator
  Fiscal Service . . . . Mr Peter Collings

Area Procurators Fiscal
 Argyll and Clyde . . . . Mr John Watt . . . . Tel: (0141) 887 5225
 Ayrshire . . . . Ms Geraldine Watt . . . Tel: (01563) 536211
 Central . . . . Ms Michelle Macleod . Tel: (01786) 462021
 Dumfries and Galloway . . . . Ms Ruth McQuaid . . . . Tel: (01387) 263034
 Fife . . . . Mr Cameron Ritchie . . Tel: (01592) 268661
 Glasgow . . . . Ms Lesley Thomson . . Tel: (0844) 561 2220
 Grampian . . . . Ms Anne Currie . . . . . . Tel: (01224) 585111
 Highlands and Islands . . . . Mr Andrew Laing . . . . Tel: (01463) 246494
 Lanarkshire . . . . Ms Janet Cameron . . . . Tel: (01698) 284000
 Lothians and Borders . . . . Ms Morag McLaughlin Tel: (0131) 226 4962
 Tayside . . . . Mr Tom Dysart . . . . . . Tel: (01382) 227535

Crown Office and Procurator Fiscal Service (Continued)

Corporate Services

Deputy Chief Executive, Corporate
Services . . . . Mr Peter Collings . . . . . Tel: (0131) 247 2675
Director of Communications . . . . . Ms Alison McInnes. . . . Tel: (0131) 247 2674
Director of Estates . . . . Mr Keith Connal. . . . . . Tel: (0131) 247 2676
Director of Finance. . . . . Mr Mark Howells . . . . . Tel: (0131) 247 3103
Director of Human Resources . . . . Ms Janice Irvine . . . . . . Tel: (0131) 222 3116
Director of IT. . . . . Ms Linda Herbert . . . . . Tel: (0131) 226 0824
Head, Policy . . . . Mr John Logue . . . . Tel: (0131) 247 2705
Ultimus Haeres QLTR . . . . Mr Andrew Brown . . . . Tel: (0131) 247 2618

Operations

Deputy Crown Agent, Operations . Mr John Dunn . . . . Tel: (0131) 247 2713
Head of Appeals Unit. . . . . Mr Fraser Gibson . . . . . Tel: (0131) 247 2715
Head of Civil Recovery Unit and
   International Co-operation Unit . Ms Kate Frame . . . . Tel: (0845) 606 6212
Head of High Court Unit . . . . Mr David Green . . . . . . Tel: (0131) 247 2716
Head of National Casework . . . . . . Ms Katie Stewart . . . . . Tel: (0131) 247 3408

Strategic Delivery

Chief of Strategic Delivery . . . . Ms Catherine Dyer . . . . Tel: (0844) 561 2074

Legal Team

Solicitor to the Scottish
Government . . . . Mr Murray Sinclair. . . . Tel: (0131) 244 0531
Deputy Solicitors . . . . Mr Patrick Layden . . . . Tel: (0131) 244 0959
                                     Ms Jane McLeod. . . . . . Tel: (0131) 244 0494
Constitutional and Civil Law . . . . . Mr Paul Johnston . . . . . Tel: (0131) 244 0576
Criminal Justice, Police and Fire. . . Mr Gordon McNicoll . . Tel: (0131) 244 1493
Development, Land and
Local Government . . . . Ms Elspeth MacDonald Tel: (0131) 244 0553
Education, Enterprise and Reviews Mr John Paterson . . . . . Tel: (0131) 244 2022
Food and Environment. . . . . Mr Stuart Foubister . . . Tel: (0131) 244 1408
Health and Community Care . . . . . Ms Gillian Russell . . . . . Tel: (0131) 244 0577
Litigation. Ms Shirley Ferguson . . . Tel: (0131) 244 0574
Litigation and Employment . . . . . . Mr Craig French. . . . . . Tel: (0131) 244 5333
Rural Affairs . . . . Mr Alan Williams . . . . . Tel: (0131) 244 0507
Transport, Culture and
Procurement . . . . Ms Caroline Lyon. . . . . Tel: (0131) 244 0535

Executive Agencies

EXECUTIVE AGENCIES

Note: This part of the Directory is divided into two sections. This first section details, (in alphabetical order), those Executive Agencies which are based in Scotland. The second section lists other useful Agency contacts, which are based elsewhere in the UK.

Accountant in Bankruptcy
1 Pennyburn Road, Kilwinning, Ayrshire, KA13 6SA
Tel: (0300) 200 2600 Fax: (0300) 200 2601
Helpline: (0300) 200 2777
E-mails: ce@aib.gsi.gov.uk
[firstname.surname]@aib.gov.uk
Web: www.aib.gov.uk

Accountability: Scottish Government – Justice Department

Established: April 2002. The Accountant in Bankruptcy is appointed under the Bankruptcy (Scotland) Act 1985 as amended.

The Agency's main statutory functions are to:
- Generally supervise the process of sequestration in Scotland and to ensure that those involved in that process – principally trustees and commissioners – properly carry out their responsibilities, and to take appropriate action when they fail to do so;
- Maintain a public register of sequestrations, protected trust deeds and company insolvencies;
- Undertake the functions of commissioners in sequestrations where none may be, or are, elected;
- Act as interim and permanent trustee in sequestrations where no insolvency practitioner is appointed or elected to do so;
- Act as Administrator under the Debt Arrangement Scheme.

The Accountant also has responsibility for administering the Government's policies in respect of personal insolvency and the process of corporate insolvency in Scotland and to monitor the implementation of these policies.

Chief Executive . . . . Mrs Rosemary Winter-Scott
Private Secretary . . . . Mrs Sharron Jeffrey

Management Board
Head of Case Operations and Policy . Mr John Cook
Head of Relocation, Corporate
Strategy and IT . . . . Mr David Wallace

EXECUTIVE AGENCIES

Forest Enterprise – Scotland
1 Highlander Way
Inverness Business Park
Inverness, IV2 7GB
Tel: (01463) 232811 Fax: (01463) 243846
E-mail: frances.mackenzie@forestry.gsi.gov.uk
Web: www.forestry.gov.uk

Accountability: Scottish Government Rural Affairs – Rural Affairs and the Environment

Established: 1st April 2003

Forest Enterprise aims to produce the environmental, financial, social and other outputs sought by ministers and the National Committee for Scotland, in a way which meets government objectives and international commitments, and which sustains both the environmental quality and the productive potential of the forest estate.

Chief Executive . . . . Dr Hugh Insley
Personal Secretary. . . . . Miss Frances MacKenzie . Tel: (01463) 232811

Management Board
Executive Members
Head of Operations. . . . . Mr Les Bryson . . . . Tel: (01463) 232811
Human Resources Business Partner . . Ms Alison McSheaffrey . . Tel: (0131) 334 8303
Communities, Recreation and
   Tourism Manager. . . . . Mr Alan Stevenson. . . . . . Tel: (01463) 232811
Environment Manager . . . . Miss Moira Baptie . . . . . . Tel: (01463) 232811
Finance Manager. . . . . Mr Alan Duncan . . . . Tel: (01463) 232811
Land Agent Scotland . . . . Mr Laurie Tyson . . . . Tel: (01387) 272440
Forest Planning Manager . . . . Ms Nicol Sinclair . . . . Tel: (01463) 232811

Other Key Staff
Information Officers . . . . Mr Charlton Clark . . . . . . Tel: (0131) 314 6508
                                             Mr Steve Williams . . . . . . Tel: (0131) 314 6508
Press Officer . . . . Mr Paul Munro. . . . . Tel: (0131) 314 6503
Secretariat and Partnership Manager . Ms Nicky Whitaker. . . . . . Tel: (01463) 232811

EXECUTIVE AGENCIES

Historic Scotland
Longmore House, Salisbury Place
Edinburgh, EH9 1SH
Tel: (0131) 668 8600 Fax: (0131) 668 8888
E-mail: via Website
Web: www.historic-scotland.gov.uk

Accountability: Scottish Government – Finance and Sustainable Growth

Established: 1st April 1991

Historic Scotland is responsible for protecting and promoting public understanding and enjoyment of Scotland's ancient monuments and archaeological sites and landscapes, historic buildings, parks, gardens and designed landscapes. This includes, in particular, the maintenance and conservation of the Palace of Holyroodhouse, the Scottish Royal Parks and the monuments in the care of the Scottish Government.

Chief Executive . . . . Mr John Graham . . . . Tel: (0131) 668 8693

Management Board
Executive Members
Director of Finance . . . . Ms Laura Petrie . . . . Tel: (0131) 668 8874
Director of Human Resources . . . . . . Mr Brian O'Neil . . . . Tel: (0131) 668 8667
Director of Policy . . . . Ms Lucy Blackburn . . . . . Tel: (0131) 668 8727
Director of Properties in Care. . . . . . Mr Peter Bromley. . . . . . . Tel: (0131) 668 8735
Director of Technical Conservation
    Group *(Acting)*. . . . . Mr David Mitchell . . . . . . Tel: (0131) 668 8929
Chief Inspector . . . . Mr Malcolm Cooper. . . . . Tel: (0131) 668 8728

Non-Executive Members
Mr Marc Ellington *(Marketing, Tourism and Management Consultant)*
Professor John Lennon *(Professor and Director, Moffat Centre for Travel and Tourism,*
    Business Development, Glasgow Caledonian University)
Mr David McGibbon *(Project Consultant, McGibbon Associates)*
Ms Ann Marie Stannard *(Partner, Company Grants Team Ltd)*
Ms Sheila Terry *(Former Head of Planning and Transportation, Falkirk Council)*
Mr Raymond Young *(Chair, Rural Housing Service)*

Other Key Staff
Deputy Chief Inspector. . . . . Mr Jim Mcdonald . . . . Tel: (0131) 668 8582
Head of Archaeology Programmes
    and Grants Advice . . . . Mr Noel Fojut. . . . . Tel: (0131) 668 8650
Head of Communications and Media. Mr Pat Connor . . . . Tel: (0131) 668 8700
Head of Conservation and
    Maintenance . . . . Mrs Sarah Morris . . . . Tel: (0131) 668 8812
Head of Policy Liaison and
    Modernisation . . . . Mr Miles Oglethorpe . . . . Tel: (0131) 668 8611
Head of Understanding and Access . . Ms Doreen Grove. . . . . . . Tel: (0131) 668 8793
Head of Investment and Projects . . . . Mr Martin Fairley. . . . . . . Tel: (0131) 668 8691
Head of Listing . . . . Dr Debbie Mays. . . . . Tel: (0131) 668 8709
Head of Major Projects. . . . . Mr Chris Watkins . . . . Tel: (0131) 668 8783

Historic Scotland – Other Key Staff (Continued)

Head of National Policy . . . . Dr Gordon Barclay . . . . . . Tel: (0131) 668 8919
Head of Scheduling. . . . . Dr Sally Foster . . . . Tel: (0131) 668 8658
Head of Strategy and Operations . . . . Ms Lesley Macinnes . . . . . Tel: (0131) 668 8653
Head of Visitor Services and
    Business Development . . . . Ms Kari Coghill . . . . Tel: (0131) 668 8614

Technical Conservation Group
  Enquiry Service . . . . Mr Graeme McKindy. . . . Tel: (0131) 668 8668

General Enquiry Line . . . . *enquiries*. . . . . Tel: (0131) 668 8600

Regional Offices
Central Region – Properties in Care
Argylls Lodging, Castle Wynd, Stirling, FK8 1EG . . . . Tel: (01786) 450000
                                                                      Fax: (01786) 464678
North Region - Properties in Care
Fort George, Nr Ardersier, Invernesshire, IV1 2TD . . . . Tel: (01667) 462777
                                                                      Fax: (01667) 462698
South Region - Properties in Care
Croft-an-Righ, Edinburgh, EH8 8ED . . . . Tel: (0131) 550 7614

Edinburgh Castle
Castle Manager . . . . Ms Barbara Smith. . . . . . . Tel: (0131) 225 9846
                                                                      Ext: 253
                                                                      Fax: (0131) 220 4733

Holyroodhouse . . . . *Palace* . . . . Tel: (0131) 557 8415
                                      Park. . . . . Tel: (0131) 556 3407
                                      Gardens . . . . Tel: (0131) 556 4160

HM Inspectorate of Education *(Scotland)*
Denholm House
Almondvale Business Park
Almondvale Way
Livingston, EH54 6GA
Tel: (01506) 600200 Fax: (01506) 600313
E-mails: [firstname.surname]@hmie.gsi.gov.uk
enquiries@hmie.gsi.gov.uk
Web: www.hmie.gov.uk

Accountability: Scottish Government - Education and Lifelong Learning

Established: 1st April 2001

HM Inspectors undertake first-hand, independent evaluations on the quality of education and services for children. Each year the Inspectorate investigates and publishes reports on key aspects of education and Services for Children. By collation, analysis and publication of the evidence and conclusions from all evaluations, it aims to identify and promote best practice in improving standards and quality.

HM Senior Chief Inspector . . . . Mr Graham Donaldson
   Business Manager . . . . Ms Veronica Thomson . . . Tel: (01506) 600365
   Fax: (01506) 600388

Directorates
Directorate 1 - Pre-school/Independent/Care and Welfare
   HM Chief Inspector . . . . Mr Alaistair Delaney . . . . . Tel: (01506) 600200

Directorate 2 - Primary
   HM Chief Inspector . . . . Mr Alaistair Delaney . . . . . Tel: (01506) 600200

Directorate 3 - Secondary/Special Educational Needs
   HM Chief Inspector . . . . Mr Kenneth Muir . . . . Tel: (0141) 242 5719

Directorate 4 - Further Education/Teacher Education
   HM Chief Inspector . . . . Mr Kenneth Muir . . . . Tel: (01506) 600240

Directorate 5 - Education Authorities/Community Learning and Development
   HM Chief Inspector . . . . Ms Gill Robinson . . . . Tel: (01506) 600250

Directorate 6 - Services for Children Unit
   HM Chief Inspector . . . . Mr Neil McKechnie . . . . . Tel: (01506) 600260

Key Staff
Corporate Services Director . . . . Mr Stuart Robinson . . . . . Tel: (01506) 600333

EXECUTIVE AGENCIES

HM Inspectorate of Education (Scotland) (Continued)

HMIE Headquarters
Business Management and
   Communications Unit . . . . Ms Laura Burnham . . . . . Tel: (01506) 600265
Corporate Planning Team . . . . Mr Jim Gallacher . . . . Tel: (01506) 600235
Finance Team . . . . Mrs Gillian Howells . . . . . Tel: (01506) 600334
Information Systems Unit . . . . Mr Allan Ryan . . . . Tel: (01506) 600315
Integrated Inspections Unit . . . . Ms Avril Martin . . . . Tel: (01506) 600389
Services for Children Unit . . . . Ms Jacqueline Crawford . . Tel: (01506) 600374
Statistics Team . . . . *Vacant* . . . . Tel: (01506) 600314

Area Offices
HMIE Aberdeen
Greyfriars House, Gallowgate, Aberdeen, AB10 1LQ . . . . Tel: (01224) 624544
   Fax: (01224) 625370

HMIE Clydebank
Ground Floor Suite, Unit 7, Blair Court, 5 North Avenue,
   Clydebank Business Park, Clydebank, G81 2LA . . . . Tel: (0141) 435 3550
   Fax: (0141) 435 3555

HMIE Dundee
1st Floor, Endeavour House, 1 Greenmarket,
   Dundee, DD1 4QB . . . . Tel: (01382) 576700
   Fax: (01382) 576701

HMIE Edinburgh
T1 Saughton House, Broomhouse Drive,
   Edinburgh, EH11 3XD . . . . Tel: (0131) 244 8293
   Fax: (0131) 244 8424

HMIE Glasgow
1st Floor, Europa Building, 450 Argyle Street,
   Glasgow, G2 8LG . . . . Tel: (0141) 242 0100
   Fax: (0141) 242 5757

HMIE Inverness
28 Longman Road, Longman East, Inverness, IV1 1SF . . . . Tel: (01463) 253115
   Fax: (01463) 253075

HMIE Livingston
Denholm House, Almondvale Business Park,
   Almondvale Way, Livingston, EH54 6GA . . . . Tel: (01506) 600200
   Fax: (01506) 600313

Marine Scotland

47 Robb's Loan
Edinburgh, EH14 1TY
Tel: (0131) 244 6060
E-mail: marinescotland@scotland.gsi.gov.uk
Web: www.scotland.gov.uk

Accountability: Scottish Government – Marine Directorate

Established: 1st April 2009 to combine the functions and resources of the former Fisheries Research Services and the Scottish Fisheries Protection Agency.

Marine Scotland's mission is to manage Scotland's seas for prosperity and environmental sustainability - supporting the Scottish Government's overall purpose of sustainable economic growth and vision for marine and coastal areas.

Director . . . . Mr Mike Neilson

Head of Aquaculture, Freshwater
      Fisheries nd Licensing Policy . . . . Ms Linda Rosborough

Head of Compliance . . . . Mr Paul Du Vivier

Head of Marine Planning and Policy . Mr Willie Cowan

Head of Performance . . . . Mr Willie Cowan

Head of Priority Projects . . . . Ms Fiona Harrison

Head of Science . . . . Mr Robin Cook

Head of Sea Fisheries Policy . . . . Mr David Brew

Mental Health Tribunal for Scotland
First Floor, Bothwell House
Hamilton Business Park
Caird Park, Hamilton, ML3 0QA
Tel: (01698) 390000
Tel: (0800) 345 7060 *(Service Users' and Carers')*
Tel: (01698) 390000 *(Healthcare Professionals* and *Tribunal Members Information)*
E-mail: mhts@scotland.gsi.gov.uk Web: www.mhtscot.org

Accountability: Scottish Government – Health and Wellbeing

Established: 5th October 2005 under the Mental Health (Care and Treatment) (Scotland) Act 2003.

The Tribunal makes and reviews decisions on the compulsory treatment of people with a mental disorder; previously these hearings took place in Sheriff Courts. Each tribunal is heard by a three member panel: a legal member, also known as the Convener, who will be a solicitor or advocate of at least seven years' standing, a medical member who will be a psychiatrist experienced in the diagnosis and treatment of mental disorders and a general member who has experience or qualifications in social care facilities (including Mental Health Officers, Social Workers with mental health experience, carers for service users, and service users). All will have relevant qualifications in dealing with people with mental health disorders.

President . . . . Dr Joe Morrow
    Private Secretary to the President . . Ms Anne Kippen

Chief Executive . . . . Mr Paul Smart

Communications Officer . . . . Ms Agnes Ferrie

National Archives of Scotland
HM General Register House, 2 Princes Street, Edinburgh, EH1 3YY
Tel: (0131) 535 1314 Fax: (0131) 535 1360
E-mail: enquiries@nas.gov.uk
Web: www.nas.gov.uk

Accountability: Scottish Government - Culture, External Affairs and the Constitution.

Established: 1st April 1993. The mission of the National Archives of Scotland is to preserve, protect and promote the nation's records; to provide the best possible inclusive and accessible archive that educates, informs and engages the people of Scotland and the world.

Chief Executive (Keeper of the
Records of Scotland) . . . . Mr George MacKenzie
PA/Business Manager . . . . Ms Catherine Dowe . . . . . . Tel: (0131) 535 1311

Management Board:
Executive Members
Deputy Keepers
   Corporate Services . . . . Mr David Brownlee . . . . . Tel: (0131) 535 1313
   Record Services . . . . *Vacant*
Head of Accommodation . . . . Mr Bob Phillips . . . . Tel: (0131) 535 1330
Head of Collections Development . . . Dr David Brown . . . . Tel: (0131) 535 1339
Head of Conservation Services . . . . . Ms Linda Ramsay . . . . Tel: (0131) 270 3305
Head of Court and Legal Records
   (Acting) . . . . Ms Laura Mitchell . . . . . . Tel: (0131) 270 3312
Head of Finance and Administration . Mr Jim Grady . . . . Tel: (0131) 535 1304
Head of Government Records . . . . . . Mr Bruno Longmore . . . . Tel: (0131) 535 1412
Head of Information and
   Communications Technology . . . . Mr Rob Mildren . . . . Tel: (0131) 270 3310
Head of Reader Services . . . . Ms Alison Horsburgh . . . . Tel: (0131) 535 1306

General Enquiry Line . . . . Tel: (0131) 535 1314

Other Offices
Thomas Thomson House, 99 Bankhead Crossway North,
   Edinburgh, EH11 4DX . . . . Tel: (0131) 270 3300
                                                   Fax: (0131) 270 3317

West Register House, Charlotte Square, Edinburgh, EH2 4DJ . . . Tel: (0131) 535 1400
                                                   Fax: (0131) 535 1436

Registers of Scotland
Meadowbank House
153 London Road
Edinburgh, EH8 7AU
Tel: (0131) 659 6111 Fax: (0131) 479 3688
E-mail: keeper@ros.gov.uk Web: www.ros.gov.uk

Accountability: Scottish Government

Established: 6th April 1990. Agency status was confirmed in April 1994 and in January 1999, following Reviews.

Registers of Scotland is responsible for registering titles to property and other deeds in Scottish Property and Court Registers.

Note: Unless otherwise indicated, the main telephone number should be used to contact staff – Tel: (0131) 659 6111. Individual extensions are listed below.

Keeper and Chief Executive . . . . Ms Sheenagh Adams . . . . Tel: (0131) 659 6111
Ext: 3299
Chief Executive Management Team
Deputy Keeper (Legal and
Corporate Services) . . . . Ms Catriona Hardman . . . Tel: (0131) 659 6111

Deputy Keeper (Service Delivery) Mr Andy Smith . . . . Tel: (0131) 659 6111
Ext: 3658
Corporate Communications and
Planning Director . . . . Mr Chris Dempsey . . . . . . Tel: (0131) 659 6111
Ext: 3745
Finance Director . . . . Ms Laura Petrie . . . . Tel: (0131) 659 6111
Ext: 3695
Human Resources and
Estates Director . . . . Mr Billy Harkness . . . . Tel: (0131) 659 6111
Ext: 3733
Information Office Director . . . . Mr Jim Bailey . . . . Tel: (0131) 659 6111

Registration Director . . . . Mr John King . . . . Tel: (0131) 659 6111
Ext: 3754
Glasgow Office
Hanover House, 24 Douglas Street, Glasgow, G2 7NQ
Business Manager . . . . Mrs Anne Ward . . . . Tel: (0141) 306 1522

Customer Service Centres
Erskine House, 68 Queen Street, Edinburgh, EH2 4NF. . . . . Tel: (0845) 607 0161
Fax: (0131) 200 3932
*9 George Square, Glasgow, G2 1DY . . . . Tel: (0845) 607 0164
Fax: (0141) 306 1721
Customer Services Director . . . . Mrs Anne Slater . . . . Tel: (0131) 659 6111
Ext: 5840

Scottish Court Service
Hayweight House
23 Lauriston Street
Edinburgh, EH3 9DQ
Tel: (0131) 229 9200 Fax: (0131) 221 6894
E-mails: enquiries@scotcourts.gov.uk
[initial.surname]@scotcourts.gov.uk
Web: www.scotscourts.gov.uk

Accountability: Scottish Government – Justice Department

Established: 3rd April 1995

The Scottish Court Service provides administrative, organisational and technical services to support the Judiciary in the delivery of Justice within the Court of Session, High Court of Justiciary and 49 Sheriff Courts located throughout Scotland.

Chief Executive . . . . Ms Eleanor Emberson . . . Tel: (0131) 221 6820

Directors
Director of Field Services . . . . Mr Eric McQueen . . . . . . Tel: (0131) 221 6807
Deputy Director of Field Services . . . Mr David Forrester. . . . . . Tel: (0141) 418 5200
Deputy Director of Field Services
   (Development). . . . . Mr Cliff Binning. . . . . Tel: (0141) 772 3079
Director of Policy and Strategy. . . . . . Mr Neil Rennick. . . . . Tel: (0131) 221 6804
Director of Operational Support. . . . . Mr Gordon Wales. . . . . . . Tel: (0131) 221 6808

Other Key Staff
Head of Corporate Communications . Ms Susan Whiteford. . . . . Tel: (0131) 221 6814

General Enquiry Line. . . . . Tel: (0131) 229 9200

Scottish Housing Regulator
Highlander House
58 Waterloo Street
Glasgow, G2 7DA
Tel: (0141) 271 3810 Fax: (0141) 221 0117
E-mail: shr@scottishhousingregulator.gsi.gov.uk
Web: www.scottishhousingregulator.gov.uk

Accountability: Scottish Government – Minister for Housing

Established: 1st April 2008, under the Housing (Scotland) Act 2001

The Regulator registers and regulates independent social landlords, and inspects housing and homeless services provided by local authorities.

Chief Executive . . . . Ms Karen Watt

Management Board
Executive Members
Head of Inspection . . . . Mr Michael Cameron
Head of Support and Intervention . . . Ms Christine Macleod
Head of Policy and
    Corporate Services. . . . . Mr Iain Muirhead
Head of Business Analysis . . . . Mr Ian Brennan

Non-Executive Members
Mr Alex Codie MBE
Mrs Mairi Keddie
Ms Ray MacFarlane

Scottish Prison Service
Calton House, 5 Redheughs Rigg
Edinburgh, EH12 9HW
Tel: (0131) 244 8745 Fax: (0131) 244 8774
E-mail: gaolinfo@sps.gov.uk
Web: www.sps.gov.uk

Accountability: Scottish Government and Scottish Parliament

Established: 1st April 1993

The mission statement of the Scottish Prison Service is to keep in custody those committed by the courts; to maintain good order in each prison; to care for prisoners with humanity; and to provide prisoners with a range of opportunities to exercise personal responsibility and to prepare for release.

Chief Executive . . . . Mr Mike Ewart . . . . Tel: (0131) 244 8522

Management Board
Executive Members
Director of Finance and
    Business Services . . . . Mr William Pretswell . . . . Tel: (0131) 244 8679
Director of Health and Care . . . . Dr Andrew Fraser. . . . . . . Tel: (0131) 244 4104
Director of Human Resources . . . . . . Mr Stephen Swan . . . . Tel: (0131) 244 8573
Director of Partnerships and
    Commissioning . . . . Mr Eric Murch . . . . Tel: (0131) 244 8561
Director of Prisons . . . . Ms Rona Sweeney . . . . . . Tel: (0131) 244 8769

Non-Executive Members
Mr Allan Burns
Ms Rachel Gwyon
Ms Jane Martin
Ms Susan Matheson
Mr Harry McGuigan
Mr Bill Morton
Ms Zoe Van Zwanenberg

Other Key Staff
Deputy Director (Prisons) . . . . Mr David Croft . . . . Tel: (0131) 244 8551
Head of Corporate Affairs . . . . Mr Tom Fox. . . . . Tel: (0131) 244 8463
Head of Estates . . . . Mr Andrew Craig . . . . Tel: (0131) 244 8695
Head of Interventions and Offender
    Case Management. . . . . Mr Charles Kelly . . . . Tel: (0131) 244 8422

General Enquiry Line. . . . . Tel: (0131) 244 8745

Scottish Public Pensions Agency
7 Tweedside Park
Tweedbank
Galashiels, TD1 3TE
Tel: (01896) 893100 *(NHS Scheme)*
Tel: (01896) 893000 *(for Teachers and Other Schemes)*
Fax: (01896) 893214
Web: www.scotland.gov.uk/sppa

Accountability: Scottish Government - Finance and Sustainable Growth Directorate

Established: 1st April 1993

The Scottish Public Pensions Agency regulates the public service pension schemes in Scotland and administers those covering the health service (NHSSS), the teaching profession (STSS), agricultural colleges, research institutes, the Scottish Legal Aid Board and Members of the Scottish Parliament.

Chief Executive . . . . Mr Neville Mackay
    Private Secretary . . . . Ms Lila Tereszczyn . . . . . Tel: (01896) 893232

Management Board
Director of Corporate Services . . . . . . Mr Chris Fenton. . . . . Tel: (01896) 893000
Director of IT and Development . . . . Mrs Pamela Brown . . . . . . Tel: (01896) 893238
Director of Operations . . . . Mr Ian Clapperton . . . . . . Tel: (01896) 893200
Director of Policy . . . . Mr Chad Dawtry . . . . Tel: (01896) 893221

Helplines
NHS Scheme . . . . Tel: (01896) 893000
Teacher's Scheme. . . . . Tel: (01896) 893000
Other Schemes . . . . Tel: (01896) 893000

Social Work Inspection Agency

Ladywell House, Ladywell Road, Edinburgh, EH12 7TB
Tel: (0131) 244 4735 Fax: (0131) 244 5496
E-mail: [firstname.surname]@swia.gsi.gov.uk
Web: www.swia.gov.uk

Accountability: Scottish Government – Education Department

Established: April 2005

SWIA inspects all social work services in Scotland and reports publicly and to Parliament on the quality of these services, locally and nationally.

The Agency aims to inspect all local authority social work services on a three-year cycle. It will undertake joint inspection work with colleagues such as HM Inspectorate of Education, to produce all-round reports and reviews.

When appointed the Agency also:
• Carries out investigations
• Provides professional support to policy development
• Undertakes other tasks that need up-to-date professional knowledge and expertise

Chief Social Work Inspector	Ms Alexis Jay	Tel: (0131) 244 6515
Personal Assistant	Mrs Barbara-Anne Travers	Tel: (0131) 244 4735

Management Board

Depute Social Work Inspectors	Mr David Cumming	Tel: (0141) 249 6801
	Mr Richard Fowles	Tel: (0141) 249 6869
	Mr Marc Hendrikson	Tel: (0131) 244 3526
	Mr Gillian Ottley	Tel: (0131) 244 3603
Corporate Manager	Mr Andrew Wilkinson	Tel: (0131) 244 4885
Office Manager	Mr Gary Mack	Tel: (0131) 244 4887
Budget Centre Liaison Officer	Mr Jim Stevendale	Tel: (0131) 244 2423

Non-Executive Members
Mr Hamish Hamill
Dr Sandra Nutley

Social Work Inspection Agency (Continued)

Other Key Staff

Social Work Inspectors . . . . Ms Linda Connolly . . . . . . Tel: (0141) 249 6829
Ms Margaret-Anne Gilbert Tel: (0131) 244 5420
Ms Jo Harrison . . . . Tel: (0141) 249 6836
Mr Gerry Hart . . . . Tel: (0141) 249 6863
Mr Ian Kerr . . . . Tel: (0141) 249 6839
Ms Katie Lamb . . . . Tel: (0141) 249 6834
Ms Rosie Lawrence . . . . . Tel: (0141) 244 3690
Mr Tom Leckie . . . . Tel: (0131) 244 3795
Mr Paolo Mazzoncini . . . . Tel: (0141) 249 6802
Ms Audrey Mistry . . . . . . Tel: (0131) 244 3529
Ms Christine Naismith . . . Tel: (0131) 244 3710
Mr Willie Paxton . . . . Tel: (0131) 244 5494
Mr Stephen Porter . . . . . . Tel: (0141) 249 6805
Ms Chris Robinson . . . . . . Tel: (0131) 244 5493
Mr David Rowbotham . . . Tel: (0131) 244 5091
Ms Irene Scullion . . . . Tel: (0141) 249 6831
Ms Martha Shortreed . . . . Tel: (0131) 244 7089
Ms Judith Tait . . . . Tel: (0131) 244 4087
Mr John Waterhouse . . . . . Tel: (0131) 244 5449
Ms Clare Wilson . . . . Tel: (0141) 329 6835

Inspection Support Managers . . . . Ms Nina Barrat . . . . Tel: (0131) 244 3693
Ms Brenda Evans . . . . Tel: (0131) 244 3691
Ms Susan Fallon . . . . Tel: (0131) 244 4745
Ms Marion Hughes . . . . . . Tel: (0141) 249 6799
Ms Janet Hunter . . . . Tel: (0131) 244 5468
Ms Dorothy Smith . . . . . . Tel: (0131) 244 4744
Mr Jamie Steed . . . . Tel: (0141) 249 6527

Student Awards Agency for Scotland
Gyleview House
3 Redheughs Rigg
Edinburgh, EH12 9HH
Tel: (0845) 111 1711 Fax: (0131) 244 5887
Web: www.saas.gov.uk

Accountability: Scottish Government – Education Directorate

Established: April 1994

The Student Awards Agency for Scotland provides assistance to eligible Scottish students undertaking courses of higher education throughout the United Kingdom. The Agency also performs related functions in connection with Student Loans, Hardship Funds and Educational Endowments.

The Agency also deals with Individual Learning Accounts in partnership with Learndirect Scotland. All the Agency's functions are carried out on behalf of the Scottish Ministers.

Chief Executive . . . . Mr Tracey Slaven . . . . Tel: (0131) 244 5867
    Executive Assistant . . . . Miss Linda Pender . . . . . . Tel: (0131) 244 5890

Management Board
Executive Members
Head of Finance . . . . Ms Audrey Shimmons . . . Tel: (0131) 244 4462
Head of Information Systems and
    Operational Policy . . . . Mr Graham Gunn . . . . . . Tel: (0131) 244 5845
Customer Services Manager . . . . Miss Audrey Heatlie . . . . . Tel: (0131) 244 5884

Non-Executive Members
Mr Allan Forsyth *(Former Assistant Principal, Cardonald College)*
Mr Dugald Mackie *(Former Vice Principal, University of Manchester)*
Dr Bruce Nelson *(Academic Registrar and Deputy Secretary, University of Edinburgh)*

Transport Scotland
Buchanan House
58 Port Dundas Road
Glasgow, G4 0HF
Tel: (0141) 272 7100
E-mail: info@transportscotland.gsi.gov.uk
Web: www.transportscotland.gov.uk

Accountability: Scottish Government – Finance and Sustainable Growth

Established: 1st January 2006

Transport Scotland is responsible for helping to deliver the Government's £3 billion capital investment programme over the next decade, overseeing the safe and efficient running of Scotland's trunk roads and rail networks and establishing and running a national scheme for concessionary travel in Scotland.

The Agency has six Directorates:
- Business Improvement and Corporate Services;
- Finance and Corporate Services;
- Major Transport Infrastructure Projects (MTRIPS);
- Rail Delivery;
- Strategy and Investment;
- Trunk Roads: Network Management

Chief Executive . . . . Mr David Middleton

Management Board
Executive Members
Director, Business Improvement
    and Corporate Services . . . . Dr Richard Scott
Director, Finance . . . . Ms Sharon Fairweather
Director, Rail Delivery . . . . Mr Bill Reeve
Director, Strategy and Investment . . . Mrs Frances Duffy
Director, Major Transport
    Infrastructure Projects . . . . Mr Ainslie McLaughlin
Director, Trunk Road Management
    and Chief Road Engineer . . . . Mr Jim Barton

Other Key Staff
Head of Communications . . . . Ms Lucy Adamson . . . . . . Tel: (0141) 272 7197

Other Executive Agencies

Note: This is not an exhaustive list. More information on Executive Agencies throughout the UK can be found in "The Directory of Executive Agencies & Public Bodies – 'Quangos'" – published annually by Carlton Publishing and Printing Ltd.

Animal Health
C3, Government Buildings
Whittingdon Road, Worcester, WR5 2LQ
Tel: (01905) 763355
E-mail: corporate.centre@animalhealth.gsi.gov.uk
Web: www.defra.gov.uk/animalhealth

Chief Executive . . . . Ms Catherine Brown

Director (Scotland) . . . . Mr Rupert Hine

Ayr Office
Russell House, King Street
Ayr, KA8 0BE
Tel: (01292) 268525 Fax: (01292) 291351
E-mail: AH.ayr@animalhealth.gsi.gov.uk

Galashiels Office
Cotgreen Road, Tweedbank
Galashiels, TD1 3SG
Tel: (01896) 758806 Fax: (01896) 756803
E-mail: AH.galashiels@animalhealth.gsi.gov.uk

Inverness Office
Government Buildings, Longman House
28 Longman Road, Longman East
Inverness, IV1 1SF
Tel: (01463) 253098 Fax: (01463) 711495
E-mail: AH.inverness@animalhealth.gsi.gov.uk

Inverurie Office
Thainstone Court
Inverurie, Aberdeenshire, AB51 5YA
Tel: (01467) 626610 Fax: (01467) 626611
E-mail: AH.inverurie@animalhealth.gsi.gov.uk

Perth Office
Strathearn House, Broxden Business Park
Lamberkine Drive, Perth, PH1 1RX
Tel: (01738) 602211 Fax: (01738) 602240
E-mail: AH.perth@animalhealth.gsi.gov.uk

Buying Solutions
3rd Floor, Royal Liver Building, Pier Head, Liverpool, L3 1PE
Tel: (0870) 268 2222
E-mail: info@buyingsollutions.gsi.gov.uk
Web: www.buyingsolutions.gov.uk

Chief Executive .... Ms Alison Littley

Central Office of Information
(Trading as COI)
Hercules House, Hercules Road, London, SE1 7DU
Tel: (020) 7928 2345
E-mail: [firstname.surname]@coi.gsi.gov.uk
Web: www.coi.gov.uk

Chief Executive .... Mr Mark Lund

Child Support Agency
National Helpline, PO Box 55, Brierley Hill
West Midlands, DY5 1YL
Tel: (0845) 713 3133 Fax: (0845) 713 8924
E-mail: generalenquiries@csa.gov.uk
Web: www.csa.gov.uk

Chief Executive .... Ms Janet Paraskwa

Falkirk Office
Parklands, Callendar Business Park, Callendar Road, Falkirk, FK1 1XT
Tel: (0845) 713 6000

Area Director................. Ms Linda Brown

Companies House
Crown Way, Cardiff, CF14 3UZ
Tel: (0303) 1234 500 Fax: (029) 2038 0900
E-mail: enquiries@companieshouse.gov.uk
Web: www.companieshouse.gov.uk

Chief Executive and
  Registrar of Companies for
  England and Wales . . . . Mr Gareth Jones OBE

Edinburgh Office
4th Floor, Edinburgh Quay 2, 139 Fountainbridge, Edinburgh, EH3 9FF
Tel: (0303) 123 4500

Registrar . . . . Ms Dorothy Blair

Driver and Vehicle Licensing Agency
Longview Road, Morriston, Swansea, SA6 7JL
Tel: (0870) 240 0009 (Fax: (0870) 850 1285
E-mails: drivers.dvla@gtnet.gov.uk
vehicles.dvla@gtnet.gov.uk
Web: www.dvla.gov.uk
dvlaregistrations.co.uk *(Personalised Registrations)*

Chief Executive . . . . Mr Noel Shanahan

Driving Standards Agency
The Axis Building, 112 Upper Parliament Street, Nottingham, NG1 6LP
Tel: (0115) 936 6666
E-mail: customer.services@dsa.gsi.gov.uk
Web: www.dsa.gsi.gov.uk

Chief Executive . . . . Ms Rosemary Thew

The Food and Environment Research Agency
Sand Hutton, York, YO41 1LZ
Tel: (01904) 462000 Fax: (01904) 462111
E-mail: science@fera.gsi.gov.uk
Web: www.defra.gov.uk/fera

Chief Executive . . . . Mr Adrian Belton

EXECUTIVE AGENCIES

Forest Research
Alice Holt Lodge, Farnham, Surrey, GU10 4LH
Tel: (01420) 22255 Fax: (01420) 23653
E-mail:research.info@forestry.gsi.gov.uk
Web: http://wwwforestresearch.gov.uk

Chief Executive . . . . Dr James Pendlebury

Scotland Office
Northern Research Station, Roslin, Midlothian, EH25 9SX
Tel: (0131) 445 2176 Fax: (0131) 445 5124

Research Liaison Officer . . . . Mr Steve Penny

Government Car and Despatch Agency
46 Ponton Road, London, SW8 5AX
Tel: (020) 7217 3839
E-mail: info@gcda.gsi.gov.uk
Web: www.gcda.gov.uk

Chief Executive . . . . Mr Roy Burke

Identity and Passport Service
Globe House, 89 Eccleston Square, London, SW1V 1PN
Tel: (0300) 222 0000
Web: www.ips.gov.uk

Chief Executive . . . . Mr James Hall

Glasgow Passport Office
3 Northgate, 96 Milton Street, Cowcaddens, Glasgow, G4 0BT
Tel: (0300) 222 0000

Regional Manager . . . . Mr Robert Wilson

Intellectual Property Office
Concept House, Cardiff Road, Newport, South Wales, NP10 8QQ
Tel: (0845) 950 0505 Fax: (01633) 814444
E-mail: enquiries@ipo.gov.uk
Web: www.ipo.gov.uk

Chief Executive . . . . Mr Ian Fletcher

Jobcentre Plus
Caxton House, Tithill Street, London, SW1H 9NA
Tel: (020) 7273 6006
Web: www.jobcentreplus.gov.uk

Chief Executive . . . . Mr Darra Singh

Scotland Office
2nd Floor, 21 Hersihell Street
Anniesland, Glasgow, G13 1HT
Tel: (0141) 950 5100

Contact . . . . Ms Julie Matthews

Maritime and Coastguard Agency
Spring Place, 105 Commercial Road, Southampton, SO15 1EG
Tel: (023) 8032 9100 Fax: (023) 8032 9298
E-mail: infoline@mcga.gov.uk
Web: www.mcga.gov.uk

Chief Executive . . . . Mr Peter Cardy

Scotland and Northern Ireland Region
Aberdeen Maritime Rescue Co-ordination Centre
4th Floor, Marine House, Aberdeen, AB11 5PB
Tel: (01224) 597907 Fax: (01224) 571920
E-mail: aberdeen_ma@mcga.gov.uk

Regional Director. . . . . Mr Bill McFadyen

Meat Hygiene Service
Kings Pool, Peasholme Green, York, YO1 7PR
Tel: (01904) 455501 Fax: (01904) 455502
Web: www.food.gov.uk

Chief Executive . . . . Mr Steve McGrath

Medicines and Healthcare Products Regulatory Agency
Market Towers, 1 Nine Elms Lane, London, SW8 5NQ
Tel: (020) 7084 2000 Fax: (020) 7084 2353
E-mail: info@mhra.gov.uk
Web: www.mhra.gov.uk

Chairman. Professor Sir Alasdair Breckenridge CBE

Met Office
Fitzroy Road, Exeter, EX1 3PB
Tel: (0870) 900 0100 Fax: (0870) 900 5050
E-mail: enquiries@metoffice.gov.uk
Web: www.met-office.gov.uk

Chief Executive . . . . Mr John Hirst

Scotland and Northern Ireland Met Office
Saughton House, Broomhouse Drive, Edinburgh, EH11 3XQ
Tel: (0131) 3XQ

Chief Adviser . . . . Mr Alex Hill

Aberdeen Office
Met Office, Davidson House, Campus 1, Aberdeen Science and Technology Park
Bridge of Don, Aberdeen, AB22 8GT
Tel: (01224) 407550 Fax: (01224) 407559

Manager. . . . . Mr Peter Buchanan

National Archives
Ruskin Avenue, Kew, Richmond, Surrey, TW9 4DU
Tel: (020) 8876 3444 Fax: (020) 8878 8905
E-mails: enquiry@nationalarchives.gov.uk
[firstname.surname]@nationalarchives.gov.uk
Web: www.nationalarchives.gov.uk

Chief Executive and Keeper of
Public Records . . . . Ms Natalie Ceeney

National Measurement Office
Stanton Avenue, Teddington, Middlesex, TW11 0JZ
Tel: (020) 8943 7272 Fax: (020) 8943 7270
E-mail: info@nmo.gov.uk
Web: www.nmo.bis.gov.uk

Chief Executive . . . . Mr Peter Mason

National Savings and Investments
Charles House, 375 Kensington High Street, London, W14 8SD
Tel: (020) 7348 9200
E-mail: customerenquiries@nsandi.com
Web: www.nsandi.com

Chief Executive . . . . Ms Jane Platt

Ordnance Survey
Romsey Road, Southampton, SO16 4GU
Tel: (023) 8079 2000 Fax: (023) 8079 2615
E-mail: customerservices@ordnancesurvey.co.uk
Web: www.ordnancesurvey.co.uk

Director General and Chief
Executive . . . . Dr Vanessa Lawrence CB

Scotland Office
Lochside House, 3 Lochside Way, Edinburgh Park, Edinburgh, EH12 9DT
Tel: (0845) 605 0505

Operations Manager . . . . Mr Peter Morrison

Pension, Disability and Carers Services Agency
PO Box 50101
London, SW1P 2WU
Tel: (020) 7449 7512 Fax: (020) 7449 7543
E-mail: terry.moran1@dwp.gsi.gov.uk
Webs: www.dwp.gov.uk/dcs
www.direct.gov.uk

Chief Executive . . . . Mr Terry Moran

Royal Mint
Llantrisant, Pontyclun, CF72 8YT
Tel: (01443) 222111 Fax: (01443) 623326
E-mail: information.office@royalmint.gov.uk
Web: www.royalmint.com

Chief Executive and
Accounting Officer . . . . Mr Andrew Stafford

Rural Payments Agency
Kings House, Kings Road, Reading, RG1 3BU
Tel: (0118) 958 3626 Fax: (0118) 959 7736
E-mail: enquiries.reading@rpa.gsi.gov.uk
Web: www.rpa.gov.uk

Chief Executive . . . . Mr Tony Cooper

Helpline Numbers
External Trade. . . . . Tel: (0191) 226 5050
Freephone Fraudline . . . . Tel: (0800) 347 347
Milk Quotas and Dairy Subsidies . . Tel: (0139) 266 6466
Securities . . . . Tel: (0118) 953 1723
Slaughter Scheme . . . . Tel: (0118) 968 7333

Service Personnel and Veterans Agency
Tomlinson House, Norcross, Blackpool, FY5 3WP
Tel: (0800) 169 2277
E-mail: veterans.help@spva.gsi.gov.uk
Web: www.veterans-uk.info

Chief Executive . . . . Mrs Cathy Barnes

Treasury Solicitor
One Kemble Street
London, WC2B 4TS
Tel: (020) 7210 3012 Fax: (020) 7210 3420
E-mail: [firstname.surname]@tsol.gsi.gov.uk Web: www.tsol.gsi.gov.uk

HM Procurator-General and
Treasury Solicitor . . . . Mr Paul Jenkins QC

Tribunals Service
8th Floor
102 Petty France, London, SW1H 9AJ
Tel: (020) 3334 3400 Fax: (020) 3334 3006
Web: www.tribunals.gov.uk

Chief Executive . . . . Mr Kevin Sadler

Asylum and Immigration Tribunals

Glasgow Office
Eagle Building, 215 Bothwell Street, Glasgow, G2 7EZ
Tel: (0141) 242 7562

Office Manager. . . . . Ms Caroline Mulholland

EXECUTIVE AGENCIES

Tribunal Service (Continued)
Criminal Injuries Compensation

Glasgow Office
Wellington House, 134-136 Wellington Street, Glasgow, G2 2XL
Tel: (0141) 354 8527

Office Manager................. Mr Tony Callaghan

Employment Tribunals

Aberdeen Office
Atholl House, 84-88 Guild Street, Aberdeen, AB11 6LT
Tel: (01224) 593137

Office Manager................. Ms Debbie Taylor

Dundee Office
13 Albert Square, Dundee, DD1 1DD
Tel: (01382) 221578

Edinburgh Office
54-56 Melville Street, Edinburgh, EH3 7HF
Tel: (0131) 226 5584

Glasgow Office
Eagle Building, 215 Bothwell Street, Glasgow, G2 7TS
Tel: (0141) 204 0730

Office Manager................. Mrs Mary Williamson

Social Security and Child Support Tribunals

Glasgow Office
Wellington House, 134-136 Wellington Street, Glasgow, G2 2XL
Tel: (0141) 354 8400
E-mail: SSCSA-Glasgow@tribunals.gsi.gov.uk

Regional Manager .... Mr Stephen Toal

UK Border Agency
11th Floor, Whitgift Centre, C Block
Wellesley Road, Croydon, CR9 3LU
Tel: (0870) 606 7766 Fax: (020) 8760 4310
Web: www.bia.homeoffice.gov.uk

Chief Executive .... Ms Lin Homer

UK Debt Management Office
Eastcheap Court, 11 Philpot Lane, London EC3M 8UD
Tel: (020) 7862 6500 Fax: (020) 7862 6509
E-mail: [firstname.surname]@dmo.gsi.gov.uk
Web: www.dmo.gov.uk

Chief Executive . . . . Mr Robert Stheeman CB

UK Hydrographic Office
Admiralty Way, Taunton, Somerset, TA1 2DN
Tel: (01823) 337900 Fax: (01823) 284077
E-mail: helpdesk@ukho.gov.uk
Web: www.ukho.gov.uk

Chief Executive . . . . Mr Mike Robinson

Valuation Office Agency
New Court, Carey Street, London, WC2A 2JE
Tel: (020) 7506 1700 Fax: (020) 7506 1998
E-mail: customerservices@voa.gsi.gov.uk
Web: www.voa.gov.uk

Chief Executive . . . . Ms Penny Cinivwicz

Edinburgh Office
50 Frederick Street, Edinburgh, EH2 1NG
Tel: (0131) 465 0700 Fax: (0131) 465 0799

Chief Valuer . . . . Mr Alan Ainslie

Vehicle Certification Agency
1 Eastgate Office Centre
Eastgate Road, Bristol, BS5 6XX
Tel: (0117) 9512 5151 Fax: (0117) 952 4103
E-mail: enquiries@vca.gov.uk
Web: www.vca.gov.uk

Chief Executive . . . . Mr Paul Markwick

Vehicle and Operator Services Agency
Berkeley House, Croydon Street, Bristol, BS5 0DA
Tel: (0117) 954 3211 Fax: (0117) 954 3209
E-mail: enquiries@vosa.gov.uk
Web: www.vosa.gov.uk

Chief Executive . . . . Mr Alastair Peoples

Veterinary Laboratories Agency
Woodham Lane, New Haw, Addlestone, Surrey, KT15 3NB
Tel: (01932) 341111 Fax: (01932) 347046
E-mail: enquiries@vla.defra.gsi.gov.uk
Web: www.defra.gov.uk/corporate/vla

Chief Executive . . . . Professor Peter Borriello

VLA Lasswade
Veterinary Laboratory, Pentlands Science Park
Bush Loan, Penicuik, Midlothian, EH26 0PZ
Tel: (0131) 445 6169 Fax: (0131) 445 6166
E-mail: lasswade@vla.defra.gsi.gov.uk

Veterinary Medicines Directorate
Woodham Lane, New Haw, Addlestone, Surrey, KT15 3LS
Tel: (01932) 336911 Fax: (01932) 336618
E-mail: [initial.surname]@vmd.defra.gsi.gov.uk
Web: www.vmd.gov.uk

Director and Chief Executive. . . . . . Professor Steve Dean

Wilton Park
Wiston House
Steyning, West Sussex, BN44 3DZ
Tel: (01903) 815020
E-mail: admin@wiltonpark.org.uk
Web: www.wiltonpark.org.uk

Chief Executive . . . . Mr Richard Burge

Public Bodies

Note: (i) This part of the Directory is divided into two sections. This first section details (in alphabetical order) these Public Bodies whose remit is specific to Scotland. The second section lists (by subject) other selected Public Bodies.

(ii) The Public Bodies listed here are officially known as Non-Department Public Bodies (or Quangos).

Additional Support Needs Tribunal for Scotland

Europa Building, 450 Argyle Street, Glasgow, G2 8LG
Tel: (0845) 120 2906 Fax: (0141) 242 0360
E-mail: inquiries@asntscotland.gov.uk
Web: www.asntscotland.gov.uk

Established:
2005, following the commencement of Section 17 of the Education (Additional Support for Learning) (Scotland) Act 2004.

Function:
The 2004 Act replaces the system for assessment and recording of children and young people with special educational needs with a new framework around additional support needs. The Tribunal hears appeals, called "references" from parents and young people on matters relating to co-ordinated support plans. Co-ordinated support plans will be prepared for children with enduring additional support needs, arising from complex or multiple factors, who need a range of support from different services.

President . . . . .Ms Jessica Burns

Secretary . . . . .Ms Sally Burns

Advisory Committee on Sites of Special Scientific Interest

23 Chester Street, Edinburgh, EH3 7ET
Tel: (0131) 225 1230 Fax: (0131) 225 5582
E-mail: acsssi@scottwilson.com

Established:
1992, under the Natural Heritage (Scotland) Act of 1991.

Function:
To advise Scottish Natural Heritage where there are sustained scientific objections to the notification of Sites of Special Scientific Interest.

Chairman . . . . .Professor Donald Davidson

Secretariat . . . . .Mr Scott Wilson

Architecture+Design Scotland (A+DS)
Bakehouse Close, 146 Canongate
Edinburgh, EH8 8DD
Tel: (0131) 556 6699 Fax: (0131) 556 6633
E-mail: info@ads.org.uk
Web: www.ads.org.uk

Established:
2005. It replaced the Royal Fine Art Commission for Scotland which was established in 1927, by Royal Warrant.

Functions:
Architecture+Design Scotland is Scotland's national champion for good architecture, design and planning in the built environment. Established by the Scottish Executive in April 2005 A+DS has a wide and proactive role in advocating the benefits of good design through Research, Enabling and Design Review activities.

Chairman . . . . .Mr Raymond Young CBE

Chief Executive *(Acting)* . . . . .Mr Trevor Muir OBE

Audit Scotland
(Accounts Commission for Scotland / Auditor General Scotland)
110 George Street
Edinburgh, EH2 4LH
Tel: (0845) 146 1010 Fax: (0845) 146 1009
E-mail: info@audit-scotland.gov.uk
Web: www.audit-scotland.gov.uk

Established:
2000, under the Public Finance and Accountability (Scotland) Act 2000.

Functions:
Audit Scotland provides services to the Auditor General and Accounts Commission. The Auditor General holds the Scottish Government and other public spending bodies (except local authorities, police forces and fire and rescue services) to account for the proper efficient and effective use of public funds. The Accounts Commission does this for local authorities, police forces and fire and rescue services.

Auditor General . . . . .Mr Robert Black

Chairman of the
Accounts Commission . . . . .Mr John Baillie

Bòrd na Gàidhlig
The Gaelic Development Agency

Darach House, Stoneyfield Business Park
Stoneyfield, Inverness, IV2 7PA
Tel: (01463) 225454 Fax: (01463) 716217
E-mail: ofios@bord-na-gaidhlig.org.uk
Web: www.bord-na-gaidhlig.org.uk

Established:
2006, under the Gaelic Language (Scotland) Act 2005

Functions:
Under the Gaelic Language (Scotland) Act 2005, Bòrd na Gàidhlig is responsible for promoting and facilitating Gaelic in Scotland, and for advising on Gaelic language, education and culture. The Bòrd is also responsible for delivering the Government's National Plan for Gaelic, and developing Gaelic language plans with public authorities and other partners across Scotland.

Chairman . . . . .Mr Arthur Cormack

Chief Executive . . . .*Vacant*

Boundary Commission for Scotland

Secretariat, 3 Drumsheugh Gardens
Edinburgh, EH3 7QJ
Tel: (0131) 538 7510 Fax: (0131) 538 7511
E-mail: secretariat@scottishboundaries.gov.uk
Web: www.bcomm-scotland.gov.uk

Established:
1944, constituted in accordance with the Parliamentary Constituencies Act of 1986, as amended. Roles are defined by that Act and by Schedule 1 of the Scotland Act 1998, as amended.

Functions:
To keep under review the boundaries of Westminster constituencies in Scotland and the Scottish Parliament constituencies and regions.

Chairman . . . .*Speaker of the House of Commons*

Deputy Chairman .Hon Lord Woolman

Secretary . . . . .Dr Hugh Buchanan

Commissioners . . . . .Dr Elspeth Graham
Mr Kenneth McDonald

Building Standards Advisory Committee

c/o Denholm House, Almondvale Business Park
Livingston, EH54 6GA
Tel: (01506) 600407 Fax: (01506) 600401
E-mail: alan.murchison@scotland.gsi.gov.uk
Web: www.sbsa.gov.uk

Established:
1959, under the Building (Scotland) Act 1959 and continued under the Building (Scotland) Act 2003.

Functions:
The precise remit of the Committee is to advise Scottish Ministers on the exercise of their functions under the Building (Scotland) Act 2003. The Committee is also responsible for keeping the operation of the building regulations under review and making recommendations to Scottish Ministers in connection with the regulations.

Members of the Committee have been appointed by Scottish Ministers and are selected to provide a broad spectrum of technical knowledge relevant to construction. They are not selected to represent particular interest groups.

Chair . . . . .Mr David Wedderburn

Secretary . . . . .Mr Alan Murchison

Cairngorms National Park Authority

14 The Square, Grantown on Spey
Moray, PH26 3HG
Tel: (01479) 873535 Fax: (01479) 873527
E-mail: enquiries@cairngorms.co.uk
Web: www.cairngorms.co.uk

Established:
2003, under The National Parks (Scotland) Act 2000.

Function:
The Park Authority manages and coordinates a range of activities aimed at caring for the Cairngorms National Park, and helps others protect, improve and enjoy it.

Convener . . . . .Mr David Green

Chief Executive . . . . .Ms Jane Hope

Caledonian Maritime Assets
Municipal Buildings, Fore Street, Port Glasgow, PA14 5EQ
Tel: (01475) 749920 Fax: (01475) 745109
E-mail: info@cmassets.co.uk
Web: www.cmassets.co.uk

Established:
1973, as Caledonia MacBrayne Ltd under the Transport Act 1968 by change of name of Caledonian Steam Packet Company Ltd (incorporated in 1889). The Scottish Transport Group was formed with responsibility for David MacBrayne Ltd and the Caledonian Steam Packet Company Ltd. In January 1973, the STG reorganised its shipping services and Caledonian MacBrayne was formed from the Caledonian Steam Packet Company Ltd and David MacBrayne Ltd.

On 1st October 2006, corporate restructuring related to the provision of the Clyde and Hebrides ferry services took place. CalMac Ferries Ltd commenced trading in taking over operation of the Clyde and Hebrides ferry services as successor to Caledonian MacBrayne Ltd. As a separate element of this corporate restructuring, Caledonian MacBrayne Ltd. had its name changed to Caledonian Maritime Assets Ltd and retained ownership of the vessels and piers which are required for the operation of the Clyde and Hebrides ferry services.

Under the new arrangements, Caledonian Maritime Assets Ltd leases the vessels and piers to the operator of the Clyde and Hebrides ferry services, currently CalMac Ferries Ltd Caledonian Maritime Assets Ltd is wholly owned by Scottish ministers.

Function:
The operation of the main network of ferry services to the islands and peninsulas in the west coast of Scotland.

Chairman . . . . .Mr Grenville Johnston OBE

Managing Director .Mr Guy Platten

Central Scotland Forest Trust
Hillhouse Ridge, Shottskirk Road, Shotts, ML7 4JS
Tel: (01501) 822015 Fax: (01501) 823919
E-mail: enquiries@csft.co.uk
Web: www.csft.co.uk

Established: 2005

Functions:
To lead and secure the creation of the Central Scotland Forest and to support social forestry widely

Chairman . . . . .Mr David Crawley

Chief Executive . . . . .Mr Simon Rennie MBE

Children's Panels
Area 2b(s) South, Victoria Quay
Edinburgh, EH6 6QQ
Tel: (0131) 244 3545 Fax: (0131) 244 3547
E-mail: childrens.hearings@scotland.gsi.gov.uk
Web: www.childrenshearingsscotland.gov.uk

Established:
1971, under the Social Work (Scotland) Act 1968, which was replaced by the Children (Scotland) Act 1995.

Functions:
Panel members sit on Children's Hearings which make decisions in respect of children referred to a Hearing by the Principal Reporter. These children are considered to be in need of compulsory measures of supervision because they are at risk or have offended.

Note: There is one Panel for each local authority.

Crofters Commission
Castle Wynd
Inverness, IV2 3EQ
Tel: (01463) 663450 Fax: (01463) 711820
E-mail: info@crofterscommission.org.uk
Web: www.crofterscommission.org.uk

Established:
1955, by the Crofters (Scotland) Act 1955. It now operates under the Crofters (Scotland) Act 1993, as amended by the Crofting Reform etc. Act 2007.

Functions:
1. To regulate crofting;
2. To promote the interests of crofters;
3. To advise Scottish Ministers on crofting matters.

Convener . . . . .Mr Drew Ratter

Chief Executive . . . . .Mr Nick Reiter

Deer Commission for Scotland
Great Glen House, Leachkin Road
Inverness, IV3 8NW
Tel: (01463) 725000 Fax: (01463) 725048
E-mail: enquiries@dcs.gov.uk
Web: www.dcs.gov.uk

Established:
1959, under the Deer (Scotland) Act 1959; subsequently consolidated into the Deer
(Scotland) Act 1996.

Functions:
To further the conservation, control and sustainable management of deer in Scotland;
and keep under review all relevant matters, including the welfare of deer.

Chairman ....Lord Dalhousie

Chief Executive ....Mr Nick Halfhide

Fisheries (Electricity) Committee
Room 408A, Pentland House, 47 Robb's Loan
Edinburgh, EH14 1TY
Tel: (0131) 244 5245 Fax: (0131) 244 6313
E-mail: andrew.dailly@scotland.gsi.gov.uk
Web: www.scotland.gov.uk/topics/fisheries/salmon-trout-coarse-17604/913

Established:
1943, under the Hydro-Electric Development (Scotland) Act 1943; consolidated in the
Electricity (Scotland) Act 1979 and extended in 1986. Its continuance was provided for
in the Electricity Act 1989.

Functions:
The Committee's statutory function is to advise and assist Scottish Ministers and any
person engaging in, or proposing to engage in the generation of hydro-electric power
(including wave and tidal) on any question relating to the effect of hydro-electric works
on fisheries or stocks of fish. The Committee also advises on the effects of the water
systems of thermal generating stations on fisheries and stocks of fish.

Chairman ....Mr James Cockburn

Secretary ....Ms Karen Shepherd

General Teaching Council for Scotland
Clerwood House, 96 Clermiston Road
Edinburgh, EH12 6UT
Tel: (0131) 314 6000 Fax: (0131) 314 6001
E-mail: gtcs@gtcs.org.uk
Web: www.gtcs.org.uk

Established:
1965, under the Teaching Council (Scotland) Act 1965. It has responsibility for maintaining and enhancing professional standards in schools and colleges and contributing to maintaining and enhancing the quality of teaching and learning in Scotland.

Functions:
1. Maintaining a register of qualified teachers;
2. Overseeing standards of entry to the profession and advising Scottish Ministers;
3. Accrediting and reviewing initial teacher eduction, Chartered Teacher and Headship Programmes;
4. Exercising disciplinary powers in relation to registration in terms of professional conduct and competence;
5. Supporting probationer teachers by means of seminars, visits and publishing guidelines;
6. Making recommendations to Scottish Ministers on the supply of teachers.
7. Making recommendations to Scottish Ministers on the continuing professional development and staff development review of teachers.

Convener . . . . .Ms May Ferries

Vice-Convener . . . . .Mr James Thewliss

Chief Executive . . . . .Mr Anthony Finn

Press/Media Contact . . . . .Mr Martin Osler

Highlands and Islands Airports Ltd
Inverness Airport, Inverness, IV2 7JB
Tel: (01667) 462445 Fax: (01667) 464300
E-mail: info@hial.co.uk
Web: www.hial.co.uk

Established:
1986, as a wholly owned subsidiary company of the Civil Aviation Authority. Ownership was transferred to the Scottish Office in 1995, and to the Scottish Executive on devolution.

Functions:
It is responsible for the management and operation of ten airports in the Highlands and Islands of Scotland: Barra, Benbecula, Campbeltown, Inverness, Islay, Kirkwall, Stornoway, Sumburgh, Tiree and Wick. Since 1st December 2007, HIAL has operated Dundee Airport via a wholly owned subsidiary, Dundee Airport Ltd.

Chairman . . . . .Lt. Col Grenville Johnston OBE

Managing Director .Mr Inglis Lyon

Company Secretary .Mr Norman Ross

Highlands and Islands Enterprise
Cowan House
Inverness Retail and Business Park
Inverness, IV2 7GF
Tel: (01463) 234171 Fax: (01463) 244469
E-mail: info@hient.co.uk
Web: www.hie.co.uk

Established:
1991, under the Enterprise and New Towns Act 1990.

Functions:
1. To prepare, co-ordinate, promote and undertake measures for the economic and social development of the Highlands and Islands;
2. To maintain and enhance skills and capacities relevant to employment; and to assist people in establishing themselves as self-employed in the region;
3. To improve further the environment in the Highlands and Islands of Scotland.

Chairman . . . . .Mr William Roe

Chief Executive . . . . .Mr Sandy Cumming CBE

Head of Communications . . . . .Mr Chris Roberts

Justices of the Peace Advisory Committee
GW.14, St Andrew's House
Edinburgh, EH1 3DG
Tel: (0131) 244 2130 Fax: (0131) 224 2623

Established:
1949, based on the recommendations the Royal Commission on Justices of the
Peace 1948.

Functions:
To keep under review the strength of the Commission of the Peace in its particular area;
and to advise Scottish Ministers on the appointment of new Justices. The Committees
have responsibility for determining both when new appointments are desirable and whom
to recommend for appointment. Minister will not normally appoint a Justice of the Peace
except on the unanimous recommendation of the appropriate Justices of the Peace
Advisory Committee.

There is an advisory committee for each Commission Area, usually chaired by the Lord-
Lieutenant. The Chairman and members are appointed by the Scottish Ministers.

Contact . . . . .Mr Richard Wilkins

Lands Tribunal for Scotland
George House, 126 George Street,
Edinburgh, EH2 4HH
Tel: (0131) 271 4350 Fax: (0131) 271 4399
E-mail: mail@lands-tribunal-scotland.org.uk
Web: www.lands-tribunal-scotland.org.uk

Established:
1971, under the Land Tribunal Act 1949. The Tribunal was originally set up in Scotland
to deal with the discharge or variation of restrictive land obligations, but there are now
various jurisdictions in relation to land tenure and the main areas are listed below.

Functions:
The Tribunal is a judicial body which deals mainly with:
  1. Land valuations in rating appeals;
  2. Applications in connection with disputes relating to council house purchase;
  3. Disputed Compensation claims in respect of compulsory purchase etc;
  4. Variation and discharge of title conditions;
  5. Other matters under the Title Conditions (Scotland) Act 2003;
  6. Appeals against the Keeper of the Registers of Scotland;
  7. Valuation under rural right to buy schemes.

Membership comprises the President, Mr John Wright QC, and two part-time surveyor
members, Mr Ian Darling FRICS and Mr Kenneth Barclay FRICS.

President . . . . .Hon Lord McGhie

Clerk . . . . .Mr Neil Tainsh

Learning and Teaching Scotland

Headquarters
The Optima, 58 Robertson Street
Glasgow, G2 8DU
Tel: (0141) 282 5000 Fax: (0141) 282 5050

Associate Office
Level 9, City House, Overgate, Dundee, DD1 1UH
Tel: (01382) 443600 Fax: (01382) 443645/6
E-mail: enquiries@ltscotland.org.uk
Web: www.ltscotland.org.uk

Established:
2000, from a merger of the Scottish Consultative Council on the Curriculum (Scottish CCC) and the Scottish Council for Educational Technology (SCET).

Functions:
Learning and Teaching Scotland is sponsored by the Scottish Government. It is the main organisation for the development and support of the Scottish curriculum..

Its role is to provide advice, support, resources and staff development to enhance the quality of learning and teaching in Scotland, combining expertise in the curriculum 3-18 with advice on the use of ICT in education.

It works in close partnership with the Scottish Government, HMIE, the SQA, ADES, COSLA, education authorities, schools and with a range of professional associations, playing a key role in the drive to improve learning and teaching.

Chairman . . . . .Mr John Mulgrew

Chief Executive . . . . .Mr Bernard McLeary

Local Government Boundary Commission for Scotland
3 Drumsheugh Gardens, Edinburgh, EH3 7QJ
Tel: (0131) 538 7510 Fax; (0131) 538 7511
E-mail: secretariat@scottishboundaries.gov.uk
Web: www.lgbc-scotland.gov.uk

Established:
1973, under the Local Government (Scotland) Act 1973.

Functions:
Reviews number and boundaries of electoral wards for local authorities, and boundaries of local authority areas.

Chairman ....Mr Peter Mackay CB

Deputy Chairman ....Mr William Magee

Secretary ....Dr Hugh Buchanan

Commissioners ....Mr Brian Clark
Mr Kenneth McDonald
Ms Paula Sharp

Loch Lomond and The Trossachs National Park Authority
Carrochan, Carrochan Road
Balloch, G83 8EG
Tel: (01389) 722600 Fax: (01389) 722633
E-mail: info@lochlomond-trossachs.org
Web: www.lochlomond-trossachs.org

Established:
2002, under the National Parks (Scotland) Act 2000.

Functions:
The Authority is responsible for the Loch Lomond and the Trossachs National Park

Convener ....Dr Michael Cantlay

Chief Executive ....Ms Fiona Logan

PR Officer ....Ms Ruth Crosbie

Mobility and Access Committee for Scotland
Area 2D, Dockside, Victoria Quay
Edinburgh, EH6 6QQ
Tel: (0131) 244 0869 Fax: (0131) 244 7281
E-mail: macs@scotland.gsi.gov.uk
Web: www.scotland.gov.uk/topics/transport/macs

Established:
2002, under Section 72 of the Transport (Scotland) Act 2001.

Functions:
To advise Scottish Ministers on the transport needs of disabled people and how to improve the accessibility of transport for them.

Convener ....Mrs Anne MacLean OBE

Secretary ....Miss Judith Ballantine

National Galleries of Scotland
Dean Gallery, 73 Bedford Road, Edinburgh, EH4 3DS
Tel: (0131) 624 6200 Fax: (0131) 223 7126
E-mail: enquiries@nationalgalleries.org
Web: www.nationalgalleries.org

Established:
The galleries were established by a Treasury Minute in 1850. This was amended by the National Galleries of Scotland Act 1906, and amended again by the National Heritage (Scotland) Act 1985.

Functions:
The Galleries' Mission Statement is:
The National Galleries of Scotland cares for, develops, researches and displays the national collection of Scottish and international fine art and, with a lively and innovative programme of exhibitions, education and publications, aims to engage, inform and inspire the broadest possible public.

The Galleries comprise the National Gallery of Scotland, the Scottish National Portrait Gallery, the Scottish National Gallery of Modern Art and the Dean Gallery, The Royal Scottish Academy Building, the Art Centre Granton, and partner galleries at Duff House, Banff and Paxton House's Picture Gallery, Berwickshire.

Chairman ....Mr Ben Thomson

Director-General ....Mr John Leighton

National Galleries of Scotland (Continued)

National Gallery of Scotland
The Mound, Edinburgh, EH2 2EL

Director . . . . .Mr Michael Clarke

Scottish National Gallery of Modern Art
75 Belford Road, Edinburgh, EH4 3DR

Director . . . . .Dr Simon Groom

Scottish National Portrait Gallery
1 Queen Street, Edinburgh, EH2 1JD

Director . . . . .Mr James Holloway

Chief Operating Officer . . . . .Mrs Nicola Catterall
Director of Development and
  Communications . . . . .Mrs Catrin Tilley
Keeper of Conservation . . . . .Ms Jacqueline Ridge

National Library of Scotland
George IV Bridge
Edinburgh, EH1 1EW
Tel: (0131) 623 3700 Fax: (0131) 623 3701
E-mail: enquiries@nls.uk
Web: www.nls.uk

Established:
1925, under the National Library of Scotland Act 1925. It was previously the library of the Faculty of Advocates, founded in 1689.

Functions:
The National Library of Scotland is a major European research library and is the world's leading centre for the study of Scotland and the Scots - an information treasure trove for Scotland's knowledge, history and culture.

The collections are of world-class importance and include many of Scotland's literary treasures. Key areas include rare books, manuscripts, maps, music, official publications, business information, science and technology, and the modern and foreign collections. The Scottish Screen Archive merged with NLS in 2007.

The Library holds well over 14 million items, including printed items, approximately 100,000 manuscripts and nearly 2 million maps. Every week it collects approximately 6,000 new items via Legal Deposit.

Digital collections and digitisation are other important areas of work and many features can be seen online at www.nls.uk.

Throughout the year NLS also hosts a wide ranging programme of free exhibitions and events, including the permanent John Murray Archive exhibition. For information on events being held at the Library, please see www.nls.uk/news/events.html.

Chairman of the Trustees . . . . .Professor Michael Anderson

National Librarian and
Chief Executive . . . . .Mr Martyn Wade

Press Officers . . . . .Mr Bruce Blacklaw
Ms Karen Gallacher

National Museums Scotland
Chambers Street
Edinburgh, EH1 1JF
Tel: (0131) 225 7534
E-mail: info@nms.ac.uk
Web: www.nms.ac.uk

Established:
1985, under the National Heritage (Scotland) Act 1985.

Functions:
National Museums Scotland preserves, interprets and make accessible for all, the past and present of Scotland, of other nations and cultures, and of the natural world.

National Museums Scotland comprises: National Museum of Scotland, National War Museum, National Museum of Flight, National Museum of Costume, National Museum of Rural Life and the National Museums Collection Centre.

Chairman of the Trustees . . . . .Sir Angus Grossart

Director . . . . .Dr Gordon Rintoul

Director of Collections . . . . .Ms Jane Carmichael

Director of Estates and Facilities
     Management . . . . .Ms Fiona Bell

Director of Finance and Resources . . . . .Mr Andrew Patience

Director of Marketing and
     Development . . . . .Ms Catherine Holden

Director of Public Programmes . . . . .Ms Sally Manuireva

Managing Director, NMS Enterprises . . . . . .Mr Peter Williamson

Communications Manager . . . . .Ms Susan Gray

Parole Board for Scotland
Room X5, Saughton House, Broomhouse Drive
Edinburgh, EH11 3XD
Tel: (0131) 244 8373 Fax: (0131) 244 4304
E-mail: parole.board@scotland.gsi.gov.uk
Web: www.scottishparoleboard.gov.uk

Established:
1968. It now operates and its proceedings are governed by the Prisons (Scotland) Act 1989, the Prisoners and Criminal Proceedings (Scotland) Act 1993, the Convention Rights (Compliance) (Scotland) Act 2001 and the Criminal Justice (Scotland) Act 2003.

Functions:
To consider whether prisoners should be granted parole and to direct Scottish Ministers accordingly.

Chairman ....Mr Alexander Cameron

Head, Parole Board Executive ....Mrs Alessia Morris

Passengers' View Scotland
Area 2D Dockside, Victoria Quay, Edinburgh, EH6 6QQ
Tel: (0131) 244 5306
E-mail: ptuc@scotland.gsi.gov.uk
Web: www.scotland.gov.uk/topics/transport/ptuc

Established:
2007. It replaced the Bus User Complaints Tribunal which was established in 2002 and is also known as the Public Transport Users' Committee for Scotland.

Functions:
To advise Scottish Ministers in relation to public transport policy.

Convener ....Mr James King

Secretary ....Mr James King

Pensions Appeal Tribunals for Scotland

George House, 126 George Street
Edinburgh, EH2 4HH
Tel: (0131) 271 4340 Fax: (0131) 271 4398
E-mail: info@patscotland.org.uk
Web: www.patscotland.org.uk

Established:
Originally set up during the First World War, it was established in its present format in 1943, under the Pensions Appeal Tribunals Act 1943.

Functions:
To arrange and organise appeal hearings; and to issue decisions following from them. Appeals arise from the refusal of applications to the Ministry of Defence for entitlement or re-assessment of war pensions.

President ....Mr Colin McEachran QC

Secretary ....Mr William Barclay

Police Complaints Commissioner for Scotland

PO Box 26300
Hamilton, ML3 3AR
Tel: (0808) 178 5577
E-mail: enquiries@pcc-scotland.org
Web: www.pcc-scotland.org

Established:
2007, under the Police, Public Order and Criminal Justice (Scotland) Act 2006.

Functions:
- To scrutinise independently the manner in which police organisations deal with complaints from the public they serve;
- To ensure that police organisations in Scotland have in place appropriate procedures for handling complaints and that these procedures are followed effectively;
- To prepare reports for Scottish Ministers about how complaints are being dealt with, both general reports commenting on police organisations as a whole, and specific reports dealing with particular issues which may arise; and
- To drive up standards and consistency in the way police complaints are handled across the Scottish Police Service.

Commissioner ....Mr John McNeill

Director ....Mr Ian Todd

Private Rented Housing Panel for Scotland
3rd Floor, 140 West Campbell Street
Glasgow, G2 4TZ
Tel: (0141) 572 1170 Fax: (0131) 572 1171
E-mail: admin@prhp.scotland.gov.uk
Web: www.prhp.scotland.gov.uk

Established:
1965, under the Rent Act 1965.

Functions:
To provide members for Rent Assessment Committees. These Committees consider objections to 'fair rents' fixed by Rent Officers under the Rent (Scotland) Act 1984. They also determine market rents for short assured tenancies and for terms for statutory assured tenancies under the Housing (Scotland) Act 1988.

President . . . . .Mrs Isabel Montgomery

Vice-President . . . . .Mr Robert Buchan

Secretary . . . . .Mrs Sara James

Risk Management Authority
St James House, 25 St James Street, Paisley, PA3 2HQ
Tel: (0141) 567 3112 Fax: (0131) 567 3111
E-mail: info@rmascotland.gsi.gov.uk
Web: www.rmascotland.gov.uk

Established:
January 2005 by Scottish Ministers.

Functions:
To play a key role in helping to protect the public from serious violent and sexual offenders and to be a national centre for good practice in risk assessment and risk management in Scotland, by advising and assisting statutory, voluntary and private sector agencies in their addressing the risk posed by serious offenders.

Convenor . . . . .Mr Peter Johnston

Chief Executive . . . . .Ms Yvonne Gailey

Royal Botanic Garden Edinburgh
20A Inverleith Row
Edinburgh, EH3 5LR
Tel: (0131) 552 7171 Fax: (0131) 248 2901
E-mail: info@rbge.org.uk
Web: www.rbge.org.uk

Established:
A Physic Garden was first established in 1670. The present Botanic Garden, occupying about 31 hectares, was established at Inverleith in 1823. There are, in addition, three Regional Gardens, providing a range of climatic and soil conditions: Benmore Botanic Garden, near Dunoon, Argyll; Logan Botanic Garden; near Stranraer, Wigtownshire; and Dawyck Botanic Garden, near Stobo, in Peeblesshire.

In 1992 the Botanics Trading Company Limited was established as the Garden's commercial wing. It operates for and on behalf of the Garden's Board of Trustees; and it annually gift-aids its profit to them.

Functions:
It aims to explore and explain the world of plants. Its role is to pursue whole plant science, notably through research of the highest quality on the origins, diversity and relationships of plants, their significance in the environment, and their conservation. In particular it:
1. Carries out investigations and research into the science of plants and related subjects; and disseminates the results;
2. Maintains and develops collections of living plants and preserved plant material, books, archives and other related objects;
3. Keeps the collections as national reference collections; and makes them available for the purpose of study;
4. Provides advice, information and education on science of plants and related subjects;
5. Provides other services, including quarantine, in relation to plants;
6. Allows members of the public to enter the Gardens to gain knowledge and enjoyment.

Chairman of the Trustees . . . . .Sir George Mathewson CBE

Regius Keeper . . . . .Professor Stephen Blackmore FRSE

Press Officer . . . . .Ms Shauna Hay

Royal Commission on the Ancient and Historical Monuments of Scotland

John Sinclair House
16 Bernard Terrace
Edinburgh, EH8 9NX
Tel: (0131) 662 1456 Fax: (0131) 662 1477
E-mail: info@rcahms.gov.uk
Web: www.rcahms.gov.uk

Established:
1908, by Royal Warrant.

Functions:
1. To survey and record the man-made environment of Scotland;
2. To compile and maintain a record of Scotland's archaeology and architecture;
3. To promote understanding of this information.

Chairman . . . . .Professor John Hume OBE

Chief Executive . . . . .Mrs Diana Murray

Scotland's Commissioner for Children and Young People

85 Holyrood Road, Edinburgh, EH8 8AU
Tel: (0131) 558 3733 Fax: (0131) 556 3378
E-mail: info@sccyp.org.uk
Web: www.sccyp.org.uk

Established:
2003, under the Commissioner for Children and Young People (Scotland) Act 2003.

Functions:
To promote and safeguard the rights of children and young people.

To achieve this, the Commissioner will:
1. Generate widespread awareness and understanding of the rights of children and young people;
2. Consider and review the adequacy and effectiveness of any law, policy and practice as it relates to the rights of children and young people;
3. Promote best practice by service providers;
4. Commission and undertake research on matters relating to the rights of children and young people.

Commissioner . . . . .Mr Tam Baillie

Press/Media Contact . . . . .Ms Ezmie McCutcheon

Scottish Advisory Committee on Distinction Awards
Scottish Health Service Centre, Crewe Road South
Edinburgh, EH4 2LF
Tel: (0131) 275 7741 Fax: (0131) 315 2369
E-mail: committee@shsc.csa.scot.nhs.uk
Web: www.sacda.scot.nhs.uk

Established: 1998.

Functions:
To decide, on behalf of Scottish ministers, which medical and dental consultants working in the NHS in Scotland should receive distinction awards for outstanding professional work.

Chairman . . . . .Professor Colin Suckling OBE

Medical Director . . . . .Professor John Reid OBE

Secretary . . . . .Mrs Fiona Kennedy

Scottish Agricultural Wages Board
Pentland House, 47 Robb's Loan, Edinburgh, EH14 1TY
Tel: (0131) 244 6397 Fax: (0131) 244 6551
E-mail: ronnie.grady@scotland.gsi.gov.uk
Web: www.scotland.gov.uk

Established:
1949, by the Agricultural Wages (Scotland) Act 1949.

Functions:
To make Orders fixing minimum wage rates, holiday entitlements and other conditions for workers employed in agriculture in Scotland. Such Orders are enforceable in law.

Chairman . . . . .Mr John Menzies

Secretary . . . . .Mr Ronnie Grady

Scottish Arts Council

12 Manor Place, Edinburgh, EH3 7DD
Tel: (0131) 226 6051 Fax: (0131) 225 9833
E-mail: help.desk@scottisharts.org.uk
Web: www.scottisharts.org.uk

Established:
1967, by Royal Charter. In 1994 the Scottish Arts Council became autonomous from the Arts Council of Great Britain.

Functions:
The Scottish Arts Council is the main arts development agency in Scotland. The Scottish Arts Council champions the arts for Scotland, investing £60 million from Scottish Executive and National Lottery funding and working with partners to support and develop artistic excellence and creativity throughout Scotland. It encourages support for the arts from other organisations (including local authorities, economic development agencies, private sponsors and charitable trusts).

It promotes development of the arts throughout Scotland; and it provides an information and advice service.

Chairman . . . . .Dr Richard Holloway

**Chief Executive and Head of Audience
and Organisational Development** . . . . . . .Mr Jim Tough

**Deputy Chief Executive and Director of
Planning and Communications** . . . . .Ms Morag Arnot

Directors of Arts . . . . .Mr Iain Munro
Mr David Taylor

Director of Finance .Ms Myriam Madden

Scottish Charities Appeals Panel
2W, St Andrews House, Regent Road, Edinburgh, EH1 3DG
Tel: (0131) 244 5578
E-mail: scap@scotland.gov.uk
Web: www.scap.gov.uk

Established:
2007, by the Charities and Trustee Investment (Scotland) Act 2005.

Functions:
- To provide fair, independent and informed adjudication of appeals against Office of the Scottish Charity Regulator's decisions, in accordance with the Act and the Rules of Procedure;
- To be accessible to users, working through flexible but consistent, impartial, efficient and effective proceedings;
- To make decisions that reflect best practice, whilst keeping the time and costs involved for all parties to a minimum.

Chair . . . . .Ms Saria Akhter

Secretary . . . . .Ms Vanessa Glynn

Scottish Children's Reporter Administration
Ochil House
Springkerse Business Park
Stirling, FK7 7XE
Tel: (01786) 459500 Fax: (01786) 459532
E-mail: netta.maciver@scra.gsx.gov.uk
Web: www.scra.gov.uk

Established:
1996, under the Local Government (Scotland) Act 1994.

Functions:
It facilitates the performance of the Principal Reporter's statutory functions, which concern children who may require compulsory care and supervision.

It manages the staff of the Reporter service throughout Scotland and provides suitable accommodation for Children's Hearings throughout Scotland.

Chairman . . . . .Mr Douglas Bulloch

Principal Reporter . . . . .Ms Netta MacIver OBE

Corporate Development Director . . . . .Mr Eddie McConnell

Scottish Commission for the Regulation of Care (The Care Commission)

Compass House, 11 Riverside Drive, Dundee, DD1 4NY
Tel: (01382) 207100 Fax: (01382) 207288
E-mail: enquiries@carecommission.com
Web: www.carecommission.com

Established:
2002, under the Regulation of Care (Scotland) Act 2001.

Functions:
To ensure, through a regulatory system, improvement in the quality of care services in Scotland, respecting the rights of people who use those services to dignity, privacy, choice and safety.

Convener . . . . .Professor Frank Clark CBE

Chief Executive . . . . .Ms Jacquie Roberts

Director of Adult Services Regulation . . . . . .Ms Marcia Ramsay

Director of Children's Services
   Regulation . . . . .Mr Ronnie Hill

Director of Corporate Services . . . . .Mr Gordon Weir

Director of Healthcare Regulation . . . . .Ms Susan Brimelow

Director of Strategic Development . . . . .Mr David Wiseman

Communications Manager . . . . .Ms Karen Anderson

Regional Offices
Central East
Compass House, 11 Riverside Drive, Dundee, DD1 4NY
Tel: (01382) 207200 Fax: (01382) 207288

Regional Manager .Mr Lorne Findlay

Central West
4th Floor, 1 Smithhills Street, Paisley, PA1 1EB
Tel: (0141) 843 4230 Fax: (0141) 843 4289

Regional Manager .Ms Gill Swapp

North
Johnstone House, Rose Street, Aberdeen, AB10 1UD
Tel: (01224) 793870 Fax: (01224) 793899

Regional Manager .Mr Chris Stadames

Scottish Commission for the Regulation of Care (Continued)

South East
Stuart House, Eskmill, Musselburgh, EH21 7PB
Tel: (0131) 653 4100 Fax: (01382) 653 4149

Regional Manager .Ms Lawrie Davidson

South West
Princes Gate, Castle Street, Hamilton, ML3 6BU
Tel: (01698) 208150 Fax: (01698) 282162

Regional Manager .Mr Henry Mathias

Scottish Crime and Drug Enforcement Agency (SCDEA)
Osprey House, Inchinnan Road
Paisley, PA3 2RE
Tel: (0141) 302 1000 Fax: (0141) 302 1090
E-mail: staffoffice@scdea.pnn.police.uk
Web: www.scdea.police.uk

Established:
2006, under the Police, Public Order and Criminal Justice (Scotland) Act 2006.

Functions:
- To prevent and detect serious organised crime;
- To contribute to the reduction of such crime in other ways and to the mitigation of its consequences;
- To gather, store and analyse information relevant to:
    (i) the prevention, detection, investigation or prosecution of offences; or
    (ii) the reduction of crime in other ways or the mitigation of its consequences.

Director-General and Deputy
Chief Constable .Mr Gordon Meldrum

Scottish Criminal Cases Review Commission
5th Floor, Portland House
17 Renfield Street, Glasgow, G2 5AH
Tel: (0141) 270 7030 Fax: (0141) 270 7040
E-mail: info@sccrc.org.uk
Web: www.sccrc.org.uk

Established:
1999, by Section 194A of the Criminal Procedure (Scotland) Act 1995 as amended by Section 25 of the Crime and Punishment (Scotland) Act 1997.

Functions:
The Commission reviews alleged miscarriages of justice in Scottish criminal convictions. After reviewing a case, if the Commission believes that a miscarriage of justice may have occurred and it is in the interests of justice, it may refer the case to the High Court in Edinburgh where the case will be heard as if it were a normal appeal.

Chairman . . . . .Mrs Jean Couper CBE

Chief Executive . . . . .Mr Gerard Sinclair

Scottish Enterprise
Atrium Court, 50 Waterloo Road
Glasgow, G2 6HQ
Tel: (0141) 248 2700 Fax: (0141) 228 2040
Network Helpline: (0845) 607 8787
E-mail: network.helpline@scotnet.co.uk
Web: www.scottish-enterprise.com

Established:
1991, under the Enterprise and New Towns (Scotland Act) 1990.

Functions:
Scottish Enterprise is Scotland's main economic, enterprise innovation and investment agency. Its ultimate goal is to stimulate growth of Scotland's economy.

To achieve this it helps ambitious and innovative businesses grow and become more successful. It also works with public and private sector partners to develop the business environment in Scotland. It delivers a range of dedicated support services locally, nationally, and internationally. Its activities help businesses with the appetite and capacity to grow to:
• Improve efficiencies;
• Access new sources of funding, and
• Conquer new markets.

Scottish Enterprise (Continued)

To build a world-class economy it is interested in industries that have real competitive advantage in Scotland, particularly:
- Energy;
- Life sciences;
- Tourism;
- Financial services;
- Food and drink, and
- Digital markets and enabling technologies.

Scottish Enterprise works in partnership with universities, colleges, local authorities and other public sector bodies to achieve these goals and to maximise its contribution to the Scottish Government's Economic Strategy. It is mainly funded by the Scottish Government, although it also raises part of its budget from other sources, such as property rental and the disposal of assets.

Chairman . . . . .Mr Crawford Gillies

Chief Executive . . . . .Mr Jack Perry

Scottish Environment Protection Agency
Erskine Court, Castle Business Park
Stirling, FK9 4TR
Tel: (01786) 457700 Fax: (01786) 446885
E-mail: info@sepa.org.uk
Web: www.sepa.org.uk

Established:
1996, under the Environment Act 1995.

Function:
Its main duty is to protect the environment in Scotland by regulating pollution of land, air and water.

Chairman . . . . .Professor David Sigsworth

Chief Executive . . . . .Dr Campbell Gemmell

Head of Communications . . . . .Ms Monica Straughan

Scottish Further and Higher Education Funding Council

Donaldson House, 97 Haymarket Terrace
Edinburgh, EH12 5HD
Tel: (0131) 313 6500 Fax: (0131) 313 6501
E-mail: info@sfc.ac.uk
Web: www.sfc.ac.uk

Established:
2005, under the terms of the Further and Higher Education (Scotland) Act 2005. The Council replaced the former Scottish Further Education Funding Council and the Scottish Higher Education Funding Council.

Functions:
The Council's main role is to distribute funding to colleges and universities in Scotland for the support of learning and teaching, research and other activities.

The Council also:
- Provides advice to Scottish Ministers on the needs of the further and higher education sectors and on other policy and funding issues that are relevant to further education and higher education;
- Works with the sectors to develop coherent strategies in support of Ministerial priorities and to ensure that there is coherent provision of high quality FE and HE;
- Has a statutory duty to ensure that the quality of FE and HE in colleges and universities is assessed and enhanced;
- Monitors the financial health of the colleges and universities;
- Supports management and governance in colleges and universities by providing guidance and disseminating good practice on many issues;
- Facilitates and supports desirable strategic changes in the sectors;
- Establishes targets and indicators of performance, and gathers evidence and data to monitor progress, and
- Is responsible for developing policies to promote sustainable development.

Chair . . . . .Mr John McClelland CBE

Chief Executive . . . . .Mr Mark Batho

**Head of Corporate Communications
and External Relations** . . . . .Mr Stephen Crowe

Scottish Industrial Development Advisory Board
Atrium Court, 50 Waterloo Street
Glasgow, G2 6HQ
Tel: (0141) 242 8432 ext: 5674
E-mail: allan.mccabe@scotland.gsi.gov.uk
Web: www.scottishbusinessgrants.gov.uk

Established:
1972, under the Industry Act 1972 and the Scottish Development Agency Act 1975.

Functions:
To advise Scottish Ministers on the exercise of their powers under section 7 of the Industrial Development Act 1982, as devolved under the Scotland Act 1999.

Chairman . . . . .Mr Neil MacDonald

Secretary . . . . .Mr Allan McCabe

Scottish Land Court
George House, 126 George Street
Edinburgh, EH2 4HH
Tel: (0131) 271 4360 Fax: (0131) 271 4399
Web: www.scottish-land-court.org.uk

Established:
The Scottish Land Court was established in terms of the Small Landholders (Scotland) Act 1911 to adjudicate on disputes between tenants and landlords of agricultural subjects in Scotland. The Court is presently constituted in terms of the Scottish Land Court Act 1993.

Functions:
The Land Court adjudicates on disputes in relation to agricultural subjects in terms of:
1. Crofters (Scotland) Act 1993 Crofting Reform (Scotland) Act 2003;
2. Small Landholders (Scotland) Acts 1886 to 1931
3. Agricultural Holdings (Scotland) Acts 1991 and 2003
4. Appeals from decisions of Scottish Ministers in relation to farming subsidies and grants;
5. Appeals from decisions of the Crofters Commission;
6. Certain other miscellaneous jurisdictions.

Membership comprises the Chairman, the Deputy Chairman, one full-time agricultural Member (Mr David Houston) and two part-time agricultural Members (Mr John Smith and Mr Angus Macdonald). To help meet the anticipated workload, Sheriff R J Macleod has been seconded to the Court as Deputy Chairman.

Chairman . . . . .Hon Lord McGhie

Principal Clerk . . . . .Mr Keith Graham

Scottish Law Commission
140 Causewayside, Edinburgh, EH9 1PR
Tel: (0131) 668 2131 Fax: (0131) 662 4900
E-mail: info@scotlawcom.gov.uk
Web: www.scotlawcom.gov.uk

Established:
1965, under the Law Commissions Act 1965.

Functions:
To promote the systematic reform and development of Scots law. This involves preparing reports containing recommendations for reform and submitting them to the Scottish or UK Ministers.

Chairman ....Hon Lord Drummond Young

Chief Executive ....Mr Malcolm McMillan

Scottish Legal Aid Board
44 Drumsheugh Gardens, Edinburgh, EH3 7SW
Tel: (0131) 226 7061 Fax: (0131) 220 4878
Tel: (0845) 122 8686 *(Legal Aid Helpline)*
E-mail: general@slab.org.uk
Web: www.slab.org.uk

Established:
1987, under the Legal Aid (Scotland) Act 1986.

Functions:
- Advising Scottish Ministers on how legal aid is working, and ways to develop it;
- Managing the Legal Aid Fund;
- Deciding whether to grant applications for legal aid;
- Examining solicitors' and advocates' accounts for legal aid work, and paying them for the work they have done;
- Deciding what people have to pay towards the cost of legal assistance and dealing with all collections, refunds and queries;
- Registering firms and solicitors under the Board's Code of Practice in relation to criminal legal assistance and monitoring their continuing compliance;
- Registering firms for civil legal assistance, monitoring each firm's administrative arrangements, and funding quality assurance which is operated by the Law Society of Scotland;
- Investigating and tackling abuse of legal aid;
- Exploring, for example by running pilot schemes, different ways of delivering a legal aid service.

Chairman ....Mr Iain A Robertson CBE

Chief Executive ....Mr Lindsay Montgomery CBE

Scottish Local Authorities Remuneration Committee

Local Democracy Team, Finance and Central Services Division
Victoria Quay, Edinburgh, EH6 6QQ
Tel: (08457) 741741 Fax: (0131) 244 7058

Established:
February 2006, under the Local Governance (Scotland) Act 2004.

Functions:
To prepare and submit to Scottish Ministers advice in relation to the payment by local authorities of remuneration (including pensions) and allowances to, and reimbursement of, expenses incurred by members of local authorities, and the payment of severance payments in relation to members of local authorities. Ministers have also set clear criteria of which the Committee must take account, including the affordability and public acceptability of its advice.

Chairman ....Mr Ian Livingstone CBE

Scottish Natural Heritage

Great Glen House, Leachkin Road, Inverness, IV3 8NW
Tel: (01463) 725000 Fax: (01463) 725067
E-mail: enquiries@snh.gov.uk
Web: www.snh.org.uk

Established:
1992, under the Natural Heritage (Scotland) Act 1991.

Functions:
It advises ministers and others about the management and use of Scotland's natural heritage; and carries out executive duties on behalf of the ministers.
In particular its role is:
  1. To secure the conservation and enhancement of Scotland's unique and precious natural heritage, including wildlife, habitats and landscape;
  2. To advise on policies and promote projects that aim to improve the natural heritage and support its sustainable use;
  3. To help people enjoy Scotland's natural heritage responsibly, understand it more fully and use it wisely so it can be sustained for future generations.

Chairman ....Mr Andrew Thin

Deputy Chairman ....Mr Keith Geddes

Chief Executive ....Dr Ian Jardine

Press and Public Relations Officer ....Ms Heather Kinnin

Scottish Police Services Authority
Elphinstone House
65 West Regent Street, Glasgow, G2 2AF
Tel: (0141) 585 8300 Fax: (0141) 331 1596
Web: www.spsa.police.uk

Established:
2007, under the Police, Public Order and Criminal Justice (Scotland) Act 2006.

Functions:
It provides:
- one of the world's only 'crime scene to court' forensic services supporting both the investigation and prosecution of crime;
- innovative ICT solutions and support for 1,300 applications, 17,000 PCs and laptops, and 21,000 handheld radios across 250 sites;
- vital police information and intelligence systems to over 50 agencies throughout the UK; and
- national training to over 3,000 police officers every year through the award-winning Scottish Policy College.

In addition, we maintain the specialist frontline officers and intelligence staff for the Scottish Crime and Drug Enforcement Agency (SCDEA).

Convener . . . . .Mr Vic Emery OBE

**Director-General, Scottish Crime
and Drug Enforcement Agency** . . . . .Deputy Chief Constable Gordon Meldrum

Director, Forensic Services . . . . .Mr Tom Nelson

Director, Scottish Police College . . . . .Assistant Chief Constable John Geates

Head of Criminal Justice . . . . .Superintendent Carol McLean

Chief Information Officer . . . . .Ms Jan Thompson

Scottish Qualifications Authority
The Optima Building, 58 Robertson Street, Glasgow, G2 8DQ
Tel: (0845) 279 1000 Fax: (0845) 213 5000
E-mail: customer@sqa.org.uk
Web: www.sqa.org.uk

Established:
1997, under the Education (Scotland) Act 1996.

Functions:
The Scottish Qualifications Authority (SQA) is the national body in Scotland for the development, assessment, certification and accreditation of qualifications other than degrees and some professional qualifications.

Chairman . . . . .Mr Graham Houston

Chief Executive . . . . .Dr Janet Brown

Media Consultant .Mr Derek Douglas

Scottish Screen
249 West George Street, Glasgow, G2 4QE
Tel: (0845) 300 7300
E-mail: info@scottishscreen.com
Web: www.scottishscreen.com

Established:
1997, as a company limited by guarantee.

Functions:
Scottish Screen is the national development agency for the screen industries in Scotland. It exists to inspire audiences, support new and established talent and businesses, and promote Scotland as a creative place to make great films, award-winning television and world renowned digital entertainment.

Chairman . . . . .Dr Richard Halloway

Chief Executive . . . . .Mr Ken Hay

Head of Inward Investment and
Communications . . . . .Ms Celia Stevenson

Scottish Social Services Council
Compass House, 11 Riverside Drive, Dundee, DD1 4NY
Tel: (01382) 207101 Fax: (01382) 207215
Information Line: (0845) 6030891
E-mail: enquiries@sssc.uk.com
Web: www.sssc.uk.com

Established:
1st October 2001, under the Regulation of Care (Scotland) Act 2001.

Functions:
- to establish registers of key groups of social services staff;
- to publish codes of practice for all social services workers and their employers;
- to regulate the training and education of the workforce;
- to undertake the functions of the Sector Skills Council: Skills for Care and Development
- to promote education and training

Convener . . . . .Mr Garry Coutts

Chief Executive . . . . .Ms Anna Fowlie

Communications Manager . . . . .Ms Nicky Scott

Public Affairs Adviser . . . . .Ms Lorraine Gray

Scottish Water
Castle House, 6 Castle Drive, Carnegie Campus
Dunfermline, KY11 8GG
Tel: (01383) 848200 Fax: (01383) 848371
E-mail: customer.service@scottishwater.co.uk
Web: www.scottishwater.co.uk
Established:
2002, under the Water Industry (Scotland) Act 2002.

Functions:
The provision of water and waste water services to communities in Scotland.

Chairman . . . . .Mr Ronnie Mercer

Chief Executive . . . . .Mr Richard Ackroyd

Skills Development Scotland

150 Broomielaw, Atlantic Quay, Glasgow, G2 8LU
Tel: (0141) 225 6710 Fax: (0141) 225 6711
E-mail: info@skillsdevelopmentscotland.co.uk
Web: www.skillsdevelopmentscotland.co.uk

Established:
2008. It is a non-departmental public body and a company limited by guarantee.

Functions:
Skills Development Scotland is the new national skills body for Scotland delivering: Careers Scotland, Get Ready for Work, ILA Scotland, learndirect scotland, learndirect scotland for business, Modern Apprenticeships, Skillseekers, The Big Plus and Training for Work.

Chairman . . . . .Mr William Roe

Chief Executive . . . . .Mr Damien Yeates

Corporate Communications . . . . .Ms Audrey Simpson

sportscotland

Doges, Templeton on the Green
62 Templeton Street, Glasgow, G40 1DA
Tel: (0141) 534 6500
E-mail: sportscotland.enquiries@sportscotland.org.uk
Web: www.sportscotland.org.uk

Established:
1972, by Royal Charter.

Functions:
The development of sport in Scotland. It has an executive role; and it is also responsible for distributing National Lottery funding for sports programmes in Scotland.

Chairman . . . . .Ms Louise Martin CBE

Chief Executive . . . . .Mr Stewart Harris

Standards Commission for Scotland

44 Drumsheugh Gardens, Edinburgh, EH3 7SW
Tel: (0131) 260 5368 Fax: (0131) 220 5941
E-mail: enquiries@standardscommission.org.uk
Web: www.standardscommissionscotland.org.uk

The Office of the Chief Investigating Officer

44 Drumsheugh Gardens, Edinburgh, EH3 7SW
Tel: (0300) 011 0550 Fax: (0131) 220 5941
E-mail: investigations@ethicalstandards.org.uk
Web: www.standardscommissionscotland.org.uk

Established:
2001, under the Ethical Standards in Public Life (Scotland) Act 2000.

Functions:
The Standards Commission for Scotland is an independent body set up to encourage high standards in public life through the promotion and enforcement of Codes of Conducts for Councillors and Members of Public Bodies. Complaints about misconduct by Councillors and Members of Public Bodies are investigated by the Chief Investigating Officer, whose function is entirely separate from the Commission, The Commission adjudicates on reports of alleged breaches submitted by the Chief Investigating Officer.

The Commission may decide to direct the Chief Investigating Officer to carry out further investigation, hold a Hearing, or take no action. If the Commission holds a Hearing and decides that there has been a breach of the Code, the Commission will impose a sanction of censure, or suspension (for up to one year), or disqualification from the office (for up to five years).

Convener . . . . .Mrs Wendy Goldstraw

Chief Investigating Officer . . . . .Mr D Stuart Allan

Secretary to the Commission . . . . .Ms Janet Nixon

VisitScotland
Ocean Point One, 94 Ocean Drive
Edinburgh, EH6 6JH
Tel: (0131) 472 2222 Fax: (0131) 472 2250
E-mail: [firstname.surname]@visitscotland.com
Web: www.visitscotland.org

Established:
1969, under the Development of Tourism Act 1969 as the Scottish Tourist Board. VisitScotland gained additional responsibilities for the promotion abroad of Scotland, as a destination for foreign tourists under the Tourism (Overseas Promotion) (Scotland) Act 1984. It was renamed VisitScotland in August 2001. (The name was formally changed under the Tourist Boards (Scotland) Act 2006.

Functions:
Its principal functions are:
1. To encourage tourists to visit Scotland;
2. To encourage the provision of tourist facilities and amenities in Scotland;
3. To advise government and public bodies on matters relating to tourism in Scotland.

Chairman . . . . .Mr Peter Lederer CBE

Chief Executive . . . . .Mr Philip Riddle OBE

Head of Communications . . . . .Mrs Barbara Clark

Water Industry Commission for Scotland
Ochil House, Springkerse Business Park
Stirling, FK7 7XE
Tel: (01786) 430200 Fax: (01786) 462018
E-mail: enquiries@watercommission.co.uk
Web: www.watercommission.co.uk

Established:
2005, under the Water Services (Scotland) Act 2005. It replaced the Water Industry Commissioner for Scotland.

Functions:
To promote the interests of persons whose premises are connected, or might reasonably become connected, to the public water supply system or the public sewerage system or both relating to the provision to them of water and sewage services.

Chairman . . . . .Sir Ian Byatt

Chief Executive . . . . .Mr Alan Sutherland

Other Public Bodies

Note: (i) This is not an exhaustive list. More information on Non Departmental Public Bodies can be found in 'The Guide to Executive Agencies & Public Bodies – 'Quangos'' published annually by Carlton Publishing and Printing.

Administration of Radioactive Substances Advisory Committee
ARSAC Secretariat, HPA, Chilton, Didcot, Oxford, OX11 0RQ
Tel: (01235) 887887 Fax: (01235) 834925
E-mail: arsac@hpa.org.uk
Web: www.arsac.org.uk

Chairman . . . . .Dr Thomas Nunan

Secretary . . . . .Mr Steve Ebdon-Jackson

Administrative Justice and Tribunals Council Scottish Committee
George House, 126 George Street, Edinburgh, EH2 4HH
Tel: (0131) 271 4300 Fax: (0131) 271 4309
E-mail: gordon.quinn@ajtc.gsi.gov.uk
Web: www.ajtc.gov.uk/scottish

Chairman . . . . .Mr Richard Henderson

Secretary . . . . .Ms Debbie Davidson

Advisory Board on the Registration of Homeopathic Products
c/o Market Towers, 1 Nine Elms Lane, London, SW8 5NQ
Tel: (020) 7084 2451
E-mail: info@mhra.gsi.gov.uk
Web: www.mhra.gov.uk

Chairman . . . . .Dr Timothy Chambers OBE

Secretary . . . . .Mr Leslie Whitbread

Advisory Committee on Antimicrobial Resistance and Healthcare Associated Infections
ARHAI Scientific Secretariat, Health Protection Agency
61 Colindale Avenue, London, NW9 5DF
Tel: (020) 8327 6689
Web: www.dh.gov.uk/ab/arhai

Chairman . . . . .Professor Roger Finch

Secretary . . . . .Dr Marika Collin

Advisory Committee on Borderline Substances
NHS Purchasing and Supply Agency
80 Lightfoot Street
Chester, CH2 3AD
Tel: (01244) 586767 Fax: (01244) 586760
E-mail: ACBS@pasa.nhs.uk
Web: www.pasa.nhs.uk

Chairman . . . . .Sir Mike Rowlands

Secretary . . . . .Mr Philip Grieve

Advisory Committee on Dangerous Pathogens
Virus Reference Department, Health Protection Agency
61 Colindale Avenue, London, NW9 5EQ
Tel: (020) 8200 6868
E-mail: acdp@hpa.org.uk
Web: www.dh.gov.uk/ab/acdp/index.htm

Chairman . . . . .Professor George Griffin

Secretary . . . . .Mrs Amanda Furlonger *(DEFRA)*
Mr Lee Wilson *(HSE)*

Advisory Committee on Hazardous Substances
Area 2A, Nobel House
17 Smith Square
London, SW1P 3JR
Tel: (020) 7238 5400
E-mail: chemicals.strategy@defra.gsi.gov.uk
Web: www.defra.gov.uk/environment/quality/chemicals.achs

Chairman . . . . .Professor Stephen Holgate CBE

Secretary . . . . .Dr Paola Casjanelli

Advisory Committee on Historic Wreck Sites
c/o English Heritage, 1 Waterhouse Square
138-142 Holborn, London, EC1N 2ST
Tel: (020) 7973 3243 Fax: (020) 7973 3111
Web: www.culture.gov.uk

Chairman . . . . .Mr Tom Hassall OBE

Clerk . . . . .Ms Sarah Baylis

Advisory Committee on Pesticides
Mallard House, Kings Pool
3 Peasholme Green
York, YO1 7PX
Tel: (01904) 455702 Fax: (01904) 455711
E-mail: acp@hse.gsi.gov.uk
Web: www.pesticides.gov.uk

Chairman . . . . .Professor Jon Ayres

Secretary . . . . .Mrs Jayne Wilder

Advisory Committee on Releases to the Environment
Area 8A, Nobel House, 17 Smith Square
London, SW1P 3JR
Tel: (020) 7238 2051 Fax: (020) 7238 6009
E-mail: acre.secretariat@defra.gsi.gov.uk
Web: www.defra.gov.uk/environment/acre

Chairman . . . . .Professor Chris Pollock CBE

Secretary . . . . .Dr Louise Ball

Advisory Council on the Misuse of Drugs
3rd Floor, Seacole Building, 2 Marsham Street, London, SW1P 4DF
Tel: (020) 7035 0454
E-mail: acmd@drugs.gov.uk
Web: www.drugs.gov.uk/drug-laws/acmd

Chairman . . . . .Professor David Nutt

Secretary . . . . .Mr William Reynolds

Advisory Group on Hepatitis
Expert Advice Support Office, Health Protection Agency
61 Colindale Avenue, London, NW9 5EQ
Tel: (020) 8327 6688 Fax (020) 8327 6007
E-mail: agh@hpa.org.uk
Web: www.advisorybodies.doh.gov.uk/agh.index.htm

Chairman . . . . .Professor William Irving

Scientific Secretary . . . . .Mr Chris Lucas

Agriculture and Horticulture Development Board
Stoneleigh Park, Kenilworth, Warwickshire, CV8 2TL
Tel: (0247) 669 2051
Web: www.adhb.org.uk

Chairman . . . . .Dr John Bridge

Chief Executive . . . . .Mr Kevin Roberts

Air Quality Expert Group
Area 3C, Ergon House, 17 Smith Square, London, SW1P 3JR
Tel: (020) 7238 3059 Fax: (020) 7238 1657
E-mail: air.quality@defra.gsi.gov.uk
Web: www.defra.gov.uk/environment/airquality/panels/aqeg/group/index.htm

Chairman . . . . .Professor Mike Pilling

Secretary . . . . .Dr Clare Bayley

Alcohol Education and Research Council
Room 178, Queen Anne Business Centre
28 Broadway, London, SW1H 9JX
Tel: (020) 7340 9502
E-mail: info@aerc.org.uk
Web: www.aerc.org.uk

Chairman . . . . .Professor Robin Davidson

Director . . . . .Professor Ray Hodgson

Animal Procedures Committee
3rd Floor, Seacole SW Quarter
2 Marsham Street, London, SW1P 4DF
Tel: (020) 7035 4578 Fax: (020) 7035 1113
E-mail: apc.secretariat@homeoffice.gov.uk
Web: www.apc.gov.uk

Chairman . . . . .Ms Sara Nathan

Secretary . . . . .Mr Phil Banks

Armed Forces' Pay Review Body
Office of Manpower Economics, Kingsgate House
66-74 Victoria Street, London, SW1E 6SW
Tel: (020) 7215 8534 Fax: (020) 7215 4445
Web: www.ome.uk.com

Chairman . . . . .Professor David Greenway

Secretary . . . . .Mr Tony Symmonds

Asylum and Immigration Tribunal
Field House, 15 Breams Buildings
London, EC4A 1DZ
Tel: (0845) 600 0877 Fax: (020) 7073 4007
E-mail: alex.jary@tribunals.gsi.gov.uk
Web: www.ait.gov.uk

President . . . . *Vacant*

Deputy Presidents . . . . Judge E Arfon-Jones
Judge Mark Ockelton

Centre Manager *(Field House)* . . . . .Mr Mike Reed

Asylum Support Tribunal
Christopher Wren House, 113 High Street,
Croydon, CR0 1QG
Tel: (0844) 798 1212 Fax: (0844) 798 3945
Web: www.asylum-support-tribunal.gov.uk

Chief Adjudicator . . . . .Ms Sehba Haroon Storey

Audit Commission
1st Floor, Millbank Tower
Millbank, London, SW1P 4HQ
Tel: (0844) 798 1212 Fax: (0844) 798 3945
E-mail: enquiries@audit-commission.gov.uk
Web: www.audit-commission.gov.uk

Chair . . . . .Mr Michael O'Higgins

Chief Executive . . . . .Mr Steve Bundred

Bank of England
Threadneedle Street, London, EC2R 8AH
Tel: (020) 7601 4444 Fax: (020) 7601 5460
E-mail: enquiries@bankofengland.co.uk
Web: www.bankofengland.co.uk

Governor . . . . .Mr Mervyn King

Secretary of the Bank . . . . .Mr Andrew Wardlow

BBC Trust
Room 211, 35 Marylebone High Street, London, W1U 4AA
Tel: (020) 7208 9377
E-mail: trust.enquiries@bbc.co.uk
Web: www.bbc.co.uk/bbctrust

Chairman . . . . .Sir Michael Lyons

Scotland Office:
Broadcasting House, Queen Margaret Drive, Glasgow, G12 8DG
Tel: (0141) 339 8844 Fax: (0141) 334 0614

Trustee, BBC Trust Scotland . . . . .Mr Jeremy Peat

Controller, BBC Scotland . . . . .Mr Ken MacQuarrie

Big Lottery Fund
1 Plough Place, London, EC4A 1DE
Tel: (0300) 500 5050 Fax: (020) 7842 4010
E-mail: general.enquiries@biglotteryfund.org.uk
Web: www.biglotteryfund.org.uk

Chairman . . . . .Professor Sir Clive Booth

Chief Executive . . . . .Mr Peter Wanless

Scotland Office
1 Atlantic Quay, 1 Robertson Street,
Glasgow, G2 8JB
Tel: (0141) 242 1400   Fax: (0141) 242 1401
E-mail: enquiries.scotland@biglotteryfund.org.uk

Chairman, Scotland . . . . .Ms Alison Magee

Director for Scotland . . . . .Mr Dharmendra Kanani

Biotechnology and Biological Sciences Research Council
Polaris House, North Star Avenue,Swindon, SN2 1UH
Tel: (01793) 413200 Fax: (01793) 413201
Web: www.bbsrc.ac.uk

Chairman . . . . .Professor Sir Tom Blundell

Chief Executive . . . . .Professor Douglas Kell

British Council
10 Spring Gardens, London, SW1A 2BN
Tel: (020) 7930 8466 Fax: (020) 7839 6347
E-mail: general enquiries@british council.org
Web: www.britishcouncil.org

Chairman *(Acting)* . . . . .Mr Gerard Lemos

Director-General . . . . .Mr Martin Davidson CMG

British Hallmarking Council
1 Colmore Square, Birmingham, B4 6AA
Tel: (0870) 763 1414 Fax: (0870) 763 1814
E-mail: david.gwyther@martjohn.com
Web: www.britishhallmarkingcouncil.gov.uk

Chairman . . . . .Mr Tom Murray

Secretary . . . . .Mr David Gwyther

British Library
96 Euston Road, London, NW1 2DB
Tel: (0870) 444 1500 Fax: (020) 7412 7340
E-mail: customer.services@bl.uk
Web: www.bl.uk

Chairman, British Library Board . . . . .Sir Colin Lucas

Chief Executive . . . . .Dame Lynne Brindley

British Museum
Great Russell Street, London, WC1B 3DG
Tel: (020) 7232 8000
E-mail: information@thebritishmuseum.ac.uk
Web: www.thebritishmuseum.ac.uk

Chairman of the Trustees . . . . .Sir Niall Fitzgerald

Director . . . . .Mr Neil MacGregor

British Nuclear Fuels plc
1100 Daresbury Park, Daresbury, Warrington, Cheshire, WA4 4GB
Tel: (01925) 832000 Fax (01925) 822711
E-mail: [firstname.surname@bnfl.com
Web: www.bnfl.com

Chairman . . . . .Mr Gordon Campbell

Chief Executive . . . . .Mr Michael Parker

British Pharmacopeia Commission
10th Floor, Market Towers, 1 Nine Elms Lane, London, SW8 5NQ
Tel: (020) 7084 2561 Fax: (020) 7084 2566
E-mail: bpcom@mhra.gsi.gov.uk
Web: www.pharmacopoeia.gov.uk

Chairman ....Professor David Woolfson

Secretary and Scientific Director ....Dr Gerard Lee

British Transport Police Authority
The Forum, 5th Floor, 74-80 Camden Street
London, NW1 0EG
Tel: (020) 7383 0259 Fax: (020) 7383 2655
E-mail: general.enquiries@btpa.police.uk
Web: www.bt-police.co.uk

Chairman, British Transport
Police Authority ....Ms Millie Banerjee CBE

Chief Executive and Clerk *(Acting)* ....Mr Paul Coen

Chief Constable ....Mr Andrew Trotter

Authority Member for Scotland ....Mr James King

Scotland Office
90 Cowcaddens Road, Glasgow, G4 0LU
Tel 0141 335 3899 Fax: (0141) 335 2155

Area Commander ....Superintendent Ronnie Mellis

British Waterways Board
64 Clarendon Road
Watford, Hertfordshire, WD17 1DA
Tel: (01923) 201120 Fax: (01923) 201400
E-mail: enquiries.hq@bwmedia.co.uk
Web: www.britishwaterways.co.uk

Chairman ....Mr Tony Hales CBE

Chief Executive ....Mr Robin Evans

Scotland Office
Canal House, Apple Cross Street, Glasgow, G4 9SP
Tel 0141 332 6936 Fax: (0141) 331 1688
E-mail: enquiries.scotland@britishwaterways.co.uk

Director, Scotland ....Mr Steve Dunlop

Business Council for Britain
1 Victoria Street, London, SW1H 0ET
Tel: (020) 7215 2781
E-mail: bcbsecretariat@berr.gsi.gov.uk

Chairman ....Mr Mervyn Davies CBE

Central Advisory Committee on Pensions and Compensation
Service Personnel Policy Pensions, MoD Main Building
Whitehall, London, SW1A 2HB
Tel: (01253) 332886
Web: www.veterans-uk.info

Chairman ....Mr Kevan Jones MP

Secretary ....Mr Lee Mansfield

Channel 4 Television Corporation
124 Horseferry Road, London, SW1P 2TX
Tel: (020) 7396 4444 Fax: (020) 7306 8397
E-mail: viewer_enqs@channel4.co.uk
Web: www.channel 4.com

Chairman ....Lord [Terry] Burns

Chief Executive *(Acting)* ....Ms Anne Bulford

Child Maintenance and Enforcement Commission
Caxton House, Tothill Street, London, SW1H 9NA
Tel: (0845) 713 3133
Web: www.childmaintenance.org

Chair ....Ms Janet Paraskeva

Chief Executive ....Mr Stephen Geraghty

Civil Aviation Authority
CAA House, 45-59 Kingsway, London, WC2B 6TE
Tel: (020) 7453 6030
Web: www.caa.co.uk

Chairman ....Dame Deirdre Hutton

Chief Executive ....Mr Andrew Haines

Civil Nuclear Constabulary
Culham Science Centre, Abingdon, Oxfordshire, OX14 3DB
Tel: (01235) 466606 Fax: (01235) 466279
Web: www.cnc.police.uk

Chief Constable ....Mr Richard Thompson

Civil Service Appeal Board
Room G32, 22 Whitehall, London, SW1A 2WH
Tel: (020) 7276 3832 Fax: (020) 7276 3836
E-mail: keithwright@cabinet-office.x.gsi.gov.uk
Web: www.civilserviceappealboard.gov.uk

Chairman . . . . .Mr John Davies OBE

Secretary . . . . .Mr Keith Wright

Coal Authority
200 Lichfield Lane, Mansfield
Nottinghamshire, NG18 4RG
Tel: (01623) 637000 Fax: (01623) 622072
E-mail: thecoalauthority@coal.gov.uk
Web: www.coal.gov.uk

Chairman . . . . .Dr Helen Mounsey

Chief Executive . . . . .Mr Philip Lawrence

Commission for Integrated Transport
2nd Floor, 55 Victoria Street, London, SW1H 0EU
Tel: (020) 7944 8131
E-mail: cfit@dft.gsi.gov.uk
Web: www.cfit.gov.uk

Chairman . . . . .Mr Peter Hendy CBE

Secretary . . . . .Mr Matt Coleman

Commission on Human Medicines
4/1, Market Towers, 1 Nine Elms Lane
London, SW18 5NQ
Tel: (020) 7084 2451 Fax: (020) 7084 2453
E-mail: leslie.whitbread@mhra.gsi.gov.uk
Web: www.mhra.gov.uk

Chairman . . . . .Professor Sir Gordon Duff

Secretary . . . . .Mr Leslie Whitbread

Committee on Carcinogenicity of Chemicals in Food, Consumer Products and the Environment
Wellington House, 133-155 Waterloo Road
London, SE1 8UG
Tel: (020) 7972 4946 Fax: (020) 7972 1001
Web: www.advisorybodies.doh.gov.uk/com/index.htm

Chairman . . . . .Professor David Phillips

Contact . . . . .Ms Sue Kennedy

Committee on Climate Change
4th Floor, Manning House
22 Carlisle Place, London, SW1P 1JA
Tel: (020) 7592 1520 Fax: (020) 7592 1583
E-mail: enquiries@theccc.gsi.gov.uk
Web: www.theccc.gov.uk

Chairman . . . . .Lord [Adair] Turner

Chief Executive . . . . .Mr David Kennedy

Committee on Medical Aspects of Radiation in the Environment
c/o Health Protection Agency, Radiation Protection Division
Chilton, Didcot, Oxfordshire, OX11 0RQ
Tel: (01235) 822629 Fax: (01235) 832447
E-mail: comare@hpa.org
Web: www.comare.org.uk

Chairman . . . . .Professor Alex Elliott

Secretariat . . . . .Dr Roy Hamlet

Committee on Mutagenicity of Chemicals in Food, Consumer Products and the Environment
Room 523, Wellington House
133-155 Waterloo Road, London, SE1 8UG
Tel: (020) 7972 4946 Fax: (020) 7972 1001
E-mail: khandu.mistry@dh.gsi.gov.uk
Web: www.iacom.org.uk

Chairman . . . . .Professor Peter Farmer

Contact . . . . .Mr Khandu Mistry

Committee on Standards in Public Life
35 Great Smith Street
London, SW1P 3BQ
Tel: (020) 7276 2595 Fax: (020) 7276 2585
E-mail: public@standards.x.gsi.gov.uk
Web: www.public-standards.gov.uk

Chairman . . . . .Sir Christopher Kelly KCB

Secretary . . . . .Ms Ruth Alaile

Committee on the Medical Effects of Air Pollutants
Health Protection Agency
Centre for Radiation and Chemical Hazards
Chilton, Didcot, Oxfordshire, OX11 0RQ
Tel: (01235) 822895
E-mail: sue.kennedy@hpa.org.uk
Web: www.advisorybodies.doh.gov.uk/comeap

Chairman . . . . .Professor Jon Ayres

Secretary . . . . .Ms Sue Kennedy

Competition Commission
Victoria House, Southampton Row
London, WC1B 4AD
Tel: (020) 7271 0100 Fax: (020) 7271 0367
E-mail: info@cc.gsi.gov.uk
Web: www.competition-commission.org.uk

Chairman . . . . .Mr Peter Freeman

Chief Executive and Secretary . . . . .Mr David Saunders

Consumer Credit Appeals Tribunal
15-19 Bedford Avenue
London, WC1B 3AS
Tel: (020) 7612 9700 Fax: (020) 7436 4151
E-mail: ccat@tribunals.gsi.gov.uk
Web: www.financeandtribunals.gov.uk

President . . . . .Sir Stephen Oliver

Consumer Focus
4th Floor, Artillery House
Artillery Row, London, SW1P 1RT
Tel: (020) 7799 7900 Fax: (020) 7799 7901
Web: www.consumerfocus.org.uk

Chairman . . . . .Lord [Larry] Whitty

Chief Executive . . . . .Mr Ed Mayo

Consumer Focus Scotland
100 Queen Street, Glasgow, G1 3DN
Tel: (0141) 226 5261

Copyright Tribunal
Concept House, Cardiff Road, Newport
South Wales, NP10 8QQ
Tel: (01633) 811035 Fax: (01633) 811175
Minicom: 08459 222250
E-mail: copyright.tribunal@patent.gov.uk
Web: www.ipo.gov.uk/tribunal

Chairman . . . . .His Honour Judge Fysh QC

Secretary . . . . .Mrs Sally Howls

Council for Healthcare Regulatory Excellence
1st Floor, Kierran Cross, 11 The Strand, London, WC2N 5HR
Tel: (020) 7389 8030 Fax: (020) 7389 8040
Web: www.chre.org.uk

Chairman . . . . .Baroness [Jill] Pitkeathley OBE

Chief Executive . . . . .Mr Harry Cayton OBE

Council for Science and Technology
Bay 261, Kingsgate House
66-74 Victoria Street, London, SW1E 6SW
Tel: (020) 3300 8510 Fax: (020) 3300 8980
E-mail: cstinfo@dti.gsi.gov.uk
Web: www.cst.gov.uk

Co-Chairmen . . . . .Professor John Beddington *(Government's Chief Scientific Adviser)*
Professor Janet Finch

Secretary . . . . .Dr Peter Brooke

Criminal Injuries Compensations Appeals Panel
11th Floor, Cardinal Tower, 12 Farringdon Road
London, EC1M 3HS
Tel: (020) 7549 4600 Fax: (020) 7549 4643
E-mail: enquiries-cicap@tribunals.gsi.gov.uk
Web: www.tribunals.gov.uk

Chairman . . . . .Mr Roger Goodier

Senior Operations Officer . . . . .Mrs Jo Taylor

Scotland Office
Wellington House, 134-136 Wellington Street, Glasgow, G2 2XL
Tel: (0141) 354 8555 Fax: (0141) 354 8520

Criminal Injuries Compensations Authority
Tay House, 300 Bath Street, Glasgow, G2 4LN
Tel: (0800) 358 3601 Fax: (0141) 332 1560
Web: www.cica.gov.uk

Chief Executive . . . . .Ms Carole Oatway

Darwin Initiative Advisory Committee
Area 3D, Nobel House
17 Smith Square, London, SW1P 3JR
Tel: (020) 7238 5250
E-mail: darwin@defra.gsi.gov.uk
Web: www.darwin.defra.gov.uk

Chairman . . . . .Professor David Macdonald

Secretary . . . . .Mr Eric Blencowe

Disability Living Allowance Advisory Board
Caxton House, 6-12 Tothill Street
London, SW1H 9NA
Tel: (020) 7962 8982 Fax: (020) 7962 0647
E-mail: dlaab-consultation@dlp.gsi.gov.uk
Web: www.dwp.gov.uk/ndpb/dlaab

Chairman . . . . .Mrs Anne Spight MBE

Medical Secretary . . . . .Dr Roger Thomas

Disabled Persons Transport Advisory Committee
Zone 2/23, Great Minster House
76 Marsham Street, London, SW1P 4DR
Tel: (020) 7944 8012 Fax: (020) 7944 6998
E-mail: dptac@dft.gov.uk
Web: www.dptac.gov.uk

Chairman ....Mr Dai Powell OBE

Secretary ....Mr Jimi Adeleye

Economic and Social Research Council
Polaris House, North Star Avenue, Swindon, SN2 1UJ
Tel: (01793) 413000 Fax: (01793) 413001
E-mail: [firstname.surname]@esrc.ac.uk
Web: www.esrc.ac.uk

Chairman ....Dr Alan Gillespie CBE

Chief Executive ....Professor Ian Diamond

Electoral Commission
Trevelyan House, Great Peter Street
London, SW1P 2HW
Tel: (020) 7271 0500 Fax: (020) 7271 0505
E-mail: info@electoralcommission.org.uk
Web: www.electoralcommission.org.uk

Chairman ....Ms Jenny Watson

Chief Executive ....Mr Peter Wardle

Scotland Office
38 Thistle Street, Edinburgh, EH2 1EN
Tel: (0131) 225 0200 Fax: (0131) 225 0205
E-mail: infoscotland@electoral commission.org.uk
Web: www.electoralcommission.org.uk

Head of Office ....Mr Andy O'Neill

Employment Tribunals
Victory House, 30-34 Kingsway, London, WC2B 6EX
Tel: (020) 7273 8603
Web: www.ets.gov.uk

President Scotland ....Mr Colin Milne

Secretary Scotland ....Doug Easton

Engineering and Physical Sciences Research Council
Polaris House, North Star Avenue
Swindon, SN2 1ET
Tel: (01793) 444000 Helpline: (01793) 444100
E-mails: [firstname.surname]@epsrc.ac.uk
infoline@epsrc.ac.uk *(Helpline)*
Web: www.epsrc.ac.uk

Chairman . . . . .Mr John Armitt

Chief Executive . . . . .Professor David Delpy

Scotland Office
Optima Building, 58 Robertson Street
Glasgow, G2 8DU
Tel: (0845) 604 5510: (0141) 228 5912
E-mail: scotland@eoc.org.uk
Web: www.eoc.org.uk

Commissioner for Scotland . . . . .Ms Morag Alexander

Director . . . . .Mr Ross Micklem

Equality and Human Rights Commission
2nd Floor, Arndale House, The Arndale Centre
Manchester, M4 3AQ
Tel: (0161) 829 8110 Fax: (0161) 829 8110
E-mail: info@equalityhumanrights.com
Web: www.equalityhumanrights.com

Chairman . . . . .Sir Trevor Phillips

Chief Executive *(Acting)* . . . . .Mr Neil Kinghan

Scotland Office
Optima Building, 58 Robertson Street, Glasgow, G2 8DU
Tel: (0845) 604 5510: (0141) 228 5912
E-mail: scotland@equalityhumanrights.com

Director . . . . Ms Ros Micklen

Equality 2025
Caxton House, 6-12 Tothill Street, London, SW1H 9NA
Tel: (0845) 460 2025
E-mail: info@equality2025.org
Web: www.officefordisability.gov.uk

Chairman . . . . Ms Rowan Jade

PUBLIC BODIES

Expert Advisory Group on Aids
Centre for Infections, Health Protection Agency
61 Colindale Avenue, London, NW9 5DF
Tel: (020) 8327 6057 Fax: (020) 8327 6007
E-mail: eaga@hpa.org.uk
Web: www.dh.gov.uk/ab/eaga/index.htm

Chairman . . . . .Professor Brian Gazzard

Scientific Secretary . . . . .Dr Linda Lazarus

Expert Panel on Air Quality Standards
Area 3C, Ergon House, 17 Smith Square
London, SW1P 2AL
Tel: (0845) 933 5577 Fax: (020) 7238 2188
E-mail: air.quality@defra.gsi.gov.uk
Web: www.defra.gov.uk/environment/airquality/aqs/index.htm

Chairman . . . . .Professor Stephen Holgate

Secretary . . . . .Dr Sarah Honour

First-tier Tax Tribunal
45 Bedford Square, London, WC1B 3DN
Tel: (020) 7612 9700 Fax: (020) 7436 4150
Web: www.tribunal.gov.uk/tax

President . . . . .His Honour Sir Stephen Oliver QC

Tribunal Manager . . . . .Ms Heather Neames

Edinburgh Office
George House, 126 George Street
Edinburgh, EH2 4HH
Tel: (0131) 226 3551 Fax: (0131) 220 6817

Tribunal Manager . . . . .Mrs Josephine Clancy

Gambling Commission
4th Floor, Victoria Square House, Victoria Square,
Birmingham B2 4BP
Tel: (0121) 230 6666 Fax: (0121) 230 6720
E-mail: info@gamblingcommission.gov.uk
Web: www.gamblingcommission.gov.uk

Chairman . . . . .Mr Brian Pomeroy CBE

Chief Executive .Mrs Jenny Williams

PUBLIC BODIES

Gangmasters Licensing Authority
PO Box 8538, Nottingham, NG8 9AF
Tel: (0845) 602 5020
E-mail: enquiries@gla.gsi.gov.uk
Web: www.gla.gov.uk

Chairman . . . . .Mr Paul Whitehouse

Chief Executive . . . . .Dr Ian Livsey

Gene Therapy Advisory Committee
Area 604, Wellington House
133-155 Waterloo Road, London, SE1 8UG
Tel: (020) 7972 3057 Fax: (020) 7972 4300
E-mail: gtac@dh.gsi.gov.uk
Web: www.dh.gov.uk/ab/gtac/index.htm

Chairman . . . . .Professor Martin Gore

Secretary . . . . .Dr John Connolly

Genetics and Insurance Committee
Area 604, Wellington House
133-155 Waterloo Road, London, SE1 8UG
Tel: (020) 7972 4351 Fax: (020) 7972 4300
E-mail: mb-gaic@doh.gov.uk
Web: www.dh.gov.uk/genetics/gaic.htm

Chairman . . . . .Professor David Johns CBE

Secretary . . . . .Mr Daniel Gooch

Health and Safety Executive
Redgrave Court, Merton Road, Bootle, L20 7HS
Tel: (0845) 345 0055
E-mail: chair@hse.gsi.gov.uk
Web: www.hse.gov.uk

Chairman . . . . .Ms Judith Hackitt

Chief Executive . . . . .Mr Geoffrey Podger

Scotland Office
Belford House, 59 Belford Road
Edinburgh, EH4 3UE
Tel: (0131) 247 2090 Fax: (0131) 247 2130

Director, Scotland .Mr Paul Stollard

Health Protection Agency
7th Floor, Holborn Gate, 330 High Holborn, London, WC1V 7PP
Tel: (020) 7758 2792 Fax: (020) 7759 2840
E-mail: webteam@hpa.org.uk
Web: www.hpa.org.uk

Chairman . . . . .Sir William Stewart

Chief Executive . . . . .Mr Justin McCracken

Herbal Medicines Advisory Committee
4/1 Market Towers, 1 Nine Elms Lane, London, SW8 5NQ
Tel: (020) 7084 3723
E-mail: lorraine.geear@mhra.gsi.gov.uk
Web: www.mhra.gov.uk

Chairman . . . . .Professor Philip Routledge OBE

Secretary . . . . .Ms Lorraine Geear

Honours Committees
Honours and Appointments Secretariat, Cabinet Office
Admiralty Arch (South), The Mall, London, SW1A 2WH
Tel: (020) 7276 2777 Fax: (020) 7276 2766
E-mail: honours@cabinet-office.x.gsi.gov.uk
Web: www.direct.gov.uk/honours

Ceremonial Officer . . . . .Mr Denis Brennan

House of Lords Appointments Commission
35 Great Smith Street, Westminster, London, SW1P 3BQ
Tel: (020) 7276 2005 Fax: (020) 7276 2109
E-mail: enquiry@lordsappointments.x.gsi.gov.uk
Web: www.lordsappointments.gov.uk

Chairman . . . . .Lord Jay of Ewelme

Secretary . . . . .Dr Richard Jarvis

Human Fertilisation and Embryology Authority
21 Bloomsbury Street, London, WC2B 3HF
Tel: (020) 7291 8200 Fax: (020) 7291 8201
E-mail: admin@hfea.gov.uk
Web: www.hfea.gov.uk

Chairman . . . . .Professor Lisa Jardine CBE

Chief Executive *(Acting)* . . . . .Mr Alan Doran CB

Human Genetics Commission
Room 605, Wellington House
135-155 Waterloo Road, London, SE1 8UG
Tel: (020) 7972 4351 Fax: (020) 7972 4300
E-mail: hgc@dh.gsi.gov.uk
Web: www.hgc.gov.uk

Chairman ....Professor Jonathan Montgomery

Secretary ....Dr Peter Mills

Human Tissue Authority
Finlaison House, 15-17 Furnival Street, London, EC4A 1AB
Tel: (020) 7211 3400
E-mail: enquiries@hta.gov.uk
Web: www.hta.gov.uk

Chairman ....Ms Shirley Harrison

Chief Executive ....Mr Adrian McNeil

Independent Living Fund
Equinox House, City Link, Nottingham, NG2 4LA
Tel: (0845) 601 8815/(0115) 945 0700
E-mail: funds@ilf.org.uk
Web: www.ilf.org.uk

Chairman ....Mr Stephen Jack

Chief Executive ....Mr Patrick Boyle

Independent Monitoring Boards of Prisons and Immigration Removal Centres
IMB Secretariat, 2nd Floor
Ashley House, 2 Monck Street
London, SW1P 2BQ
Tel: (020) 7035 2254 Fax: (020) 7035 2250
E-mail: imb@justice.gsi.gov.uk
Web: www.imb.gov.uk

President, National Council of
Monitoring Boards ....Dr Peter Selby

Head of Secretariat ....Mr Norman McLean

Independent Review Panel for Borderline Products
c/o Medicines and Healthcare products Regulatory Agency, Market Towers
1 Nine Elms Lane, London, SW8 5NQ
Tel: (020) 7084 3723 Fax: (020) 7084 2493
Web: www.mhra.gov.uk

Chairman . . . . .Mr Kevin Mooney

Secretary . . . . .Ms Lorraine Geear

Independent Review Panel for the Advertising of Medicines
Market Towers
1 Nine Elms Lane, London, SW8 5NQ
Tel: (020) 7084 2455 Fax: (020) 7084 2493
E-mail: fred.huckle@mhra.gsi.gov.uk
Web: www.mhra.gov.uk

Chairman . . . . .Mr James Watt

Secretary . . . . .Mr Fred Huckel

Information Centre for Health and Social Care
1 Trevelyan Square, Boar Lane, Leeds, LS1 6AB
Tel: (0845) 300 6016
E-mail: enquiries@ic.nhs.uk
Web: www.ic.nhs.uk

Chairman . . . . .Mr Michael Ramsden

Chief Executive . . . . .Mr Tim Straughan

Information Commissioner's Office
Wycliffe House, Water Lane, Wilmslow, Cheshire, SK9 5AF
Tel: (0845) 630 6060 Fax: (01625) 524510
E-mail: mail@ico.gsi.gov.uk
Web: www.ico.gov.uk

Information Commissioner . . . . .Mr Christopher Graham

Information Tribunal
Arnhem House Support Centre
PO Box 6987, Leicester, LE1 6SX
Tel: (0845) 600 0877 Fax: (0116) 249 4253
E-mail: informationtribunal@tribunals.gsi.gov.uk
Web: www.informationtribunal.gov.uk

Chairman . . . . .Professor John Angel

Tribunal Manager . . . . .Mr Graham Cresswell

Inland Waterways Advisory Council
City Road Lock, 38 Graham Street, Islington, London, N1 8JX
Tel: (020) 7253 1745 Fax: (020) 7490 7656
E-mail: iwac@iwac.gsi.gov.uk
Web: www.iwac.org.uk

Chairman . . . . .Mr John Edmonds

Policy Adviser . . . . .Mr John Manning

International Oil and Gas Business Advisory Board
Tay House, 300 Bath Street, Glasgow, G2 4DX
Tel: (0141) 228 3665 Fax: (0141) 228 3627
Web: www.uktradeinvest.gov.uk

Chairman . . . . .Mr Neil Bruce

Secretariat . . . . .Ms Eileen Barnett

Investigatory Powers Tribunal
PO Box 33220, London, SW1H 9ZQ
Tel: (020) 7035 3711
Web: www.ipt-uk.com

President . . . . .Rt Hon Lord Justice [John] Mummery

Secretary . . . . .Mr David Payne

Investors in People
7-10 Chandos Street, London, W1G 9DQ
Tel: (020) 7467 1900 Fax: (020) 7636 2386
E-mail: info@iipuk.co.uk
Web: www.investorsinpeople.co.uk

Chairman . . . . .Mr Philip Williamson CBE

Chief Executive . . . . .Mr Simon Jones

Joint Committee on Vaccination and Immunisation
Room 509, Wellington House
133-155 Waterloo Road, London, SE1 8UG
Tel: (020) 7972 3991 Fax: (020) 7972 3989
E-mail: dorian.kennedy@dh.gsi.gov.uk
Web: www.dh.gov.uk/jcvi/index.htm

Chairman . . . . .Professor Andrew Hall

Administrative Secretary . . . . .Dr Dorian Kennedy

Joint Nature Conservation Committee
Monkstone House, City Road, Peterborough, PE1 1JY
Tel: (01733) 562626 Fax: (01733)555948
E-mail: [firstname.lastname]@jncc.gov.uk
Web: www.jncc.gov.uk

Chair ....Dr Peter Bridgewater

Managing Director ....Mr Marcus Yeo

Low Pay Commission
1st Floor, Kingsgate House, 66-74 Victoria Street
London, SW1E 6SW
Tel: (020) 7215 8459 Tel: (020) 7215 8199
E-mail: lpc@lowpay.gov.uk
Web: www.lowpay.gov.uk

Chairman ....Mr David Norgrove

Secretary ....Mrs Katy Cornish

Medical Research Council
20 Park Crescent, London, W1B 1AL
Tel: (020) 7636 5422 Fax: (020) 7436 6179
E-mail: [firstname.lastname]@headoffice.mrc.ac.uk
Web: www.mrc.ac.uk

Chairman ....Sir John Chisholm

Chief Executive ....Sir Leszek Borysiewicz

Migration Advisory Committee
Advance House, 15 Wellesley Road, Croydon, CR0 2AG
Tel: (020) 8604 6027
E-mail: mac@homeoffice.gsi.gov.uk
Web: www.homeoffice.gov.uk/mac

Chairman ....Professor David Metcalf CBE

National Employer Advisory Board
Ministry of Defence, Zone 8, Zone E, London, SW1A 2HB
Tel: (020) 7897 0326
E-mail: helpline@sabre.mod.uk
Web: www.sabre.mod.uk

Chairman ....Lord Glenarthur

Secretary ....Wing Commander Charlie Anderson

National Endowment for Science, Technology and the Arts
1 Plough Place, London, EC4A 1DE
Tel: (020) 7645 2500 Fax: (020) 7645 2501
E-mail: mail@nesta.org.uk
Web: www.nesta.org.uk

Chairman . . . . .Sir Chris Powell

Chief Executive . . . . .Mr Jonathan Kestenbaum

National Lottery Commission
101 Wigmore Street, London, W1U 1QU
Tel: (020) 7016 3400 Fax: (020) 7016 3401
E-mail: publicaffairs@natlotcomm.gov.uk
Web: www.natlotcomm.gov.uk

Chairman . . . . .Dr Anne Wright CBE

Chief Executive . . . . .Mr Mark Harris

Natural Environment Research Council
Polaris House, North Star Avenue, Swindon, SN2 1EU
Tel: (01793) 411500 Fax: (01793) 411501
Web: www.nerc.ac.uk

Chairman . . . . .Mr Edmund Wallis

Chief Executive and
   Deputy Chairman . . . . .Professor Alan J Thorpe

NHS Blood and Transplant
Oak House, Reeds Crescent, Watford, WD24 4QN
Tel: (01923) 486800 Fax (01923) 486801
Donor Line Tel: (0300) 123 2323
E-mail: enquiries@nhsbt.nhs.uk
Web: www.nhsbt.nhs.uk

Chairman . . . . .Mr Bill Fullagar

Chief Executive . . . . .Ms Lynda Hamlyn

NHS Institute for Innovation and Improvement
Coventry House, University of Warwick Campus
Coventry, CV4 7AL
Tel: (0800) 555 5500
E-mail: enquiries@institute.nhs.uk
Web: www.institute.nhs.uk

Chairman ....Dame Yves Buckland

Chief Executive ....Professor Bernard Cramp

NHS Pay Review Body
Office of Manpower Economics, Kingsgate House,
66-74 Victoria Street, London, SW1E 6SW
Tel: (020) 7215 4453 Fax: (020) 7215 4445
Web: www.ome.uk.com

Chairman ....Professor Gillian Morris

Secretary ....Ms Trish Wilson

Northern Lighthouse Board
84 George Street, Edinburgh, EH2 3DA
Tel: (0131) 473 3100 Fax: (0131) 220 2093
E-mail: enquiries@nlb.org.uk
Web: www.nlb.org.uk

Chairman ....Sir Andrew Cubie CBE

Chief Executive ....Mr Roger Lockwood

Information Officer ....Mrs Lorna Hunter

Nuclear Decommissioning Authority
Herdus House, Westlakes Science and Technology Park
Moor Row, Cumbria, CA24 3HU
Tel: (01925) 802002 Fax: (01925) 802003
E-mail: enquiries@nda.gov.uk
Web: www.nda.gov.uk

Chairman ....Mr Stephen Henwood

Chief Executive ....Mr Tony Fountain

Nuclear Liabilities Fund
c/o PKF Farringdon Place, 20 Farringdon Road
London, EC1M 3AP
Tel: (020) 7065 0000 Fax: (020) 7065 0650
E-mail: david.venus@uk.pkf.com

Chairman . . . . .Lady Balfour of Burleigh

Executive Secretary . . . . .Mr David Venus

Nursing and Midwifery Council
23 Portland Place, London, W1B 1PZ
Tel: (020) 7637 7181 Fax: (020) 7436 2924
E-mail: communications@nmc-uk.org
Web: www.nmc-uk.org

Chair . . . . .Professor Tony Hazell

Chief Executive and Registrar . . . . .Mr Dickon Weir-Hughes

OFCOM
Riverside House, 2A Southwark Bridge Road
London, SE1 9HA
Tel: (020) 7981 3000 Fax: (020) 7981 3333
E-mail: contact@ofcom.org.uk
Web: www.ofcom.org.uk

Chairman . . . . .Ms Colette Bowe

Chief Executive . . . . .Mr Ed Richards

Scotland Office
Ofcom (Scotland), Sutherland House, 149 St Vincent Street
Glasgow, G2 5NW
Tel: (0141) 229 7400 Fax: (0141) 229 7433

Director . . . . .Ms Vicki Nash

Office of Fair Trading
Fleetbank House, 2-6 Salisbury Square, London, EC4Y 8JX
Tel: (020) 7211 8000 Fax: (020) 7211 8800
E-mail: enquiries@oft.gsi.gov.uk
Web: www.oft.gov.uk

Chairman . . . . .Mr Philip Collins

Chief Executive . . . . .Mr John Fingleton

Office of the Immigration Services Commissioner
5th Floor, Counting House, 53 Tooley Street
London, SE1 2QN
Tel: (020) 7211 1500 Fax: (020) 7211 1553
E-mail: info@oisc.gov.uk
Web: www.oisc.gov.uk

Immigration Services
Commissioner ....Mrs Suzanne McCarthy

Office of the Surveillance Commissioners
PO Box 29105, London, SW1V 1ZU
Tel: (020) 7828 3421 Fax: (020) 7592 1788
E-mail: oscmailbox@osc.gsi.gov.uk
Web: www.surveillancecommissioners.gov.uk

Chief Surveillance Commissioner ....Rt Hon Sir Christopher Rose

Chief Surveillance Inspector ....Mr Sam Lincoln

Oil and Pipelines Agency
York House, 23 Kingsway
London, WC2B 6UJ
Tel: (020) 7420 1670 Fax: (020) 7379 0500
E-mail: [firstname.surname]@oilandpipelines.com

Chairman ....Mr Francis Dobbyn

Chief Executive ....Mr Tony Nicholls

Olympic Lottery Distributor
1 Plough Place, London, EC4A 1DE
Tel: (020) 7880 2012 Fax: (020) 7880 2024
Web: www.olympiclotterydistributor.org.uk

Chairman ....Ms Janet Paraskeva

Chief Executive ....Mr Mike O'Connor

Passenger Focus
Whittles House, 14 Pentonville Road, London, N1 9HF
Tel: (0845) 302 2022 Fax: (020) 7713 2729
E-mail: info@passengerfocus.org.uk
Web: www.passengerfocus.org.uk

Chairman ....Mr Colin Foxall CBE

Chief Executive ....Mr Anthony Smith

Pensions Ombudsman
11 Belgrave Road, London, SW1V 1RB
Tel: (020) 7630 2200 Fax (020) 7821 0065
E-mail: enquiries@pensions-ombudsman.org.uk
Web: www.pensions-ombudsman.org.uk

Pensions Ombudsman . . . . .Mr Tony King

Deputy Pensions Ombudsman . . . . .Mr Charlie Gordon

Business Manager . . . . .Ms Jane Carey

Pensions Protection Fund
Knollys House, 17 Addiscombe Road, Croydon, Surrey, CR0 6SR
Tel: (0845) 600 2541 Fax (020) 8633 4910
E-mail: information@ppf.gsi.gov.uk
Web: www.pensionprotectionfund.org.uk

Chairman . . . . .Mr Lawrence Churchill

Chief Executive . . . . .Mr Alan Rubenstein

The Pensions Regulator
Napier House, Trafalgar Place, Brighton, BN1 4DW
Tel: (0870) 606 3636 Fax: (0870) 241 1144
E-mail: customersupport@thepensionsregulator.gov.uk
Web: www.pensionsregulator.gov.uk

Chairman . . . . .Mr David Norgrove

Chief Executive . . . . .Mr Tony Hobman

Plant Variety and Seeds Tribunal
FERA Varieties and Seeds Team, Whitehouse Lane
Huntingdon Road, Cambridge, CB3 0LF
Tel: (01233) 342322 Fax: (01233) 342386
E-mail: elspeth.nicol@fera.gsi.gov.uk
Web: www.fera.defra.gov.uk

Contact . . . . .Mrs Elspeth Nicol

Police Negotiating Body
Office of Manpower Economics, Kingsgate House,
66-74 Victoria Street, London, SW1E 6SW
Tel: (020) 7215 8101 Fax: (020) 7215 4445
Web: www.ome.uk.com/

Chairman . . . . .Mr John Randall

Secretary . . . . .Mr Steve Makogwu

Postal Services Commission
5th Floor, Hercules House, 6 Hercules Road
London, SE1 7DB
Tel: (020) 7593 2100 Fax: (020) 7593 2142
E-mail: info@psc.gov.uk
Web: www.psc.gov.uk

Chairman . . . . .Mr Nigel Stapleton

Chief Executive . . . . .Mr Tim Brown

Postgraduate Medical Education and Training Board
Hercules House, 6 Hercules Road
London, SE1 7DU
Tel: (020) 7160 6100 Fax: (020) 7160 6102
E-mail: info@pmetb.org.uk
Web: www.pmetb.org.uk

Chairman . . . . .Professor Stuart Macpherson

Chief Executive . . . . .Mr Graham Smith

Renewable Fuels Agency
Ashdown House, Sedlescombe Road North
St Leonards-on-Sea, East Sussex, TN37 7GA
Tel: (020) 7944 8555
Web: www.renewablefuelsagency.org

Chairman . . . . .Professor Ed Gallagher

Chief Executive Officer . . . . .Mr Nick Goodall

Renewables Advisory Board
C/o AEA Technology plc
Gemini Building, Fermi Avenue, Harwell IBC
Didcot, Oxfordshire, OX11 0QR
Tel: (0870) 190 6042
E-mail: RAB_secretariat@uk.aeat.com
Web: www.renewables-advisory-board.org.uk

Chairman . . . .*Secretary of State for Energy and*
Climate Change

Secretariat . . . . .Mr Nick Beale (AEA)

Review Board for Government Contracts
DCD-DCS2-AD1, Maple 2b
MoD, Abbey Wood, Bristol, BS34 8JH
Tel: (020) 7007 1512 Fax: (020) 7007 1074

Chairman ....Mr George Staple CB QC

Secretary ....Mr Alastair Scrimgoeur

Review Body on Doctors' and Dentists' Remuneration
Office of Manpower Economics, 6th Floor, Kingsgate House
66-74 Victoria Street, London, SW1E 6SW
Tel: (020) 7215 8413 Fax: (020) 7215 4445
Web: www.ome.uk.com/

Chairman ....Mr Ron Amy OBE

Secretary ....Ms Catriona Hunter

Reviewing Committee on the Export of Works of Art and Objects of Cultural Interest
The Museums, Libraries and Archives Council
Wellcome Wolfson Building, 165 Queen's Gate
South Kensington, London, SW7 5HD
Tel: (020) 7273 8270 Fax: (020) 7273 1404
E-mail: info@mla.gov.uk
Web: www.mla.gov.uk

Chairman ....Lord Inglewood

Secretary ....Ms Frances Wilson

Royal Commission on Environmental Pollution
55 Whitehall, London, SW1A 2EY
Tel: (0300) 068 6474 Fax: (0300) 068 6475
E-mail: enquiries@rcep.org.uk
Web: www.rcep.org.uk

Chairman ....Sir John Lawton FRS

Secretary ....Dr John Roberts

Royal Mail Group Ltd
100 Victoria Embankment
London, EC4Y 0HQ
Tel: (020) 7449 8000 Fax: (020) 7250 2960
Web: www.royalmail.com

Chairman . . . . .Mr Donald Brydon CBE

Chief Executive . . . . .Mr Adam Crozier

Science Advisory Council
Area 1A, Nobel House, 17 Smith Square,London, SW1P 3JR
Tel: (020) 7238 4993
E-mail: science.advisory.council@defra.gsi.gov.uk
Web: www.defra.gov.uk/science/sac/advisory.htm

Chairman . . . . .Professor Chris Gaskell

Secretary . . . . .Dr William Eason

Scientific Advisory Committee on Nutrition
Room 704, Wellington House
133-135 Waterloo Road, London, SE1 8UG
Tel: (020) 7972 1339 Fax: (020) 7972 4877
Web: www.sacn.gov.uk

Chairman . . . . .Professor Alan Jackson

Secretaries . . . . .Dr Sheela Reddy *(Department of Health)*
Dr Elain Stone *(Food Standards
Agency)*

Sea Fish Industry Authority
18 Logie Mill, Logie Green Road, Edinburgh, EH7 4HS
Tel: (0131) 558 3331 Fax: (0131) 558 1442
E-mail: seafish@seafish.co.uk
Web: www.seafish.org

Chairman . . . . .Mr Charles Howeson

Chief Executive . . . . .Mr John Rutherford

Security Commission
26 Whitehall, London, SW1A 2WH
Tel: (020) 7276 5642 Fax: (020) 7276 5651
E-mail: martin.fuller@cabinet-office.x.gsi.gov.uk
Web: www.cabinetoffice.gov.uk/security

Chairman . . . . .Rt Hon Lord Justice Mantell

Secretary . . . . .Mr Martin Fuller

Security Vetting Appeals Panel
Room 2.42, 26 Whitehall, London, SW1A 2WH
Tel: (020) 7276 5645 Fax: (020) 7276 5651
E-mail: martin.sterling@cabinet-office.x.gsi.gov.uk

Chairman . . . . .Sir George Newman

Secretary . . . . .Mr Martin Sterling

Senior Salaries Review Body
Office of Manpower Economics, Kingsgate House
66-74 Victoria Street, London, SW1E 6SW
Tel: (020) 7215 8276
Web: www.ome.uk.com

Chairman . . . . .Mr Bill Cockburn CBE

Secretary . . . . .Mr Keith Masson

SITPRO Ltd
1st Floor, Kingsgate House, 66-74 Victoria Street, London, SW1E 6SW
Tel: (020) 7215 8150 Fax: (020) 7215 4242
E-mail: info@sitpro.org.uk
Web: www.sitpro.org.uk

Chairman . . . . .Mr Norman Rose

Chief Executive .Mr Malcolm McKinnon

Social Security Advisory Committee
Level 3 North East Spur, Adelphi Building
1-11 John Adam Street, London, WC2N 6HT
Tel: (020) 7962 8355 Fax: (020) 7962 8916
E-mail: ssac@dwp.gsi.gov.uk
Web: www.ssac.org.uk

Chairman . . . . .Sir Richard Tilt

Secretary . . . . .Ms Gill Saunders

Statistics Board
Government Building, Cardiff Road, Newport, NP10 8XG
Tel: (0845) 601 3034
Web: www.statistics.gov.uk

Chairman . . . . .Sir Michael Scholar

National Statistician . . . . .Ms Jil Matheson

Director-General .Ms Rolande Anderson

Strategic Advisory Board for Intellectual Property Policy
21 Bloomsbury Street, London, WC1B 3HF
Tel: (020) 7034 2800 Fax: (020) 7034 2826
Web: www.sabip.org.uk

Chairman . . . . .Mr Joly Dixon

Chief Executive . . . . .Mr Robert Bettley-Smith

Sustainable Development Commission
Room 101, 55 Whitehall, c/o 3-8 Whitehall Place
London, SW1A 2HH
Tel: (020) 7270 6157
E-mail: enquiries@sd-commission.org.uk
Web: www.sd-commission.gov.uk

Chairman . . . . .Mr Jonathon Porritt CBE

Director . . . . .Mr Andrew Lee

Traffic Commissioner for Scotland
Scottish Traffic Area
The Stamp Office, 10 Waterloo Place
Edinburgh, EH1 3EG
Tel: (0131) 200 4905 Fax: (0131) 229 0682
E-mail: joan.aitken@otc.gsi.gov.uk

Commissioner . . . . .Miss Joan Aitken

Treasure Valuation Committee
c/o British Museum, Great Russell Street
London, WC1B 3DG
Tel: (020) 7323 8546
Web: www.culture.gov.uk

Chairman . . . . .Professor Norman Palmer

Secretary . . . . .Mr Ian Richardson

UKAEA
The Manor Court, Harwell, Oxfordshire, OX11 0RN
Tel: (01235) 431810 Fax: (01235) 431811
Web: www.ukaea.co.uk

Chairman . . . . .Lady [Barbara] Judge

Chief Executive . . . . .Mr Norman Harrison

UK Commission for Employment and Skills
3 Califlex Business Park, Golden Smithies Lane
Wath-upon-Dearne, South Yorkshire, S63 7ER
Tel: (01709) 774800 Fax: (01709) 774802
E-mail: info@ukces.org.uk
Web: www.ukces.org.uk

Chairman ....Sir Michael Rake

Chief Executive ....Mr Chris Humphries CBE

UK Film Council
10 Little Portland Street, London, W1W 7JG
Tel: (020) 7861 7861 Fax: (020) 7861 7862
E-mail: info@ukfilmcouncil.org.uk
Web: www.filmcouncil.org.uk

Chairman ....Mr Stewart Till CBE

Chief Executive ....Mr John Woodward

UK Sport
40 Bernard Street, London, WC1N 1ST
Tel: (020) 7211 5100 Fax: (020) 7211 5246
E-mail: info@uksport.gov.uk
Web: www.uksport.gov.uk

Chairman ....Ms Sue Campbell CBE

Chief Executive ....Mr John Steele

United Kingdom Advisory Panel for Health Care Workers Infected with Bloodborne Viruses
Health Protection Agency, Centre for Infections
61 Colindale Avenue, London, NW9 5EQ
Tel: (020) 8327 6074 Fax: (020) 8200 7868
E-mail: helen.janecek@hpa.org.uk

Chairman ....Mrs Isabel Boxer

Senior Administrator ....Ms Helen Janecek

Medical Secretary ....Dr Fortune Ncube

Veterinary Products Committee

Veterinary Medicines Directorate, Woodham Lane
New Haw, Addleston, Surrey, KT15 3LS
Tel: (01932) 336911 Fax: (01932) 336618
E-mail: vpc@vmd.defra.gsi.gov.uk
Web: www.vpc.gov.uk

Chairman . . . . .Mr David Skilton

Secretary . . . . .Mr Colin Bennett

VisitBritain

1 Palace Street, London, SW1E 5HE
Tel: (020) 7578 1000
E-mail: industry.relations@visitbritain.org
Web: www.visitbritain.org

Chairman . . . . .Mr Christopher Rodrigues CBE

Chief Executive . . . . .Ms Sandie Dawe MBE

War Pensions Committees

*There are 13 War Pensions Committees, each with responsibility for a specific area
of the United Kingdom.*

Room 6406, SPVA, Norcross, Blackpool, FY5 3WP
Tel: (01253) 333834 Fax: (01253) 330437
Freephone: Tel: (0800) 169 2277
E-mail: veterans.help@spva.gsi.gov.uk

Contact . . . . .Mrs Chrissie Lancaster

Women's National Commission

Zone 4/G9, Eland House, Bressenden Place
London, SW1E 5DU
Tel: (020) 7944 0585 Fax: (020) 7544 0583
Web: www.thewnc.org.uk

Chair . . . . .Baroness [Joyce] Gould

Director . . . . .Mrs Barbara Collins

Scottish Health
Bodies

NHS BOARDS

NHS Ayrshire and Arran
3 Lister Street, Crosshouse Hospital, Kilmarnock, KA2 0BE
Tel: (01563) 577037 Fax: (01563) 577046
E-mail: comms@aaht.scot.nhs.uk
Web: www.nhsayrshireandarran.com

Chairman. . . . . Professor Bill Stevely

Chief Executive . . . . Mrs Wai-yin Hatton

Press/Media Contact: Director of Communications . Mrs Penny French

NHS Borders
Newstead, Melrose, Roxburghshire, TD6 9DB
Tel: (01896) 825500 Fax: (01896) 825580
E-mail: bordershb@borders.scot.nhs.uk
Web: www.nhsborders.org.uk

Chairman. . . . . Ms Mary Wilson

Chief Executive . . . . Mr John Glennie

Press/Media Contact . . . . Mr Robbie Pearson

NHS Dumfries and Galloway
Crichton Hall, Dumfries, DG1 4TG
Tel: (01387) 246246
E-mail: dg.feedbak@nhs.net
Web: www.nhsdg.scot.nhs.uk/dumfries

Chairman. . . . . Mr Mike Keggans

Chief Executive . . . . Mr John Burns

Press/Media Contact:
Communication Co-ordinator . . . . Mr John Glover

NHS Fife
Hayfield House, Hayfield Road, Kirkcaldy, KY2 5AH
Tel: (01592) 643355 Fax: (01592) 648142
E-mail: patientrelations.fife@nhs.net
Web: www.nhsfife.scot.nhs.uk

Chairman. . . . . Professor James McGoldrick

Chief Executive . . . . Mr George Brechin

Press/Media Contact: Communications Officer. . . . . Mr Douglas Ross

NHS Forth Valley

Carseview, Castle Business Park, Stirling, FK9 4SW
Tel: (01786) 463031
E-mail: yourhealthservice@fvhb.nhs.net
Web: www.nhsforthvalley.com

Chairman............................... Mr Ian Mullen OBE

Chief Executive .... Miss Fiona Mackenzie

Press/Media Contact: Head of Communications .... Ms Elsbeth Campbell

NHS Grampian

Summerfield House, Eday Road, Aberdeen, AB15 6RE
Tel: (0845) 456 6000 Fax: (01224) 550655
E-mail: grampian@nhs.net
Web: www.nhsgrampian.org

Chairman............................... Dr David Cameron

Chief Executive .... Mr Richard Carey

Press/Media Contact:
Director of Corporate Communications .... Mrs Laura Gray

NHS Greater Glasgow and Clyde

Dalian House, PO Box 15329, 350 St Vincent Street, Glasgow, G3 8YZ
Tel: (0141) 201 4444 Fax: (0141) 201 4400
E-mail: firstname.surname@ggc.scot.nhs.uk
Web: www.nhsggc.org.uk

Chairman............................... Mr Andrew Robertson OBE

Chief Executive .... Mr Robert Calderwood

Press/Media Contact: Communications Director. .... Mr Ally McLaws

NHS Highland

Assynt House, Beechwood Park, Inverness, IV2 3BW
Tel: (01463) 717123 Fax: (01463) 235189
E-mail: ahreception@hhb.scot.nhs.uk
Web: www.nhshighland.scot.nhs.uk

Chair .... Mr Garry Coutts

Chief Executive .... Dr Roger Gibbins

Press/Media Contact: Communications Manager ... Ms Gill Keel

NHS Lanarkshire
14 Beckford Street, Hamilton, ML3 0TA
Tel: (01698) 281313 Fax: (01698) 423134
E-mail: david.pigott@lanhb.scot.nhs.uk
Web: www.nhslanarkshire.co.uk

Chairman............................... Mr Kenneth Corsar

Chief Executive .... Mr Tim Davidson

Press/Media Contact: Head of Communications.... Ms Karen Hamilton

NHS Lothian
Deaconess House, 148 Pleasance, Edinburgh, EH8 9RS
Tel: (0131) 536 9000 Fax: (0131) 536 9164
E-mail: lothian.communications@nhs.net
Web: www.nhslothian.scot.nhs.uk

Chair .... Dr Charles Winstanley

Chief Executive .... Professor James Barbour OBE

Press/Media Contact: Head of Public Relations .... Ms Jennifer Stirton

NHS Orkney
Garden House, New Scapa Road, Kirkwall, Orkney, KW15 1BQ
Tel: (01856) 888000 Fax: (01856) 885411
E-mail: iain.crozier@nhs.net
Web: www.ohb.nhs.uk

Chairman............................... Mr John Ross Scott

Chief Executive .... Mr David Piggott

Press/Media Contact: .... Mrs Lynette Web

NHS Shetland
Brevik House, 27 South Road, Lerwick, Shetland, ZE1 0TG
Tel: (01595) 696767 Fax: (01595) 696727
E-mail: [firstname.surname]@shb.shetland.scot.nhs.uk
Web: www.shb.nhs.uk

Chairman............................... Mr Ian Kinniburgh

Chief Executive .... Miss Sandra Laureson

Press/Media Contact: .... *Via Chief Executive's Office*

NHS Tayside
Kings Cross, Clepington Road, Dundee, DD3 8EA
Tel: (01382) 818479 Fax: (01382) 424003
E-mail: generalcomments.tayside.nhs.net
Web: www.nhstayside.scot.nhs.uk

Chairman................................Mr Sandy Watson OBE

Chief Executive ....Professor Tony Wells

Press/Media Contact: Head of Communications....Mrs Shona Singers

NHS Western Isles
37 South Beach Street, Stornoway, Isle of Lewis, HS1 2BN
Tel: (01851) 702997 Fax: (01851) 704405
E mail: wihb@sol.co.uk
Web: www.wihb.scot.nhs.uk

Chairman................................Mr John MacKay OBE

Chief Executive ....Mr Gordon Jamieson

Press/Media Contact
Communications Manager.................Ms Maggie Frazer

Mental Welfare Commission for Scotland
Thistle House, 91 Haymarket Terrace
Edinburgh, EH12 5HE
Tel: (0131) 313 8777 Fax: (0131) 222 6112/3
User and Carer Freephone: (0800) 389 6809
E-mail: enquiries@mwcscot.org.uk
Web: www.mwcscot.org.uk

Established:
1960, under Section 2 of the Mental Health (Scotland) Act 1960. The Commission is an independent organisation with duties set out in mental health law. The powers, functions, constitution and duties of the organisation are currently outlined in Mental Health (Care & Treatment) (Scotland) Act 2003 and the Adults with Incapacity (Scotland) Act 2000.

Functions:
The Commission:
- Finds out whether individual care and treatment is in line with the law and good practice;
- Challenges service providers to deliver best practice in mental health and learning disability care;
- Provides information, advice and guidance to service users, carers and service providers;
- Maintains a strong and influential voice in service and policy development;
- Promotes best practice in mental health law by building up a picture of how the Mental Health (Care & Treatment) (Scotland) Act 2003 and the Adults with Incapacity (Scotland) Act 2000 are being applied across Scotland.

Chairman . . . . .Mr Jim Connechen

Director . . . . .Dr Donald Lyons

Head of Corporate Services . . . . .Ms Alison McRae

Communications Manager . . . . .Ms Anita Wiseman

NHS 24 Scotland
Caledonia House, 50 Pitches Road
Cardonald Park, Glasgow, GS1 4ED
Tel: (0141) 337 4501 Fax: (0141) 882 0188
E-mail: enquiries@nhs24.scot.nhs.uk
Web: www.nhs24.com

Established:
2001, under the NHS 24 (Scotland) Order 2001.

Functions:
To establish, implement and manage a confidential 24 hour nurse consultation telephone service across Scotland.

Chairman ....Mr Allan Watson

Chief Executive ....Mr John Turner

NHS Education for Scotland
4th Floor, Thistle House, 91 Haymarket
Edinburgh, EH12 8HE
Tel: (0131) 313 8031 Fax: (0131) 313 8122
E-mail: enquiries@nes.scot.nhs.uk
Web: www.nes.scot.nhs.uk

Established:
2002, through a merger of the National Board for Nursing, Midwifery and Health Visiting for Scotland, the Scottish Council for Postgraduate Medical and Dental Education and the Post Qualification Education Board for Pharmacists.

Functions:
To help provide better patient care by designing, commissioning, quality assuring and, where appropriate, providing education, training and lifelong learning for the NHS workforce in Scotland.

Chairman ....Mrs Ann Markham OBE

Chief Executive ....Mr Malcolm Wright

NHS Health Scotland

Woodburn House, Canaan Lane, Edinburgh, EH10 4SG
Tel: (0131) 536 5500 Fax: (0131) 536 5501
Web: www.healthscotland.com

Established:
2003, under Section 28 of the National Health Service and Community Care Act 1990, and constituted under the Health Education Board for Scotland Order 1990, as amended by the Health Education Board for Scotland Order 2003.

Functions:
Health Scotland is a Special NHS Board which provides professional national leadership with partners to help everyone in Scotland, especially the most disadvantaged, to sustain and improve their health.

It achieves this by:
- Advancing understanding of Scotland's health and how to improve it;
- Contributing evidence and expertise to policy and planning;
- Building competence and capacity for improved health;
- Positively influencing by communicating with the public.

Chairman Ms Margaret Burns CBE

Chief Executive . . . . Mr Graham Robertson

NHS National Services Scotland

Gyle Square, 1 South Gyle Crescent
Edinburgh, EH12 9EB
Tel: (0131) 275 6000 Fax: (0131) 275 7530
Web: www.nhsnss.org

Established:

1974, under the National Health Service (Scotland) Act 1978; formerly the Common Services Agency for Scotland

Functions:

These are set out in the National Health Service (Functions of the Common Services Agency) (Scotland) Order 1974 as amended: They include:

1. The provision of services to enable the Ministers, NHS Boards and NHS Divisions to carry out their functions in relation to the provision of hospital and other accommodation and residential accommodation for health staff;
2. The procurement of equipment and supplies and the provision of related scientific and technical services in support of the functions of the Ministers, NHS Boards and NHS Divisions;
3. The provision of information, advisory and management services in support of the Ministers, NHS Boards and NHS Divisions;
4. The provision of supplies of human blood for blood transfusion and related services, including the production of blood fractions;
5. Examining and checking the pricing of prescription drugs, medicines and appliances for pharmaceutical services;
6. The provision of officers, accommodation and other facilities required by the Scottish Dental Practice Board for its work in relation to the approval of estimates of dental treatment and appliances;
7. The co-ordination of personnel policies, including agreement with NHS Boards and NHS Divisions, arrangements for appointment, training and planned movement of staff and the organisation of, and participation in, training;
8. The provision of such officers as the Scottish Medical Practices Committee may require;
9. The collection and dissemination of epidemiological data and participation in epidemiological investigations;
10. The provision of legal services to NHS Boards and NHS Divisions;
11. The provision of research and development services in the field of public health;
12. The provision of professional advice on facilities management to NHS Scotland healthcare bodies on non-clinical facilities services.

Chairman . . . . .Mr Bill Matthews

Chief Executive . . . . .Mr Ian F Crichton

NHS Quality Improvement Scotland (NHS QIS)
Edinburgh
Elliott House, 8-10 Hillside Crescent, Edinburgh, EH7 5EA
Tel: (0131) 623 4300 Fax: (0131) 623 4299

Glasgow
Delta House, 50 West Nile Street, Glasgow, G1 2NP
Tel: (0141) 225 6999 Fax: (0141) 248 3778
E-mail: comments@nhshealthquality.org
Web: www.nhshealthquality.org

Established:
2003, under SSI 2002 No. 534 (Scotland) Order 2002.

Functions:
Provision of advice, guidance and support on effective clinical practice and service improvements.

Note: NHS Quality Improvement Scotland was formed by the merger of: the Clinical Standards Board for Scotland, the Health Technology Board for Scotland, the Scottish Health Advisory Service, the Nursing and Midwifery Practice Development Unit, and the Clinical Resources and Audit Group. It now also includes the Scottish Intercollegiate Guidelines Network and the Scottish Health Council.

Chairman . . . . .Professor Sir Graham Teasdale

Deputy Chairman . . . . .Mr Martyn Evans

Chief Executive . . . . .Dr Frances Elliott

Head of Communications . . . . .Mr Ken Miller

National Waiting Times Centre Board of Scotland
Golden Jubilee National Hospital
Beardmore Hotel and Conference Centre, Clydebank, G81 4HX
Tel: (0141) 951 5000 Fax: (0141) 951 5007
E-mail: enquiries@gjnh.scot.nhs.uk
Web: www.nhsgoldenjubilee.co.uk

Established:
2002, as an NHS Special Health Board

Functions:
The Golden Jubilee National Hospital helps reduce patient waiting times across Scotland.
Patients can be referred to the hospital by their regional NHS Board for hip and knee
replacements, diagnostic procedures (x-ray, MRI, ultrasound etc.), plastic surgery, eye
surgery, endoscopy procedures and other general surgery. In 2008, the centre also became
home to the West of Scotland Heart and Lung Centre.

The NHS National Waiting Times Centre is also the only NHS Board in the UK to manage
a hotel on site. The Beardmore Hotel and Conference Centre is a four-star facility
specialising in conferences, meetings and training courses at special rates for the public
sector.

Chairman . . . . .Dr Lindsay Burley

Chief Executive . . . . .Mrs Jill Young

Scottish Ambulance Service
National Headquarters, Tipperlinn Road, Edinburgh, EH10 5UU
Tel: (0131) 446 7000 Fax: (0131) 446 7001
Web: www.scottishambulance.com

Established:
1999, as a Special Health Board, replacing the Scottish Ambulance Service NHS Trust

Functions:
The provision of emergency and non-emergency ambulance services for patients
throughout Scotland.

Chairman . . . . .Mr David Garbutt

Chief Executive . . . . .Ms Pauline Howie

State Hospitals Board for Scotland
The State Hospital, Lampits Road, Carstairs
Lanarkshire, ML11 8RP
Tel: (01555) 840293 Fax: (01555) 840024
E-mail: info@tsh.org.uk
Web: www.show.scot.nhs.uk

Established:
1995, under the State Hospitals (Scotland) Act 1994.

Functions:
The State Hospital is a secure hospital administered by a special health board, subject to the same financial regime and accountability review process as all other health boards.

It aims to provide high quality forensic psychiatric care in a secure environment for patients admitted under the requirements of the Mental Health (Scotland) Act 1984 and related legislation.

Chairperson . . . . .Mr Gordon Craig

Chief Executive . . . . .Mrs Andreana Adamson

Scottish Local Authorities

Aberdeen City Council
Town House
Broad Street
Aberdeen, AB10 1FY
Tel: (01224) 522000 Fax: (01224) 644346
Web: www.aberdeencity.gov.uk

Political Control . . . . Liberal Democrat/SNP

Leader of the Council . . . . . . Cllr John Stewart . . . . Tel: (01224) 522526

Chief Executive . . . . Mrs Sue Bruce . . . . Tel: (01224) 522500

Director of Corporate
Governance . . . . Mr Stewart Carruth . . . . Tel: (01224) 522551

Director of Education,
Culture and Sport . . . . . . Mrs Annette Bruton . . . . Tel: (01224) 523458

Director of Enterprise,
Planning and
Infrastructure . . . . Mr Gordon McIntosh . . . . . . Tel: (01224) 522941

Director of Housing and
Environment . . . . Mr Pete Leonard . . . . Tel: (01224) 523899

Director of Social Care
and Wellbeing . . . . Mr Fred McBride . . . . Tel: (01224) 523797

Corporate Communications . Mr Graham Lawther . . . . . . Tel: (01224) 523188

Aberdeenshire Council

Woodhill House
Westburn Road
Aberdeen, AB16 5GB
Tel: (01467) 620981
Web: www.aberdeenshire.gov.uk

Political Control . . . . Liberal Democrat/Conservative

**Provost of the
Council** . . . . Cllr William Howatson . . . . . Tel: (01224) 665002
Fax: (01224) 664007

Leader of the Council . . . . . . Cllr Anne Robertson . . . . Tel: (01224) 665002
Fax: (01224) 664007

Chief Executive . . . . Mr Colin Mackenzie . . . . Tel: (01224) 665402
Fax: (01224) 665444

Assistant Chief Executive . . . Ms Colette Backwell . . . . Tel: (01224) 620891

Director of Corporate
Services . . . . Mr Charles Armstrong . . . . . Tel: (01224) 665409
Fax: (01224) 664888
Director of Education,
Learning and Leisure . . . . . Mr Bruce Robertson . . . . Tel: (01224) 665427
Fax: (01224) 665445
Director of Housing
and Social Work . . . . Mr Ritchie Johnson . . . . Tel: (01224) 664960
Fax: (01224) 665445
Director of Planning and
Environmental
Services . . . . Dr Christine Gore . . . . Tel: (01224) 665509
Fax: (01224) 664888
Director of Transportation
and Infrastructure . . . . Mr Iain Gabriel . . . . Tel: (01224) 665164
Fax: (01224) 662005
Head of Corporate
Communications . . . . Ms Kate Bond . . . . Tel: (01224) 664465
Fax: (01224) 665204

Angus Council
Angus House
Orchardbank Business Park
Angus, DD8 1AX
Tel: (08452) 777778
E-mail: chiefexec@angus.gov.uk
Web: www.angus.gov.uk

Political Control . . . . The Angus Alliance

Leader of the Council . . . . . . Cllr Bob Myles . . . . Tel: (01307) 473049
Fax: (01307) 461968
Chief Executive . . . . Mr David Sawers . . . . Tel: (01307) 476100

Corporate Services
Director of Corporate
   Services . . . . Mr Colin McMahon . . . . Tel: (01307) 476200
Fax: (01307) 476216
Head of Finance . . . . Mr Ian Lorimer . . . . Tel: (01307) 476222
Head of IT . . . . Mr Neil Munro . . . . Tel: (01307) 476444
Head of Law and
   Administration . . . . Ms Sheona Hunter . . . . Tel: (01307) 476262
Head of Property . . . . Mr John Pearson . . . . Tel: (01241) 435054

Education
Director of Education . . . . . . Ms Rachel Saitz . . . . Tel: (01307) 476300
Fax: (01307) 461848
Senior Managers
   Property/IT/Finance
     Support . . . . Mr Craig Clement . . . . Tel: (01307) 476333
   Pupil and Parent Support Ms Susan Duff . . . . Tel: (01307) 476363
   School and Community
     Support . . . . Mr Neil Logue . . . . Tel: (01307) 476347

Infrastructure Services
County Buildings, Market Street, Forfar, DD8 3WR
Director of Infrastructure
   Services . . . . Mr Eric Lowson . . . . Tel: (01307) 473333
Fax: (01307) 473388
Head of Economic
   Development . . . . Mr David Valentine . . . . Tel: (01307) 473358
Head of Planning and
   Transport . . . . Mr George Chree . . . . Tel: (01307) 473292
Head of Roads . . . . Mr Jeff Green . . . . Tel: (01307) 473289

Angus Council (Continued)

Neighbourhood Services
William Wallace House, Orchard Loan, Orchardbank Business Park, Forfar, DD8 1WH
Director of Neighbourhood
Services . . . . Mr Ron Ashton . . . . Tel: (01307) 474710
Fax: (01307) 474799
Head of Environmental
Management . . . . Mr John Zimny. . . . . Tel: (01307) 474771
Head of Housing. . . . . Mr Alan McKeown . . . . Tel: (01307) 474779

Social Work and Health
St Margaret's House, Orchard Loan, Orchardbank Business Park, Forfar, DD8 1WS
Director of Social
Work and Health. . . . . . . Dr Robert Peat . . . . Tel: (01307) 474839
Fax: (01307) 474899
Senior Managers
Children/Family/
Criminal Justice . . . . . Mr Tim Armstrong . . . . Tel: (01307) 462405
Community Care . . . . . . Ms Lorraine Young . . . . Tel: (01307) 474840
Support Services . . . . Mr Les Hutchinson . . . . Tel: (01307) 474866

Argyll and Bute Council
Kilmory
Lochgilphead
Argyll, PA31 8RT
Tel: (01546) 602127 Fax: (01546) 604138
E-mail: enquiries@argyll-bute.gov.uk
Web: www.argyll-bute.gov.uk

Political Control . . . . Independent/SNP

Leader of the Council . . . . . . Cllr Dick Walsh . . . . Tel: (01546) 604328
Fax: (01546) 604349

Chief Executive . . . . Ms Sally Loudon . . . . Tel: (01546) 604263
Fax: (01546) 604349

Director, Community
Services . . . . Mr Douglas Hendry . . . . Tel: (01546) 604244
Fax: (01546) 604344

Director, Corporate and
Democratic Services . . . . Mr Nigel Stewart . . . . Tel: (01546) 604272
Fax: (01546) 604444

Director, Development
Services . . . . Mr George Harper . . . . Tel: (01546) 604225
Fax: (01546) 604386

Director, Operational
Services . . . . Mr Andrew Law . . . . Tel: (01546) 604657
Fax: (01546) 603749

Communications Manager . . *Vacant* . . . . Tel: (01546) 604136
Fax: (01546) 604346

Clackmannanshire Council

Greenfield
Alloa, FK10 2AD
Tel: (01259) 450000 Fax: (01259) 452010
Web: www.clacksweb.org.uk

Political Control . . . . Labour

Leader of the Council . . . . . . Cllr Janet Cadenhead . . . . . . Tel: (01259) 452011
Fax: (01259) 452230

Chief Executive . . . . Mrs Angela Leitch . . . . Tel: (01259) 452002

Director of Development and
Environmental Services. . Mr Garry Dallas . . . . Tel: (01259) 452532
Fax: (01259) 452530

Communications and
Marketing Manager. . . . . Ms Ruth Fry . . . . Tel: (01259) 452023
Fax: (01259) 452117

Lime Tree House, Alloa, FK10 1EX
Head of Education . . . . Mr Jim Goodall . . . . Tel: (01259) 452437
Fax: (01259) 452440

Comhairle Nan Eilean Siar
(Western Isles)
Council Offices
Sandwick Road, Stornoway
Isle of Lewis, HS1 2BW
Tel: (01851) 703773 Fax: (01851) 705349
E-mail: cnes@cne-siar.gov.uk
Web: www.cne-siar.gov.uk

Political Control . . . . Independent

Convener of the Council . . . . Cllr Alex MacDonald

Leader of the Council . . . . . . Cllr Angus Campbell

Chief Executive . . . . Mr Malcolm Burr . . . . E-mail:
m.burr@cne-siar.gov.uk

Director of Development . . . Mr Calum I Maciver

Director of Education and
   Children's Services . . . . . Ms Seonag Mackinnon

Director of Finance and
   Corporate Services . . . . . Mr Robert Emmott

Director of Social and
   Community Services . . . . Mr Ian Macaulay

Director of Technical
   Services . . . . Mr Murdo Gray

Communications Officer . . . Mr Nigel Scott

Dumfries and Galloway Council

Council Offices, English Street, Dumfries, DG1 2DD
Tel: (0303) 333 3000 Fax: (01387) 260034
Web: www.dumgal.gov.uk

Political Control . . . . Conservative

Convener of the Council . . . . Cllr Patsy Gilroy . . . . Tel: (01387)260050

Chief Executive . . . . Mr Gavin Stevenson . . . . Tel: (01387) 260001

Marchmount House, Marchmount, Dumfries, DG1 1PY
Director DGFirst . . . . Mr Geoff Lewis . . . . Tel: (01387) 731001
Fax: (01387) 259730
Council Offices, English Street, Dumfries, DG1 2DD
Communications Manager . . Mrs Susan Black . . . . Tel: (01387) 260330
Fax: (01387) 260334
Council Offices, English Street, Dumfries, DG1 2HR
Director Support Services. . . Mr Gordon Lawson . . . . Tel: (01387) 260015
Fax: (01387) 260029
Group Manager,
Economic Regeneration . Mr Tony Fitzpatrick . . . . Tel: (01387) 260005

30 Edinburgh Road, Dumfries, DG1 1JG
Corporate Director of Education and
Community Services . . . . *Vacant* . . . . Tel: (01387) 260400
Fax: (01387) 260453
DGHP (Executive) . . . . Ms Zoe Forster . . . . Tel: (01387) 242501
Fax: (01387) 242509
Service Directors
Schools Services . . . . Mr Colin Grant . . . . Tel: (01387) 260439
Social Work Services. . . . Mr John Alexander. . . . . Tel: (01387) 260451

Carruthers House, English Street, Dumfries DG1 2HP
Operations Manager
Accountancy . . . . Mr Paul Garrett . . . . Tel: (01387) 260250
Fax: (01387) 260368
Brooms Road, Dumfries, DG1 2DZ
Fire Brigade -
Chief Fire Officer . . . . . . Mr David Wynne . . . . Tel:: (01387) 260988
Fax: (01387) 252686
Operations Manager,
Human Resources . . . . . . Mr Paul Clarkin . . . . Tel: (01387) 260060
Fax: (01387) 260029
Militia House, English Street, Dumfries, DG1 2HR
Director Sustainable
Development . . . . Mr Alistair Speedie . . . . Tel: (01387) 260361
Fax: (01387) 260111
Grierson House, Bankend Road, Dumfries, DG1 4ZH
Senior Social Work Officer. . Mr Allan Monteforte . . . . . . Tel: (01387) 260900
Fax: (01387) 260924

Dundee City Council
21 City Square
Dundee, DD1 3BY
Tel: (01382) 434000 Fax: (01382) 434666
E-mail: alexstephen@dundeecity.gov.uk
Web: www.dundeecity.gov.uk

Political Control . . . . Labour/Liberal Democrat

Leader of the Council . . . . . . Cllr Kevin Keenen . . . . Tel: (01382) 434450
E-mail: kevin.keenan@
dundeecity.gov.uk

Chief Executive . . . . Mr David Dorward . . . . Tel: (01382) 434201

Deputy Chief Executive
(Finance) . . . . Ms Marjorie Stewart . . . . Tel: (01382) 433555
Depute Chief Executive
(Support Services) . . . . . Ms Patricia McIlquham . . . . Tel: (01382) 434202
Assistant Chief Executive
(Community Planning) . Mr Chris Ward . . . . Tel: (01382) 434258
Director of Dundee Contract
Services . . . . Mr Ken Laing . . . . Tel: (01382) 434729
Director of Economic
Development . . . . Mr Douglas Grimmond . . . . Tel: (01382) 434251
Director of Education . . . . . . Ms Anne Wilson . . . . Tel: (01382) 433088
Director of Housing . . . . Mrs Elaine Zwirlein . . . . Tel: (01382) 434538
Director of Leisure and
Communities . . . . Mr Stewart Murdoch . . . . . . Tel: (01382) 437460
Director of Planning and
Transportation . . . . Mr Mike Galloway . . . . Tel: (01382) 433610
Director of Social Work . . . . Mr Alan Baird . . . . Tel: (01382) 433205
Head of Environmental Health
and Trading Standards . . Mr Albert Oswald . . . . Tel: (01382) 436201
Head of IT . . . . Mr Ged Bell . . . . Tel: (01382) 438123
Head of Personnel . . . . Mr Iain Martin . . . . Tel: (01382) 434433
Head of Public Relations . . . Mr Les Roy . . . . Tel: (01382) 434501

East Ayrshire Council

London Road, Kilmarnock
East Ayrshire, KA3 7BU
Tel: (01563) 576000 Fax: (01563) 576500
E-mail: the.council@east-ayrshire.gov.uk
Web: www.east-ayrshire.gov.uk

Political Control . . . . Coalition

Leader of the Council . . . . . . Cllr Douglas Reid . . . . Tel: (01563) 576027
Fax: (01563) 576275
E-mail: douglas.reid@
east-ayrshire.gov.uk

Chief Executive . . . . Ms Fiona Lees . . . . Tel: (01563) 576019
Fax: (01563) 576200
Depute Chief Executive and
Executive Director of
Corporate Support . . . . . Ms Elizabeth Morton . . . . . . Tel: (01563) 576001
Fax: (01563) 576200
Executive Director of Educational
and Social Services . . . . . Mr Graham Short . . . . Tel: (01563) 576017
Fax: (01563) 576210
Executive Director of
Neighbourhood Services . Mr William Stafford . . . . Tel: (01563) 576023
Fax: (01563) 576130
Head of Community
Support . . . . Ms Kay Gilmour . . . . Tel: (01563) 576104
Fax: (01563) 576210
Head of Democratic
Services . . . . Mr Bill Walkinshaw . . . . Tel: (01563) 576135
Fax: (01563) 576245
Head of Facilities
Management . . . . Mr Robin Gourlay . . . . Tel: (01563) 576089
Fax: (01563) 576210
Head of Legal, Procurement
and Regulatory Services . Mr David Mitchell . . . . Tel: (01563) 576061
Fax: (01563) 576179

Head of Personnel . . . . Mr Martin Rose . . . . Tel: (01563) 576092
Fax: (01563) 576067

Head of Resources . . . . Mr Euan Couperwhite . . . . . Tel: (01563) 576090
Fax: (01563) 576123
Head of Service: Schools
Support . . . . Mr Andrew Sutherland . . . . . Tel: (01563) 576126
Fax: (01563) 576210

East Ayrshire Council (Continued)

2 The Cross, Kilmarnock, KA1 1LR
Head of Information
    Technology . . . . Mr Malcolm Roulston . . . . . Tel: (01563) 576809
    Fax: (01563) 576825

Council Offices, Civic Centre North, John Dickie Street, Kilmarnock, KA1 1BY
Executive Head of Housing . Mr Chris McAleavey . . . . . . Tel: (01563) 554876
    Fax: (01563) 554890
Head of Leisure Services . . . Mr John Griffiths . . . . Tel: (01563) 578179
    Fax: (01563) 578177

Council Office, Greenholm Street, Kilmarnock, KA1 4DY
Executive Head of Finance
    and Asset Management. . Mr Alex McPhee . . . . Tel: (01563) 576300
    Fax: (01563) 576457
Head of Roads and
    Transportation . . . . Mr John Bryson . . . . Tel: (01563) 576310
    Fax: (01563) 576312

Council Offices, Civic Centre South, John Dickie Street, Kilmarnock, KA1 1BY
Executive Head of Social
    Work . . . . Ms Susan Taylor . . . . Tel: (01563) 576920
    Fax: (01563) 576644

Council Offices, Burnside Street, Kilmarnock, KA1 4BY
Head of Building and
    Works . . . . Mr Derek Spence . . . . Tel: (01563) 555501
    Fax: (01563) 555709

Council Offices, Croft Street, Kilmarnock, KA1 4DY
Head of Planning and
    Economic Development . Mr Alan Neish . . . . Tel: (01563) 576767
    Fax: (01563) 576774

East Dunbartonshire Council
Tom Johnston House
Civic Way, Kirkintilloch
East Dunbartonshire G66 4TJ
Tel: (0141) 578 8000 Fax: (0141) 777 8576
E-mail: [firstname.lastname]@eastdunbarton.gov.uk
Web: www.eastdunbarton.gov.uk

Political Control . . . . Labour/Conservative

Leader of the Council . . . . . . Cllr Rhondda Geekie . . . . . . Tel: (0141) 578 8000

Chief Executive . . . . Mr Gerry Cornes . . . . E-mail: chiefexec@
eastdunbarton.gov.uk
Directors
Community Services . . . . Mr John Simmons
Corporate and
Customer Services . . . . Ms Diane Campbell
Development and
Infrastructure . . . . Mr Derek Cunningham

Community Services
Director Community
Services . . . . Mr John Simmons

William Patrick Library, 2-4 West High Street, Kirkintilloch, G66 1AD
Head of Social Work . . . . Mr Tony Keogh . . . . Tel: (0141) 775 9000
Fax: (0141) 777 6203

Boclair House, 100 Milngavie Road, Bearsden, G61 2TQ
Head of Education . . . . Mr Tony Currie . . . . E-mail: education@
eastdunbarton.gov.uk

Head of Integrated Services . Mr Sandy McGarvey

Tom Johnston House, Civic Way, Kirkintilloch, G66 4TJ
Head of Housing and
Community Services . . . . Mr Kenny Simpson . . . . Tel: (0141) 578 8409
E-mail: housing@
eastdunbarton.gov.uk

East Dunbartonshire Council (Continued)

Corporate and Customer Services
Director Corporate and
    Customer Services . . . . Ms Diane Campbell

Head of Customer Relations and
    Organisational Development. Mrs Ann Davie

Head of Finance & ICT. . . . . . . Mr Ian Black . . . . E-mail: counciltax@
eastdunbarton.gov.uk
E-mail: rates@
eastdunbarton.gov.uk

Head of Legal and Democratic
    Services . . . . Mr Alistair Crighton

Development and Infrastructure
Director of Development and
    Infrastructure . . . . Mr Derek Cunningham . . . E-mail: commercial@
eastdunbarton.gov.uk

Head of Assets and Property
    Services . . . . Mrs Grace Irvine

Head of Development and
    Enterprise. . . . . Mr Thomas Glen

Broomhill Depot, Broomhill Industrial Estate, Glasgow, G66 1TF
Head of Roads and
    Neighbourhood Services . . . Mr David Devine . . . . Tel: (0141) 574 5600

East Lothian Council
John Muir House
Haddington
East Lothian, EH41 3HA
Tel: (01620) 827827 Fax: (01620) 827888
Web: www.eastlothian.gov.uk

Political Control . . . . SNP/Liberal Democrat

Provost . . . . Cllr Sheena Richardson . . . . Tel: (01620) 827011
Fax: (01620) 823140

Leader of the Council . . . . . . Cllr David Bevy . . . . Tel: (01620) 827012
Fax: (01620) 823140

Chief Executive . . . . Mr Alan Blackie

Director of Environment . . . Mr Pete Collins . . . . Tel: (01620) 827273
Fax: (01620) 827450

Director of Education and
Children's Services
(Acting) . . . . Mr Don Ledingham . . . . Tel: (01620) 827596
Fax: (01620) 827291

Director of Corporate
Finance and Information
Technology . . . . Mr Alex McCrorie . . . . Tel: (01620) 827204
Fax: (01620) 827446

Head of Personnel . . . . Ms Sharon Saunders . . . . . . Tel: (01620) 827632
Fax: (01620) 827612

Communications and
Democratic Services
Manager . . . . Mr David Russell . . . . Tel: (01620) 827655
Fax: (01620) 827442

Economic Development
Manager . . . . Miss Susan Smith . . . . Tel: (01620) 827282
Fax: (01620) 827482

Social Work and Housing Headquarters, 6-11 Lodge Street,
Haddington, East Lothian, EH41 3DX
Director of Community
Services . . . . Dr Sue Ross . . . . Tel: (01620) 827542
Fax: (01620) 826202

East Renfrewshire Council
Council Headquarters
Eastwood Park
Rouken Glen Road
Giffnock
East Renfrewshire, G46 6UG
Tel: (0141) 577 3000 Fax: (0141) 620 0884
E-mail: customerservices@eastrenfrewshire.gov.uk
Web: www.eastrenfrewshire.gov.uk

Political Control . . . . Labour/SNP/Liberal Democrat/Independent

Leader of the Council . . . . . . Cllr Jim Fletcher . . . . Tel: (0141) 577 3112
Fax: (0141) 577 3119
E:-mail: jim.fletcher@
eastrenfrewshire.gov.uk

Chief Executive . . . . Mrs Lorraine McMillan . . . . Tel: (0141) 577 3009
Fax: (0141) 577 3890
Deputy Chief Executive . . . . Mrs Caroline Innes . . . . Tel: (0141) 577 3161
Fax: (0141) 577 3017
Director of Community Health
  and Care Partnership . . . Mrs Julie Murray . . . . Tel: (0141) 577 3839
Fax: (0141) 577 3846
Director of Environment . . . Mr Andrew Cahill . . . . Tel: (0141) 577 3036
Fax: (0141) 577 3078
Director of Finance . . . . Mr Norie Williamson . . . . . . Tel: (0141) 577 3060
Fax: (0141) 621 0921
Public Relations Manager . . . Mr Hugh Dougherty . . . . . . Tel: (0141) 577 3851
Fax: (0141) 577 3852
Senior Public Relations
  Officer . . . . Mr George Barbour . . . . Tel: (0141) 577 3853
Fax: (0141) 577 3852

Barrhead Council Offices, 211 Main Street, Barrhead, East Renfrewshire, G78 1SY
Director of Education . . . . . . Mr John Wilson . . . . Tel: (0141) 577 3479
Fax: (0141) 577 3405

The City of Edinburgh Council
Waverley Court, 4 East Market Street
Edinburgh, EH8 8BG
Tel: (0131) 200 2000 Fax: (0131) 469 3010
E-mail: corporate.communications@edinburgh.gov.uk
Web: www.edinburgh.gov.uk

Political Control . . . . Liberal Democrat/SNP

Leader of the Council . . . . . . Cllr Jenny Dawe . . . . Tel: (0131) 529 3261
Fax: (0131) 529 4979

Chief Executive . . . . Mr Tom Aitchison . . . . Tel: (0131) 469 3002
Fax: (0131) 469 3010
Director of Children and
Families . . . . Mrs Gillian Tee . . . . Tel: (0131) 469 3322
Fax: (0131) 469 3320
Director of City
Development . . . . Mr Dave Anderson . . . . Tel: (0131) 529 3524
Fax: (0131) 529 3498
Director of Corporate
Services . . . . Mr Jim Inch . . . . Tel: (0131) 469 3067
Fax: (0131) 469 3092

Director of Finance . . . . Mr Donald McGougan . . . . Tel: (0131) 469 3005
Fax: (0131) 469 3010
Director of Health and
Social Care . . . . Mr Peter Gabbitas . . . . Tel: (0131) 553 8289
Fax: (0131) 554 4863
Director of Services for
Communities . . . . Mr Mark Turley . . . . Tel: (0131) 529 7325
Fax: (0131) 529 7103
Head of Corporate
Communications . . . . Ms Isabell Reid . . . . Tel: (0131) 529 4020
Fax: (0131) 529 7479
Head of Culture and
Sport . . . . Ms Lynne Halfpenny . . . . . . Tel: (0131) 529 3657
Fax: (0131) 529 3321

*Note: The postal address for the Council Leader is: City Chambers, High Street,
Edinburgh, EH1 1YJ*

Falkirk Council
Municipal Buildings
Falkirk, FK1 5RS
Tel: (01324) 506070 Fax: (01324) 506071
E-mail: contact.centre@falkirk.gov.uk
Web: www.falkirk.gov.uk

Political Control . . . . Labour/Independent/Conservative

Leader of the Council . . . . . . Cllr Linda Gow . . . . Tel: (01324) 506070

Chief Executive . . . . Mrs Mary Pitcaithly OBE . . . . Tel: (01324) 506070

Community Services
The Falkirk Stadium, Westfield, Falkirk, FK2 9DX
Director of Community
　　Services . . . . Ms Maureen Campbell . . . . . Tel: (01324) 506070
Head of Culture and
　　Lifelong Learning . . . . . . Ms Sue Selwyn . . . . Tel: (01324) 590903
Head of Economic
　　Development . . . . Mr Douglas Duff . . . . Tel: (01324) 590905

Corporate and Neighbourhood Services
The Forum, Calendar Business Park, Falkirk, FK1 1XR
Director of Corporate and
　　Neighbourhood Services . Mr Stuart Ritchie . . . . Tel: (01324) 506070
Head of Business Services . . Mr David McGhee . . . . Tel: (01324) 590788
Head of Estates Management Mr Carl Bullough . . . . Tel: (01324) 503020
Head of Human Resources . . Ms Karen Algie . . . . Tel: (01324) 506070
Head of ICT . . . . Mr Lawrie McFall . . . . Tel: (01324) 506070
Head of Policy and
　　Performance Review . . . . Ms Fiona Campbell . . . . Tel: (01324) 506070
Head of Service (Housing) . . Ms Jennifer Litts . . . . Tel: (01324) 590789

Development Services
Abbotsford House, David's Loan, Bainsford, Falkirk, FK3 4HQ
Director of Development
　　Services . . . . Ms Rhona Geisler . . . . Tel: (01324) 504950
Head of Environmental and
　　Regulatory Services
　　(Acting) . . . . Mr Russell Cartwright . . . . . Tel: (01324) 504950
Head of Planning and
　　Transportation Services
　　(Acting) . . . . Mr John Angell . . . . Tel: (01324) 504950
Head of Roads and Design
　　Services . . . . Mr Robert McMaster . . . . . . Tel: (01324) 504950

Falkirk Council (Continued)

Education Services
McLaren House, Marchmont Avenue, Polmont, Falkirk, FK2 0NZ
Director of Education . . . . . . Mrs Julia Swan . . . . Tel: (01324) 506600

Finance and Services
Director of Finance . . . . Mr Alex Jannetta . . . . Tel: (01324) 506300
Head of Accountancy
    Services . . . . Mr Dougie McGregor . . . . . Tel: (01324) 506353
Head of Payroll and
    Pensions . . . . Mr David Cunningham . . . . Tel: (01324) 506333
Head of Revenue
    Services . . . . Mr Jim Littlejohn . . . . Tel: (01324) 506990
Head of Treasury and
    Investment Services . . . . . Mr Bryan Smail . . . . Tel: (01324) 506337

Social Work Services
The Forum, Calendar Business Park, Falkirk, FK1 1XR
Director of Social Work
    Services *(Acting)* . . . . Ms Margaret Anderson . . . . Tel: (01324) 506400
Heads of Service -
    Children and Families
      and Criminal Justice . . . Ms Rosie Bolton
                       Ms Kathy McCarroll . . . . . . Tel: (01324) 506400
    Community Care . . . . . . Ms Marian Reddie . . . . Tel: (01324) 506400

Law and Administration Services
Head of Legal Services . . . . . Ms Rose Mary Glackin . . . . . Tel: (01324) 506070

Fife Council

Fife House, North Street, Glenrothes, KY7 5LT
Tel: (0845) 155 5555
E-mail: fife.council@fife.gov.uk
Web: www.fife.gov.uk

Political Control . . . . SNP / Liberal Democrats

Leader of the Council . . . . . . Cllr Peter Grant

Chief Executive . . . . Mr Ronnie Hinds

Executive Director for
    Education . . . . Mr Ken Greer . . . . Tel: (0845) 155 5555
                                               Ext: 443928

Executive Director for Environmental
    and Development Service) Mr Stuart Nicol . . . . Tel: (0845) 155 5555
                                               Ext: 442199

Executive Director for
    Finance and Resources . . Mr Brian Lawrie . . . . Tel: (0845) 155 5555
                                               Ext: 440972

Executive Director for Housing
    and Communities . . . . . . Mr Steve Grimmond . . . . . . Tel: (0845) 155 5555
                                               Ext: 444143

Executive Director for Performance
    and Organisational
    Support . . . . Mr Michael Enston . . . . Tel: (0845) 155 5555
                                               Ext: 441198

Executive Director for
    Social Work . . . . Mr Stephen Moore . . . . Tel: (0845) 155 5555
                                               Ext: 441201

Head of Local and
    Community Services . . . . Mr Joe Fitzpatrick . . . . Tel: (0845) 155 5555
                                               Ext: 444143

Head of Housing . . . . Mr Derek Muir . . . . Tel: (0845) 155 5555
                                               Ext: 444530

Team Leader, External
    Relations . . . . Mr Bruce Manson . . . . Tel: (0845) 155 5555
                                               Ext: 441244

Carleton House, Balgonie Road, Markinch
Head of Information
    Technology . . . . Mr Terry Trundley . . . . Tel: (0845) 155 5555
                                               Ext: 440238

Glasgow City Council

City Chambers, George Square, Glasgow, G2 1DU
Tel: (0141) 287 2000 Fax: (0141) 287 5666
E-mail: pr@glasgow.gov.uk
Web: www.glasgow.gov.uk

Political Control . . . . Labour

Leader of the Council . . . . . . Cllr Stephen Purcell

Chief Executive . . . . Mr George Black . . . . Tel: (0141) 287 4739
E-mail: george.black@
glasgow.gov.uk

Executive Director, Corporate
Services . . . . Mr Ian Drummond . . . . Tel: (0141) 287 4521
E-mail: ian.drummond@
glasgow.gov.uk

Head of Communication and
Organisational
Development . . . . Mr Colin Edgar . . . . Tel: (0141) 287 0901
E-mail: colin.edgar@
glasgow.gov.uk

Head of Corporate Policy and
Service Reform . . . . Ms Dawn Corbett . . . . . . Tel: (0141) 287 4604
E-mail: dawncorbett@
glasgow.gov.uk

229 George Street, Glasgow, G2 1QU
Executive Director of
Development and
Regeneration Services . . . Mr Steve Inch . . . . Tel: (0141) 287 7200
E-mail: steve.inch@
drs.glasgow.gov.uk

Assistant Directors . . . . Mr Gerry Gormal . . . . . . Tel: (0141) 287 8400
E-mail: gerry.gormal@
drs.glasgow.gov.uk

Mr James Cunningham . . Tel: (0141) 287 7294
E-mail: james.cunningham@
drs.glasgow.gov.uk

231 George Street, Glasgow, G1 1RX
Executive Director of Land
and Environmental
Services . . . . Mr Robert Booth . . . . . . Tel: (0141) 287 9100
E-mail: robert.booth@
glasgow.gov.uk

Assistant Directors . . . . Mr Tommy McDonald . Tel: (0141) 287 6511
E-mail: tommy.mcdonald@
eps.glasgow.gov.uk

Mr George Gillespie . . . . Tel: (0141) 287 9013
E-mail: george.gillespie@
glasgow.gov.uk

Glasgow City Council (Continued)

285 George Street, Glasgow, G2 1DU
Executive Director of Financial
Services . . . . Ms Lynn Brown . . . . Tel: (0141) 287 3837
E-mail: lynn.brown@
glasgow.gov.uk
Assistant Director . . . . Ms Morag Johnston . . . . Tel: (0141) 287 4316
E-mail: morag.johnston@
glasgow.gov.uk

Charlotte House, 78 Queen Street, Glasgow, G1 3DR
City Assessor and Electoral
Registration Officer. . . . . Mr Hugh Munro . . . . . . Tel: (0141) 287 7515
E-mail: hugh.munro@
fs.glasgow.gov.uk

Port Dundas Business Park, 100 Borron Street, Glasgow, G4 9XE
Director of Direct and
Care Services. . . . . Mr Fergus Chambers . . . Tel: (0141) 353 9130
E-mail: fergus.chambers@
dacs.glasgow.gov.uk

350 Darnick Street, Glasgow, G21 4BA
Managing Director of City
Building (Glasgow) LLP Mr Willie Docherty. . . . . Tel: (0141) 287 1785
E-mail: williedocherty@
glasgow.gov.uk

20 Trongate, Glasgow, G1 5EY
Chief Executive of Culture
and Sport (Glasgow). . . . Ms Bridget McConnell. . Tel: (0141) 287 5058
Fax: (0141) 287 5151
E-mail: bridget.mcconnell@
glasgow.gov.uk

Wheatley House, 25 Cochrane Street, Glasgow, G1 1HL
Executive Director of
Social Care Services . . . . Mr David Crawford . . . . Tel: (0141) 287 8853
E-mail: david.crawford@
glasgow.gov.uk
Service Director of
Education . . . . Ms Maureen McKenna . Tel: (0141) 287 4111
E-mail: maureen.mckenna@
education.glasgow.gov.uk
Assistant Director . . . . Mr David Williams. . . . . Tel: (0141) 287 8847
E-mail: david.williams@
sw.glasgow.gov.uk

The Highland Council

Glenurquhart Road
Inverness, IV3 5NX
Tel: (01463) 702000 Fax: (01463) 702111
E-mail: webmaster@highland.gov.uk
Web: www.highland.gov.uk

Political Control . . . . Independent

**Convener of the
Council** . . . . Cllr Sandy Park . . . . Tel: (01463) 702832
Fax: (01463) 702830

Vice Convener. . . . . Cllr Dr Michael Foxley . . . . Tel: (01463) 702832
Fax: (01463) 702830

Chief Executive. . . . . Mr Alistair Dodds. . . . . Tel: (01463) 702837
Fax: (01463) 702830

Director of Education,
Culture and Sport. . . . . . Mr Hugh Fraser . . . . Tel: (01463) 702801
Fax: (01463) 702828

Director of Finance. . . . . Mr Alan Geddes. . . . . Tel: (01463) 702301
Fax: (01463) 702310

Director of Housing and
Property . . . . Mr Steve Barron. . . . . Tel: (01463) 702853
Fax: (01463) 702879

Director of Planning and
Development. . . . . Mr Stuart Black . . . . Tel: (01463) 702251
Fax: (01463) 702298

Director of Social Work . . . . Mrs Harriet Dempster . . . . . Tel: (01463) 702860
Fax: (01463) 702855

Director of Transport,
Environmental and
Community Services. . . . Mr Neil Gillies . . . . Tel: (01463) 702601
Fax: (01463) 702606

Inverclyde Council

Municipal Buildings
Greenock, PA15 1LY
Tel: (01475) 717171 Fax: (01475) 712010
E-mail: [firstname.lastname]@inverclyde.gov.uk
Web: www.inverclyde.gov.uk

Political Control . . . . Labour

Leader of the Council . . . . . . Cllr Stephen McCabe

Chief Executive . . . . Mr John Mundell

Corporate Director of Education and
    Social Care . . . . *Vacant* . . . . Tel: (01475) 712748
                                                     Fax: (01475) 712731
Corporate Director Environment and
    Community Protection . . Mr Neil Graham . . . . Tel: (01475) 712709

Corporate Director Improvement
    and Performance . . . . Mr Paul Wallace . . . . Tel: (01475) 712700
                                                     Fax: (01475) 712731

Corporate Director Regeneration
    and Resources . . . . Mr Aubrey Fawcett . . . . Tel: (01475) 712764
                                                     Fax: (01475) 712731

Cathcart House, 6 Cathcart Square, Greenock, PA15 1LS
Physical Investment Team
    Manager, Legal and
    Administration Service . . Mr Gerard Malone . . . . Tel: (01475) 712710
                                                     Fax: (01475) 712127

Dalrymple House, Dalrymple Street, Greenock, PA15 1LD
Chief Social Work Officer . . Mr Robert Murphy . . . . Tel: (01475) 714011
                                                     Fax: (01475) 714060

The Business Store, Cathcart Street, Greenock, PA15 1DO
Head of Economic and
    Social Regeneration. . . . . Mr Stuart Jamieson. . . . . Tel: (01475) 715555
                                                     Fax: (01475) 715608

Midlothian Council
Midlothian House
Buccleuch Street
Dalkeith
Midlothian, EH22 1DJ
Tel: (0131) 270 7500 Fax: (0131) 271 3050
E-mail: enquiries@midlothian.gov.uk
Web: www.midlothian.gov.uk

Political Control . . . . Labour

Leader of the Council . . . . . . Cllr Derek Milligan. . . . . Tel: (0131) 270 7500
Fax: (0131) 270 3050

Chief Executive . . . . Mr Kenneth Lawrie . . . . Tel: (0131) 270 7500
Fax: (0131) 271 3014
Director, Corporate
Services . . . . Mr Ian Jackson . . . . Tel: (0131) 270 7500
Fax: (0131) 271 3251
Director, Strategic
Services . . . . Mr Ian L Young. . . . . Tel: (0131) 270 3402
Fax: (0131) 271 3239

Communications Manager . . Mr Stephen Fraser . . . . Tel: (0131) 271 3425
Fax: (0131) 271 3536

Dundas Buildings, 62A Potton Street, Bonnyrigg, Midlothian. EH19 3YD
Director, Commercial
Services . . . . Mr John Blair . . . . Tel: (0131) 663 1103
Fax: (0131) 654 2797

Development Unit, Strategic Services, 1 Eskdaill Court, Dalkeith, EH22 1AG
European Officer . . . . *Vacant* . . . . Tel: (0131) 271 7500
Fax: (0131) 271 3535

Fairfield House, 8 Lothian Road, Dalkeith, Midlothian, EH22 3AA
Director Education and
Communities . . . . Mr Donald MacKay . . . . Tel: (0131) 270 7500
Fax: (0131) 271 3751

Director Social Work . . . . . . Mr Colin Anderson . . . . Tel: (0131) 270 7500
Fax: (0131) 271 3624

The Moray Council

Council Offices, High Street
Elgin, IV30 1BX
Tel: (01343) 543451 Fax: (01343) 563335
E-mail: hotline@moray.gov.uk
Web: www.moray.gov.uk

Political Control . . . . Independent/Conservative

Leader of the Council . . . . . . Cllr George McIntyre . . . . . . Tel: (01343) 563111
Fax: (01343) 563199
E-mail: convener@
moray.gov.uk

Chief Executive . . . . Mr Alastair Keddie . . . . Tel: (01343) 563001
Fax: (01343) 540399
E-mail: akeddie@
moray.gov.uk

Chief Legal Officer . . . . Mr Roddy Burns . . . . Tel: (01343) 563011
Fax: (01343) 540183
E-mail: roddy.burns@
moray.gov.uk

Chief Financial Officer . . . . . Mr Mark Palmer . . . . Tel: (01343) 563103
Fax: (01343) 563221
E-mail: palmerm@
moray.gov.uk

Director of Community
Services . . . . Mr Sandy Riddell . . . . Tel: (01343) 563530
Fax: (01343) 563521
E-mail: sandy.riddell@
moray.gov.uk

Director, Environmental
Services . . . . Mr Robert Stewart . . . . Tel: (01343) 563260
Fax: (01343) 563483
E-mail: stewart@
moray.gov.uk

Director of Educational
Services . . . . Mr Donald Duncan . . . . Tel: (01343) 563134
Fax: (01343) 563478
E-mail: donald.duncan@
moray.gov.uk

Public Relations
Co-ordinator . . . . Mr Raymond Shewan . . . . . . Tel: (01343) 563046
Fax: (01343) 563311
E-mail: raymond.shewan@
moray.gov.uk

North Ayrshire Council

Cunninghame House
Friars Croft
Irvine
Ayrshire, KA12 8EE
Tel: (0845) 603 0590 Fax: (01294) 324114
Web: www.north-ayrshire.gov.uk

Political Control . . . . Labour

Leader of the Council . . . . . . Cllr David O'Neill . . . . Tel: (01294) 324172
Fax: (01294) 324114

Chief Executive . . . . Ms Elma Murray . . . . Tel: (01294) 324124
Fax: (01294) 324114
Corporate Director,
Educational Services . . . . Ms Carol Kirk . . . . Tel: (01294) 324412
Fax: (01294) 324444
Corporate Director,
Property Services . . . . . . Mr Tom Orr . . . . Tel: (01294) 324620
Fax: (01294) 324624
Corporate Director,
Social Services . . . . Ms Bernadette Docherty . . . Tel: (01294) 317725
Fax: (01294) 317701
Team Leader
(Communications) . . . . . Ms Anne Clarke . . . . Tel: (01294) 324141
Fax: (01294) 324154

Perceton House, Perceton, Irvine, Ayrshire, KA11 2DE
European Officer . . . . Ms Linda Aird . . . . Tel: (01294) 225195
Fax: (01294) 225184

North Lanarkshire Council
Civic Centre
Windmillhill Street, Motherwell, ML1 1AB
Tel: (01698) 302222 Fax: (01698) 275125
Web: www.northlanarkshire.gov.uk

Political Control . . . . Labour

Leader of the Council . . . . . . Cllr James McCabe . . . . Tel: (01698) 302226

Chief Executive . . . . Mr Gavin Whitefield . . . . . . Tel: (01698) 302452

Assistant Chief Executive . . . Mr Russell Ellerby . . . . Tel: (01698) 302251

Executive Director
  Corporate Services . . . . . Mr John O'Hagan . . . . Tel: (01698) 302344

Executive Director Finance
  and Customer Services . . Mr Alastair Crichton . . . . . . Tel: (01698) 302200

Executive Director
  Environmental Services . . Mr Paul Jukes . . . . Tel: (01698) 302746

Executive Director Learning
  and Leisure Services . . . . Ms Christine Pollock . . . . . . Tel: (01698) 302634

Executive Director Housing and
  Social Work Services . . . . Ms Mary Castles . . . . Tel: (01698) 302350

Head of Corporate
  Communications and
  Marketing . . . . Mr Stephen Penman . . . . Tel: (01698) 302591

Orkney Islands Council

Council Offices
School Place
Kirkwall
Orkney, KW15 1NY
E-mail: customerservice@orkney.gov.uk
Tel: (01856) 873535 Fax: (01856) 874615
Web: www.orkney.gov.uk

Political Control . . . . Independent

Leader of the Council . . . . . . Cllr Stephen Hagan

Chief Executive . . . . Mr Alistair Buchan . . . . E-mail: chief.executive@
orkney.gov.uk

Assistant Chief Executive . . . Ms Elaine Grieve . . . . E-mail: administration-
email@orkney.gov.uk

Director of Community
Social Services . . . . Mr Duncan MacAulay . . . . . E-mail: social.services@
orkney.gov.uk

Director of Corporate
Services . . . . Ms Elaine Grieve . . . . E-mail: social.services@
orkney.gov.uk

Director of Education and
Leisure Services . . . . Mr Leslie Manson . . . . E-mail: education@
orkney.gov.uk

Director of Finance and
Housing . . . . Mr Albert Tait . . . . E-mail: finance@
orkney.gov.uk

Director of Development and
Environment Services . . . Mr Brian Thomson . . . . E-mail: technical.services@
orkney.gov.uk

Head of Law and
Administration . . . . Ms Fiona MacDonald

Development and Officer
(EU Liaison) . . . . Mrs Phyllis Harvey

Communications Officer . . . Ms Lynette Webb

Harbour Authority Building, Scapa, Orkney, KW15 1SD
Director of Marine Services . Captain Nigel Mills . . . . E-mail: harbours@
orkney.gov.uk

Perth and Kinross Council
2 High Street
Perth, PH1 5PH
Tel: (01738) 475000 Fax: (01738) 475710
E-mail: enquiries@pkc.gov.uk
Web: www.pkc.gov.uk

Political Control . . . . SNP and Liberal Democrat Partnership

Leader of the Council . . . . . . Cllr Ian Miller . . . . Tel: (01738) 475039
Fax: (01738) 475007

Chief Executive . . . . Miss Bernadette
Malone . . . . Tel: (01738) 475001
E-mail: bmalone@pkc.gov.uk

Depute Chief Executive . . . . Mr Jim Irons . . . . Tel: (01738) 476501
E-mail: jfirons@pkc.gov.uk
Head of Strategic Management
and Improvement . . . . . . Ms Tina Yule . . . . Tel: (01738) 475002
E-mail: clyule@pkc.gov.uk
Head of Democratic
Services . . . . Ms Gillian Taylor . . . . Tel: (01738) 475135
E-mail: gataylor@pkc.gov.uk

Corporate Services
Executive Director (Corporate
Services) . . . . *Vacant* . . . . Tel: (01738) 475501
E-mail: gstevenson@pkc.gov.uk
Head of Finance . . . . Mr John Symon . . . . . Tel: (01738) 475504
E-mail: jsymon@pkc.gov.uk
Head of Human Resources . . Mr Hugh Mackenzie . . Tel: (01738) 475402
E-mail: hlmackenzie@pkc.gov.uk
Head of Legal Services . . . . . Mr Ian Innes . . . . Tel: (01738) 475503
E-mail: iinnes@pkc.gov.uk
Head of Property . . . . Mr Russell Thomson . Tel: (01738) 475901
E-mail: jrthomson@pkc.gov.uk
Head of Shared Support
Services . . . . Mr Alan Nairn . . . . . . Tel: (01738) 475502
E-mail: ajnairn@pkc.gov.uk
Head of IST . . . . Ms Karen Lawrie . . . . Tel: (01738) 476603
E-mail: klawrie@pkc.gov.uk

Education and Children's Services
Pullar House, 35 Kinnoull Street, Perth, PH1 5GD
Executive Director (Education
and Children's Services) . Mr John Fyffe . . . . Tel: (01738) 476205
E-mail: jfyffe@pkc.gov.uk
Depute Director (Education
and Children's Services) . Ms Maria Walker . . . . Tel: (01738) 476313
E-mail: mwalker@pkc.gov.uk

Perth and Kinross Council (Continued)

Head of Children's and
   Families' Services . . . . . . Mr Bill Atkinson . . . . . Tel: (01738) 476205
                                                   E-mail: batkinson@pkc.gov.uk
Head of Education Services . Mr Chris Webb. . . . . . Tel: (01738) 476312
     E-mail: cwebb@pkc.gov.uk
Head of Support Services . . . Mr Alan Taylor. . . . . . Tel: (01738) 476225
     E-mail: amtaylor@pkc.gov.uk
Head of Cultural and
   Community Services. . . . Ms Heather Jack . . . . . Tel: (01738) 476313

The Environment Service
Pullar House, 35 Kinnoull Street, Perth, PH1 5GD
Executive Director
   (Environment Service) . . Mr Jim Irons . . . . Tel: (01738) 476501
     E-mail: jfirons@pkc.gov.uk
Depute Director
   (Environment Service) . . Mr Jim Valentine. . . . . E-mail: jvalentine@pkc.gov.uk
Head of Environmental and
   Consumer Services . . . . . Mr Keith McNamara . Tel: (01738) 476404
     E-mail: kdmcnamara@pkc.gov.uk
Head of Operations and
   Support Services . . . . Mr John Walker . . . . . Tel: (01738) 476505
     E-mail: jwalker@pkc.gov.uk
Head of Planning . . . . Mr Roland Bean . . . . . Tel: (01738) 475305
     E-mail: rabean@pkc.gov.uk
Head of Public Space
   Management . . . . Mr Adam Olenjnik . . . Tel: (01738) 476520
     E-mail: aolejnik@pkc.gov.uk
5 High Street, Perth
Head of Economic
   Development. . . . . Mr Ken Macdonald . . Tel: (01738) 477942
     E-mail: kjmacdonald@pkc.gov.uk

Housing and Community Care
Pullar House, 35 Kinnoull Street, Perth, PH1 5GD
Executive Director (Housing
   and Community Care) . . Mr David Burke . . . . . Tel: (01738) 475101
     E-mail: dburke@pkc.gov.uk
Depute Director (Housing
   and Community Care) . . Mr John Walker . . . . . Tel: (01738) 476701
     E-mail: dburke@pkc.gov.uk
Head of Housing. . . . . Ms Helen Turley. . . . . Tel: (01738) 476003
     E-mail: hturley@pkc.gov.uk
Head of Planning and
   Business Support . . . . . . Mr Roland Bean . . . . . Tel: (01738) 475000
     E-mail: rabean@pkc.gov.uk
Head of Strategy and
   Support. . . . . Ms Lorna Cameron . . Tel: (01738) 475300
     E-mail: lcameron@pkc.gov.uk

5 Whitefriars Crescent, Perth, PH2 0PA
Head of Community Care . . Mr Jim Dean . . . . Tel: (01738) 476702
     E-mail: jimdean@pkc.gov.uk

Renfrewshire Council
Renfrewshire House
Cotton Street
Paisley
Renfrewshire, PA1 1TR
Tel: (0141) 842 5000 Fax: (0141) 840 3335
Web: www.renfrewshire.gov.uk

Political Control . . . . SNP / Liberal Democrat

Leader of the Council . . . . . . Cllr Derek MacKay . . . . Tel: (0141) 840 3548
Fax: (0141) 840 3366

Chief Executive . . . . Mr David Martin . . . . Tel: (0141) 840 3601
Fax: (0141) 840 3349

Director of Corporate
Services . . . . Mr Paul Gannon . . . . Tel: (0141) 840 3471
Fax: (0141) 840 3635

Director of Education and
Leisure Services . . . . Mr John Rooney . . . . Tel: (0141) 842 5601
Fax: (0141) 842 5655

Director of Environmental
Services . . . . Ms Shona MacDougall . . . . . Tel: (0141) 840 3100
Fax: (0141) 840 3233

Director of Finance
and IT . . . . Ms Sandra Black . . . . Tel: (0141) 842 5051
Fax: (0141) 842 5055

Director of Housing and
Property Services . . . . . . Ms Mary Crearie . . . . Tel: (0141) 842 5643
Fax: (0141) 842 5883

Director of Planning and
Transport . . . . Mr Bob Darracott . . . . Tel: (0141) 842 5855
Fax: (0141) 842 5040

Director of Social Work . . . . Mr Peter Macleod . . . . Tel: (0141) 842 5167
Fax: (0141) 842 5144

Head of Policy . . . . Mr Ron Morrison . . . . Tel: (0141) 840 3228
Fax: (0141) 840 3349

Scottish Borders Council
Council Headquarters
Newtown St Boswells, Melrose
Roxburghshire, TD6 0SA
Tel: (01835) 824000 Fax: (01835) 825001
Web: www.scotborders.gov.uk

Political Control . . . . Liberal Democrat/Conservative

Convener of the Council . . . . Cllr Alasdair Hutton . . . . Tel: (01835) 824000
Ext: 5942
Fax: (01835) 825059

Leader of the Council . . . . . . Cllr David Parker . . . . Tel: (01835) 824000
Ext: 5201
Fax: (01835) 825059

Chief Executive . . . . Mr David Hume . . . . Tel: (01835) 825055
Fax: (01835) 825059

Director of Education and
Lifelong and Learning . . . Mr Glenn Rodger . . . . Tel: (01835) 825095
Fax: (01835) 825091
Director of Resources . . . . . . Ms Tracey Logan . . . . Tel: (01835) 826673
Fax: (01835) 825001
Director of Planning and
Economic Development . Mr Ian Lindley . . . . Tel: (01835) 825065
Fax: (01835) 825061
Director of Social Care and
Community
Services . . . . Mr Andrew Lowe . . . . Tel: (01835) 825085
Fax: (01835) 825081
Director of Technical
Services *(Acting)* . . . . Mr Ray Oxby . . . . Tel: (01835) 825075
Fax: (01835) 825071
Head of Business
Improvement . . . . Ms Jo Tolland . . . . Tel: (01835) 824000

Corporate Communications
Officer . . . . Ms Kathleen Travers . . . . . . Tel: (01835) 825008
Fax: (01835) 825059

Scott House, Sprouston Road, Newtown St Boswells, Melrose,
Roxburghshire, TD6 0QD
Assessor and Electoral
Registration Officer . . . . . Mr Leslie Walker . . . . Tel: (01835) 825100
Fax: (01835) 825105

Shetland Islands Council
Town Hall, Lerwick, Shetland, ZE1 0HB
Tel: (01595) 693535 Fax: (01595) 744509
E-mail: general.enquiry.office@shetland.gov.uk
Web: www.shetland.gov.uk

Political Control . . . . Independent

**Convener of the
Council** . . . . Cllr Sandy Cluness . . . . Tel: (01595) 744544
Fax: (01595) 744509
E-mail: convener@
shetland.gov.uk
Chief Executive . . . . Mr David Clerk . . . . Tel: (01595) 744500
Fax: (01595) 744509
Montfield, Burgh Road, Lerwick, ZE1 0TY
Head of Service, Finance . . . Mr Graham Johnston . . . . . . Tel: (01595) 744681
Fax: (01595) 744667
6 Northness Business Park, ZE1 0LZ
Head of Housing . . . . Mr Chris Medley . . . . Tel: (01595) 744360
Fax: (01595) 744395
4 Market Street, Lerwick, Shetland, ZE1 0JN
Head of Legal and
Administration . . . . Mr Jan Riise . . . . Tel: (01595) 744550

Grantfield, Lerwick, ZE1 0NT
Executive Director,
Infrastructure Services . . Mr Gordon Greenhill . . . . . . Tel: (01595) 744800
Fax: (01595) 744804
Heads of Service:
Planning . . . . Mr Iain McDiarmid
Roads . . . . Mr Ian Halcrow
Transport . . . . Mr Michael Craigie

Hayfield House, Hayfield Lane, Lerwick, ZE1 0QD
Executive Director, Education
and Social Care . . . . Ms Hazel Sutherland . . . . . . Tel: (01595) 744000
Fax: (01595) 744010
Head of Economic
Development . . . . Mr Neil Grant . . . . Tel: (01595) 744940
Fax: (01595) 744961
Head of Children's Services . Mr Stephen Morgan . . . . Tel: (01595) 744400
Fax: (01595) 744436
Head of Schools . . . . Ms Helen Budge . . . . Tel: (01595) 744000
Fax: (01595) 692810

Port Administration Building, Sella Ness, Sullom Voe, ZE2 9QR
General Manager, Ports and
Harbours Operations . . . . Mr Roger Moore . . . . Tel: (01806) 242551
Fax: (01806) 242237

South Ayrshire Council

County Buildings
Wellington Square
Ayr, KA7 1DR
Tel: (01292) 612000 Fax: (01292) 612158
E-mail: [firstname.lastname]@south-ayrshire.gov.uk
Web: www.south-ayrshire.gov.uk

Political Control . . . . Conservative Minority

Leader of the Council . . . . . . Cllr Hugh Hunter . . . . Tel: (01292) 612390
Fax: (01292) 612376

Chief Executive . . . . Mr David Anderson . . . . Tel: (01292) 612170
Fax: (01292) 612158

Deputy Chief Executive and
Executive Director -
Development and
Environment . . . . Mr Graham Peterkin . . . . . . Tel: (01292) 612182
Fax: (01292) 612106

Executive Director -
Children and Community Mr Harry Garland . . . . Tel: (01292) 612419
Fax: (01292) 612481

Executive Director -
Corporate Services . . . . . Mrs Eileen Howat . . . . Tel: (01292) 612912
Fax: (01292) 612105

South Lanarkshire Council
Council Offices, Almada Street
Hamilton, South Lanarkshire, ML3 0AA
Tel: (01698) 454444 Fax: (01698) 454275
Web: www.southlanarkshire.gov.uk

Political Control . . . . Labour Minority

Leader of the Council . . . . . . Cllr Eddie McAvoy. . . . . Tel: (01698) 454626
Fax: (01698) 454960

Chief Executive . . . . Mr Archibald Strang. . . . . . . Tel: (01698) 454208
Fax: (01698) 454275

Executive Director Finance and
Information Technology
Resources and
Depute Chief Executive . Mrs Linda Hardie. . . . . Tel: (01698) 454530
Fax: (01698) 454682

Executive Director, Community
Resources . . . . Mr Norrie Anderson. . . . . . . Tel: (01698) 454849
Fax: (01698) 454362

Executive Director,
Corporate Resources. . . . Mr Robert McIlwain . . . . . . Tel: (01698) 454660
Fax: (01698) 454637

Executive Director,
Education Resources. . . . Mr Larry Forde . . . . Tel: (01698) 454379
Fax: (01698) 454465

Executive Director, Housing and
Technical Resources . . . . Mr Jim Hayton . . . . Tel: (01698) 454406
Fax: (01698) 454341

Executive Director,
Social Work Resources . . Mr Harry Stevenson. . . . . . . Tel: (01698) 453700
Fax: (01698) 453784

Head of Corporate Communications
and Public Affairs . . . . . . Mr Drew King . . . . Tel: (01698) 454904
Fax: (01698) 454949

Montrose House, 154 Montrose Crescent, Hamilton, ML3 6LL
Executive Director,
Enterprise Resources. . . . Mr Colin McDowall. . . . . . . Tel: (01698) 454798
Fax: (01698) 454801

Stirling Council
Viewforth
Stirling, FK8 2ET
Tel: (0845) 277 7000
E-mail: [surnameinitialfirstname]@stirling.gov.uk
Web: www.stirling.gov.uk

Political Control . . . . SNP

Leader of the Council . . . . . . Cllr Graham Houston . . . . . . Tel: (01786) 443300
Fax: (01786) 442962

Chief Executive . . . . Mr Bob Jack . . . . Tel: (01786) 443320
Fax: (01786) 443474

Assistant Chief Executive
Care, Health and
Wellbeing . . . . Ms Janice Hewitt . . . . Tel: (01786) 442677
Fax: (01786) 442933

Assistant Chief Executive
Learning, Empowerment
and Citizenship . . . . Ms Linda Kinney . . . . Tel: (01786) 442526
Fax: (01786) 442933

Assistant Chief Executive
Sustainability, Economy
and Environment . . . . . . Ms Rebecca Maxwell . . . . . . Tel: (01786) 443366
Fax: (01786) 442933

Manager, Chief Executive
Office . . . . Mr Bill Scott . . . . Tel: (01786) 443341
Fax: (01786) 442933

West Dunbartonshire Council

Council Offices
Garshake Road
Dunbarton, G82 3PU
Tel: (01389) 737000 Fax: (01389) 737070
E-mail: [firstname.surname]@west-dunbarton.gov.uk
Web: www.west-dunbarton.gov.uk

Political Control . . . . SNP

Leader of the Council . . . . . . Cllr Iain Robertson . . . . Tel: (01389) 737547
Fax: (01389) 737544

Chief Executive . . . . Mr David McMillan . . . . Tel: (01389) 737667
Fax: (01389) 737669

Director of Educational
Services . . . . Mr Terry Lanagan . . . . Tel: (01389) 737301

Director of Housing,
and Environmental and
Economic Development . Ms Elaine Melrose . . . . Tel: (01389) 737603

Director of Social Work
and Health. . . . . Mr Bill Clark. . . . . Tel: (01389) 737526

Head of Finance and ICT . . Mr David Connell . . . . Tel: (01389) 737191

Head of Legal and
Administrative Services. . Mr Andrew Fraser . . . . Tel: (01389)737800

Head of Personnel. . . . . Ms Tricia O'Neill . . . . Tel: (01389) 737584

Section Head - Forward
Planning . . . . Mr Steve Marshall . . . . Tel: (01389) 737164
Fax: (01389) 737512

Head of Corporate
Communications and
Marketing . . . . Ms Louise Mahon . . . . Tel: (01389) 737503
Fax: (01389) 737578

West Lothian Council
West Lothian House
Almondvale Boulevard
Livingston
West Lothian, EH54 6QG
Tel: (01506) 775000 Fax: (01506) 777249
Web: www.westlothian.gov.uk

Political Control . . . . SNP/Action to Save St John's Hospital

Leader of the Council . . . . . . Cllr Peter Johnston . . . . Tel: (01506) 281725
Fax: (01506) 281746

Chief Executive . . . . Mr Alex Linkston . . . . Tel: (01506) 281697
Fax: (01506) 281689
Director of Community Health
and Care Partnership . . . Mr Jim Forrest . . . . Tel: (01506) 281977
Fax: (01506) 281689
Director of Customer and
Support Services . . . . Mr Graham Hope . . . . Tel: (01506) 281762
Fax: (01506) 281689
Director of Development and
Environmental Services . . Mr Jim Dickson . . . . Tel: (01506) 281761
Fax: (01506) 281689
Director of Education and
Cultural Services . . . . Mr Gordon Ford . . . . Tel: (01506) 281657
Fax: (01506) 281689

Western Isles
(see Comhairie Nan Eilean Siar at p272)

LOCAL AUTHORITY EUROPEAN OFFICES

East of Scotland European Consortium
Scotland House, Rond-Point Schuman 6, B1040 - Brussels, Belgium
Tel: + 32 2 282 8428   Fax: + 32 2 282 8429

Aberdeen City Council, 4th Floor, Balgownie One
Conference Way, Bridge of Don, Aberdeen, AB23 8AQ
Tel: (01224) 814600   Fax: (01224) 814590
E -mail: info@esec.org.uk
Web: www.esec.org.uk

Head of Office and
   Policy Officer . . . . Ms Ingrid Dobson . . . . Tel: (01259) 814600

Highlands and Islands Partnership
Scotland House, Rond-Point Schuman 6, B1040 - Brussels, Belgium
Tel: + 32 2 282 8360   Fax: + 32 2 282 8363
E-mail: marie.orban@pop.kpn.be

Head of Office. . . . . Ms Marie-Yvonne Prevot

COSLA
Convention of Scottish Local Authorities
Roseberry House, 9 Haymarket Terrace, Edinburgh, EH12 5XZ
Tel: (0131) 474 9200   Fax: (0131) 474 9292
E-mail: carol@cosla.gov.uk   Web: www.cosla.gov.uk

Chief Executive. . . . . Mr Rory Mair

Brussels Office
Square de Meeus 1, B1000 - Brussels, Belgium
Tel: + 32 2 213 8120 Fax: + 32 2 213 8129
E-mail: elfreda@cosla.gov.uk   Web: www.cosla.gov.uk

Brussels Manager . . . . Ms Elfreda Whitty

Head of Office. . . . . Mr Serafin Pazos-Vidal

Scotland and the United Kingdom Parliament

Notes: (i) The following list includes all members representing Scottish constituencies in the House of Commons at Westminster.

(ii) All Members of Parliament can be contacted at the House of Commons, Westminster, London, SW1A 0AA Tel: (020) 7219 3000.

(iii) At the time of printing a by-election was pending in Glenrothes Constituency.

Alexander, Danny MP   Inverness, Nairn, Badenoch and Strathspey
Liberal Democrat . . . Majority 4,148 over Lab
Born . . . . 15th May 1972
Educated . . . . Lochaber High School; Oxford University
Elected . . . . 2005 MP for Inverness, Nairn, Badenoch and Strathspey
Offices Held . . . . 2005 - 08 Liberal Democrat Spokesman on Work
                            and Pensions
                            2007 - Chief of Staff to Nick Clegg MP (Liberal Democrat
                            Leader)
Commons Office . . . . . Tel: (020) 7219 8328 Fax: (020) 7219 1438
                            E-mail: alexanderdg@parliament.uk
                            Researcher – Mr Nick Davies
                            Tel: (020) 7219 2300
                            E-mail: daviesnj@parliament.uk
Constituency Office . . . 45 Huntly Street, Inverness, IV3 5HR
                            Tel: (01463) 711280 Fax: (01463) 714380
                            E-mail: danny@highlandlibdem.sorg.uk
                            Researcher – Mr Gavin Steel
                            E-mail: steelg@parliament.uk
                            Office Manager – Mr Fraser Grieve
                            E-mail: grievef@parliament.uk
                            Secretary – Ms Deidre McCreath
                            E-mail: mccreathd@parliament.uk
                            Caseworker – Ms Karen Fraser
                            E-mail: fraserk@parliament.uk
Parliamentary Interests Benefit Reform and Pensions; Environment; Housing;
                            Transport for Rural Communities;
Leisure Interests . . . . . . Fishing; Hill Walking; Sport; Travel

Alexander, Rt Hon Douglas MP Paisley and Renfrewshire South
Labour. . . . . Majority 13,232 over Lib Dem
Born. . . . . 26th October 1967 in Glasgow
Educated. . . . . Park Mains High School, Erskine; Lester B College, Vancouver;
                          University of Pennsylvania; Edinburgh University
Elected . . . . 1997 - 2005 MP for Paisley South (By-election)
                          2005 MP for Paisley and Renfrewshire South
Offices Held . . . . 2001 - 02 Minister of State, Department of
                          Trade and Industry
                          (Minister for E-Commerce and Competitiveness)
                          2002 - 04 Minister for the Cabinet Office and
                          Chancellor of the Duchy of Lancaster
                          2004 - 05 Minister of State, Department of Trade and
                          Industry (also at Foreign and Commonwealth Office)
                          2005 - 06 Minister of State, Foreign and Commonwealth Office
                          (Minister for Europe)
                          2006 - 07 Secretary of State for Scotland and Secretary of
                          State for Transport
                          2007 - Secretary of State for International Development
Commons Office . . . . . Tel: (020) 7219 1345
                          E-mail: alexanderd@parliament.uk
Constituency Office. . . 2014 Mile End Mill, Abbey Mill Business Centre,
                          Seedhill Road, Paisley, PA1 1JS
                          Tel: (0141) 561 0333 Fax: (0141) 561 0334
                          E-mail: dalexandermp@talk21.com
                          Web: www.douglasalexander.labour.co.uk
                          Constituency Assistant – Ms Joyce Llewellyn
Trade Union. . . . . Unite
Publications . . . . 1999: New Scotland, It Could Be
                          2005: Telling it like it Could Be
Parliamentary Interests Constitution; Employment; Industry

Bain, Willie MP   Glasgow North East
Labour. . . . . Majority 8,111 over SNP
Born. . . . . 1972 in Glasgow
Educated. . . . . St Roch's Secondary School; Strathclyde University
Elected . . . . 2009 - MP for Glasgow North East (By-election)
Commons Office . . . . . Tel: (020) 7219 4343
                          E-mail: bainw@parliament.uk
                          Web: www.williebain.com
Trade Union. . . . . Unite
Parliamentary Interests Crime; Anti-social Behaviour; Pensions

Banks, Gordon MP Ochil and Perthshire South
Labour. . . . . Majority 688 over SNP
Born. . . . . 14th June 1955 in Alloa, Northumberland
Educated. . . . . Lornshill Academy; Alloa; Glasgow College of Building;
                      Stirling University
Elected . . . . 2005 MP for Ochil and Perthshire South
Office Held . . . . 2006 - 09 PPS to James Purnell MP (2006 - 07 Minister of State,
                      Department for Work and Pensions, 2007 - Culture Secretary)
Commons Office . . . . . Tel: (020) 7219 8275 Fax: (020) 7219 8693
                      E-mail: banksgr@parliament.uk
                      Parliamentary Assistant – Miss Shefali Enaker
                      E-mail: enakers@parliament.uk
Constituency Office . . . 49-51 High Street, Alloa, Clackmannanshire, FK10 1JF
                      Tel: (01259) 721536 Fax: (01259) 216761
                      Constituency Office Manager – Miss Haldis Scott
                      E-mail: scotth@parliament.uk
                      Constituency Assistant – Mr John Spence
                      E-mail: spencej@parliament.uk
                      Constituency Researcher/Press Officer –
                      Mr Colin McFarlane
                      E-mail: mcfarlanec@parliament.uk
Directorships. . . . . Cartmore Building Supply Co Ltd
Trade Union. . . . . Unite
Parliamentary Interests Economy; Environment; Europe; Foreign Affairs;
                      International Development; Scotland
Leisure Interests. . . . . . Football; Guitar; Motor Sport

SCOTLAND MPs – CVs

Barrett, John MP . . . Edinburgh West
Liberal Democrat . . . Majority 13,600 over Labour
Born . . . . 11th February 1954 in Australia
Educated. . . . . Telford College; Napier Polytechnic
Elected . . . . 2001 MP for Edinburgh West
Offices Held . . . . 1995 - 2001 Councillor, Edinburgh City Council
                      2002 - 05 Liberal Democrat Spokesman on International
                        Development
                      2005 - 07 Liberal Democrat Spokesman on Scotland
                      2007 Liberal Democrat Spokesman on International
                        Development
                      2008 - Liberal Democrat Spokesman on Work and Pensions
Commons Office . . . . . Tel: (020) 7219 8244 Fax: Tel: (020) 7219 2340
                      E-mail: barrettj@parliament.uk
                      Web: www.johnbarrettmp.com
                      Parliamentary Assistant – Mr Euan Robinson
                      E-mail: robinsonet@parliament.uk
Constituency Office . . . 1A Drum Brae Avenue, Edinburgh, EH12 8TE
                      Tel: (0131) 339 0339 Fax: (0131) 476 7101
                      Constituency Assistant – Mr Ewan Irvine
Directorships . . . . ABC Productions
Parliamentary Interests Air and Rail Safety; Environment and Energy Production;
                      Overseas Aid; Transport
Leisure Interests. . . . . . Film; Music; Theatre; Travel

Begg, Anne MP. . . . . Aberdeen South
Labour. . . . . Majority 1,348 over Lib Dem
Born . . . . 6th December 1955 in Forfar
Educated. . . . . Brechin High School; Aberdeen University
Elected . . . . 1997 MP for Aberdeen South
Commons Office . . . . . Tel: (020) 7219 2140 Fax: (020) 7219 1264
                      Mobile: 07711 237743
                      E-mail: begga@parliament.uk
                      Web: www.annebegg.info
                      Parliamentary Assistant/Facilitator – Ms Sonia Campbell
                      E-mail: campbells@parliament.uk
Constituency Office . . . Admiral Court, Poynernook Road, Aberdeen, AB11 5QX
                      Tel: (01224) 252704 Fax: (01224) 252705
                      Office Manager – Mrs Pamela Fryer
                      E-mail: fryerpa@parliament.uk
                      Researcher – Mr Gavin Donoghue
                      E-mail: donoghueg@parliament.uk
                      Caseworker – Ms Kathryn Russell
                      E-mail: russellk@parliament.uk
Professional Association General Teaching Council for Scotland
Trade Unions . . . . Educational Institute of Scotland; GMB
Parliamentary Interests Scotland; Broadcasting; Welfare Reform; Energy; Disability
Leisure Interests. . . . . . Cinema; Reading; Theatre

Brown, Rt Hon Gordon MP Kirkcaldy and Cowdenbeath
Labour. . . . . Majority 18,216 over SNP
Born. . . . . 20th February 1951 in Glasgow
Educated. . . . . Kirkcaldy High School; Edinburgh University
Elected . . . . 1983 - 2005 MP for Dunfermline East
. . . . MP for Kirkcaldy and Cowdenbeath
Offices Held . . . . 1985 - 87 Opposition Spokesman on Trade and Industry
. . . . 1987 - 89 Shadow Chief Secretary to the Treasury
. . . . 1989 - 92 Shadow Trade and Industry Secretary
. . . . 1992 - 97 Shadow Chancellor of the Exchequer
. . . . 1997 - 2007 Chancellor of the Exchequer
. . . . 2007 - Prime Minister
Contacts . . . . Tel: (020) 7930 4433
. . . . E-mails: https://email.number10.gov.uk
. . . . browng@parliament.uk
. . . . Web: www.number10.gov.uk
Constituency Office . . . Unit 1B, Cowdenbeath Business Centre,
. . . . 318-324 High Street, Cowdenbeath, Fife, KY4 9QJ
. . . . Tel: (01383) 611702 Fax: (01383) 611703
. . . . Office Manager – Ms Rhona White
. . . . E-mail: whiterh@parliament.uk
. . . . Constituency Adviser – Mr Alex Rowley
. . . . Tel: (01592) 263792
. . . . E-mail: rowleya@parliament.uk
Parliamentary Interests Economy; Employment; Health. Social Security; Scotland
Leisure Interests. . . . . . Golf; Tennis; Watching all Sports

Brown, Russell MP Dumfries and Galloway
Labour. . . . . Majority 2,922 over Con
Born . . . . 17th September 1951 in Annan
Educated. . . . . Annan Academy
Elected . . . . 1997 - 2005 MP for Dumfries
2005 MP for Dumfries and Galloway
Offices Held . . . . 2002 - 03 PPS to Rt Hon Lord Williams of Mostyn
(Lord Privy Seal and Leader of the House of Lords)
2003 - 05 PPS to Rt Hon Baroness Amos
(Lord Privy Seal and Leader of the House of Lords)
2005 - 06 PPS to Rt Hon Alistair Darling MP (Secretary of
State for Transport and Secretary of State for Scotland)
2006 - 07 PPS to Rt Hon Douglas Alexander MP (Secretary of
State for Scotland)
2007 - 08 PPS to Des Browne MP then, from 2008,
Jim Murphy MP (successive Secretaries of State for Scotland)
Commons Office . . . . . Tel: (020) 7219 4429 Fax: (020) 7219 0922
Mobile: 07798 703162
E-mail: russell@brownmp.new.labour.org.uk
Web: www.russellbrown.labour.co.uk
Constituency Offices . . 5 Friars Vennel, Dumfries, DG1 2RQ
Tel: (01387) 247902 Fax: (01387) 247903
Office Administrator – Mrs Gillian Carey
E-mail: careygi@parliament.uk
Personal Assistant/Researcher – Mr Cameron Scott
Secretary – Mrs Janice Richardson
E-mail: richardsonjr@parliament.uk
13 Hanover Street, Stranraer, DG9 7SB
Tel & Fax: (01776) 705254
Secretary – Miss Sharon Lamb
E-mail: lambs@parliament.uk
Trade Union . . . . Unite
Parliamentary Interests Employment Legislation; Health and Safety
Leisure Interests. . . . . . Sport (especially Football)

Browne, Rt Hon Des MP Kilmarnock and Loudoun
Labour. . . . . Majority 8,703 over SNP
Born. . . . . 22nd March 1952 in Ayrshire
Educated. . . . . St Michael's Academy, Kilwinning; Glasgow University
Elected . . . . 1997 MP for Kilmarnock and Loudoun
Offices Held . . . . 1998 - 99 PPS to Donald Dewar
　　　　　　　　　　(Secretary of State for Scotland)
　　　　　　　　　　2000 PPS to Adam Ingram (Minister of State,
　　　　　　　　　　Northern Ireland Office)
　　　　　　　　　　2001 - Parliamentary Secretary, Northern
　　　　　　　　　　Ireland Office
　　　　　　　　　　2003 - 04 Minister of State (Minister for Work),
　　　　　　　　　　Department for Work and Pensions
　　　　　　　　　　2004 - 05 Minister of State, Home Office (Minister for
　　　　　　　　　　Citizenship, Immigration and Counter Terrorism)
　　　　　　　　　　2005 - 06 Chief Secretary, HM Treasury
　　　　　　　　　　2006 - 08 Secretary of State for Defence
　　　　　　　　　　2007 - 08 Secretary of State for Scotland
Commons Office . . . . . Tel: (020) 7219 4501
　　　　　　　　　　E-mail: browned@parliament.uk
　　　　　　　　　　Web: www.desbrownemp.co.uk
　　　　　　　　　　Researcher/Office Manager – Ms Shata Shetty
　　　　　　　　　　Tel: (020) 7219 1162
　　　　　　　　　　E-mail: shettys@parliament.uk
　　　　　　　　　　Communications Assistant – Ms Clare-Frances Lennon
　　　　　　　　　　Tel: (020) 7219 0075
　　　　　　　　　　E-mail: lennonc@parliament.uk
Constituency Office . . . 32 Grange Street, Kilmarnock,
　　　　　　　　　　Ayrshire, KA1 2DD
　　　　　　　　　　Tel: (01563) 520267 Fax: (01563) 539439
　　　　　　　　　　Web: www.kimarnockandloudoun.co.uk
　　　　　　　　　　PA – Ms Maureen Murphy
　　　　　　　　　　E-mail: murphym@parliament.uk
　　　　　　　　　　Caseworker – Mr Bruce Kirkpatrick
　　　　　　　　　　E-mail: kirkpatrickb@parliament.uk
　　　　　　　　　　Caseworker – Mr David Ross
　　　　　　　　　　E-mail: rossd@parliament.uk
Professional Association Faculty of Advocates (non-practising)
Trade Union. . . . . UNISON
Parliamentary Interests Constitution; Disability; Education; Human Rights;
　　　　　　　　　　International Affairs; Northern Ireland
Leisure Interests. . . . . . Family and Friends; Football; Reading; Swimming; Tennis

Bruce, Rt Hon Malcolm MP   Gordon

Liberal Democrat . . . Majority 11,026 over Lab

Born . . . . 17th November 1944 in Birkenhead, Merseyside

Educated . . . . Wrekin College, Shropshire;
St Andrews University; Strathclyde University;
Middlesex University; Inns of Court School of Law

Elected . . . . 1983 MP for Gordon

Offices Held . . . . 1983 - 85 Liberal Spokesman on Scotland
1986 - 87 Liberal Spokesman on Energy
1987 Alliance Spokesman on Employment
1987 - 88, 1992 - 94 Liberal Democrat
Spokesman on Trade and Industry
1988 - 90 Liberal Democrat Spokesman on
Environment and Natural Resources
1988 - 92 Leader, Scottish Liberal Democrats
1990 - 92 Liberal Democrat Spokesman on
Scottish Affairs
1992 - 94 Liberal Democrat Spokesman on
Trade and Industry
1994 - 99 Liberal Democrat Spokesman on
Treasury Matters
1999 - 2001 Chairman, Parliamentary Liberal
Democrat Party
2000 - President, Scottish Liberal Democrats
2001 - 02 Liberal Democrat Spokesman on
Environment, Food and Rural Affairs
2003 - 05 Liberal Democrat Spokesman on Trade and
Industry
2005 - Chairman International Development Committee,
House of Commons

Commons Office . . . . . Tel: (020) 7219 6233 Fax: (020) 7219 2334
E-mail: brucem@parliament.uk
Web: www.malcolmbruce.org.uk
Parliamentary Assistant – Ms Alex Hernandez
E-mail: hernandeza@parliament.uk

Constituency Office . . . 71 High Street, Inverurie, Aberdeenshire, AB51 9QJ
Tel: (01467) 623413 Fax: (01467) 624994
Constituency Caseworker – Mr Rob Milsom
E-mail: milsomr@parliament.uk
Head of Office – Mrs Rosemary Bruce
Tel: (013398) 89120 Fax: (013398) 82386
E-mail: brucer@parliament.uk

Parliamentary Interests Council of Europe; Disability (especially Deaf Children);
Economic Reform

Leisure Interests . . . . . . Theatre, Music, Golf, Walking

Cairns, David MP . . Inverclyde
Labour. . . . . Majority 11,259 over SNP
Born. . . . . 7th August 1966 in Greenock
Educated. . . . . Notre Dame High School; Gregorian University, Rome;
Franciscan Study Centre, Canterbury
Elected . . . . 2001 - 2005 MP for Greenock and Inverclyde
2005 MP for Inverclyde
Offices Held . . . . 2003 - 05 PPS to Malcolm Wicks MP (Minister for of State,
Department for Work and Pensions)
2005 - 07 Parliamentary Secretary, Scotland Office,
Department for Constitutional Affairs
2006 - 07 Parliamentary Secretary, Northern Ireland Office
2007 - 08 Minister of State, Scotland Office
Commons Office . . . . . Tel: (020) 7219 8242 Fax: (020) 7219 1772
E-mail: cairnsd@parliament.uk
Web: www.davidcairns.com
Constituency Office. . . 20 Union Street, Greenock, PA16 8JL
Tel: (01475) 791820 Fax: (01475) 791821
Parliamentary Researcher – Ms Christina Boyd
Tel: (01475) 791617
E-mail: boydc@parliament.uk
Caseworker – Ms Angela Moore
Trade Union. . . . . Community
Languages Spoken. . . . Italian
Parliamentary Interests Defence; Employment; Israel
Leisure Interests. . . . . . Travel; Watching Football;
Spending Time with Extended Family

Campbell, Rt Hon Sir Menzies CBE QC MP North East Fife
Liberal Democrat . . . Majority 12,571 over Con
Born . . . . 22nd May 1941 in Glasgow
Educated . . . . Hillhead High School, Glasgow;
                      Glasgow University; Stanford University, USA
Elected . . . . 1987 MP for North East Fife
Offices Held . . . . 1991 - 2002 Liberal Democrat Spokesman on
                      Foreign Affairs (also Defence and Europe 1997 - 2001)
                      2002 - 05 Liberal Democrat Spokesman on International Affairs
                      2003 - 06 Deputy Leader, Liberal Democrats
                      2005 - 06 Liberal Democrat Shadow Foreign Secretary
                      2006 - 07 Leader, Liberal Democrats
Commons Office . . . . . Tel: (020) 7219 6910 Fax: (020) 7219 0559
                      E-mail: campbellm@parliament.uk
                      Web: www.mingcampbell.org.uk
                      Aide – Ms Emma Collinson
                      E-mail: collinsone@parliament.uk
                      Press Officer – Ms Carrie Henderson
                      Tel: (020) 7219 1181
                      E-mail: hendersonc@parliament.uk
Constituency Office . . . 16 Millgate, Cupar, Fife, KY15 5EG
                      Tel: (01334) 656361 Fax: (01334) 654045
                      Secretary – Lady [Elspeth] Campbell
                      Tel & Fax: (0131) 346 7268
Parliamentary Interests Defence; Foreign Affairs; Legal Affairs; Sport
Leisure Interests . . . . . . Sports; Theatre; Music

Carmichael, Alistair MP   Orkney and Shetland
Liberal Democrat . . . Majority 6,627 over Lab
Born . . . . 15th July 1965 in Islay, Argyll
Educated. . . . . Islay High School, Argyll; Aberdeen University
Elected . . . . 2001 MP for Orkney and Shetland
Offices Held . . . . 2001 - 05 Liberal Democrat Spokesman on Northern Ireland
                          (also Scotland to 2004)
                          2005 - 06 Liberal Democrat Spokesman on Home Affairs
                          2006 - 07 Liberal Democrat Shadow Transport Secretary
                          2007 - Liberal Democrat Shadow Secretary for
                          Northern Ireland and Scotland
Commons Office . . . . . Tel: (020) 7219 8181 Fax: (020) 7219 1787
                          E-mail: carmichaela@parliament.uk
                          Web: www.alistaircarmichael.org.uk
                          Researcher – Mr James Phillips
                          E-mail: phillipsje@parliament.uk
Constituency Offices . . 31 Broad Street, Kirkwall, Orkney, KW15 1DH
                          Tel: (01856) 876541 Fax: (01856) 876162
                          Caseworker – Mrs Barbara Flett
                          E-mail: flettb@parliament.uk
                          171 Commercial Street, Lerwick, Shetland, ZE1 0HX
                          Tel: (01595) 690044 Fax: (01595) 690055
                          Personal Assistant – Ms Beatrice Wishart
                          E-mail: wishartb@parliament.uk
                          Constituency Assistant – Mrs Elinor Nicolson
Directorships . . . . Solicitors Will Aid Scotland (unpaid)
Parliamentary Interests Agriculture; Energy; Fishing
Leisure Interests. . . . . . Music; Theatre

Clark, Katy MP . . . . North Ayrshire and Arran
Labour. . . . . Majority 11,296 over Con
Born . . . . 3rd July 1967 in Kilwinning
Educated. . . . . Kyle Academy; University of Aberdeen;
                          Edinburgh University
Elected . . . . 2005 MP for North Ayrshire and Arran
Commons Office . . . . . Tel: (020) 7219 4113 Fax: (020) 7219 4002
                          E-mail: clarkk@parliament.uk
                          Web: www.katyclarkmp.org.uk
Constituency Office . . . 53 Main Street Kilbirnie, KA25 7DF
                          Tel: (01505) 684127 Fax: (01505) 684349
Trade Union . . . . UNISON
Parliamentary Interests Equality; Human Rights; Policy Development

Clarke, Rt Hon Tom CBE MP   Coatbridge, Chryston and Bellshill
Labour. . . . . Majority 19,519 over SNP
Born. . . . . 10th January 1941 in Coatbridge
Educated. . . . . Columba High School, Coatbridge;
                           Scottish College of Commerce
Elected . . . . 1982 MP for Coatbridge and Airdrie
                           (By-election), then (1983) Monklands West
                           and (1997 - 2005) Coatbridge and Chryston
                           2005 - MP for Coatbridge, Chryston and Bellshill
Offices Held . . . . 1975 - 82 Provost of Monklands
                           1986 - 87 Opposition Spokesman on
                           Scottish Affairs
                           1987 - 90 Opposition Spokesman on Health
                           and Social Services
                           1992 - 93 Shadow Scottish Secretary
                           1993 - 94 Opposition Spokesman on Development
                           and Co-operation
                           1994 - 97 Opposition Spokesman on Disability Rights
                           (Member Shadow Cabinet)
                           1997 - 98 Minister of State, Department for
                           Culture, Media and Sport
Commons Office . . . . . Tel: (020) 7219 5007 Fax: (020) 7219 6094
                           E-mail: clarket@parliament.uk
                           Parliamentary Assistant – Mr Sam Harty
                           Researcher – Mr Oliver Parker
Constituency Office. . . Municipal Buildings, Kildonan Street, Coatbridge, ML5 3LF
                           Tel: (01236) 600800 Fax: (01236) 600808
                           Secretary – Ms Lindsay McNeill
                           E-mail: mcneilll@parliament.uk
                           Assistant Secretary – Mrs Dianne Willis
Trade Union. . . . . GMB
Parliamentary Interests Disability Issues; International Development; International
                           Economy; The Film Industry; Scotland
Leisure Interests. . . . . . Film; Reading; Walking

Connarty, Michael MP   Linlithgow and Falkirk East
Labour . . . . Majority 11,202 over SNP
Born . . . . 3rd September 1947 in Coatbridge
Educated . . . . St Patrick's High School, Coatbridge;
   Langside College; Stirling University;
   Glasgow University; Jordanhill College of Education
Elected . . . . 1992 - 2005 MP for Falkirk East
   2005 MP for Linlithgow and Falkirk East
Offices Held . . . . 1980 - 90 Leader, Stirling District Council
   1997 - 98 PPS to Tom Clarke MP
   (Minister of State, Department for Culture,
   Media and Sport)
   2006 - Chairman, European Scrutiny Select Committee
Commons Office . . . . . Tel: (020) 7219 5071 Fax: (020) 7219 2541
   Mobile: 07973 311705
   E-mail: connartym@parliament.uk
   Web: www.mconnartymp.com
Constituency Offices . . Room 8, 5 Kerse Road, Grangemouth, Stirlingshire, FK3 8HQ
   Tel: (01324) 474832 Fax: (01324) 666811
   Senior Parliamentary Researcher – Mr Peter Hastie
   E-mail: hastiep@parliament.uk
   Secretary/Parliamentary Assistant – Ms Jackie West
   E-mail: westj@parliament.uk
   Constituency Assistant – Mr Joe Hill
   E-mail: hillj@parliament.uk
   62 Hopetoun Street, Bathgate, EH48 4PD
   Tel: (01506) 676711 Fax: (01506) 676722
   Parliamentary Assistant – Ms Yvonne Rankin
Trade Unions . . . . Communication Workers Union;
   Educational Institute of Scotland; Unite
Directorships . . . . Scottish National Jazz Orchestra (Chair unpaid)
Parliamentary Interests Chemical Industries; Energy; EU Legislation; Haemophilia;
   Middle East; Offshore Oil and Gas Industry;
   Science and Technology; Nuclear Power
Leisure Interests . . . . . . Family; Hill Walking; Jazz; Reading

Darling, Rt Hon Alistair MP Edinburgh South West
Labour. . . . . Majority 7,242 over Con
Born. . . . . 28th November 1953 in London
Educated. . . . . Loretto School; Aberdeen University
Elected . . . . 1987 - 2005 MP for Edinburgh Central
                           2005 MP for Edinburgh South West
Offices Held . . . . 1988 - 92 Opposition Spokesman on
                           Home Affairs
                           1992 - 96 Opposition Spokesman on the City
                           and Financial Services
                           1996 - 97 Shadow Chief Secretary to the Treasury
                           1997 - 98 Chief Secretary to the Treasury
                           1998 - 2001 Secretary of State for Social Security
                           2001 - 02 Secretary of State for Work and Pensions
                           2002 - 06 Secretary of State for Transport
                           2003 - 06 Secretary of State for Scotland
                           2006 - 07 Secretary of State for Trade and Industry
                           2007 - Chancellor of the Exchequer
Constituency Office. . . 22A Rutland Square, Edinburgh, EH1 2BB
                           Tel: (0131) 476 2552 Fax: (0131) 656 0368
                           E-mail: darlinga@parliament.uk
                           Personal Assistant – Mrs Isobel Forrester
                           Research Assistant – Ms Carol Wright
Parliamentary Interests Constitution; Economic Policy; Education; Health; Transport

Davidson, Ian MP . . Glasgow South West
Labour. . . . . Majority 13,896 over SNP
Born. . . . . 8th September 1950 in Jedburgh
Educated. . . . . Jedburgh Grammar School; Galashiels Academy;
                           Edinburgh University; Jordanhill College
Elected . . . . 1992 MP for Glasgow Govan, then (1997)
                           Glasgow Pollok
                           2005 MP for Glasgow South West
Commons Office . . . . . Tel: (020) 7219 3610 Fax: (020) 7219 2238
                           E-mail: davidsonig@parliament.uk
                           Web: www.epolitix.com/ian-davidson
Constituency Office. . . 3 Kilmuir Drive, Glasgow, G46 8BW
                           Tel: (0141) 621 2216 Fax: (0141) 621 2154
Trade Unions . . . . Unite
Parliamentary Interests Defence; Education; Europe; Local Government;
                           Public Accounts; Third World; Trade and Industry;
                           Trade Unions; Shipbuilding
Leisure Interests. . . . . . Rugby; Running; Swimming

Devine, Jim MP . . . . Livingston
Labour. . . . . Majority 2,860 over SNP
Born. . . . . 24th May 1953 in Blackburn
Educated. . . . . St Mary's Academy, West Lothian;
Moray House College School of
Nursing
Elected . . . . 2005 MP for Livingston (By-election)
Office Held . . . . 2006 - 07 PPS to Rosie Winton (Minister of
State, Department of Health)
Commons Office . . . . . Tel: (020) 7219 6229 Fax: (020) 7219 1964
E-mail: devinej@parliament.uk
Web: www.jimdevine.org.uk
Constituency Office. . . Suite 5, Pentland House, Livingston,
West Lothian, EH54 6NG
Tel: (01506) 497965 Fax: (01506) 497962
Caseworkers – Ms Carol Bartholomew
Ms Christine Law
E-mails: bartholomewc@parliament.uk
lawc@parliament.uk
Trade Union. . . . . UNISON
Leisure Interests. . . . . . Reading; Chess; Football; Horseracing

Donohoe, Brian MP . Central Ayrshire
Labour. . . . . Majority 10,423 over Con
Born. . . . . 10th September 1948 in Kilmarnock
Educated. . . . . Irvine Royal Academy; Kilmarnock Technical College
Elected . . . . 1992 - 2005 MP for Cunninghame South
2005 Central Ayrshire
Office Held . . . . 2008 - PPS to Lord Adonis (Minister of State, Department
of Transport
Commons Office . . . . . Tel: (020) 7219 6230 Fax: (020) 7219 5388
Mobile: 07774 646600
Pager: 07659 160413
E-mail: donohoeb@parliament.uk
Web: www.briandonohoemp.co.uk
Constituency Office. . . 17 Townhead, Irvine, Ayrshire, KA12 0BL
Tel: (01294) 276844 Fax: (01294) 313463
Secretary – Ms Ruth Brown
E-mail: brownrm@parliament.uk
Secretarial Assistant – Miss Samantha Mair
E-mail: mairs@parliament.uk
Trade Union. . . . . UNISON; Unite
Directorship . . . . Thrive
Parliamentary Interests Transport; Environment
Leisure Interests. . . . . . Gardening

Doran, Frank MP. . . Aberdeen North
Labour. . . . . Majority 6,795 over Lib Dem
Born. . . . . 13th April 1949 in Edinburgh
Educated. . . . . Dundee University
Elected . . . . 1987 - 92 MP for Aberdeen South
1997 - 2005 MP for Aberdeen Central
2005 MP for Aberdeen North
Offices Held . . . . 1988 - 92 Opposition Spokesman on Energy
1997 - 2001 PPS to Ian McCartney MP
(Minister of State, Department of Trade
and Industry 1997 - 99, Cabinet Office 1999 - 2001)
2005 - Chairman, Administration Committee,
House of Commons
Commons Office . . . . . Tel: (020) 7219 3481 Fax: (020) 7219 0682
E-mail: doranf@parliament.uk
Parliamentary Assistant – Ms Caitriana Bearryman
Constituency Office. . . 69 Dee Street, Aberdeen, AB11 6EE
Tel: (01224) 252715 Fax: (01224) 252716
Parliamentary Assistant – Ms Catriona Bearryman
Caseworkers – Ms Rebecca Groundwater
Ms Louise Smart
Parliamentary Interests Employment; Energy; Fisheries
Trade Union. . . . . GMB

Griffiths, Nigel MP Edinburgh South
Labour. . . . . Majority 405 over Lib Dem
Born. . . . . 20th May 1955
Educated. . . . . Hawick Comprehensive School; Edinburgh University;
    Moray House College of Education
Elected . . . . 1987 MP for Edinburgh South
Offices Held . . . . 1980 - 87 Chairman, Housing Committee,
    Edinburgh City Council
    1987 - 89 Opposition Whip
    1989 - 97 Opposition Spokesman on Consumer Affairs
    1997 - 98; 2001 - 05 Parliamentary Secretary,
    Department of Trade and Industry
    2005 - 07 Deputy Leader of the House of Commons
Commons Office . . . . . Tel: (020) 7219 2424
    E-mail: ngriffithsmp@parliament.uk
    Web: www.nigelgriffiths.co.uk
Constituency Office. . . 31 Minto Street, Edinburgh, EH9 2BT
    Tel: (0131) 662 4520
    E-mail: tellnigel@parliament.to
    Personal Assistant – Mrs Elizabeth Lyon
Trade Unions . . . . Unite; USDAW
Language Spoken . . . . French
Publications . . . . 1981: Guide to Council Housing in Edinburgh
    1981: Welfare Rights Survey
    1982: Council Housing on the Point of Collapse
    1982 - 86: Welfare Rights Guide
    1983: A Guide to DHSS Claims and Appeals
    1983: Welfare Rights Advice for Doctors,
    Health Visitors and Social Workers
    1988: Rights Guide for Mentally Handicapped People
    2000/2003/2005: 300 Gains from a Labour Government
Parliamentary Interests Arts; Disability; Economic Policy; Education;
    Health and Social Service; Housing; Scotland
Leisure Interests. . . . . . Squash; Travel; Live Entertainment; Badminton; Reading;
    Hill Walking/Rock Climbing; Architecture; Scuba Diving

Hamilton, David MP Midlothian
Labour . . . . Majority 7,265 over Lib Dem
Born . . . . 24th October 1950 in Dalkeith, Midlothian
Educated . . . . Dalkeith High School
Elected . . . . 2001 MP for Midlothian
Commons Office . . . . . Tel: (020) 7219 8257 Fax: (020) 7219 2532
E-mail: hamiltonda@parliament.uk
Web: www.davidhamiltonmp.co.uk
Resarcher – Mr Robert Geaney
Tel: (020) 219 1780
E-mail: geaneyr@parliament.uk
Constituency Office . . . 95 High Street, Dalkeith, Midlothian, EH22 1AX
Tel: (0131) 654 1585 Fax: (0131) 654 1586
Caseworker – Ms Maureen Curran
E-mail: curranm@parliament.uk
Office Manager/Personal Assistant – Mrs Jean Hamilton
Tel: (0131) 654 4332
E-mail: hamiltonj@parliament.uk
Directorships Cre8te
Midlothean Innovation Technology Trust (Chairman unpaid)
Trade Union . . . . NUM
Parliamentary Interests Biotechnology; Cyprus; Defence; Energy; Europe; Gibraltar
Leisure Interests . . . . . . Current Affairs; Films; Grandchildren

Harris, Tom MP . . . . Glasgow South
Labour . . . . Majority 10,832 over Lib Dem
Born . . . . 20th February 1964 in Irvine, Ayrshire
Educated . . . . Garnock Academy, Kilbirnie, Ayrshire;
Napier College, Edinburgh
Elected . . . . 2001 MP for Glasgow Cathcart
2005 MP for Glasgow South
Offices Held . . . . 2003 - 05 PPS to John Spellar (Minister of State,
Northern Ireland Office)
2005 – 06 PPS to Patricia Hewitt (Secretary of State for Health)
2006 - 08 Parliamentary Secretary, Department for Transport
Commons Office . . . . . Tel: (020) 7219 8237 Fax: (020) 7219 1769
E-mail: tomharrismp@parliament.uk
Web: www.tomharrismp.com
Parliamentary Researcher – Mr David Packer
E-mail: packerd@parliament.uk
Constituency Office . . . c/o Queen's Park Football Club, Somerville Drive,
Glasgow, G42 9BA
Tel: (0141) 649 9780 Fax: (0141) 636 9349
Researcher – Mr Donald Campbell
E-mail: campbelld@parliament.uk
Campaign Assistant – Mr Malcolm Cunning
E-mail: cunningm@parliament.uk
Trade Union . . . . Unite
Parliamentary Interests Transport; Asylum and Immigration; Drug Laws; Europe;
Health; Middle East; Northern Ireland; Trade Union;
Welfare Reform
Leisure Interests . . . . . . Badminton; Cinema; Astronomy; Hill Walking

Hood, Jimmy MP . . . Lanark and Hamilton East
Labour. . . . . Majority 11,947 over Lib Dem
Born. . . . . 16th May 1948 in Lesmahagow, Clydesdale
Educated. . . . . Motherwell College; Nottingham University
Elected . . . . 1987 - 2005 MP for Clydesdale
2005 MP for Lanark and Hamilton East
Office Held . . . . 1992 - 98, 2001 - 06 Chairman, European Scrutiny
Committee, House of Commons
Commons Office . . . . . Tel: (020) 7219 4585 Fax: (020) 7219 5872
Mobile: 07876 772233
E-mail: hoodj@parliament.uk
Web: www.jimhoodmp.co.uk
Constituency Office . . . Council Offices, South Vennel,
Lanark, ML11 7JT
Tel: (01555) 673177 Fax: (01555) 673188
Secretary/Personal Assistant – Miss Helen Davidson
E-mail: davidsonh@parliament.uk
Office Assistant – Ms Karen McKay
E-mail: mckayk@parliament.uk
Parliamentary Interests Health Service; Home Affairs; Alcohol Abuse;
Industrial Relations
Trade Union. . . . . Unite
Leisure Interests. . . . . . Gardening; Reading; Writing; Walking

Hosie, Stewart MP . . Dundee East
SNP . . . . Majority 383 over Lab
Born . . . . 1963 in Dundee
Educated . . . . Carnoustie High School; Bell Street Tech
Elected . . . . 2005 MP for Dundee East
Offices Held . . . . 2005 - SNP Spokesman on Economy, Home Affairs,
　　　　　　　　　　　　Treasury and Women
　　　　　　　　　　　　2007 - SNP Spokesman on Home Office and Women
　　　　　　　　　　　　2007 - Deputy Leader and Chief Whip,
　　　　　　　　　　　　SNP Westminster Group
Commons Office . . . . . Tel: (020) 7219 8164 Fax: (020) 7219 6716
　　　　　　　　　　　　E-mail: hosies@parliament.uk
　　　　　　　　　　　　Web: www.stewarthosie.com
　　　　　　　　　　　　Office Manager – Mr Luke Skipper
　　　　　　　　　　　　Tel: (020) 7219 1602
　　　　　　　　　　　　E-mail: skipperl@parliament.uk
Constituency Office . . . 8 Old Glamis Road, Dundee, DD3 8HP
　　　　　　　　　　　　Tel & Fax: (01382) 623200
　　　　　　　　　　　　E-mail: stewart@stewarthosie.com
　　　　　　　　　　　　Constituency Assistants – Mr Kevin Cordell
　　　　　　　　　　　　　　　　　　　　　Mr Craig Melville
　　　　　　　　　　　　Tel: (01382) 903211 Fax: (01382) 903205
　　　　　　　　　　　　E-mails: kevin@stewarthosie.com
　　　　　　　　　　　　　　　　craig@stewarthosie.com
　　　　　　　　　　　　Press Officer – Mr Andrew Scott
　　　　　　　　　　　　Tel: (01382) 903202 Fax: (01382) 903205
　　　　　　　　　　　　E-mail: media@dundeesmp.org
Parliamentary Interests Economy; Home Affairs; Treasury

Ingram, Rt Hon Adam MP East Kilbride, Strathaven and Lesmahagow
Labour. . . . . Majority 14,723 over SNP
Born. . . . . 1st February 1947 in Glasgow
Educated. . . . . Cranhill Secondary School, Glasgow;
  Open University
Elected . . . . 1987 - 2005 MP for East Kilbride
  2005 MP for East Kilbride, Strathaven and Lesmahagow
Offices Held . . . . 1984 - 87 Leader, East Kilbride District Council
  1988 - 92 PPS to Neil Kinnock (Leader of the Opposition)
  1993 - 95 Opposition Spokesman on Social Security
  1995 - 97 Opposition Spokesman on Trade and Industry
  1997 - 2001 Minister of State, Northern Ireland Office
  2001 - 07 Minister of State, Ministry of Defence
  (Minister for the Armed Forces)
Commons Office . . . . . Tel: (020) 7219 4093
  Mobile: 07899 877025
  E-mail: adam_ingram@compuserve.com
  Researcher/Parliamentary Assistant – Mr Michael Courtney
  E-mail: courtneym@parliament.uk
Constituency Office . . . Civic Centre, Andrew Street, East Kilbride, G74 1AB
  Tel: (01355) 806016 Fax: (01355) 806035
  Secretary/Personal Assistant – Mrs Maureen Ingram
  Secretary – Mr John Muldoon
  Senior Research Assistant – Mr Michael McCann
Trade Union. . . . . Unite
Parliamentary Interests Defence; Energy; Industry; Northern Ireland
Leisure Interests. . . . . . Cooking; Fishing; Reading

Joyce, Eric MP . . . . . Falkirk
Labour. . . . . Majority 13,475 over SNP
Born. . . . . 13th October 1960 in Perth, Scotland
Educated. . . . . University of Stirling; University of Bath; University of Keele
Elected . . . . 2000 - 2005 MP for Falkirk West (By-election)
                     2005 MP for Falkirk
Office Held . . . . 2003 - 05 PPS to Mike O'Brien MP (Minister of State, Foreign
                     and Commonwealth Office and Department of
                     Trade and Industry)
                     2005 - 06 PPS to Margaret Hodge MP (Minister for Work)
                     (Minister of State, Department for Work and Pensions then,
                     from 2006, (Minister of State, Department of Trade and
                     Industry)
                     2006 - 09 PPS to John Hutton MP, (Secretary of State for
                     Work and Pensions, 2007 - Secretary of State for Business,
                     Enterprise and Regulatory Reform)
                     2009 - PPS to Bob Ainsworth MP (Secretary of State for
                     Defence)
Commons Office . . . . . Tel: (020) 7219 2779 Fax: (020) 7219 2090
                     E-mail: ericjoycemp@parliament.uk
Constituency Office. . . Burnfoot Lane, Falkirk, FK1 5BH
                     Tel: (01324) 638919 Fax: (01324) 679449
                     Secretary – Mrs May McIntyre
                     E-mail: mcintyrem@parliament.uk
Trade Union. . . . . UNISON
Publications . . . . 1997: Arms and the Man, Renewing the Armed Forces
Parliamentary Interests Defence; Economy; Education; Foreign Affairs;
                     International Development; Training; Work
Leisure Interests. . . . . . Climbing; Judo; Most Sports

Kennedy, Rt Hon Charles MP Ross, Skye and Lochaber
Liberal Democrat . . . Majority 14,249 over Lab
Born . . . . 25th November 1959 in Inverness
Educated . . . . Lochaber High School, Fort William;
Glasgow University; Indiana University, USA
Elected . . . . 1983 MP for Ross, Cromarty and Skye
then (1997 - 2005) for Ross, Skye and
Inverness West
2005 MP for Ross, Skye and Lochaber
Offices Held . . . . 1983 - 87 SDP Spokesman on Health and
Social Security, Scotland
1986 - 88 SDP Scottish Spokesman
1988 - 89 Liberal Democrat Spokesman on
Trade and Industry
1989 - 92 Liberal Democrat Spokesman on
Health
1990 - 94 Liberal Democrat Party President
1992 - 97 Liberal Democrat Spokesman on
Europe
1997 - 99 Liberal Democrat Spokesman on
Agriculture, Fisheries, Food and
Rural Affairs
1999 - 2006 Leader, Liberal Democrats
Commons Office . . . . . Tel: (020) 7219 0356 Fax: (020) 7219 4881
E-mail: kennedyc.@parliament.uk
Web: www.charleskennedy.org.uk
Head of Office – Ms Siân Norris-Copson
E-mail: norriscopsons@parliament.uk
Researcher – Mr Peter Wasson
Tel: (020) 7219 5741
E-mail: wassonp@parliament.uk
Constituency Office . . . 5 McGregor's Court, Dingwall, IV15 9HS
Tel: (01349) 862152 Fax: (01349) 866829
E-mail: charles@highlandlibdems.org.uk
Web: www.highlandlibdems.org.uk
Constituency Assistant – Ms Sarah Southcott
E-mail: southcotts@parliament.uk
Constituency Researcher – Mr Gavin Steele
Tel: (01463) 711280 Fax: (01463) 714960
E-mail: gavin@highlandlibdems.org.uk
Leisure Interests . . . . . . Reading; Music; Cinema

Lazarowicz, Mark MP   Edinburgh North and Leith
Labour. . . . . Majority 2,153 over Lib Dem
Born. . . . . 8th August 1953
Educated. . . . . St Andrews University; Edinburgh University
Elected . . . . 2001 MP for Edinburgh North and Leith
Offices Held . . . . 1986 - 93 Leader, Edinburgh City Council
           2007 - 08 PPS to David Cairns MP (Minister of State,
           Scotland Office)
Commons Office . . . . . Tel: (020) 7219 8222 Fax: (020) 7219 1761
           E-mail: lazarowiczm@parliament.uk
           Web: www.marklazarowicx.org.uk
           Researcher – Mr Gary Calder
           E-mail: calderg@parliament.uk
Constituency Office . . . 5 Croall Place, Leith, Edinburgh, EH7 4LT
           Tel: (0131) 557 0577 Fax: (0131) 557 5759
           E-mail: mark@marklazarowicz.org.uk
           Office Manager – Mrs Karen Doran
           E-mail: doranka@parliament.uk
           Constituency Assistant – Ms Alannah Turner
Trade Union. . . . . Unite
Parliamentary Interests Consumer Affairs; Constitutional Reform; Environment;
           Finance and Economy; Transport

MacNeil, Angus MP   Na h-Eileanan An Iar
SNP . . . . Majority 1,441 over Lab
Born. . . . . 21st July 1971 in Scotland
Educated. . . . . Nicholson Institute, Stornoway's,
           Strathclyde University; Angus University
Elected . . . . 2005 MP for Na h-Eileanan An Iar
Office Held . . . . 2005 - SNP Spokesman on Environment, Food, Rural Affairs,
           Fishing, Tourism and Transport
Commons Office . . . . . Tel: (020) 7219 8476 Fax: (020) 7219 6716
           Mobile: 07733 077799
           E-mail: macneila@parliament.uk
           Researcher – Mr Christopher Mullins-Silverstein
           Tel: (020) 7219 3225
           E-mail: mullinssilversteinc@parliament.uk
Constituency Office . . . 31 Bayhead Street, Lewis, Stornoway, HS2 2DU
           Tel: (01851) 702272 Fax: (01851) 701767
           Caseworkers: Mrs Rona Macdonald
                      Mr Kenneth Macleod
           E-mails: macdonaldm@parliament.uk
                  macleodk@parliament.uk
Trade Union. . . . . Educational Institute of Scotland
Language Spoken . . . . Gaelic
Parliamentary Interests Transport; Fishing; Economy; Independence
Leisure Interests. . . . . . Crofting; Football; Boats

Mason, John MP . . . Glasgow East
SNP . . . . Majority 365 over Labour
Born . . . . 15th May 1957 in Rutherglen
Elected . . . . 2008 - MP for Glasgow East (By-election)
Offices Held . . . . 1998 - 2008 SNP Group Leader, Glasgow City Council
                             2008 - SNP Party Spokesman on Work and Pensions
Parliamentary Office . . Tel: (020) 7219 6148
                             Mobile: 07792 277614
                             E-mail: masonj@parliament.uk
                             Web: www.johnmasonmp.org
Constituency Office . . . 888 Shettleson Road, Glasgow, G32 7XN
                             Tel: (0141) 778 8270
                             Office Manager – Mr Grant McLennan
                             E-mail: mclennang@parliament.uk
Leisure Interests . . . . . . Church; Walking; Watching Football

McAvoy, Rt Hon Tommy MP   Rutherglen and Hamilton West
Labour . . . . Majority 16,112 over Liberal Democrat
Born . . . . 14th December 1943 in Rutherglen
Educated . . . . St Columbkilles School, Rutherglen
Elected . . . . 1987 - 2005 MP for Glasgow Rutherglen
                             2005 MP for Rutherglen and Hamilton West
Offices Held . . . . 1996 - 97 Opposition Whip
                             1997 - 2008 Government Whip (Comptroller of
                               HM Household)
                             2008 - Government Deputy Chief Whip (Treasurer of
                               HM Household)
                             2008 – Chairman, Joint Parliamentary Committee
                               on Security
Commons Office . . . . . Tel: (020) 7219 5009
                             E-mail: mail@tommymcavoymp.org.uk
                             Web: www.epolitix.com/tommy-mcavoy
Constituency Office . . . Unit 7, Strathclyde Business Centre, 416 Hamilton Road,
                             Cambuslang, G72 7XR
                             Tel: (0141) 641 6946 Fax: (0141) 641 8583
                             Web: www.tommymcavoy.labour.co.uk

McFall, Rt Hon John MP Dunbartonshire West
Labour . . . . Majority 12,553 over SNP
Born . . . . 4th October 1944 in Dunbarton
Educated . . . . Glasgow University
Elected . . . . 1987 - 2005 MP for Dunbarton
                        2005 MP for Dunbartonshire West
Offices Held . . . . 1989 - 92 Opposition Whip
                        1992 - 97 Opposition Spokesman on Scotland
                        1997 - 98 Government Whip
                           (Lord Commissioner, HM Treasury)
                        1998 - 99 Parliamentary Secretary,
                           Northern Ireland Office
                        2001 - Chairman, Treasury Select Committee,
                           House of Commons
Commons Office . . . . . Tel: (020) 7219 3521 Fax: (020) 7219 6141
                        E-mail: mcfallj@parliament.uk
                        Web: www.john.mcfall.com
Constituency Office . . . 125 College Street, Dunbarton, G82 1NH
                        Tel: (01389) 734214 Fax: (01389) 761498
                        E-mail: john.mcfall@blueyonder.co.uk
Leisure Interests . . . . . . Golf; Reading; Running

McGovern, Jim MP Dundee West
Labour . . . . Majority 5,379 over SNP
Born . . . . 17th November 1956 in Glasgow
Educated . . . . Lawside R C Academy, Dundee
Elected . . . . 2005 MP for Dundee West
Office Held . . . . 2007 - 08 PPS to Pat McFadden MP (Minister of State,
                        Department for Business, Enterprise and Regulatory Reform)
Commons Office . . . . . Tel: (020) 7219 4938 Fax: (020) 7219 4812
                        E-mail: mcgovernj@parliament.uk
                        Web: www.jimmcgovern.co.uk
                        Researchers – Mr Michael Marra
                                       Ms Victoria Mitchell
                        E-mails: marram@parliament.uk
                                       mitchellv@parliament.uk
Constituency Office . . . 7 West Wynd, Dundee, DD1 4JQ
                        Tel: (01382) 322100 Fax: (01382) 322696
                        Secretary – Mrs Jane O'Neill
                        E-mail: oneilj@parliament.uk
                        Caseworker – Mrs Emma Purvis
                        E-mail: purvise@parliament.uk
Trade Union . . . . GMB
Parliamentary Interests Employment Rights
Leisure Interests . . . . . . Watching Football (Celtic FC)

McGuire, Rt Hon Anne MP Stirling

Labour. . . . . Majority 4,767 over Con
Born. . . . . 26th May 1949 in Glasgow
Educated. . . . . Our Lady and St Francis School, Glasgow;
                  Glasgow University;
                  Notre Dame Teacher Training College, Glasgow
Elected . . . . 1997 MP for Stirling
Offices Held . . . . 1997 - 98 PPS to Donald Dewar (Secretary of State for
                  Scotland)
                  1998 - 2001 Assistant Government Whip
                  2001 - 02 Government Whip (Lord
                  Commissioner, HM Treasury)
                  2002 - 03 Parliamentary Secretary,
                  Scotland Office
                  2003 - 05 Parliamentary Secretary, Department for
                  Constitutional Affairs
                  2005 - Parliamentary Secretary, Department for Work and
                  Pensions (Minister for Disabled People)
Commons Office . . . . . Tel: (020) 7219 5829 Fax: (020) 7219 2503
                  E-mail: mcguirea@parliament.uk
                  Web: www.annemcguiremp.org.uk
Constituency Office . . . 22 Viewfield Street, Stirling, FK8 1UA
                  Tel: (01786) 446515 Fax: (01786) 446513
                  Office Manager – Mr Graham Fraser
                  E-mail: fraserg@parliament.uk
Trade Union. . . . . GMB
Parliamentary Interests Europe; Rural Development; Urban Regeneration;
                  Voluntary Sector
Leisure Interests. . . . . . Football; Scottish Traditional Music; Walking

McKechin, Ann MP Glasgow North
Labour . . . . Majority 3,338 over Lib Dem
Born . . . . 22nd April 1961 in Paisley
Educated . . . . Paisley Grammar School; Strathclyde University
Elected . . . . 2001 - 2005 MP for Glasgow Maryhill
                          2005 MP for Glasgow North
Office Held . . . . 2008 - Parliamentary Secretary, Scotland Office
Commons Office . . . . . Tel: (020) 7219 8239 Fax: (020) 7219 1770
                          Mobile: 07751 482722
                          E-mail: mckechina@parliament.uk
                          Web: www.annmckechinmp.net
                          Research Assistant – Mr Tom Tabori
                          Tel: (020) 7219 5472
                          E-mail: taborit@parliament.uk
Constituency Office . . . 154/156 Raeberry Street, Maryhill, Glasgow, G20 6EA
                          Tel: (0141) 946 1300 Fax: (0141) 946 1412
                          Research Officer – Mr Martin Rhodes
                          E-mail: rhodesm@parliament.uk
                          Secretary/Caseworkers – Ms Yvonne Boyle
                                             Mr James Burns
                                             Ms Pat Rice
Professional Association Law Society of Scotland
Trade Union . . . . Unite
Parliamentary Interests Employment Rights; Health and Safety;
                          International Development
Leisure Interests . . . . . . Art History; Dancing; Films

McKenna, Rosemary CBE MP Cumbernauld, Kilsyth and Kirkintilloch East
Labour . . . . Majority 11,562 over SNP
Born . . . . 8th May 1941 in Renfrewshire
Educated . . . . St Augustine's Comprehensive, Glasgow;
            Notre Dame College of Education, Glasgow
Elected . . . . 1997 - 2005 MP for Cumbernauld and Kilsyth
            2005 MP for Cumbernauld, Kilsyth and Kirkintilloch East
Offices Held . . . . 1984 - 96 Leader Provost, Cumbernauld and Kilsyth
            Council (President, COSLA, 1994 - 96)
            2001 PPS to Brian Wilson MP (Minister of State
            Foreign and Commonwealth Office)
            2005 – Chairman, Committee on Selection, House of Commons
Commons Office . . . . . Tel: (020) 7219 4135 Fax: (020) 7217 2544
            E-mail: mckennar@parliament.uk
            Web: www.rosemarymckenna@labour.org.uk
Constituency Office . . . Lennox House, Lennox Road, Cumbernauld, G67 1LB
            Tel: (01236) 457788 Fax: (01236) 453303
            Parliamentary Assistant – Ms Gillian Dalrymple
            E-mail: dalrymmpleg@parliament.uk
Trade Union . . . . Unite
Parliamentary Interests Access to Technology; Education and Training; Media; Sport
Leisure Interests . . . . . . Family Gatherings; Reading; Travel

Moffat, Anne MP . . . East Lothian
Labour . . . . Majority 7,620 over Lib Dem
Born . . . . 30th March 1958 in Dunfermline
Educated . . . . Woodmill High School
Elected . . . . 2005 MP for East Lothian (elected as Anne Picking)
Office Held . . . . 2007 - PPS to Alan Johnson MP (Secretary of State for
            Health, then Home Secretary)
Commons Office . . . . . Tel: (020) 7219 8220 Fax: (020) 7219 1760
            E-mail: moffata@parliament.uk
            Web: www.epolitix.com/anne-moffat
Constituency Office . . . Unit 14, Cockenzie Business Centre, 23 Edinburgh Road,
            Cockenzie, EH32 0XL
            Tel: (01875) 818430 Fax: (01875) 819462
            Senior Political Assistant – Ms Karie Murphy
            E-mail: murphyk@parliament.uk
Trade Union . . . . UNISON
Parliamentary Interests Economy; Energy; Health; Small Businesses; Social Justice
Leisure Interests . . . . . . Reading; Sailing; Walking

Moore, Michael MP Berwickshire, Roxburgh and Selkirk
Liberal Democrat . . . Majority 5,901 over Con
Born . . . . 3rd June 1965 in Dundonald, Northern Ireland
Educated . . . . Strathallan School; Jedburgh Grammar School;
Edinburgh University
Elected . . . . 1997 - 2005 MP for Tweeddale, Ettrick and Lauderdale
2005 MP for Berwickshire, Roxburgh and Selkirk
Offices Held . . . . 1999 - 2001 Liberal Democrat Spokesman on Transport
1999; 2001 Liberal Democrat Spokesman on Scottish Affairs
2001 - 05 Liberal Democrat Deputy Spokesman on Foreign
Affairs
2002 - Deputy Leader, Scottish Liberal Democrats
2005 - 06 Liberal Democrat Spokesman on Defence
2006 - 07 Liberal Democrat Spokesman on Foreign Affairs
2007 - Liberal Democrat Spokesman on International
Development
2008 Liberal Democrat Spokesman on Scotland and
Northern Ireland
Commons Office . . . . . Tel: (020) 7219 2236 Fax: (020) 7219 0263
E-mail: michaelmooremp@parliament.uk
Web: www.michaelmoore.org.uk
Researchers – Mr Adam Clarke
Mr Ben Stevenson
E-mails: clarkea@parliament.uk
stevensonb@parliament.uk
Constituency Office . . . 11 Island Street, Galashiels, TD1 1NZ
Tel: (01896) 663650 Fax: (01896) 663655
Caseworker– Mrs Margaret Lundie
E-mail: lundiem@parliament.uk
Personal Assistant – Mrs Angela Jackson
E-mail: jacksona@parliament.uk
Casework Assistant – Mrs Alison Moore
E-mail: mooreal@parliament.uk
Professional Association Institute of Chartered Accountants of Scotland
Parliamentary Interests Defence; Corporate Social Responsibility; Europe;
Foreign Affairs; Transport; Textiles
Leisure Interests . . . . . . Hillwalking; Jazz; Rugby

Mundell, David MP . . . . . . Dumfriesshire, Clydesdale and Tweeddale
Conservative . . . . Majority 1,738 over Lab
Born . . . . 27th May 1962 in Dumfries
Educated . . . . Lockerbie Academy; Edinburgh University;
Strathclyde University
Elected . . . . 2005 - Elected MP for Dumfriesshire, Clydesdale
and Tweeddale
Offices Held . . . . 1999 – 2005 Member, Scottish Parliament
2005 - Shadow Scottish Secretary
Commons Office . . . . Tel: (020) 7219 4895 Fax: (020) 7219 2707
Mobile: 07850 725403
E-mail: mundelld@parliament.uk
Web: www.davidmundell.com
Special Adviser – Mr Allan Rae
Mobile: 07753 763201
E-mail: allan.rae@conservatives.com
Constituency Office . . . . . . 2 Holm Street, Moffat, Dumfriesshire, DG10 9EB
Tel: (0800) 731 9590 Fax: (01683) 222796
Senior Caseworker – Ms Helen Dickson
Tel: (01683) 222746
E-mail: dicksonh@parliament.uk
Assistant Caseworker – Mrs Karen McQueen
Tel: (01683) 222746
E-mail: mcqueenk@parliament.uk
Diary Secretary – Ms Maryann Benson
Tel: (01683) 222770
E-mail: bensonm@parliament.uk
Press Officer – Mrs Jane Anderson-Clark
Tel: (01683) 247135
E-mail: clarkaj@parliament.uk
Political Career . . . . 1984 - 86 Councillor, Annandale and Eskdale
District Council
1986 - 87 Councillor, Dumfries and Galloway Region
1999 - 2005 Member, Scottish Parliament
1999 - 2001 Conservative Deputy Spokesman on
Education, Arts, Culture and Sport, Scottish Parliament
2001 - 02 Conservative Deputy Spokesman on
Enterprise and Lifelong Learning, Scottish Parliament
2002 - 05 Conservative Spokesman on Transport,
Communications and IT, Scottish Parliament
2005 - Shadow Secretary of State for Scotland
Languages Spoken . . . . . . French; German
Parliamentary Interests . . . Business; Commerce; Rural Affairs; USA
Leisure Interests . . . . Golf

Murphy, Rt Hon Jim MP East Renfrewshire
Labour............Majority 6,657 over Con
Born..............23rd August 1967 in Glasgow
Educated..........Bellarmine Secondary School;
                    Milnerton High School, Cape Town;
                    Strathclyde University
Elected ....1997 - 2005 MP for Eastwood
                    2005 MP for East Renfrewshire (seat renamed)
Offices Held ....2001 - 02 PPS to Helen Liddell MP (Secretary of State
                    for Scotland)
                    2002 - 05 Assistant Government Whip
                    2005 - 06 Parliamentary Secretary, Cabinet Office
                    2006 - 07 Minister of State for Employment and
                        Welfare Reform, Department of Work and Pensions
                        (Minister for Work)
                    2007 - 08 Minister of State, Foreign Office (Minister
                        for Europe)
                    2008 - Secretary of State for Scotland
Commons Office .....Tel: (020) 7219 4615 Fax: (020) 7219 5657
                    E-mail: jimmurphymp@parliament.uk
                    Web: www.jimmurphymp.com
Constituency Office ...238 Ayr Road, Newtown Mearns, East Renfrewshire, G77 6AA
                    Tel: (0141) 577 0100 Fax: (0141) 616 3613
                    Personal Assistant – Ms Marion Anderson
                    Researcher/Press Officer – Mr Paul Kelly
                    Researcher – Mr Neil Bibby
Parliamentary Interests Consumer Affairs; Defence; International Issues; Sport;
                    Treasury Issues
Leisure Interests......Cinema; Football; Golf; Travelling in Scotland

Osborne, Sandra MP Ayr, Carrick and Cumnock
Labour . . . . Majority 9,997 over Con
Born . . . . 23rd February 1956 in Paisley
Educated . . . . Camphill Secondary School, Paisley;
Annlesland College; Jordanhill College;
Strathclyde University
Elected . . . . 1997 - 2005 MP for Ayr
2005 MP for Ayr, Carrick and Cumnock
Offices Held . . . . 1999 - 2001 PPS to Brian Wilson MP
(Minister of State, Scotland Office)
2001 - 02 PPS to George Foulkes MP
(Minister of State, Scotland Office)
2002 - 03 PPS to Helen Liddell MP
(Secretary of State for Scotland)
Commons Office . . . . . Tel: (020) 7219 6402
E-mail: osbornes@parliament.uk
Web: www.epolitix.com/sandra-osborne
Constituency Office . . . 139 Main Street, Ayr, KA8 8BX
Tel: (01292) 262906 Fax: (01292) 885661
Office Manager – Ms Lisa Stewart
Parliamentary Assistant – Ms Kay Runcimay
Trade Union . . . . Unite
Parliamentary Interests Foreign Affairs; Housing; International Development;
Poverty; Women's Issues
Leisure Interests . . . . . . Family; Reading; Walking

Reid, Alan MP . . . . . Argyll and Bute
Liberal Democrat . . . Majority 5,636 over Con
Born . . . . 7th August 1954
Educated. . . . . Prestwick Academy; Ayr Academy; Strathclyde University;
                               Jordanhill College; Bell College
Elected . . . . 2001 MP for Argyll and Bute
Office Held . . . . 2001 - 03 Liberal Democrat Spokesman on Scottish Fisheries
                               2002 - 05 Liberal Democrat Whip
                               2003 - 05 Liberal Democrat Spokesman for Scotland
                               2005 - Liberal Democrat Spokesman on
                                   Information Technology
                               2006 - Liberal Democrat Spokesman on Northern Ireland
                               2007 - Liberal Democrat Spokesman on Scotland
                               2009 - Liberal Democrat Whip
Commons Office . . . . . Tel: (020) 7219 8127 Fax: (020) 7219 1737
                               E-mail: reida@parliament.uk
Constituency Office . . . 95 Alexandra Parade, Dunoon, Argyll, PA23 8AL
                               Tel: (01369) 704840 Fax: (01369) 701212
                               Office Manager – Mrs Helen Duffy
                               E-mail: duffyh@parliament.uk
                               Caseworker – Ms Alison Tarkenter
                               E-mail: tarkentera@parliament.uk
                               Constituency Researcher – Mr Tony Miles
                               E-mail: milest@parliament.uk
Trade Union . . . . Association of University Teachers
Parliamentary Interests Elderly; Environment; Employment; Farming;
                               Fishing Industry; Fuel Tax; Health; International Affairs;
                               Local Issues; Rural Development
Leisure Interests. . . . . . Chess; Reading; Walking; Watching TV

Reid, Rt Hon Dr John MP Airdrie and Shotts
Labour . . . . Majority 14,084 over SNP
Born . . . . 8th May 1947 in Bellshill, Scotland
Educated . . . . St Patrick's Secondary School, Coatbridge; Stirling University
Elected . . . . 1987 - 2005 MP for Motherwell North, then (1997)
　　　　　　　　　　　　Hamilton North and Bellshill
　　　　　　　　　　　　2005 MP for Airdrie and Shotts
Offices Held . . . . 1990 - 97 Opposition Spokesman on Defence
　　　　　　　　　　　　1997 - 98 Minister of State, Ministry of Defence
　　　　　　　　　　　　1998 - 99 Minister for Transport, Department
　　　　　　　　　　　　for Environment, Transport and the Regions
　　　　　　　　　　　　1999 - 2001 Secretary of State on Scotland
　　　　　　　　　　　　2001 - 02 Secretary of State on Northern Ireland
　　　　　　　　　　　　2002 - 03 Party Chairman and Minister without Portfolio
　　　　　　　　　　　　2003 Leader of the House of Commons and
　　　　　　　　　　　　President of the Council
　　　　　　　　　　　　2003 - 05 Secretary of State for Health
　　　　　　　　　　　　2005 - 06 Secretary of State for Defence
　　　　　　　　　　　　2006 - 07 Home Secretary
Commons Office . . . . . Tel: (020) 7219 4118
　　　　　　　　　　　　E-mail: reidj@parliament.uk
　　　　　　　　　　　　Web: www.johnreidmp.com
　　　　　　　　　　　　Parliamentary Assistant – Ms Pamela Nash
　　　　　　　　　　　　E-mail: nashp@parliament.uk
Constituency Office . . . 115 Graham Street, Airdire, ML6 6DE
　　　　　　　　　　　　Tel: (01236) 748777 Fax: (01236) 748666
　　　　　　　　　　　　Personal Assistant – Ms Mary McKenna
　　　　　　　　　　　　Mobile: 07721 399181
　　　　　　　　　　　　E-mail: mckennam@parliament.uk
　　　　　　　　　　　　Secretary – Ms Connie Mezynski
　　　　　　　　　　　　E-mail: mezynskic@parliament.uk
Languages Spoken . . . . French
Trade Union . . . . Unite
Parliamentary Interests Defence; Foreign Affairs; The Economy
Leisure Interests . . . . . . Crossword Puzzles; Football

Rennie, Willie MP .. Dunfermline and West Fife
Liberal Democrat ... Majority 1,800 over Lab
Born .... 27th September 1967
Elected .... 2006 MP for Dunfermline and West Fife (By-election)
Educated .... Paisley College; Glasgow College
Offices Held .... 2006 - 07 Liberal Democrat Spokesman on Defence
2007 - Liberal Democrat Whip
2008 – Chair, Liberal Democrat Parliamentary
Campaigns Team
Commons Office ..... Tel: (020) 7219 5054 Fax: (020) 7219 2810
E-mail: renniew@parliament.uk
Researcher – Mr Josh Green
E-mail: fosterjs@parliament.uk
Caseworker – Ms Cheryl Krueger
E-mail: kruegerc@parliament.uk
Caseworker – Caron Lindsay
E-mail: lindsayc@parliment.uk
Constituency Office ... 1st Floor, 1 High Street, Dunfermline, KY12 7DL
Tel: (01383) 841700
E-mail: willie@dunfermlinelibdems.org.uk
Web: www.dunfermlinelibdems.org.uk
Constituency Assistant – Ms Elspeth Finlay
Administrator – Ms Dot Hobson
Parliamentary Interests Asthma; Defence; Health; Science
Leisure Interests ...... Running

Robertson, Angus MP   Moray
SNP . . . . Majority 5,676 over Con
Born . . . . 28th September 1969 in Wimbledon
Educated. . . . . Broughton High School, Edinburgh;
Aberdeen University
Elected . . . . 2001 MP for Moray
Offices Held . . . . 2002 - SNP Spokesman on Defence, Europe and
International Affairs
2005 - 07 Deputy Leader, Social Democrat Party
Westminster Group
2007 - Leader, Social Democrat Party Westminster Group
Commons Office . . . . . Tel: (020) 7219 8259 Fax: (020) 7219 1781
E-mail: robertsona@parliament.uk
Chief of Staff – Mr Luke Skipper
Tel: (020) 7219 3494
E-mail: skipperl@parliament.uk
Constituency Office . . . 9 Wards Road, Elgin, Moray, IV30 1NL
Tel: (01343) 551111 Fax: (01343) 556355
E-mail: info@moraymp.org
Web: www.moraymp.org
Office Manager – Mrs Sue Boulton
E-mail: boultons@parliament.uk
Parliamentary Officers – Ms Carron Anderson
Mr Graham Leadbetter
E-mail: andersonc@parliament.uk
Languages Spoken. . . . German
Trade Union. . . . . NUJ
Parliamentary Interests Defence; International and European Affairs; Fishing; Oil;
Scottish Independence; Sustainable Development;
Whisky; Youth Issues
Leisure Interests. . . . . . Books; Films; Football; Golf; History; Music; Rugby; Skiing;
Socialising; Travel

Robertson, John MP Glasgow North West
Labour. . . . . Majority 10,093 over Lib Dem
Born. . . . . 17th April 1952 in Glasgow
Educated. . . . . Shawlands Academy, Glasgow; Langside College;
                     Stow College
Elected . . . . 2000 - 2005 MP for Glasgow Anniesland (By-election)
                     2005 MP for Glasgow North West
Offices Held . . . . 2005 - 08 PPS to Kim Howells MP (Minister for the Middle
                     East, Foreign and Commonwealth Office)
                     2008 – PPS to Yvette Cooper MP (Chief Secretary to the
                     Treasury then from 2009, Secretary for Work
                     and Pensions)
Commons Office . . . . . Tel: (020) 7219 6964 Fax: (020) 7219 1096
                     Mobile: 07976 746090
                     E-mail: robertsonjo@parliament.uk
                     Web: www.johnrobertsonmp.co.uk
                     Parliamentary Assistant – Mr Andrew Woodcock
                     E-mail: woodcocka@parliament.uk
Constituency Office . . . 131 Dalsetter Avenue, Glasgow, G15 8TE
                     Tel: (0141) 944 7298 Fax: (0141) 944 7121
                     E-mail: jrmpoffice@btinternet.com
                     Secretary/Caseworker – Ms Rachel Paton
                     E-mail: patonr@parliament.uk
                     Assistant Secretary/Caseworker – Mr Alan Cook
                     E-mail: cookal@parliament.uk
                     Parliamentary Assistant – Mr Bill Tynan
                     E-mail: tynanb@parliament.uk
Trade Unions . . . . Unite; Connect
Parliamentary Interests Defence; International Development;
                     Scottish Affairs; Works and Pensions;
                     Foreign and Commonwealth Office
Leisure Interests. . . . . . Cricket; Football; Golf; Music; Reading

Roy, Frank MP . . . . . Motherwell and Wishaw
Labour. . . . . Majority 15,222 over SNP
Born . . . . 29th August 1958 in Motherwell
Educated. . . . . Our Lady's High School, Motherwell;
Glasgow Caledonian University
Elected . . . . 1997 MP for Motherwell and Wishaw
Offices Held . . . . 1998 PPS to Helen Liddell MP (Minister of
State, Scotland Office)
1998 - 2001 PPS to John Reid MP, then Helen Liddell MP
(successive Secretaries of State for Scotland)
2005 - 06 Assistant Government Whip
2006 - Government Whip (Lord Commissioner,
HM Treasury)
Commons Office . . . . . Tel: (020) 7219 6467 Fax: (020) 7219 6866
E-mail: royf@parliament.uk
Web: www.frankroy.org.uk
Assistant – Miss Sarah McGuire
Tel: (020) 7219 1038
E-mail: mcguirese@parliament.uk
Constituency Office . . . 265 Main Street, Wishaw, Lanarkshire, ML2 7NE
Tel: (01698) 303040 Fax: (01698) 303060
Personal Assistant – Mr John Pentland
E-mail: pentlandj@parliament.uk
Senior Caseworker – Mrs Mary Clark
E-mail: clarkmm@parliament.uk
Caseworker – Mrs Myra McKim
E-mail: mckim@parliament.uk
Trade Union . . . . GMB
Parliamentary Interests Foreign Affairs; Social Security
Leisure Interests . . . . . . Football; Gardening

Roy, Lindsay . . . . . . Glenrothes
Labour . . . . Majority 6,737 over SNP
Born . . . . 19th January 1949 in Perth
Educated. . . . . Perth Academy; University of Edinburgh
Elected . . . . 2008 MP for Glenrothes (By-election)
Commons Office . . . . . Tel: (020) 7219 5485 Fax: (020) 7219 0791
E-mail: royl@parliament.uk
Web: www.lroymp.org.uk
Senior Parliamentary Assistant –
Ms Kirsty McCullagh
Tel: (020) 7219 8273
E-mail: mccullaghk@parliament.uk
Constituency Office . . . 83a Woodside Way, Glenrothes,
Fife, KY7 5DW
Tel: (01592) 758662 Fax: (01592) 758662
Senior Caseworkers – Mrs Jeanette Kidd
Ms Julie MacDougall
E-mails: Kiddj@parliament.uk
macdougalljul@parliament.uk
Parliamentary Assistant – Mr David Ross
E-mail: rossd@parliament.uk
Senior Parliamentary Assistant –
Mr Scott Brady
Tel: (01592) 751549
E-mail: bradys@parliament.uk
Parliamentary Assistant – Mr Brian Kemp
Tel: (01592) 751549
E-mail: kempb@parliament.uk
Professional Association International Confederation of Principals;
School Leaders Scotland
Language Spoken . . . . French
Parliamentary Interests Business; Innovation; Skills; Education;
Sport and Culture; Security
Leisure Interests. . . . . . Mountain Biking; Soccer; Angling

Salmond, Rt Hon Alex MP MSP Banff and Buchan
SNP . . . . Majority 11,837 over Con
Born . . . . 31st December 1954 in Linlithgow
Educated . . . . Linlithgow Academy; St Andrews University
Elected . . . . 1987 MP for Banff and Buchan
Offices Held . . . . 1987 - 90 Deputy Leader, Scottish National Party
1990 - 2000 Leader, Scottish National Party
1999 - 2001 Member, Scottish Parliament
2000 - 07 Leader, SNP Group at Westminster
2004 - Leader, Scottish National Party
2007 – Member, Scottish Parliament
2007 - First Minister, Scotland
Commons Office . . . . . Tel: (020) 7219 4500 Fax: (020) 7219 6716
E-mail: salmonda@parliament.uk
Parliamentary Assistant – Mr Alexander Anderson
Tel: (020) 7219 0074
E-mail: andersona@parliament.uk
Constituency Office . . . 17 Maiden Street, Peterhead, Aberdeenshire, AB42 1EE
Tel: (01779) 470444 Fax: (01779) 474460
Web: www.westminster snp.org
Office Manager – Ms Jennifer Harkins
E-mail: harkinsj@parliament.uk
Parliamentary Assistant – Mr Rob Merson
E-mail: mersonr@parliament.uk
Parliamentary Interests Constitution; Foreign Affairs; Fisheries; Scotland
Leisure Interests . . . . . . Golf; Horse Racing; Reading

Sarwar, Mohammad MP Glasgow Central
Labour. . . . . Majority 8,531 over Lib Dem
Born. . . . . 18th August 1952 in Pakistan
Educated. . . . . University of Faisalabad, Pakistan
Elected . . . . 1997 - 2005 MP for Glasgow Govan
 2005 MP for Glasgow Central
Offices Held . . . . 1995 - 97 Convener, General Purposes Committee,
 Glasgow City Council
 2005 - Chairman, Scottish Affairs Committee,
 House of Commons
Commons Office . . . . . Tel: (020) 7219 5024 Fax: (020) 7219 5898
 E-mail: sarwar@sarwar.org.uk
 Web: www.sarwar.org.uk
 Researcher – Ms Caroline Erickson
 Tel: (020) 7219 0547
 E-mail: ericksonc@parliament.uk
 Assistant – Mr Yassar Abbas
 Tel: (020) 7219 0547
 E-mail: abbasy@parliament.uk
Constituency Office . . . 247 Paisley Road West, Glasgow, G51 1NE
 Tel: (0141) 427 5250 Fax: (0141) 427 5938
 Researcher – Ms Caroline Erickson
 E-mail: ericksonc@parliament.uk
 Assistant – Ms Siobhan McCrone
 E-mail: mccrones@parliament.uk
 Staff – Mr Malcolm Cunning
 E-mail: cunningm@parliament.uk
Languages Spoken. . . . Punjabi; Urdu
Parliamentary Interests International Development; Shipbuilding; Senior Citizens
Leisure Interests. . . . . . Abseiling; Charitable Work; Relaxing with Family and Friends

Sheridan, Jim MP. . . . Paisley and Renfrewshire North
Labour. . . . . Majority 11,001 over SNP
Born. . . . . 24th November 1952 in Glasgow
Elected . . . . 2001 - 2005 MP for Renfrewshire West
2005 MP for Paisley and Renfrewshire North
Commons Office . . . . . Tel: (020) 7219 8314
Pager: 07626 409536
E-mail: jim@james-sheridan-mp.org.uk
Web: www.james-sheridan-mp.org.uk
Constituency Office. . . Mirren Court Three, 123 Renfrew Road,
Paisley, PA3 4EA
Tel: (0141) 847 1457 Fax: (0141) 847 1395
E-mail: enquiries@james-sheridan-mp.org.uk
Caseworker – Miss Joanne Sheridan
E-mail: joanne@james-sheridan-mp.org.uk
Personal Assistant – Mrs Jacqueline Thompson
Tel: (0141) 847 1459
E-mail: jacqui@james-sheridan-mp.org.uk
Researcher – Mr Daniel Harris
Tel: (0141) 847 1458
E-mail: daniel@james-sheridan-mp.org.uk
Caseworker – Mrs Jean McGuinness
Tel: (0141) 847 1458
E-mail: jean@james-sheridan-mp.org.uk
Trade Union. . . . . Unite
Parliamentary Interests Employment Legislation; Foreign Affairs; Home Affairs;
International Development; Social Inclusion
Leisure Interests. . . . . . Football; Exercise; Current Affairs

Smith, Sir Robert MP West Aberdeenshire and Kincardine
Liberal Democrat . . . Majority 7,471 over Con
Born . . . . 15th April 1958
Educated . . . . Merchant Taylors School; University of Aberdeen
Elected . . . . 1997 MP for West Aberdeenshire and
                            Kincardine
Offices Held . . . . 1997 - 99 Liberal Democrat Spokesman on
                            Transport and Environment
                            1999 - 2001 Liberal Democrat Whip
                            and Spokesman on Scottish Affairs
                            2001 - 06 Liberal Democrat Deputy Chief Whip
                            2005 - 06 Liberal Democrat Spokesman on Energy and
                            Trade and Industry
                            2007 - Liberal Democrat Deputy Shadow Leader of the
                            House of Commons
                            2008 - Liberal Democrat Deputy Chief Whip
Commons Office . . . . . Tel: (020) 7219 3531 Fax: (020) 7219 4526
                            E-mail: robert.smithmp@parliament.uk
                            Researcher – Mr Robbie McRory
                            E-mail: falconera@parliament.uk
Constituency Office . . . 6 Dee Street, Banchory, Kincardineshire, AB31 5ST
                            Tel: (01330) 820330 Fax: (01330) 820338
                            Office Manager – Ms Sheila Thomson
                            Casework Assistant – Mrs Alison Auld
Parliamentary Interests Electoral Reform; Off Shore Industry;
                            Rural Affairs
Leisure Interests . . . . . . Hill Walking; Sailing

Strang, Rt Hon Gavin MP Edinburgh East
Labour. . . . . Majority 6,202 over Lib Dem
Born. . . . . 10th July 1943 in Dundee
Educated. . . . . Morrison's Academy, Perthshire; Edinburgh University;
            Churchill College, Cambridge
Elected . . . . 1970 - 2005 MP for Edinburgh East, then (1997)
            Edinburgh East and Musselburgh
            2005 MP for Edinburgh East
Offices Held . . . . 1974 Parliamentary Secretary, Department of Energy
            1974 - 79 Parliamentary Secretary, Ministry of
              Agriculture, Fisheries and Food
            1979 - 83 Opposition Spokesman on Agriculture,
              Fisheries and Food
            1987 - 89 Opposition Spokesman on Employment
            1992 - 97 Shadow Minister of Agriculture,
              Food and Rural Affairs
            1997 - 98 Minister for Transport
Commons Office . . . . . Tel: (020) 7219 5155 Fax: (020) 7219 5815
            E-mail: strangg@parliament.uk
            Web: www.gavinstrangmp.co.uk
            Researcher – Ms Kate Davies
            E-mail: daviesk@parliament.uk
Constituency Office . . . 54 Portobello High Street, Edinburgh, EH15 1DA
            Tel: (0131) 669 6002 Fax: (0131) 669 9162
            Case Worker – Ms Angela Gillan
            E-mail: gillana@parliament.uk
Trade Union. . . . . Unite
Language Spoken . . . . French
Parliamentary Interests Agriculture; AIDS; Aviation
Leisure Interests. . . . . . Cycling; Golf; Swimming; Watching Football

Swinson, Jo MP . . . . East Dunbartonshire
Liberal Democrat . . . Majority 4,061 over Lab
Born . . . . 5th February 1980
Educated . . . . Douglas Academy; Milngavie; London School of Economics
Elected . . . . 2005 MP for East Dunbartonshire
Offices Held . . . . 2005 - 06 Liberal Democrat Spokesman on
Culture, Media and Sport
2006 - 07 Liberal Democrat Shadow Secretary for Scotland
2007 - 08 Liberal Democrat Shadow Minister for
Women and Equalities
2008 - Liberal Democrat Shadow Minister for
Foreign Affairs
Commons Office . . . . . Tel: (020) 7219 8088 Tel: (020) 7219 0555
E-mail: swinsonj@parliament.uk
Web: www.joswinson.org.uk
Researcher – Ms Hannah Wright
E-mail: wrighth@parliament.uk
Constituency Office . . . 4 Springfield House, Emerson Road, Bishopbriggs, G64 1QE
Tel: (0141) 762 2209 Fax: (0141) 762 5604
Personal Assistant/Diary Manager – Ms Julie Davidson
E-mail: davidsonj@parliament.uk
Caseworker – Miss Karen Hurst
Tel: (0141) 762 5608
E-mail: hurstk@parliament.uk
Political Assistant – Mr Jamie McHale
Tel: (0141) 762 8444
E-mail: mchalej@parliament.uk
Parliamentary Interests Corporate Responsibility; Environment; Equality Issues;
Voting Reform
Leisure Interests . . . . . . Gym; Hill Walking; Reading; Running

Thurso, John MP ... Caithness, Sutherland and Easter Ross
Liberal Democrat ... Majority 8,168 over Lab
Born .... 10th September 1953 in Thurso
Educated. .... Eton College
Elected .... 2001 MP for Caithness, Sutherland and
                Easter Ross
Offices Held .... 1995 - 99 Member of the House of Lords (as
                Viscount Thurso)
                2001 - 06 Liberal Democrat Spokesman on Scotland
                2003 - 05 Liberal Democrat Spokesman on Transport
                2005 - 06 Liberal Democrat Shadow Secretary
                for Scotland
                2008 - 09 Liberal Democrat Shadow Business, Enterprise
                and Regulatory Reform Secretary
                2009 - Liberal Democrat Shadow Business, Innovation
                and Skills Secretary
Commons Office ..... Tel: (020) 7219 1752 Fax: (020) 7219 3797
                E-mail: thursoj@parliament.uk
                Web: www.johnthurso.org.uk
                Staff – Mrs Bridget Beechey
                Miss Maggie Harrison
                Tel: (020) 7219 3448
                E-mails: beecheyb@parliament.uk
                harrisonm@parliament.uk
Languages Spoken. ... French
Professional Association Hotel and Catering International Management
                Association (Fellow);
                Tourism Society (President)
Directorships .... Fitness Industry Association (Chairman)
                International Wine and Spirit Competition Ltd (Chairman)
                Millennium and Copthorne Hotels plc (Deputy Chairman)
Parliamentary Interests Scotland; Tourism; Lords Reform; Transport
Leisure Interests. ..... Country Pursuits

Weir, Mike MP..... Angus
SNP .... Majority 1,601 over Con
Born.............. 24th March 1957 in Arbroath
Educated........... Arbroath High School; Aberdeen University
Elected .... 2001 MP for Angus
Office Held .... 2005 - SNP Spokesman on Work and Pensions, Business,
Enterprise, Energy and Environment
Commons Office ..... Tel: (020) 7219 8125 Fax: (020) 7219 1736
E-mail: weirm@parliament.uk
Constituency Offices .. 16 Brothock Bridge, Arbroath, Angus, DD11 1NG
Tel: (01241) 874522
Web: www.angussnp.org
Parliamentary Assistant – Mr Donald Morrison
E-mail: morrisondo@parliament.uk
Secretary – Mrs Joyce Morrison
E-mail: morrisonj@parliament.uk
10a George Street, Montrose, DD10 8EN
Tel: (01674) 675743
Constituency Assistant – Mr Stewart Mowatt
E-mail: mowatts@parliament.uk
Professional Association Law Society of Scotland
Parliamentary Interests Disability; Environment; Health; Industrial Development;
Rural Affairs

Wishart, Pete MP . . . Perth and North Perthshire
SNP . . . . Majority 1,521 over Con
Born . . . . 9th March 1962
Educated. . . . . Queen Anne High School, Dunfermline;
                       Moray House College of Education
Elected . . . . 2001 MP for North Tayside
                       2005 MP for Perth and North Perthshire
Offices Held . . . . 2001 - 05 SNP Spokesman on Transport,
                       Local Government and the Regions and
                       Culture Media and Sport
                       2001 - 07 SNP Chief Whip
                       2001 - 05 SNP Spokesman on Transport, Local Government
                       and Regions, Culture Media and Sport and Overseas Aid
                       2005 - SNP Spokesman on Media, Culture and Sport
Commons Office . . . . . Tel: (020) 7219 8303
                       E-mail: wishartp@parliament.uk
                       Web: www.peterwishartmp.com
Constituency Offices . . 35 Perth Street, Blairgowrie, Perthshire, PH10 6DL
                       Tel: (01250) 876576 Fax: (01250) 876991
                       Office Manager – Miss Elaine Wylie
                       9 York Place, Perth, PH2 8ER
                       Tel: (01738) 639598 Fax: (01738) 587637
                       Constituency Assistants – Mrs Dawn Chapman
                                          Mr Scott Telfer
Trade Union . . . . Musicians Union
Parliamentary Interests Intellectual Property Protection; Music; Scottish Football
Leisure Interests. . . . . . Music; Hillwalking; Travel

Notes: *(i) The following list includes all members representing Scottish constituencies in the House of Commons and Westminster.*
(ii) The following abbreviations are used herein:

Con..*Conservative Party*
Lab..*Labour Party*
Lib Dem ....*Liberal Democrat Party*
SNP...*Scottish National Party*

A

Aberdeen North ....Frank Doran (Lab)
Aberdeen South...Anne Begg (Lab)
Airdrie and Shotts..Rt Hon John Reid (Lab)
Angus ....Mike Weir (SNP)
Argyll and Bute..Alan Reid (Lib Dem)
Ayr, Carrick and Cumnock..Sandra Osborne (Lab)

B

Banff and Buchan..Rt Hon Alex Salmond MSP (SNP)
Berwickshire, Roxburgh and Selkirk....................................Michael Moore (Lib Dem)

C

Caithness, Sutherland and Easter Ross ....John Thurso (Lib Dem)
Central Ayrshire ....Brian Donohoe (Lab)
Coatbridge, Chryston and Bellshill ....Rt Hon Tom Clarke (Lab)
Cumbernauld, Kilsyth and Kirkintilloch East......................Rosemary McKenna (Lab)

D

Dumfries and Galloway ....Russell Brown (Lab)
Dumfriesshire, Clydesdale and Tweeddale................................David Mundell (Con)
Dundee East...Stewart Hosie (SNP)
Dundee West ....Jim McGovern (Lab)
Dunfermline and West Fife ....Willie Rennie (Lib Dem)

E

East Dunbartonshire ....Jo Swinson (Lib Dem)
East Kilbride, Strathaven and Lesmahagow......................Rt Hon Adam Ingram (Lab)
East Lothian ....Anne Moffat (Lab)
East Renfrewshire...Jim Murphy (Lab)
Edinburgh East...Rt Hon Gavin Strang (Lab)

Edinburgh North and Leith ....Mark Lazarowicz (Lab)
Edinburgh South ....Nigel Griffiths (Lab)
Edinburgh South West.......................................Rt Hon Alistair Darling (Lab)
Edinburgh West ....John Barrett (Lib Dem)

F
Falkirk ....Eric Joyce (Lab)

G
Glasgow Central...Mohammad Sarwar (Lab)
Glasgow East..John Mason (SNP)
Glasgow North...Ann McKechin (Lab)
Glasgow North East ....Willie Bain (Lab)
Glasgow North West..John Robertson (Lab)
Glasgow South...Tom Harris (Lab)
Glasgow South West ....Ian Davidson (Lab)
Glenrothes ....Lindsay Roy (Lab)
Gordon ....Rt Hon Malcolm Bruce (Lib Dem)

I
Inverclyde ....David Cairns (Lab)
Inverness, Nairn, Badenoch and Strathspey.....................Danny Alexander (Lib Dem)

K
Kilmarnock and Loudoun...................................Rt Hon Des Browne (Lab)
Kirkcaldy and Cowdenbeath ....Rt Hon Gordon Brown (Lab)

L
Lanark and Hamilton East ....Jimmy Hood (Lab)
Linlithgow and East Falkirk ....Michael Connarty (Lab)
Livingston ....Jim Devine (Lab)

M
Midlothian..David Hamilton (Lab)
Moray ....Angus Robertson (SNP)
Motherwell and Wishaw ....Frank Roy (Lab)

N
Na h-Eileanan an Iar ....Angus MacNeil (SNP)
North Ayrshire and Arran...Katy Clark (Lab)
North East Fife ....Rt Hon Sir Menzies Campbell (Lib Dem)

O

Ochil and South Perthshire ....Gordon Banks (Lab)
Orkney and Shetland ....Alistair Carmichael (Lib Dem)

P

Paisley and Renfrewshire North...Jim Sheridan (Lab)
Paisley and Renfrewshire South.................................Rt Hon Douglas Alexander (Lab)
Perth and North Perthshire...Pete Wishart (SNP)

R

Ross, Skye and Lochaber....................................Rt Hon Charles Kennedy (Lib Dem)
Rutherglen and Hamilton West...................................Rt Hon Thomas McAvoy (Lab)

S

Stirling ....Rt Hon Anne McGuire (Lab)

W

West Aberdeenshire and Kincardine.................................Sir Robert Smith (Lib Dem)
West Dunbartonshire..Rt Hon John McFall (Lab)

Conservative

M

Mundell, David...Dumfriesshire, Clydesdale and Tweeddale

Labour

A

Alexander, Rt Hon Douglas ....Paisley and Refrewshire South

B

Bain, Willie ....Glasgow North East
Banks, Gordon..Ochil and South Perthshire
Begg, Anne...Aberdeen South
Brown, Rt Hon Gordon..Kirkcaldy and Cowdenbeath
Brown, Russell ....Dumfries and Galloway
Browne, Rt Hon Des ....Kilmarnock and Loudoun

C

Cairns, David...Inverclyde
Clark, Katy ....North Ayrshire and Arran
Clarke, Rt Hon Tom..Coatbridge, Chryston and Bellshill
Connarty, Michael ....Linlithgow and East Falkirk

D

Darling, Rt Hon Alistair ....Edinburgh South West
Davidson, Ian...Glasgow South West
Devine, Jim...Livingston
Donohoe, Brian...Central Ayrshire
Doran, Frank...Aberdeen North

G

Griffiths, Nigel...Edinburgh South

H

Hamilton, David...Midlothian
Harris, Tom ....Glasgow South
Hood, Jimmy...Lanark and Hamilton East

I

Ingram, Rt Hon Adam ....East Kilbride, Strathaven and Lesmahagow

Labour (Continued)

J

Joyce, Eric..Falkirk

L

Lazarowicz, Mark ....Edinburgh North and Leith

M

McAvoy, Rt Hon Tommy................Rutherglen and Hamilton West
McFall, Rt Hon John ....West Dunbartonshire
McGovern, Jim..Dundee West
McGuire, Rt Hon Anne ....Stirling
McKechin, Ann ....Glasgow North
McKenna, Rosemary ....Cumbernauld, Kilsyth and Kirkintilloch East
Moffat, Anne ....East Lothian
Murphy, Rt Hon Jim......................................East Renfrewshire

O

Osborne, Sandra................................Ayr, Carrick and Cumnock

R

Reid, Rt Hon Dr John................................Airdrie and Shotts
Robertson, John ....Glasgow North West
Roy, Frank................................Motherwell and Wishaw
Roy, Lindsay..Glenrothes

S

Sarwar, Mohammad ....Glasgow Central
Sheridan, Jim ....Paisley and Renfrewshire North
Strang, Rt Hon Gavin ....Edinburgh East

Liberal Democrat

A

Alexander, Danny ....Inverness, Nairn, Badenoch and Strathspey

B

Barrett, John..Edinburgh West
Bruce, Malcolm ....Gordon

C

Campbell, Rt Hon Sir Menzies ....North East Fife
Carmichael, Alistair ....Orkney and Shetland

Liberal Democrat (Continued)

K
Kennedy, Rt Hon Charles ....Ross, Skye and Lochaber

M
Moore, Michael.......................................Berwickshire, Roxburgh and Selkirk

R
Reid, Alan ....Argyll and Bute
Rennie, Willie ....Dunfermline and West Fife

S
Smith, Sir Robert...West Aberdeenshire and Kincardine
Swinson, Jo...East Dunbartonshire

T
Thurso, John...Caithness, Sutherland and Easter Ross

Scottish National Party

H
Hosie, Stewart...Dundee East

M
MacNeil, Angus ....Na h-Eileanan An Iar
Mason, John...Glasgow East

R
Robertson, Angus ....Moray

S
Salmond, Rt Hon Alex MSP ....Banff and Buchan

W
Weir, Mike ....Angus
Wishart, Peter ....Perth and North Perthshire

MEMBERS OF THE HOUSE OF COMMONS –
ALPHABETICAL LIST WITH PARTY AND CONSTITUENCY

Note: MPs can be contacted at: House of Commons, London, SW1A 0AA,
Tel: (020) 7219 3000.

Name	Party	Constituency

A

Abbott, Diane	Labour	Hackney North and Stoke Newington
Adams, Gerry	Sinn Fein	Belfast West
Afriyie, Adam	Conservative	Windsor
Ainger, Nick	Labour	Carmarthen West and South Pembrokeshire
Ainsworth, Rt Hon Bob	Labour	Coventry North East
Ainsworth, Peter	Conservative	East Surrey
Alexander, Danny	Liberal Democrat	Inverness, Nairn, Badenoch and Strathspey
Alexander, Rt Hon Douglas	Labour	Paisley and Renfrewshire South
Allen, Graham	Labour	Nottingham North
Amess, David	Conservative	Southend West
Ancram, Rt Hon Michael	Conservative	Devizes
Anderson, David	Labour	Blaydon
Anderson, Janet	Labour	Rossendale and Darwen
Arbuthnot, Rt Hon James	Conservative	North East Hampshire
Armstrong, Rt Hon Hilary	Labour	North West Durham
Atkins, Charlotte	Labour	Staffordshire Moorlands
Atkinson, Peter	Conservative	Hexham
Austin, Ian	Labour	Dudley North
Austin, John	Labour	Erith and Thamesmead

B

Bacon, Richard	Conservative	South Norfolk
Bain, Willie	Labour	Glasgow North East
Bailey, Adrian	Labour	West Bromwich West
Bain, William	Labour	Glasgow North East
Baird, Vera	Labour	Redcar
Baker, Norman	Liberal Democrat	Lewes
Baldry, Tony	Conservative	Banbury
Balls, Rt Hon Ed	Labour	Normanton
Banks, Gordon	Labour	Ochil and South Perthshire
Barker, Gregory	Conservative	Bexhill and Battle
Barlow, Celia	Labour	Hove
Baron, John	Conservative	Billericay
Barrett, John	Liberal Democrat	Edinburgh West
Barron, Rt Hon Kevin	Labour	Rother Valley
Battle, Rt Hon John	Labour	Leeds West
Bayley, Hugh	Labour	City of York

Name	Party	Constituency
Beckett, Rt Hon Margaret	Labour	Derby South
Begg, Anne	Labour	Aberdeen South
Beith, Rt Hon Alan	Liberal Democrat	Berwick-upon-Tweed
Bell, Sir Stuart	Labour	Middlesbrough
Bellingham, Henry	Conservative	North West Norfolk
Benn, Rt Hon Hilary	Labour	Leeds Central
Benton, Joe	Labour	Bootle
Benyon, Richard	Conservative	Newbury
Bercow, Rt Hon John	Speaker	Buckingham
Beresford, Sir Paul	Conservative	Mole Valley
Berry, Dr Roger	Labour	Kingswood
Betts, Clive	Labour	Sheffield Attercliffe
Binley, Brian	Conservative	Northampton South
Blackman, Liz	Labour	Erewash
Blackman-Woods, Dr Roberta	Labour	Durham City
Blears, Rt Hon Hazel	Labour	Salford
Blizzard, Bob	Labour	Waveney
Blunkett, Rt Hon David	Labour	Sheffield Brightside
Blunt, Crispin	Conservative	Reigate
Bone, Peter	Conservative	Wellingborough
Borrow, David	Labour	South Ribble
Boswell, Tim	Conservative	Daventry
Bottomley, Peter	Conservative	Worthing West
Bradshaw, Rt Hon Ben	Labour	Exeter
Brady, Graham	Conservative	Altrincham and Sale West
Brake, Tom	Liberal Democrat	Carshalton and Wallington
Brazier, Julian	Conservative	Canterbury
Breed, Colin	Liberal Democrat	South East Cornwall
Brennan, Kevin	Labour	Cardiff West
Brokenshire, James	Conservative	Hornchurch
Brooke, Annette	Liberal Democrat	Mid Dorset and North Poole
Brown, Rt Hon Gordon	Labour	Kirkcaldy and Cowdenbeath
Brown, Lyn	Labour	West Ham
Brown, Rt Hon Nick	Labour	Newcastle-upon-Tyne East and Wallsend
Brown, Russell	Labour	Dumfries and Galloway
Browne, Rt Hon Desmond	Labour	Kilmarnock and Loudoun
Browne, Jeremy	Liberal Democrat	Taunton
Browning, Angela	Conservative	Tiverton and Honiton
Bruce, Rt Hon Malcolm	Liberal Democrat	Gordon
Bryant, Chris	Labour	Rhondda
Buck, Karen	Labour	Regent's Park and Kensington North
Burden, Richard	Labour	Birmingham Northfield

Name	Party	Constituency
Burgon, Colin	Labour	Elmet
Burnham, Rt Hon Andrew	Labour	Leigh
Burns, Simon	Conservative	West Chelmsford
Burrowes, David	Conservative	Enfield Southgate
Burstow, Paul	Liberal Democrat	Sutton and Cheam
Burt, Alastair	Conservative	North East Bedfordshire
Burt, Lorely	Liberal Democrat	Solihull
Butler, Dawn	Labour	Brent South
Butterfill, Sir John	Conservative	Bournemouth West
Byers, Rt Hon Stephen	Labour	North Tyneside
Byrne, Liam	Labour	Birmingham Hodge Hill

C

Name	Party	Constituency
Cable, Dr Vincent	Liberal Democrat	Twickenham
Caborn, Rt Hon Richard	Labour	Sheffield Central
Cairns, David	Labour	Inverclyde
Cameron, Rt Hon David	Conservative	Witney
Campbell, Alan	Labour	Tynemouth
Campbell, Gregory	Democratic Unionist	Londonderry East
Campbell, Rt Hon Menzies	Liberal Democrat	North East Fife
Campbell, Ronnie	Labour	Blyth Valley
Carmichael, Alistair	Liberal Democrat	Orkney and Shetland
Carswell, Douglas	Conservative	Harwich
Cash, William	Conservative	Stone
Caton, Martin	Labour	Gower
Cawsey, Ian	Labour	Brigg and Goole
Challen, Colin	Labour	Morley and Rothwell
Chapman, Ben	Labour	Wirral South
Chaytor, David	Labour	Bury North
Chope, Christopher	Conservative	Christchurch
Clapham, Michael	Labour	Barnsley West and Penistone
Clappison, James	Conservative	Hertsmere
Clark, Greg	Conservative	Tunbridge Wells
Clark, Katy	Labour	North Ayrshire and Arran
Clark, Paul	Labour	Gillingham
Clarke, Rt Hon Charles	Labour	Norwich South
Clarke, Rt Hon Kenneth	Conservative	Rushcliffe
Clarke, Rt Hon Tom	Labour	Coatbridge and Chryston and Bellshill
Clegg, Rt Hon Nick	Liberal Democrat	Sheffield Hallam
Clelland, David	Labour	Tyne Bridge
Clifton-Brown, Geoffrey	Conservative	Cotswold
Clwyd, Rt Hon Ann	Labour	Cynon Valley
Coaker, Vernon	Labour	Gedling
Coffey, Ann	Labour	Stockport
Cohen, Harry	Labour	Leyton and Wanstead

Name	*Party*	*Constituency*
Connarty, Michael	Labour	Linlithgow and East Falkirk
Conway, Derek	Independent Conservative	Old Bexley and Sidcup
Cook, Frank	Labour	Stockton North
Cooper, Rosie	Labour	West Lancashire
Cooper, Rt Hon Yvette	Labour	Pontefract and Castleford
Corbyn, Jeremy	Labour	Islington North
Cormack, Sir Patrick	Conservative	South Staffordshire
Cousins, Jim	Labour	Newcastle-upon-Tyne Central
Cox, Geoffrey	Conservative	Torridge and West Devon
Crabb, Stephen	Conservative	Preseli Pembrokeshire
Crausby, David	Labour	Bolton North East
Creagh, Mary	Labour	Wakefield
Cruddas, Jon	Labour	Dagenham
Cryer, Ann	Labour	Keighley
Cummings, John	Labour	Easington
Cunningham, Jim	Labour	Coventry South
Cunningham, Tony	Labour	Workington
Curry, Rt Hon David	Conservative	Skipton and Ripon
Curtis-Thomas, Claire	Labour	Crosby

D

Darling, Rt Hon Alistair	Labour	Edinburgh South West
Davey, Edward	Liberal Democrat	Kingston and Surbiton
David, Wayne	Labour	Caerphilly
Davidson, Ian	Labour	Glasgow South West
Davies, Dai	Independent	Blaenau Gwent
Davies, David TC	Conservative	Monmouth
Davies, Philip	Conservative	Shipley
Davies, Quentin	Labour	Grantham and Stamford
Davis, Rt Hon David	Conservative	Haltemprice and Howden
Dean, Janet	Labour	Burton
Denham, Rt Hon John	Labour	Southampton Itchen
Devine, Jim	Labour	Livingston
Dhanda, Parmjit	Labour	Gloucester
Dismore, Andrew	Labour	Hendon
Djanogly, Jonathan	Conservative	Huntingdon
Dobbin, Jim	Labour	Heywood and Middleton
Dobson, Rt Hon Frank	Labour	Holborn and St Pancras
Dodds, Nigel	Democratic Unionist	Belfast North
Doherty, Pat	Sinn Fein	West Tyrone
Donaldson, Rt Hon Jeffrey	Democratic Unionist Party	Lagan Valley
Donohoe, Brian	Labour	Central Ayrshire
Doran, Frank	Labour	Aberdeen North
Dorrell, Rt Hon Stephen	Conservative	Charnwood

MEMBERS OF THE HOUSE OF COMMONS –
ALPHABETICAL LIST WITH PARTY AND CONSTITUENCY

Name	Party	Constituency
Dorries, Nadine	Conservative	Mid Bedfordshire
Dowd, Jim	Labour	Lewisham West
Drew, David	Labour	Stroud
Duddridge, James	Conservative	Rochford and Southend East
Duncan, Alan	Conservative	Rutland and Melton
Duncan Smith, Rt Hon Iain	Conservative	Chingford and Woodford Green
Dunne, Philip	Conservative	Ludlow
Durkan, Mark	SDLP	Foyle

E

Name	Party	Constituency
Eagle, Angela	Labour	Wallasey
Eagle, Maria	Labour	Liverpool Garston
Efford, Clive	Labour	Eltham
Ellman, Louise	Labour	Liverpool Riverside
Ellwood, Tobias	Conservative	Bournemouth East
Engel, Natascha	Labour	North East Derbyshire
Ennis, Jeff	Labour	Barnsley East and Mexborough
Etherington, Bill	Labour	Sunderland North
Evans, Nigel	Conservative	Ribble Valley
Evennett, David	Conservative	Bexleyheath and Crayford

F

Name	Party	Constituency
Fabricant, Michael	Conservative	Lichfield
Fallon, Michael	Conservative	Sevenoaks
Farrelly, Paul	Labour	Newcastle-under-Lyme
Farron, Tim	Liberal Democrat	Westmorland and Lonsdale
Featherstone, Lynne	Liberal Democrat	Hornsey and Wood Green
Field, Rt Hon Frank	Labour	Birkenhead
Field, Mark	Conservative	Cities of London and Westminster
Fisher, Mark	Labour	Stoke-on-Trent Central
Fitzpatrick, Jim	Labour	Poplar and Canning Town
Flello, Robert	Labour	Stoke-on-Trent South
Flint, Rt Hon Caroline	Labour	Don Valley
Flynn, Paul	Labour	Newport West
Follett, Barbara	Labour	Stevenage
Foster, Don	Liberal Democrat	Bath
Foster, Michael Jabez	Labour	Hastings and Rye
Foster, Michael John	Labour	Worcester
Fox, Dr Liam	Conservative	Woodspring
Francis, Dr Hywel	Labour	Aberavon

Name	Party	Constituency
Francois, Mark	Conservative	Rayleigh
Fraser, Christopher	Conservative	South West Norfolk

G

Gale, Roger	Conservative	North Thanet
Galloway, George	Respect	Bethnal Green and Bow
Gapes, Mike	Labour	Ilford South
Gardiner, Barry	Labour	Brent North
Garnier, Edward	Conservative	Harborough
Gauke, David	Conservative	South West Hertfordshire
George, Andrew	Liberal Democrat	St Ives
George, Rt Hon Bruce	Labour	Walsall South
Gerrard, Neil	Labour	Walthamstow
Gibb, Nick	Conservative	Bognor Regis and Littlehampton
Gidley, Sandra	Liberal Democrat	Romsey
Gildernew, Michelle	Sinn Fein	Fermanagh and South Tyrone
Gillan, Cheryl	Conservative	Chesham and Amersham
Gilroy, Linda	Labour	Plymouth Sutton
Godsiff, Roger	Labour	Birmingham Sparkbrook and Small Heath
Goggins, Rt Hon Paul	Labour	Wythenshawe and Sale East
Goldsworthy, Julia	Liberal Democrat	Falmouth and Camborne
Goodman, Helen	Labour	Bishop Auckland
Goodman, Paul	Conservative	Wycombe
Goodwill, Robert	Conservative	Scarborough and Whitby
Gove, Michael	Conservative	Surrey Heath
Gray, James	Conservative	North Wiltshire
Grayling, Chris	Conservative	Epsom and Ewell
Green, Damian	Conservative	Ashford
Greening, Justine	Conservative	Putney
Greenway, John	Conservative	Ryedale
Grieve, Dominic	Conservative	Beaconsfield
Griffith, Nia	Labour	Llanelli
Griffiths, Nigel	Labour	Edinburgh South
Grogan, John	Labour	Selby
Gummer, Rt Hon John	Conservative	Suffolk Coastal
Gwynne, Andrew	Labour	Denton and Reddish

H

Hague, Rt Hon William	Conservative	Richmond (Yorks)
Hain, Rt Hon Peter	Labour	Neath
Hall, Mike	Labour	Weaver Vale
Hall, Patrick	Labour	Bedford

MEMBERS OF THE HOUSE OF COMMONS –
ALPHABETICAL LIST WITH PARTY AND CONSTITUENCY

Name	Party	Constituency
Hamilton, David	Labour	Midlothian
Hamilton, Fabian	Labour	Leeds North East
Hammond, Philip	Conservative	Runnymede and Weybridge
Hammond, Stephen	Conservative	Wimbledon
Hancock, Mike	Liberal Democrat	Portsmouth South
Hands, Greg	Conservative	Hammersmith and Fulham
Hanson, Rt Hon David	Labour	Delyn
Harman, Rt Hon Harriet	Labour	Camberwell and Peckham
Harper, Mark	Conservative	Forest of Dean
Harris, Dr Evan	Liberal Democrat	Oxford West and Abingdon
Harris, Tom	Labour	Glasgow South
Harvey, Nick	Liberal Democrat	North Devon
Haselhurst, Rt Hon Sir Alan	Conservative	Saffron Walden
Havard, Dai	Labour	Merthyr Tydfil and Rhymney
Hayes, John	Conservative	South Holland and The Deepings
Heal, Sylvia	Labour	Halesowen and Rowley Regis
Heald, Oliver	Conservative	North East Hertfordshire
Healey, John	Labour	Wentworth
Heath, David	Liberal Democrat	Somerton and Frome
Heathcoat-Amory, Rt Hon David	Conservative	Wells
Hemming, John	Liberal Democrat	Birmingham Yardley
Henderson, Doug	Labour	Newcastle-upon-Tyne North
Hendrick, Mark	Labour	Preston
Hendry, Charles	Conservative	Wealden
Hepburn, Stephen	Labour	Jarrow
Heppell, John	Labour	Nottingham East
Herbert, Nick	Conservative	Arundel and South Downs
Hermon, Lady [Sylvia]	Ulster Unionist	North Down
Hesford, Stephen	Labour	Wirral West
Hewitt, Rt Hon Patricia	Labour	Leicester West
Heyes, David	Labour	Ashton-under-Lyne
Hill, Rt Hon Keith	Labour	Streatham
Hillier, Meg	Labour	Hackney South and Shoreditch
Hoban, Mark	Conservative	Fareham
Hodge, Rt Hon Margaret	Labour	Barking

Name	Party	Constituency
Hodgson, Sharon	Labour	Gateshead East and Washington West
Hoey, Kate	Labour	Vauxhall
Hogg, Rt Hon Douglas	Conservative	Sleaford and North Hykeham
Hollobone, Philip	Conservative	Kettering
Holloway, Adam	Conservative	Gravesham
Holmes, Paul	Liberal Democrat	Chesterfield
Hood, Jimmy	Labour	Lanark and Hamilton East
Hoon, Rt Hon Geoff	Labour	Ashfield
Hope, Philip	Labour	Corby
Hopkins, Kelvin	Labour	Luton North
Horam, John	Conservative	Orpington
Horwood, Martin	Liberal Democrat	Cheltenham
Hosie, Stewart	SNP	Dundee East
Howard, Rt Hon Michael	Conservative	Folkestone and Hythe
Howarth, David	Liberal Democrat	Cambridge
Howarth, Rt Hon George	Labour	Knowsley North and Sefton East
Howarth, Gerald	Conservative	Aldershot
Howell, John	Conservative	Henley
Howells, Rt Hon Dr Kim	Labour	Pontypridd
Hoyle, Lindsay	Labour	Chorley
Hughes, Rt Hon Beverley	Labour	Stretford and Urmston
Hughes, Simon	Liberal Democrat	North Southwark and Bermondsey
Huhne, Chris	Liberal Democrat	Eastleigh
Humble, Joan	Labour	Blackpool North and Fleetwood
Hunt, Jeremy	Conservative	South West Surrey
Hunter, Mark	Liberal Democrat	Cheadle
Hurd, Nick	Conservative	Ruislip-Northwood
Hutton, Rt Hon John	Labour	Barrow and Furness

I

Name	Party	Constituency
Iddon, Dr Brian	Labour	Bolton South East
Illsley, Eric	Labour	Barnsley Central
Ingram, Rt Hon Adam	Labour	East Kilbride, Strathaven and Lesmahagow
Irranca-Davies, Huw	Labour	Ogmore

J

Name	Party	Constituency
Jack, Rt Hon Michael	Conservative	Fylde
Jackson, Glenda	Labour	Hampstead and Highgate
Jackson, Stewart	Conservative	Peterborough
James, Siân	Labour	Swansea East
Jenkin, Hon Bernard	Conservative	North Essex

Name	Party	Constituency
Jenkins, Brian	Labour	Tamworth
Johnson, Rt Hon Alan	Labour	Hull West and Hessle
Johnson, Diana	Labour	Hull North
Jones, David	Conservative	Clwyd West
Jones, Helen	Labour	Warrington North
Jones, Kevan	Labour	North Durham
Jones, Lynne	Labour	Birmingham Selly Oak
Jones, Martyn	Labour	Clwyd South
Jowell, Rt Hon Tessa	Labour	Dulwich and West Norwood
Joyce, Eric	Labour	Falkirk

K

Name	Party	Constituency
Kaufman, Rt Hon Gerald	Labour	Manchester Gorton
Kawczynski, Daniel	Conservative	Shrewsbury and Atcham
Keeble, Sally	Labour	Northampton North
Keeley, Barbara	Labour	Worsley
Keen, Alan	Labour	Feltham and Heston
Keen, Ann	Labour	Brentford and Isleworth
Keetch, Paul	Liberal Democrat	Hereford
Kelly, Rt Hon Ruth	Labour	Bolton West
Kemp, Fraser	Labour	Houghton and Washington East
Kennedy, Rt Hon Charles	Liberal Democrat	Ross, Skye and Lochaber
Kennedy, Rt Hon Jane	Labour	Liverpool Wavertree
Key, Robert	Conservative	Salisbury
Khan, Rt Hon Sadiq	Labour	Tooting
Kidney, David	Labour	Stafford
Kilfoyle, Peter	Labour	Liverpool Walton
Kirkbride, Julie	Conservative	Bromsgrove
Knight, Rt Hon Greg	Conservative	East Yorkshire
Knight, Jim	Labour	South Dorset
Kramer, Susan	Liberal Democrat	Richmond Park
Kumar, Dr Ashok	Labour	Middlesbrough South and East Cleveland

L

Name	Party	Constituency
Ladyman, Dr Stephen	Labour	South Thanet
Laing, Eleanor	Conservative	Epping Forest
Lait, Jacqui	Conservative	Beckenham
Lamb, Norman	Liberal Democrat	North Norfolk
Lammy, David	Labour	Tottenham
Lancaster, Mark	Conservative	North East Milton Keynes
Lansley, Andrew	Conservative	South Cambridgeshire

MEMBERS OF THE HOUSE OF COMMONS – ALPHABETICAL LIST WITH PARTY AND CONSTITUENCY

Name	Party	Constituency
Laws, David	Liberal Democrat	Yeovil
Laxton, Bob	Labour	Derby North
Lazarowicz, Mark	Labour	Edinburgh North and Leith
Leech, John	Liberal Democrat	Manchester Withington
Leigh, Edward	Conservative	Gainsborough
Lepper, David	Labour	Brighton Pavilion
Letwin, Rt Hon Oliver	Conservative	West Dorset
Levitt, Tom	Labour	High Peak
Lewis, Ivan	Labour	Bury South
Lewis, Dr Julian	Conservative	New Forest East
Liddell-Grainger, Ian	Conservative	Bridgwater
Lidington, David	Conservative	Aylesbury
Lilley, Rt Hon Peter	Conservative	Hitchin and Harpenden
Linton, Martin	Labour	Battersea
Lloyd, Tony	Labour	Manchester Central
Llwyd, Elfyn	Plaid Cymru	Meirionnydd Nant Conwy
Lord, Sir Michael	Conservative	Central Suffolk and North Ipswich
Loughton, Tim	Conservative	East Worthing and Shoreham
Love, Andrew	Labour	Edmonton
Lucas, Ian	Labour	Wrexham
Luff, Peter	Conservative	Mid Worcestershire

M

Name	Party	Constituency
Mackay, Rt Hon Andrew	Conservative	Bracknell
MacKinlay, Andrew	Labour	Thurrock
Maclean, Rt Hon David	Conservative	Penrith and the Border
MacNeil, Angus	SNP	Na h-Eileanan an Iar
MacShane, Rt Hon Denis	Labour	Rotherham
Mactaggart, Fiona	Labour	Slough
McAvoy, Rt Hon Tommy	Labour	Rutherglen and Hamilton West
McCabe, Stephen	Labour	Birmingham Hall Green
McCafferty, Christine	Labour	Calder Valley
McCarthy, Kerry	Labour	Bristol East
McCarthy-Fry, Sarah	Labour	Portsmouth North
McCartney, Rt Hon Ian	Labour	Makerfield
McCrea, Rev Dr William	Democratic Unionist	South Antrim
McDonagh, Siobhain	Labour	Mitcham and Morden
McDonnell, Dr Alasdair	SDLP	Belfast South
McDonnell, John	Labour	Hayes and Harlington
McFadden, Pat	Labour	Wolverhampton South East

Name	Party	Constituency
McFall, Rt Hon John	Labour	West Dumbartonshire
McGovern, Jim	Labour	Dundee West
McGrady, Eddie	SDLP	South Down
McGuiness, Martin	Sinn Fein	Mid Ulster
McGuire, Anne	Labour	Stirling
McIntosh, Anne	Conservative	Vale of York
McIsaac, Shona	Labour	Cleethorpes
McKechin, Ann	Labour	Glasgow North
McKenna, Rosemary	Labour	Cumbernauld, Kilsyth and Kirkintilloch
McLoughlin, Rt Hon Patrick	Conservative	West Derbyshire
McNulty, Rt Hon Tony	Labour	Harrow East
Mahmood, Khalid	Labour	Birmingham Perry Barr
Main, Anne	Conservative	St Albans
Malik, Shahid	Labour	Dewsbury
Malins, Humfrey	Conservative	Woking
Mallaber, Judy	Labour	Amber Valley
Mann, John	Labour	Bassetlaw
Maples, John	Conservative	Stratford-on-Avon
Marris, Robert	Labour	Wolverhampton South West
Marsden, Gordon	Labour	Blackpool South
Marshall-Andrews, Robert	Labour	Medway
Martlew, Eric	Labour	Carlisle
Mason, John	SNP	Glasgow East
Mates, Rt Hon Michael	Conservative	East Hampshire
Maude, Rt Hon Francis	Conservative	Horsham
May, Rt Hon Theresa	Conservative	Maidenhead
Meacher, Rt Hon Michael	Labour	Oldham West and Royton
Meale, Alan	Labour	Mansfield
Mercer, Patrick	Conservative	Newark
Merron, Gillian	Labour	Lincoln
Michael, Rt Hon Alun	Labour	Cardiff South and Penarth
Milburn, Rt Hon Alan	Labour	Darlington
Miliband, Rt Hon David	Labour	South Shields
Miliband, Rt Hon Edward	Labour	Doncaster North
Miller, Andrew	Labour	Ellesmere Port and Neston
Miller, Maria	Conservative	Basingstoke
Milton, Anne	Conservative	Guildford
Mitchell, Andrew	Conservative	Sutton Coldfield
Mitchell, Austin	Labour	Great Grimsby
Moffatt, Anne	Labour	East Lothian
Moffatt, Laura	Labour	Crawley

Name	Party	Constituency
Mole, Chris	Labour	Ipswich
Moon, Madeleine	Labour	Bridgend
Moore, Michael	Liberal Democrat	Berwickshire, Roxburgh and Selkirk
Moran, Margaret	Labour	Luton South
Morden, Jessica	Labour	Newport East
Morgan, Julie	Labour	Cardiff North
Morley, Rt Hon Elliott	Labour	Scunthorpe
Moss, Malcolm	Conservative	North East Cambridgeshire
Mountford, Kali	Labour	Colne Valley
Mudie, George	Labour	Leeds East
Mulholland, Greg	Liberal Democrat	Leeds North West
Mullin, Chris	Labour	Sunderland South
Mundell, David	Conservative	Dumfriesshire, Clydesdale and Tweeddale
Munn, Meg	Labour	Sheffield Heeley
Murphy, Conor	Sinn Fein	Newry and Armagh
Murphy, Denis	Labour	Wansbeck
Murphy, Rt Hon Jim	Labour	East Renfrewshire
Murphy, Rt Hon Paul	Labour	Torfaen
Murrison, Dr Andrew	Conservative	Westbury

N

Naysmith, Dr Doug	Labour	Bristol North West
Neill, Bob AM	Conservative	Bromley and Chislehurst
Newmark, Brooks	Conservative	Braintree
Norris, Dan	Labour	Wansdyke

O

Oaten, Mark	Liberal Democrat	Winchester
O'Brien, Rt Hon Mike	Labour	North Warwickshire
O'Brien, Stephen	Conservative	Eddisbury
O'Hara, Eddie	Labour	Knowsley South
Olner, Bill	Labour	Nuneaton
Opik, Lembit	Liberal Democrat	Montgomeryshire
Osborne, George	Conservative	Tatton
Osborne, Sandra	Labour	Ayr, Carrick and Cumnock
Ottaway, Richard	Conservative	Croydon South
Owen, Albert	Labour	Ynys Môn

Name	Party	Constituency

P

Paice, James	Conservative	South East Cambridgeshire
Paisley, Rt Hon Rev Dr Ian	Democratic Unionist	North Antrim
Palmer, Dr Nick	Labour	Broxtowe
Paterson, Owen	Conservative	North Shropshire
Pearson, Ian	Labour	Dudley South
Pelling, Andrew	Conservative	Croydon Central
Penning, Mike	Conservative	Hemel Hempstead
Penrose, John	Conservative	Weston-Super-Mare
Pickles, Eric	Conservative	Brentwood and Ongar
Plaskitt, James	Labour	Warwick and Leamington
Pope, Greg	Labour	Hyndburn
Pound, Stephen	Labour	Ealing North
Prentice, Bridget	Labour	Lewisham East
Prentice, Gordon	Labour	Pendle
Prescott, Rt Hon John	Labour	Hull East
Price, Adam	Plaid Cymru	Carmarthen East and Dinefwr
Primarolo, Rt Hon Dawn	Labour	Bristol South
Prisk, Mark	Conservative	Hertford and Stortford
Pritchard, Mark	Conservative	The Wrekin
Prosser, Gwyn	Labour	Dover
Pugh, Dr John	Liberal Democrat	Southport
Purchase, Ken	Labour	Wolverhampton North East
Purnell, Rt Hon James	Labour	Stalybridge and Hyde

R

Rammell, Bill	Labour	Harlow
Randall, John	Conservative	Uxbridge
Raynsford, Rt Hon Nick	Labour	Greenwich and Woolwich
Redwood, Rt Hon John	Conservative	Wokingham
Reed, Andrew	Labour	Loughborough
Reed, Jamie	Labour	Copeland
Reid, Alan	Liberal Democrat	Argyll and Bute
Reid, Rt Hon Dr John	Labour	Airdrie and Shotts
Rennie, William	Liberal Democrat	Dunfermline and West Fife
Rifkind, Rt Hon Sir Malcolm	Conservative	Kensington and Chelsea
Riordan, Linda	Labour	Halifax
Robathan, Andrew	Conservative	Blaby
Robertson, Angus	SNP	Moray
Robertson, Hugh	Conservative	Faversham and Mid Kent
Robertson, John	Labour	Glasgow North West

Name	Party	Constituency
Robertson, Laurence	Conservative	Tewkesbury
Robinson, Geoffrey	Labour	Coventry North West
Robinson, Rt Hon Peter	Democratic Unionist	Belfast East
Rogerson, Dan	Liberal Democrat	North Cornwall
Rooney, Terry	Labour	Bradford North
Rosindell, Andrew	Conservative	Romford
Rowen, Paul	Liberal Democrat	Rochdale
Roy, Frank	Labour	Motherwell and Wishaw
Ruane, Chris	Labour	Vale of Clwyd
Ruddock, Joan	Labour	Lewisham Deptford
Ruffley, David	Conservative	Bury St Edmunds
Russell, Bob	Liberal Democrat	Colchester
Russell, Christine	Labour	City of Chester
Ryan, Rt Hon Joan	Labour	Enfield North

S

Name	Party	Constituency
Salmond, Rt Hon Alex MSP	SNP	Banff and Buchan
Salter, Martin	Labour	Reading West
Sanders, Adrian	Liberal Democrat	Torbay
Sarwar, Mohammad	Labour	Glasgow Central
Scott, Lee	Conservative	Ilford North
Seabeck, Alison	Labour	Plymouth Devonport
Selous, Andrew	Conservative	South West Bedfordshire
Shapps, Grant	Conservative	Welwyn Hatfield
Sharma, Virendra	Labour	Ealing Southall
Shaw, Jonathan	Labour	Chatham and Aylesford
Sheerman, Barry	Labour	Huddersfield
Shepherd, Richard	Conservative	Aldridge-Brownhills
Sheridan, James	Labour	Paisley and Renfrewshire North
Short, Rt Hon Clare	Labour	Birmingham Ladywood
Simmonds, Mark	Conservative	Boston and Skegness
Simon, Siôn	Labour	Birmingham Erdington
Simpson, Alan	Labour	Nottingham South
Simpson, David	Democratic Unionist	Upper Bann
Simpson, Keith	Conservative	Mid Norfolk
Singh, Marsha	Labour	Bradford West
Skinner, Dennis	Labour	Bolsover
Slaughter, Andrew	Labour	Ealing, Acton and Shepherd's Bush
Smith, Rt Hon Andrew	Labour	Oxford East
Smith, Angela C	Labour	Sheffield Hillsborough
Smith, Chloe	Conservative	Norwich North
Smith, Rt Hon Angela E	Labour	Basildon
Smith, Geraldine	Labour	Morecambe and Lunesdale
Smith, Rt Hon Jacqui	Labour	Redditch

Name	Party	Constituency
Smith, John	Labour	Vale of Glamorgan
Smith, Sir Robert	Liberal Democrat	West Aberdeenshire and Kincardine
Snelgrove, Anne	Labour	South Swindon
Soames, Hon Nicholas	Conservative	Mid Sussex
Soulsby, Sir Peter	Labour	Leicester South
Southworth, Helen	Labour	Warrington South
Spellar, Rt Hon John	Labour	Warley
Spelman, Caroline	Conservative	Meriden
Spicer, Sir Michael	Conservative	West Worcestershire
Spink, Dr Robert	Independent	Castle Point
Spring, Richard	Conservative	West Suffolk
Stanley, Rt Hon Sir John	Conservative	Tonbridge and Malling
Starkey, Dr Phyllis	Labour	Milton Keynes South West
Steen, Anthony	Conservative	Totnes
Stewart, Ian	Labour	Eccles
Stoate, Dr Howard	Labour	Dartford
Strang, Rt Hon Gavin	Labour	Edinburgh East
Straw, Rt Hon Jack	Labour	Blackburn
Streeter, Gary	Conservative	South West Devon
Stringer, Graham	Labour	Manchester Blackley
Stuart, Gisela	Labour	Birmingham Edgbaston
Stuart, Graham	Conservative	Beverley and Holderness
Stunell, Andrew	Liberal Democrat	Hazel Grove
Sutcliffe, Gerry	Labour	Bradford South
Swayne, Desmond	Conservative	New Forest West
Swinson, Jo	Liberal Democrat	East Dunbartonshire
Swire, Hugo	Conservative	East Devon
Syms, Robert	Conservative	Poole

T

Name	Party	Constituency
Tami, Mark	Labour	Alyn and Deeside
Tapsell, Sir Peter	Conservative	Louth and Horncastle
Taylor, Dari	Labour	Stockton South
Taylor, David	Labour	North West Leicestershire
Taylor, Ian	Conservative	Esher and Walton
Taylor, Matthew	Liberal Democrat	Truro and St Austell
Taylor, Dr Richard	Independent	Wyre Forest
Teather, Sarah	Liberal Democrat	Brent East
Thomas, Gareth	Labour	Harrow West
Thornberry, Emily	Labour	Islington South and Finsbury
Thurso, John	Liberal Democrat	Caithness, Sutherland and Easter Ross
Timms, Rt Hon Stephen	Labour	East Ham
Timpson, Edward	Conservative	Crewe and Nantwich

MEMBERS OF THE HOUSE OF COMMONS –
ALPHABETICAL LIST WITH PARTY AND CONSTITUENCY

Name	Party	Constituency
Tipping, Paddy	Labour	Sherwood
Todd, Mark	Labour	South Derbyshire
Touhig, Rt Hon Don	Labour	Islwyn
Tredinnick, David	Conservative	Bosworth
Trickett, Jon	Labour	Hemsworth
Truswell, Paul	Labour	Pudsey
Turner, Andrew	Conservative	Isle of Wight
Turner, Dr Desmond	Labour	Brighton Kemptown
Turner, Neil	Labour	Wigan
Twigg, Derek	Labour	Halton
Tyrie, Andrew	Conservative	Chichester

U
Ussher, Kitty	Labour	Burnley

V
Vaizey, Edward	Conservative	Wantage
Vara, Shailesh	Conservative	North West Cambridgeshire
Vaz, Rt Hon Keith	Labour	Leicester East
Viggers, Sir Peter	Conservative	Gosport
Villiers, Theresa	Conservative	Chipping Barnet
Vis, Dr Rudi	Labour	Finchley and Golders Green

W
Walker, Charles	Conservative	Broxbourne
Wallace, Ben	Conservative	Lancaster and Wyre
Walley, Joan	Labour	Stoke-on-Trent North
Walter, Robert	Conservative	North Dorset
Waltho, Lynda	Labour	Stourbridge
Ward, Claire	Labour	Watford
Wareing, Robert	Labour	Liverpool West Derby
Waterson, Nigel	Conservative	Eastbourne
Watkinson, Angela	Conservative	Upminster
Watson, Tom	Labour	West Bromwich East
Watts, Dave	Labour	St Helens North
Webb, Professor Steven	Liberal Democrat	Northavon
Weir, Michael	SNP	Angus
Whitehead, Dr Alan	Labour	Southampton Test
Whittingdale, John	Conservative	Maldon and East Chelmsford
Wicks, Malcolm	Labour	Croydon North
Widdecombe, Rt Hon Ann	Conservative	Maidstone and the Weald
Wiggin, Bill	Conservative	Leominster
Willetts, David	Conservative	Havant

Name	Party	Constituency
Williams, Rt Hon Alan	Labour	Swansea West
Williams, Betty	Labour	Conwy
Williams, Hywel	Plaid Cymru	Caernarfon
Williams, Mark	Liberal Democrat	Ceredigion
Williams, Roger	Liberal Democrat	Brecon and Radnorshire
Williams, Stephen	Liberal Democrat	Bristol West
Willis, Phil	Liberal Democrat	Harrogate and Knaresborough
Willott, Jenny	Liberal Democrat	Cardiff Central
Wills, Michael	Labour	North Swindon
Wilshire, David	Conservative	Spelthorne
Wilson, Phil	Labour	Sedgefield
Wilson, Rob	Conservative	Reading East
Wilson, Sammy	Democratic Unionist	East Antrim
Winnick, David	Labour	Walsall North
Winterton, Ann	Conservative	Congleton
Winterton, Sir Nicholas	Conservative	Macclesfield
Winterton, Rt Hon Rosie	Labour	Doncaster Central
Wishart, Peter	SNP	Perth and North Perthshire
Wood, Mike	Labour	Batley and Spen
Woodward, Rt Hon Shaun	Labour	St Helens South
Woolas, Phil	Labour	Oldham East and Saddleworth
Wright, Anthony	Labour	Great Yarmouth
Wright, David	Labour	Telford
Wright, Iain	Labour	Hartlepool
Wright, Jeremy	Conservative	Rugby and Kenilworth
Wright, Dr Tony	Labour	Cannock Chase
Wyatt, Derek	Labour	Sittingbourne and Sheppey

Y

Name	Party	Constituency
Yeo, Tim	Conservative	South Suffolk
Young, Rt Hon Sir George	Conservative	North West Hampshire
Younger-Ross, Richard	Liberal Democrat	Teignbridge

UK GOVERNMENT – CABINET

Prime Minister, First Lord of the Treasury
and Minister for the Civil Service . . . . .Rt Hon Gordon Brown MP

Leader of the House of Commons,
Lord Privy Seal and Minister for
Women and Equalities . . . . .Rt Hon Harriet Harman QC MP
*(also Labour Party Chair and
Deputy Leader of the Labour Party)*

First Secretary of State and Secretary of
State for Business, Innovation and Skills . . . . .Rt Hon Lord Mandelson

Chancellor of the Exchequer . . . . .Rt Hon Alistair Darling MP

Secretary of State for Foreign and
Commonwealth Affairs . . . . .Rt Hon David Miliband MP

Secretary of State for Justice and
Lord Chancellor . . . . .Rt Hon Jack Straw MP

Secretary of State for the Home
Department . . . . .Rt Hon Alan Johnson MP

Secretary of State for Environment, Food
and Rural Affairs . . . . .Rt Hon Hilary Benn MP

Secretary of State for International
Development . . . . .Rt Hon Douglas Alexander MP

Secretary of State for Communities and
Local Government . . . . .Rt Hon John Denham MP

Secretary of State for Children, Schools
and Families . . . . .Rt Hon Ed Balls MP

Secretary of State for Energy and
Climate Change . . . . .Rt Hon Edward Miliband MP

Secretary of State for Health . . . . .Rt Hon Andy Burnham MP

Secretary of State for Northern Ireland . . . . .Rt Hon Shaun Woodward MP

Leader of the House of Lords and
Chancellor of the Duchy of Lancaster . . . . . . .Rt Hon Baroness Royall of Blaisdon

Minister for the Cabinet Office, Olympics
and Paymaster General . . . . .Rt Hon Tessa Jowell MP

Secretary of State for Scotland . . . . .Rt Hon Jim Murphy MP

Secretary of State for Work and Pensions . . . . . .Rt Hon Yvette Cooper MP

Chief Secretary to the Treasury . . . . .Rt Hon Liam Byrne MP

Secretary of State for Wales . . . . .Rt Hon Peter Hain MP

Secretary of State for Defence . . . . .Rt Hon Bob Ainsworth MP

Secretary of State for Transport . . . . .Rt Hon Lord Adonis

Secretary of State for Culture, Media
and Sport . . . . .Rt Hon Ben Bradshaw MP

The following Ministers also attend Cabinet meetings:

Chief Whip and Parliamentary Secretary
to the Treasury . . . . .Rt Hon Nick Brown MP

Minister for Housing and Planning . . . . .Rt Hon John Healey MP

Minister for Employment and
Welfare Reform . . . . .Rt Hon Jim Knight MP

Minister for Science and Innovation . . . . .Rt Hon Lord Drayson

Minister of State, Department for Business,
Innovation and Skills . . . . .Rt Hon Pat McFadden MP

Note: The term Parliamentary Secretary is used here to denote Parliamentary Under Secretary of State.

Prime Minister

10 Downing Street, London, SW1A 2AA
Tel: (020) 7270 3000
Web: www.number-10.gov.uk

**Prime Minister, First Lord of the
Treasury and Minister for the
Civil Service** . . . . Rt Hon Gordon Brown MP

Department for Business, Innovation and Skills

1 Victoria Street, London, SW1H 0ET
Tel: (020) 7215 5000
E-mail: bis.gov.uk@contact-us
Web: www.bis.gov.uk

Secretary of State . . . . Rt Hon Lord Mandelson
Ministers of State . . . . Rt Hon Pat McFadden MP *(Business, Innovation and Skills)*
Kevin Brennan MP *(Further Education, Skills, Apprenticeships and Consumer Affairs) (also at Department for Children, Schools and Families)*
Rt Hon David Lammy MP *(Higher Education and Intellectual Property)*
Rt Hon Rosie Winterton MP *(Regional Economic Development and Co-ordination) (also at Department for Communities and Local Government)*
Rt Hon Lord Drayson *(Science and Innovation) (also at Ministry of Defence)*
Lord Davies of Abersoch *(Trade, Investment and Small Business) (also at Foreign and Commonwealth Office)*
Parliamentary Secretaries . . . . Ian Lucas MP *(Business and Regulatory Reform)*
Rt Hon Stephen Timms *(Digital Britain) (also at the Treasury)*
Lord Young of Norwood Green *(Postal Affairs and Employment Relations)*

Cabinet Office
70 Whitehall, London, SW1A 2AS
Tel: (020) 7276 1234
E-mail: [firstname.surname]@cabinet-office.x.gsi.gov.uk
Web: www.cabinetoffice.gov.uk

Ministers of State . . . . Rt Hon Tessa Jowell MP *(also Minister for the Olympics, Paymaster General, and Minister for London)*
Rt Hon Angela E Smith MP *(Third Sector)*
Parliamentary Secretary . . . . Dawn Butler MP *(Youth Citizens and Youth Engagement)*

Department for Children, Schools and Families
Sanctuary Buildings, Great Smith Street, London, SW1P 3BT
Tel: (0870) 000 2288
E-mail: info@dcsf.gsi.gov.uk
Web: www.dcsf.gov.uk

Secretary of State . . . . Rt Hon Ed Balls MP
Ministers of State . . . . Kevin Brennan MP *((also at Department for Business, Innovations and Skills)*
Vernon Coaker MP *(Schools and Learners)*
Rt Hon Dawn Primarolo MP *(Children, Young People and Families)*
Parliamentary Secretaries . . . . Iain Wright MP *(14-19 Reform and Apprenticeships)*
Baroness Morgan of Drefelin *(Children, Young People and Families)*
Diana Johnson MP *(Schools)*

Department for Communities and Local Government
Eland House, Bressenden Place, London, SW1E 5DU
Tel: (020) 7944 4400
E-mail: contactus@communities.gsi.gov.uk
Web: www.communities.gov.uk

Secretary of State . . . . Rt Hon John Denham MP
Ministers of State . . . . Rt Hon Rosie Winterton MP *(Local Government)*
(also at Department for Business, Innovations and Skills)
Rt Hon John Healey MP *(Housing and Planning)*
Parliamentary Secretaries . . . . Ian Austin MP
Barbara Follett MP
Shahid Malik MP
Lord McKenzie of Luton *(also at Department for Work and Pensions)*

UK GOVERNMENT MINISTERS BY DEPARTMENT

Department for Culture, Media and Sport
2-4 Cockspur Street, London, SW1Y 5DH
Tel: (020) 7211 6200
E-mail: enquiries@culture.gov.uk
Web: www.culture.gov.uk

Secretary of State . . . . Rt Hon Ben Bradshaw MP
Minister of State . . . . Rt Hon Margaret Hodge *(Culture and Tourism)*
Parliamentary Secretaries . . . . Siôn Simon MP *(Creative Industries)*
Gerry Sutcliffe MP *(Sport)*

Ministry of Defence
5th Floor, Main Building, Whitehall
London, SW1A 2HB
Tel: (020) 7218 9000
Web: www.mod.uk

Secretary of State . . . . Rt Hon Bob Ainsworth MP
Ministers of State . . . . Rt Hon Lord Drayson *(also at Department for Business, Innovations and Skills)*
Bill Rammell MP *(Armed Forces)*
Parliamentary Secretaries . . . . Quentin Davies MP *(Defence Equipment and Support)*
Kevan Jones MP *(Veterans)*
Rt Hon Baroness Taylor of Bolton *(International Defence and Security) (also at Foreign and Commonwealth Office)*

Department for Energy and Climate Change
3-8 Whitehall Place, London, SW1A 2HH
Tel: (0300) 060 4000
E-mail: [firstname.surname]@decc.gsi.gov.uk
Web: www.decc.gov.uk

Secretary of State . . . . Rt Hon Edward Miliband MP
Ministers of State . . . . Joan Ruddock MP
Lord Hunt of Kings Heath
Parliamentary Secretary . . . . David Kidney MP

UK GOVERNMENT MINISTERS BY DEPARTMENT

Department for Environment, Food and Rural Affairs
Nobel House, 17 Smith Square, London, SW1P 3JR
Tel: (0845) 933 5577
E-mail: helpline@defra.gsi.gov.uk
Web: www.defra.gov.uk

Secretary of State . . . . Rt Hon Hilary Benn MP
Minister of State . . . . Jim Fitzpatrick MP *(Food, Farming and Environment)*
Parliamentary Secretaries . . . . Huw Irranca-Davies MP *(Marine and Natural)*
Dan Norris MP *(Rural Affairs and Environment)*
Rt Hon Lord Davies of Oldham

Foreign and Commonwealth Office
King Charles Street, London, SW1A 2AH
Tel: (020) 7270 1500
Web: www.fco.gov.uk

Secretary of State . . . . Rt Hon David Miliband MP
Ministers of State . . . . Ivan Lewis MP *(Foreign and Commonwealth Affairs)*
Lord Davies of Abersoch MP *(UK Trade and Investment) (also at Department for Business, Innovation and Skills)*
Baroness Kinnock of Holyhead *(Africa and the UN)*
Parliamentary Secretaries . . . . Chris Bryant MP *(Europe and Asia)*
Baroness Taylor of Bolton *(also at Ministry of Defence)*

Government Equalities Office
5th Floor, Eland House, Bressenden Place
London, SW1E 5DU
Tel: (020) 7944 0601
E-mail: enquiries@geo.gsi.gov.uk
Web: www.equalities.gov.uk

Ministers of State . . . . Rt Hon Harriet Harman QC MP *(also Leader of the House of Commons, Lord Privy Seal, Minister for Women and Equality and Labour Party Chair and Deputy Leader)*
Maria Eagle MP *(also at Ministry of Justice)*
Parliamentary Secretary . . . . Michael Jabez Foster MP

Department of Health
Richmond House, 79 Whitehall
London, SW1A 2NS
Tel: (020) 7210 4850
E-mail: dhmail@dh.gsi.gov.uk
Web: www.dh.gov.uk

Secretary of State . . . . Rt Hon Andy Burnham MP
Ministers of State . . . . Phil Hope MP *(Care Services) (also Minister for the East Midlands)*
Gillian Merron MP *(Public Health)*
Rt Hon Mike O'Brien MP *(Health Services)*
Parliamentary Secretary . . . . Ann Keen MP *(Health Services)*

Home Office
2 Marsham Street, London, SW1P 4DF
Tel: (020) 7035 4848
E-mail: public.enquiries@homeoffice.gsi.gov.uk
Web: www.homeoffice.gov.uk

Secretary of State . . . . Rt Hon Alan Johnson MP
Ministers of State . . . . Rt Hon David Hanson MP *(Crime and Policing)*
Phil Woolas MP *(Borders and Immigration) (also at HM Treasury and Minister for the North West)*
Parliamentary Secretaries . . . . Alan Campbell MP *(Crime Reduction)*
Meg Hillier MP *(Identity)*
Lord [Alan] West of Spithead *(Security and Counter-Terrorism)*

Department for International Development
1 Palace Street, London, SW1E 5HE
Tel: (0845) 300 4100
E-mail: enquiry@dfid.gov.uk
Web: www.dfid.gov.uk

Secretary of State . . . . Rt Hon Douglas Alexander MP
Minister of State . . . . Gareth Thomas MP
Parliamentary Secretary . . . . Michael Foster MP

Ministry of Justice
102 Petty France, London, SW1H 9AJ
Tel: (020) 7210 8500
E-mail: general.queries@justice.gsi.gov.uk
Web: www.justice.gov.uk

Secretary of State and
Lord Chancellor . . . . Rt Hon Jack Straw MP
Ministers of State . . . . Maria Eagle MP *(also at Government Equalities
Office)*
Rt Hon Michael Wills MP
Parliamentary Secretaries . . . . Bridget Prentice MP
Claire Ward MP
Lord Bach

Law Officers
Attorney General's Chambers, 20 Victoria Street, London, SW1H 0NF
Tel: (020) 7271 2492
E-mail: correspondenceunit@attorneygeneral.gsi.gov.uk
Web: www.attorneygeneral.gov.uk

Attorney General . . . . Rt Hon Baroness Scotland of Asthal QC
Solicitor General . . . . Vera Baird QC MP
Advocate General for
Scotland. Lord Davidson of Glen Cova QC

Office of the Leader of the House of Commons
26 Whitehall, London SW1A 2WH
Tel: (020) 7276 1005
E-mail: leader@commonsleader.x.gsi.gov.uk
Web: www.commonsleader.gov.uk

Lord Privy Seal and Leader
of the House of Commons . . . . Rt Hon Harriet Harman QC MP
*(also Minister for Women and Equality, and
Labour Party Chair and Deputy Leader)*
Parliamentary Secretary . . . . Barbara Keeley MP

Northern Ireland Office
11 Millbank, London SW1P 4PN
Tel: (020) 7210 3000
Block B, Castle Buildings, Stormont Estate, Belfast, BT4 3SG
Tel: (028) 9052 0700
Web: www.nio.gov.uk

Secretary of State . . . . Rt Hon Shaun Woodward MP
Minister of State. . . . . Rt Hon Paul Goggins MP

UK GOVERNMENT MINISTERS BY DEPARTMENT

Privy Council Office
2 Carlton Gardens, London, SW1Y 5AA
Tel: (020) 7210 1033
E-mail: pcosecretariat@pco.x.gsi.gov.uk
Web: www.privycouncil.org.uk

Lord President of the Council . . . . Rt Hon Lord Mandelson *(also at*
Department for Business, Innovation
and Skills)

Scotland Office
Dover House, Whitehall, London, SW1A 2AU
Tel: (020) 7270 6754
1 Melville Crescent, Edinburgh, EH3 7HW
Tel: (0131) 244 9010
E-mail: scotlandoffice.gov@scotlandoffice/58.html
Web: www.scotlandoffice.gov.uk

Secretary of State . . . . Rt Hon Jim Murphy MP
Parliamentary Secretary . . . . Ann McKechin MP

Department for Transport
Great Minster House, 76 Marsham Street, London, SW1P 4DR
Tel: (020) 7944 8300
E-mail: FAX9643@dft.gsi.gov.uk
Web: www.dft.gov.uk

Secretary of State . . . . Rt Hon Lord Adonis
Minister of State . . . . Rt Hon Sadiq Khan MP
Parliamentary Secretaries . . . . Paul Clark MP
Chris Mole MP

H M Treasury
1 Horseguards Road, London, SW1A 2HQ
Tel: (020) 7270 4558
E-mail: ministers@hm-treasury.gov.uk
Web: www.hm-treasury.gov.uk

Chancellor of the Exchequer . . . . . . Rt Hon Alistair Darling MP
Chief Secretary . . . . Rt Hon Liam Byrne MP
Financial Secretary . . . . Rt Hon Stephen Timms MP
Economic Secretary . . . . Ian Pearson MP
Exchequer Secretary . . . . Sarah McCarthy-Fry MP

Wales Office
Gwydyr House, Whitehall, London, SW1A 2NP
Tel: (020) 7270 0534
National Assembly for Wales, Cardiff Bay, Cardiff, CF99 1NA
Tel: (029) 2082 5111
E-mail: wales.office@walesoffice.gsi.gov.uk
Web: www.walesoffice.gov.uk

Secretary of State . . . . Rt Hon Peter Hain MP
Parliamentary Secretary . . . . Wayne David MP

Department for Work and Pensions
Caxton House, Tothill Street, London, SW1A 9DA
Tel: (020) 7962 8000
Web: www.dwp.gov.uk

Secretary of State . . . . Rt Hon Yvette Cooper MP
Ministers of State . . . . Angela Eagle MP *(Pensions and the Ageing Society)*
Rt Hon Jim Knight MP *(Employment and Welfare Reform) (also Minister for the South West)*
Parliamentary Secretaries . . . . Helen Goodman MP
Jonathan Shaw MP *(Disabled People) (also Minister for the South East)*
Lord McKenzie of Luton *(also at Department for Communities and Local Government)*

Government Whips (Commons)
9 Downing Street, London, SW1A 2AG
Tel: (020) 7276 2020

Government Chief Whip and Parliamentary
Secretary to the Treasury . . . . Rt Hon Nick Brown MP
(also Minister for the North East)

Deputy Chief Whip and Treasurer of
Her Majesty's Household . . . . Rt Hon Tommy McAvoy MP

Comptroller of Her Majesty's
Household . . . . Rt Hon John Spellar MP

Vice-Chamberlain of Her
Majesty's Household . . . . Helen Jones MP

Lords Commissioners of the Treasury . . . . Bob Blizzard MP
Tony Cunningham MP
Steve McCabe MP
Frank Roy MP
Dave Watts MP

Assistant Whips . . . . Lyn Brown MP
Dawn Butler MP
Mary Creagh MP
John Heppell MP
Sharon Hodgson MP
Kerry McCarthy MP
George Mudie MP
Mark Tami MP
David Wright MP

Government Whips (Lords)
House of Lords, Westminster, London, SW1A 0PW
Tel: (020) 7219 3131

**Captain of the Gentlemen-At-Arms
and Chief Whip** . . . . Rt Hon Lord Bassam of Brighton

**Captain of the Yeomen of the Guard
and Deputy Chief Whip** . . . . Rt Hon Lord Davies of Oldham

Lords in Waiting . . . . Lord Brett
Lord Faulkner of Worcester
Lord Tunnicliffe
Lord Young of Norwood Green

Baronesses in Waiting . . . . Baroness Crawley
Baroness Farrington of Ribbleton
Baroness Thornton

Scottish Affairs Committee of the House of Commons

Chairman . . . . Mohammad Sarwar

Members . . . . Alistair Carmichael
Katy Clark
Ian Davidson
Jim Devine
Jim McGovern
David Mundell
Lindsay Roy
Charles Walker
Ben Wallace
Pete Wishart

Clerk . . . . Ms Nerys Welfoot
Enquiries (020) 7219 2173

House of Commons

*If writing to MPs or officials of the House of Commons the following
address should be used:*

House of Commons
London, SW1A 0AA

The House of Commons switchboard
number is: (020) 7219 3000

House of Lords

The address of the House of Lords is:

The House of Lords
London, SW1A 0PW

The House of Lords switchboard number is: (020) 7219 3000

Scotland Office

SCOTLAND OFFICE

Dover House, Whitehall,
London, SW1A 2AU
Tel: (020) 7270 6754
Web: www.scotlandoffice.gov.uk

1 Melville Crescent,
Edinburgh, EH3 7HW
Tel: (0131) 244 9010

Secretary of State for
Scotland . . . . Rt Hon Jim Murphy MP
Principal Parliamentary
Private Secretary . . . . Ms Kate Richards. . . . . Tel: (020) 7270 6728

Minister of State
(Scotland) . . . . Ms Ann McKechin MP
Private Secretary . . . . Ms Barbara Reid . . . . . Tel: (020) 7270 6806

Scotland Office Management Group
Head of Department,
Scotland Office. . . . . Mr Alasdair McIntosh . Tel: (020) 7270 6769

1 Melville Crescent, Edinburgh, EH3 7HW
Head of Briefing Services Division . Mr John Henderson . . . Tel: (0131) 244 9071

Chief Press Officer, Scotland Office Mr Clark Dunn . . . . . . Tel: (0131) 244 9053

Dover House, Whitehall, London, SW1A 2AU
Head of Parliamentary and
Constitutional Division . . . . Miss Laura Thomas . . . Tel: (020) 7270 6802

Parliamentary Clerk, Scotland
Office . . . . Miss Karen McNeill . . . Tel: (020) 7270 6746

European Union
and Scotland

European Parliament
60 Rue Wiertz, B-1047 Brussels, Belgium
Tel: 00 32 2284 3457 Fax: 00 32 2284 3530
Web: www.europarl.eu.int

Hudghton, Ian MEP

Political Allegiance	SNP
European Political Group	Verts/ALE
Born	19th September 1951 in Forfar
UK Office	8 Old Glamis Road, Dundee, DD3 8HP
	Tel: (01382) 903206 Fax: (01382) 903205
	Web: www.hudghtonmep.com
UK-Based Staff	Parliamentary Assistant – Kate Young
	Secretary/PA – Lily Hudghton
Brussels Office	Room No: 08H 124, Bâtiment Altiero Spinelli,
	60 Rue Wiertz, B-1047, Brussels, Belgium
	Tel: + 32 2 284 5499 Fax: + 32 2 284 9499
	E-mail: ian.hudghton@europarl.europa.eu
Strasbourg Numbers	Tel: + 33 3 88 17 5499 Fax: + 33 3 88 17 9499
Professional Career	1970 - 94 Proprietor, Decorating Business
Political Career	1988 - 96 Housing Convener,
	Angus District Council
	1996 - 99 Leader, Angus Council
	1998 - Member of the European Parliament
	(Scotland)
	2005 - Spokesman on Europe, SNP Shadow
	Cabinet
	2005 - President, SNP
Committee Membership	Fisheries Committee *(Member)*
	Regional Development Committee *(Member)*
	Internal Market and Consumer Protection
	Committee *(Substitute)*
Inter-Parliamentary Delegations	EU- Canada *(Member)*
	EU - Croatia *(Substitute)*

Lyon, George MEP

Political Allegiance	Liberal Democrat
European Political Group	ALDE
Born	16th July 1956 in Rothesay
UK Office	9 Newton Terrace, Glasgow, G3 7PJ
	Tel: (0141) 222 2480
	E-mail: george@georgelyon.org.uk
	Web: www.georgelyon.org.uk
Brussels Office	Room No: 10G 210, Bâtiment Altiero Spinelli,
	60 Rue Wiertz, B-1047, Brussels, Belgium
	Tel: + 32 2 284 5628
	E-mail: george.lyon@europarl.europa.eu
Strasbourg Numbers	Tel: + 33 3 88 17 5628
Professional Career	1972 - Farmer
Political Career	1999 - 2007 Member of the Scottish Parliament
	2009 - Member of the European Parliament
	(Scotland)
Committee Membership	Agriculture and Rural Development Committee
	(Member)
	Internal Market and Consumer Protection
	Committee *(Substitute)*
Inter-Parliamentary Delegation	EU- Australia and New Zealand *(Member)*
	EU- Canada *(Substitute)*
Leisure Interests	Football; Cycling; Rural Issues

Martin, David MEP

Political Allegiance	Labour
European Political Group	PES
Born	26th August 1954 in Edinburgh
UK Office	Midlothian Innovation Centre, Roslin, Midlothian, EH25 9R3 Tel: (0131) 440 9040 E-mail: david@martinmep.com Web: www.martinmep.com
UK-Based Staff	Political Adviser – Colin Bartie
Brussels Office	Room 13G 354, Bâtiment Altiero Spinelli, 60 Rue Wiertz, B-1047, Brussels, Belgium Tel: + 32 2 284 5539 Fax: + 32 2 284 9539 E-mail: david.martin@europarl.europa.eu
Strasbourg Numbers	Tel: + 33 3 88 17 5539 Fax: + 33 3 88 17 9539
Professional Career	1970 - 74 Stockbroker's Assistant
Political Career	1982 - 84 Councillor, Lothians Regional Council 1984 - 2004 Member of the European Parliament (Formerly Lothians, now Scotland) 1987 - 89 Leader, European Parliamentary Labour Party 1989 - 2004 Vice President, European Parliament
Committee Membership	International Trade Committee *(Member)* Human Rights Committee *(Member)* Constitutional Affairs Committee *(Substitute)*
Inter-Parliamentary Delegation	EU-Australia and New Zealand *(Member)* EU-Palestine *(Substitute)*
Other European Parliament Posts	1989 - 2004 Vice-President, European Parliament
Parliamentary Subject Interests	Trade; Environment; Climate Change; Animal Welfare

Smith, Alyn MEP

Political Allegiance . . . . Scottish National Party
European Political Group . . . . . . EFA
Born. . . . . 15th September 1973 in Glasgow
UK Office. . . . . Gordon Lamb House, 3 Jacksons Entry,
Edinburgh, EH8 8JP
Tel: (0131) 525 8926 Fax: (0131) 525 8901
Web: www.alynsmith.eu
Brussels Office . . . . Room No: 08H 149, Bâtiment Altiero Spinelli,
60 Rue Wiertz, B-1047, Brussels, Belgium
Tel: + 32 (0)7 284 9187
E-mail: alyn.smith@europarl.europa.eu
Strasbourg Numbers . . . . Tel: + 33 (0)3 88 17 9187
Political Career. . . . . 2004 - Member of the European Parliament (Scotland)
Committee Membership. . . . . Agriculture and Rural Development Committee *(Member)*
Constitutional Affairs Committee *(Substitute)*
Culture and Education Committee *(Substitute)*
Inter-Parliamentary Delegation. . EU-Switzerland, Ireland and Norway and EEA
(Member)

Stevenson, Struan MEP
Political Allegiance . . . . Conservative
European Political Group . . . . . . ECR
Born. . . . . 4th April 1948 in Ballantrae, Ayrshire
UK Office. . . . . 83 Princes Street, Edinburgh, EH2 2ER
Tel: (0131) 247 6890 Fax: (0131) 247 6891
E-mail: struan.stevenson@europarl.europa.eu
Web: www.scottishconservatives.com
UK-Based Staff . . . . Policy Advisor and Parliamentary Assistant –
Belinda Don
E-mail: belinda.don@scottishconservatives.com
Brussels Office . . . . Bâtiment Altiero Spinelli, 60 Rue Wiertz, B-1047,
Brussels, Belgium
Tel: + 32 2 284 7710 Fax: + 32 2 284 9710
E-mail: struan.stevenson@europarl.europa.eu
Brussels-Based Staff . . . . Parliamentary Assistants – Miss Anna Dmitnjeura
Miss Kathryn Strack
Strasbourg Numbers . . . . Tel: + 33 3 88 17 7710 Fax: + 33 3 88 17 9710
Professional Career . . . . 1968 - 2004 Director, J and R Stevenson Ltd
1986 - 90 Director, Demarco Gallery
1992 - 94 Director, Saferworld
1994 - 99 Director, PS Communication Consultants
Political Career. . . . . 1974 - 92 Councillor, Kyle and Carrick District
Council (Leader 1986-88)
1986 - 88 Conservative Group Leader, COSLA
1999 - Member of the European Parliament (Scotland)
2001 - 04 Chairman, Fisheries Committee,
European Parliament
Committee Membership. . . . . Fisheries Committee *(Chairman 2001 - 2004) (Member)*
Environment, Public Health and Food Safety
Committee *(Substitute)*
Inter-Parliamentary Delegation . . EU - Iraq *(Chairman)*
Parliamentary Subject Interests . . Scotland; Agriculture; Fisheries
Leisure Interests . . . . Contemporary Art; Opera; Poetry; Photography;
Hill Walking

Stihler, Catherine MEP
Political Allegiance . . . . Labour
European Political Group . . . . PSE
Born . . . . 30th July 1973 in Bellshill
UK Office . . . . 25 Church Street, Inverkeithing, Fife, KY11 1LG
Tel: (01383) 417799 Fax: (01383) 413335
E-mail: stihlermep@btconnect.com
UK-Based Staff . . . . Press and Campaigns Organiser –
Fiona Fairley
Office Manager – Yvonne Thorpe
Brussels Office . . . . Room No: 13G 217 Bâtiment Altiero Spinelli
60 Rue Wiertz, B-1047, Brussels, Belgium
Tel: + 32 2 284 5462
E-mail: catherine.stihler@europarl.europa.eu
Brussels-Based Staff . . . . Political Adviser – Stephen O'Donnell
Assistant – Emma Gillan
Political Career . . . . 1997 - 99 PA to Anne Begg MP
1999 - Member of the European Parliament
(Scotland)
2000 - 03 President, Public Health Intergroup
2004 - Deputy Leader, European Parliamentary
Labour Party
Committee Membership . . . . Internal Market and Consumer Protection
Committee *(Member)*
Economic and Monetary Affairs Committee
(Substitute)
Inter-Parliamentary Delegations . . . . EU Switzerland, Iceland and Norway and EEA
(Member)
EU-Chile *(Substitute)*
Parliamentary Subject Interests . . . . . Disability Issues; Environment; European Security;
Public Health; Volunteering
Leisure Interests . . . . Films; Music; Running; Yoga

ECONOMIC AND SOCIAL COMMITTEE – SCOTLAND MEMBERS

Note: Members of the Committee from Scotland (ie: currently resident in Scotland or listed organisations based in Scotland)

Boyle, Sandy
UK Political Allegiance . . . . Labour
Born . . . . 23rd December 1945 in Falkirk
Occupation . . . . Former Banker / Economics
Former Deputy Director General Secretary, UNIFI
Home Address . . . . 9 Learmouth Street, Falkirk, FK1 5AG
Tel: (01324) 626708 Fax: (01324) 624910
E-mail: sandyboyle@blueyonder.co.uk
Group . . . . Group II - Workers (nominated by STUC/TUC)
Membership of Committee Sections . . External Relations
Single Market, Production and Consumption

Burns, Brendan
Occupation . . . . Director, Burns, Burns and Burns
Work Address . . . . Burns, Burns and Burns, Killen Cottage,
Killen Avoch, Ross-shire, IV9 8RQ
Tel: (01381) 622244
E-mail: brendan.burns@eesc.europe.eu
Group . . . . Group I - Employers
Membership of Committee Sections . . Agriculture, Rural Development and the Environment
Single Market, Production and Consumption

Fraser, Kenneth
UK Political Allegiance . . . . None
Born . . . . 24th April 1941 in Perth
Education . . . . Perth High School;
Dundee College of Technology
Occupation . . . . Company Director
Home Address . . . . Wester Clatto, Blebo Craigs, Cupar,
Fife, KY15 5UE
Tel: (01334) 850632 Fax: (01334) 850097
E-mail: kfraser@frasercorporate.co.uk
Group . . . . Group I - Employers
Membership of Committee Sections . . Agriculture, Rural Development and the Environment
Transport, Energy, Infrastructure and the Information Society

O'Neill, Maureen

UK Political Allegiance	None
Born	11th May 1948 in Kampala, Uganda
Occupation	Director, Faith in Older People
Work Address	Faith in Older People, 21a Grosvenor Crescent, Edinburgh, EH12 5EL
	Tel: (0131) 346 7981
	E-mail: maureenponeill@yahoo.co.uk
	Web: www.faithinolderpeople.org.uk
Home Address	Brinsdale, 40 Corstorphine Road, Edinburgh, EH12 6HS
	Tel: (0131) 346 8609
	E-mail: maureenponeill@yahoo.co.uk
Group	Group III - Various Interests
Membership of Committee Sections	Employment, Social Affairs and Citizenship External Relations

Scottish Executive European Union Office

9th Floor, Scotland House, 6 Rond Point Schuman, 1040 Brussels
Tel: (+32) 2 282 8330 Fax: (+32) 2 282 8345
E-mail: [firstname.surname]@scotland.gsi.gov.uk
Web: www.scotlandeuropa.com

Head of Office .... Mr Donald Henderson

Deputy Head of Office .... Mr Ian Campbell

Senior Policy Adviser .... Mr Craig Egner

COMMITTEE OF THE REGIONS –
SCOTLAND MEMBERS

Note: Both Full and Alternate Members of the Committee from Scotland are listed below.

Garvie, Cllr Graham
UK Political Allegiance. . . . . Liberal Democrat
Born . . . . 11th March 1942 in Edinburgh
Occupation. . . . . Management Consultant
Work Address. . . . . 12 Broughton Place, Edinburgh, EH1 1RX
Tel & Fax: (01721) 721010
Home Address . . . . 34 Kirkland Street, Peebles, EH45 8EV
Current Local Authority Position . . . . . . Councillor, Scottish Borders Council
Local Authority Address . . . . Scottish Borders Council,
Council Headquarters, Newton St Boswells,
Melrose, TD6 0SA
Tel: (01835) 825155
E-mail: ggarvie@scotborders.gov.uk
Previous Local Authority Position . . . . . . Chief Executive, Tweeddale District Council
(1985 - 96)
Type of Committee Member . . . . Alternate

McCabe, Cllr Jim
UK Political Allegiance. . . . . Labour
Work Address. . . . . North Lanarkshire Council, Civic Centre,
Windmill Street, Motherwell, ML1 1AB
Tel: (01698) 302226 Fax: (01698) 302462
E-mail: mccabej@northlan.gov.uk
Current Local Authority Position . . . . . . Leader, North Lanarkshire Council
Type of Committee Member . . . . Alternate

McChord, Cllr Corrie OBE
UK Political Allegiance. . . . . Labour
Born . . . . 17th September 1946 in Stirling
Home Address . . . . 41 Mayfield Court, St Ninians,
Stirling, FK7 0BX
Current Local Authority Position . . . . . . Leader, Labour Group, Stirling Council
Local Authority Address . . . . Viewforth, Stirling, FK8 2ET
Tel: (01786) 443378 Fax: (01786) 442636
E-mail: mcchordc@stirling.gov.uk
Previous Local Authority Position . . . . . . Leader and Vice Convener, Central Regional
Council, Scotland (1990 - 96)
Commission Membership . . . . Constitutional Affairs and European
Governance
Sustainable Development
West Balkans Working Group `
Type of Committee Member . . . . Full Member

Other Contacts

Note: This section includes details of public bodies not listed elsewhere in this Directory, and also other selected useful contacts.

BROADCASTING

STV North Ltd
The Television Centre, Craigsham Business Park
West Tullos, Aberdeen, AB12 3QH
Tel: (01224) 848848 Fax: (01224) 848800
Web: www.stv.tv

Director of Broadcasting . . . . Mr Bobby Hain

CBI

CBI Scotland
16 Robertson Street, Glasgow, G2 8DS
Tel: (0141) 222 2184 Fax: (0141) 222 2187
Web: www.cbi.org.uk

Director . . . . Mr Iain McMillan CBE

CHURCHES

The Church of Scotland
121 George Street, Edinburgh, EH2 4YN
Tel: (0131) 225 5722 Fax: (0131) 220 3113
E-mail: mediarelations@cofscotland.org.uk
Web: www.churchofscotland.co.uk

Moderator . . . . Rt Rev William C Hewitt

Scottish Churches Parliamentary Office
Scottish Churches Parliamentary Officer
43-45 High Street
Edinburgh, EH1 1SR
Tel: (0131) 558 8137
Web: www.actsparl.org

Parliamentary Officer . . . . Ms Chloe Clemmons

Scottish Episcopal Church
General Synod Office, 21 Grosvenor Crescent
Edinburgh, EH12 5EE
Tel: (0131) 225 6357 Fax: (0131) 346 7247
E-mail: office@scotland.anglican.org
Web: www.scotland.anglican.org

Secretary General . . . . Mr John F Stuart

CIVIL SERVICE
National School of Government
(formerly The Civil Service College)
Sunningdale Park, Larch Avenue, Ascot
Berkshire, SL5 OQE
Tel: (01344) 634000 Fax: (01344) 634233
Web: www.nationalschool.gov.uk

Principal and Chief Executive . . . . . Mr Rod Clark

National School of Government in Scotland
23 Walker Street, Edinburgh, EH3 7HX
Tel: (0131) 225 4208 Fax: (0131) 225 8165

Contact . . . . Mrs Diane Gordon

CROPS
Scottish Crop Research Institute
Mylnefield, Invergowrie, Dundee, DD2 5DA
Tel: (01382) 562731 Fax: (01382) 562426
E-mail: mail@scri.ac.uk
Web: www.scri.ac.uk

Chairman . . . . .Mr Peter Berry

Director . . . . .Professor Peter Gregory

Press Officer . . . . .Mr Phil Taylor

DEVELOPMENT AND INDUSTRY

Scottish Council for Development and Industry
23 Chester Street, Edinburgh, E3 7ET
Tel: (0131) 225 7911 Fax: (0131) 220 2116
E-mail: enquiries@scdi.org.uk
Web: www.scdi.org.uk

Chairman . . . . .Ms Shonaig Macpherson CBE

Chief Executive . . . . .Dr Lesley Sawers

General Manager . . . . .Mr Iain McTaggart

Highlands and Islands
Ballantyne House, 84 Academy Street
Inverness, IV1 1LU
Tel: (01463) 231878 Fax: (01463) 243568
E-mail: lesley.rhind@scdi.org.uk

Regional Manager . . . . Mr Gareth Williams

Scottish Council for Development and Industry (Continued)

North East
c/o Conoco Phillips (UK) Ltd, Rubislaw House
Anderson Drive, Aberdeen AB15 6FZ
Tel: (01224) 205868 Fax:(01224) 205889
E-mail: ian.armstrong@scdi.org.uk

Regional Manager . . . . Mr Ian Armstrong

West
Campsie House, 17 Park Circus Place, Glasgow, G3 6AH
Tel: (0141) 332 9119 Fax: (0141) 333 0039
E-mail: enquiries@scdi.org.uk

Regional Manager . . . . Mr Ian McTaggart

EDUCATION

Queen Victoria School
Dunblane, Perthshire, FK15 0JY
Tel: (01786) 822288 Fax: (0131) 310 2926
E-mail: enquiries@qvs.org.uk
Web: www.qvs.org.uk

Head . . . . Mrs Wendy Bellars

Scottish Further Education Unit
Argyll Court, Castle Business Park,
Stirling, FK9 4TY
Tel: (01786) 892000 Fax: (01786) 892001
E-mail: sfeu@sfeu.ac.uk
Web: www.sfeu.ac.uk

Chair . . . . .Ms Christina Potter

Chief Executive *(Acting)* . . . . .Dr Ray Harris

EUROPEAN UNION

COSLA
Convention of Scottish Local Authorities
Square de Meeüs
B1000 - Brussels, Belgium
Tel: +32 2 213 8120 Fax: +32 2 213 8129
E-mail: serafin@cosla.gov.uk
Web: www.cosla.gov.uk

Director . . . . Mr Serafin Pazos-Vidal

European Union (Continued)

European Commission Office in Scotland
9 Alva Street,
Edinburgh, EH2 4PH
Tel: (0131) 225 2058 Fax: (0131) 226 4105
E-mail: neil.mitchison@ec.europa.eu
Webs: www.europa.eu
www.europe.org.uk/regions/scotland

Head of Office . . . . Mr Neil Mitchison

Objective 3 Partnership (Scotland) Ltd
European Social Fund
2nd Floor, Caithness House,
127 Vincent Street,
Glasgow, G2 5JF
Tel: (0141) 582 0401 Fax: (0141) 582 0478
E-mail: enquiries@objective3.org
Web: www.objective3.org

Chief Executive . . . . Ms Christine Mulligan

Scotland Europa
Scotland House,
6 Rond-Point Schuman, B-1040 Etterbeek, Brussels
Tel: (+32) 2 282 8330
E-mail: information.desk@scotent.co.uk
Web: www.scotland.gov.uk/euoffice

Chief Executive . . . . Mr Donald MacInnes

FOOD

Scottish Food Advisory Committee
Food Standards Agency Scotland
St Magnus House, 6th Floor, 25 Guild Street
Aberdeen, AB11 6NJ
Tel: (01224) 285104 Fax: (01224) 285167
E-mail: jane.ferries@foodstandards.gsi.gov.uk
Web: www.food.gov.uk/scotland

Chairman . . . . .Professor Graeme Millar CBE

Secretary . . . . .Mr Ryan Bruce

FORESTRY

Forestry Commission Scotland
Silvan House, 231 Corstophine Road, Edinburgh, EH12 7AT
Tel: (0131) 334 0303 Fax: (0131) 314 6152
E-mail: fcscotland@forestry.gsi.gov.uk
Web: www.forestry.gov.uk/scotland

Director .... Dr Bob McIntosh

FRAUD

Serious Fraud Office
Elm House, 10-16 Elm Street, London, WC1X 0BJ
Tel: (020) 7239 7000 Fax: (020) 7837 1689
Web: www.sfo.gov.uk

Director .... Mr Richard Alderman

FURTHER EDUCATION COLLEGES

Aberdeen College
Gallowgate, Aberdeen, AB25 IBN
Tel: (01224) 612000 Fax: (01224) 612001
E-mail: enquiry@abcol.ac.uk
Web: www.abcol.ac.uk

Adam Smith College
Stenton Road, Glenrothes, Fife, KY6 2RA
Tel: (01592) 772233 Fax: (01592) 568182
E-mail: enquiries@adamsmith.ac.uk
Web: www.adamsmithcollege.ac.uk

Angus College
Keptie Road, Arbroath, Angus, DD11 3EA
Tel: (01241) 432600 Fax: (01241) 876169
E-mail: marketing@angus.ac.uk
Web: www.angus.ac.uk

Anniesland College
19 Hatfield Drive, Glasgow, G12 OYE
Tel: (0141) 357 3969 Fax: (0141) 357 6557
E-mail: reception@anniesland.ac.uk
Web: www.anniesland.ac.uk

Further Education Colleges (Continued)

Association of Scottish Colleges
Argyll Court, Castle Business Park
Stirling, FK9 4TY
Tel: (01786) 892100 Fax: (01786) 892109
E-mail: enquiries@ascol.org.uk
Web: www.ascol.org.uk

Chairman . . . . Mr Ian Macpherson MBE

Ayr College
Dam Park, Ayr, KA8 0EU
Tel: (01292) 265184 Fax: (01292) 263889
E-mail: enquiries@ayrcoll.ac.uk
Web: www.ayrcoll.ac.uk

Banff and Buchan College
Henderson Road, Fraserburgh, Aberdeenshire, AB43 9GA
Tel: (01346) 586100 Fax: (01346) 515370
E-mail: info@banff-buchan.ac.uk
Web: www.banff-buchan.ac.uk

Barony College
Parkgate, Dumfries, DG1 3NE
Tel: (01387) 860251 Fax: (01387) 860395
E-mail: admin@barony.ac.uk
Web: www.barony.ac.uk

Borders College
Scottish Borders Campus, Nether Road, Galashiels, Selkirkshire, TD1 3HF
Tel: (0870) 050 5152 Fax: (01896) 758179
E-mail: enquiries@borderscollege.ac.uk
Web: www.borderscollege.ac.uk

Cardonald College
690 Mosspark Drive, Glasgow, G52 3AY
Tel: (0141) 272 3333 Fax: (0141) 272 3444
E-mail: enquiries@cardonald.ac.uk
Web: www.cardonald.ac.uk

Carnegie College
Halbeath, Dunfermline, KY11 8DY
Tel: (0844) 248 0115 Fax: (0844) 248 0116
E-mail: info@carnegiecollege.ac.uk
Web: www.carnegiecollege.ac.uk

Further Education Colleges (Continued)

Central College Glasgow
300 Cathedral Street, Glasgow, G1 2TA
Tel: (0141) 552 3941 Fax: (0141) 553 2368
E-mail: information@central-glasgow.ac.uk
Web: www.centralcollege.ac.uk

Clydebank College
College Square, Queens' Quay, Clydebank, Dunbartonshire, G81 1NX
Tel: (0141) 951 7400 Fax: (0141) 951 7401
E-mail: info@clydebank.ac.uk
Web: www.clydebank.ac.uk

Coatbridge College
Kildonan Street, Coatbridge, Lanarkshire, ML5 3LS
Tel: (01236) 422316 Fax: (01236) 440266
E-mail: mail@coatbridge.ac.uk
Web: www.coatbridge.ac.uk

Cumbernauld College
Tryst Road, The Town Centre, Cumbernauld, G67 1HU
Tel: (01236) 731811 Fax: (01236) 723416
E-mail: cumbernauld_college@cumbernauld.ac.uk
Web: www.cumbernauld.ac.uk

Dumfries & Galloway College
College Gate, Bankend Road, Dumfries, DG1 4FD
Tel: (01387) 273400 Fax: (01387) 250006
E-mail: info@dumgal.ac.uk
Web: www.dumgal.ac.uk

Dundee College
Old Glamis Road, Dundee, Angus, DD3 8LE
Tel: (01382) 834834 Fax: (01382) 858117
E-mail: enquiry@dundeecollege.ac.uk
Web: www.dundeecoll.ac.uk

Edinburgh's Telford College
350 Granton Road, Edinburgh, EH5 1QE
Tel: (0131) 559 4000 Fax: (0131) 559 4111
E-mail: mail@ed-coll.ac.uk
Web: www.ed-coll.ac.uk

Elmwood College
Carslogie Road, Cupar, Fife, KY15 4JB
Tel: (01334) 658800 Fax: (01334) 658888
E-mail: contact@elmwood.ac.uk
Web: www.elmwood.ac.uk

Further Education Colleges (Continued)

Forth Valley College
Grangemouth Road, Alloa, FK2 9AD
Tel: (01324) 403000 Fax: (01324) 403222
E-mail: info@forthvalley.ac.uk
Web: www.forthvalley.ac.uk

Glasgow College of Nautical Studies
21 Thistle Street, Glasgow, G5 9XB
Tel: (0141) 565 2500 Fax: (0141) 565 2599
E-mail: enquiries@gcns.ac.uk
Web: www.glasgow-nautical.ac.uk

Glasgow Metropolitan College
60 North Hanover Street, Glasgow, G1 2BP
Tel: (0141) 566 6222 Fax: (0141) 566 6226
E-mail: enquiries@glasgowmet.ac.uk
Web: www.glasgowmet.ac.uk

Inverness College
3 Longman Road, Longman Street, Inverness, IV1 1SA
Tel: (01463) 273000 Fax: (01463) 711977
E-mail: inverness.college@inverness.uhi.ac.uk
Web: www.inverness.uhi.ac.uk

James Watt College
Finnart Street, Greenock, Strathclyde, PA16 8HF
Tel: (01475) 724433 Fax: (01475) 888079
E-mail: enquiries@jameswatt.ac.uk
Web: www.jameswatt.ac.uk

Jewel and Esk College
Newbattle Road, Dalkeith, EH22 3AE
Tel: (0131) 660 1010 Fax: (0131) 663 2276
E-mail: info@jec.ac.uk
Web: www.jev.ac.uk

John Wheatley College
2 Haghill Road, Glasgow, G31 3SR
Tel: (0141) 588 1500 Fax: (0141) 763 2384
E-mail: advice@jwheatley.ac.uk
Web: www.jwheatley.ac.uk

Kilmarnock College
Holehouse Road, Kilmarnock, Ayrshire, KA3 7AT
Tel: (01563) 523501 Fax: (01563) 538182
E-mail: enquiries@kilmarnock.ac.uk
Web: www.kilmarnock.ac.uk

Further Education Colleges (Continued)

Langside College
50 Prospecthill Road, Glasgow, G42 9LB
Tel: (0141) 649 4991 Fax: (0141) 632 5252
E-mail: enquireuk@langside.ac.uk
Web: http//:www.langside.ac.uk

Lews Castle College
Stornoway, Isle of Lewis, HS2 0XR
Tel: (01851) 770000 Fax: (01851) 770001
E-mail: aofficele@lews.uhi.ac.uk
Web: www.lews.uhi.ac.uk

Moray College
Moray Street, Elgin, IV30 1JJ
Tel: (01343) 576000 Fax: (01343) 576005
E-mail: mc.admissions@moray.ac.uk
Web: www.moray.ac.uk

Motherwell College
1 Enterprise Way, Motherwell, ML1 2TX
Tel: (01698) 232323 Fax: (01698) 232527
E-mail: mcol@motherwell.co.uk
Web: www.motherwell.ac.uk

Newbattle Abbey College
Newbattle Road, Dalkeith, Midlothian, EH22 3LL
Tel: (0131) 663 1921 Fax: (0131) 654 0598
E-mail: office@newbattleabbeycollege.ac.uk
Web: www.newbattleabbeycollege.ac.uk

North Glasgow College
110 Flemington Street, Glasgow, G21 4BX
Tel: (0141) 558 9001 Fax: (0141) 558 9905
E-mail: infocentre@north-gla.ac.uk
Web: www.northglasgowcollege.ac.uk

North Highland College
Ormlie Road, Thurso, Caithness, KW14 7EE
Tel: (01847) 896161 Fax: (01847) 893872
E-mail: info@northhighland.ac.uk
Web: www.nhcscotland.com

Oatridge College
Ecclesmachan, Broxburn, West Lothian, EH52 6NH
Tel: (01506) 864800 Fax: (01506) 853373
E-mail: info@oatridge.ac.uk
Web: www.oatridge.ac.uk

Orkney College
East Road, Kirkwall, Orkney, KW15 1LX
Tel: (01856) 569000 Fax: (01856) 569001
E-mail: orkney.college@orkney.uhi.ac.uk
Web: www.orkney.uhi.ac.uk

Further Education Colleges (Continued)

Perth College
Crieff Road, Perth, PH1 2NX
Tel: (01738) 877000 Fax: (01738) 877001
E-mail: pc.enquiries@perth.uhi.ac.uk
Web: www.perth.ac.uk

Reid Kerr College
Renfrew Road, Paisley, PA3 4DR
Tel: (0141) 581 2222 Fax: (0141) 581 2204
E-mail: sservices@reidkerr.ac.uk
Web: www.reidkerr.ac.uk

Sabhal Mòr Ostaig (Skye)
Sleat, Isle of Skye, IV44 8RQ
Tel: (01471) 888000 Fax: (01471) 888001
E-mail: trusadh@smo.uhi.ac.uk
Web: www.smo.uhi.ac.uk

Shetland College
Gremista, Lerwick, ZE1 0PX
Tel: (01595) 695514 Fax: (01595) 694830
E-mail: admin.offices@shetland.uhi.ac.uk
Web: www.shetland.uhi.ac.uk

South Lanarkshire College
College Way, East Kilbride, G75 0NE
Tel: (01355) 807780 Fax: (01355) 807781
E-mail: admissions@slc.ac.uk
Web: www.south-lanarkshire-college.ac.uk

Stevenson College Edinburgh
Bankhead Avenue, Edinburgh, EH11 4DE
Tel: (0131) 535 4600 Fax: (0131) 535 4666
E-mail: info@stevenson.ac.uk
Web: www.stevenson.ac.uk

Stow College
43 Shamrock Street, Glasgow, G4 9LD
Tel: (0141) 332 1786 Fax: (0141) 332 5287
E-mail: enquiries@stow.ac.uk
Web: www.stow.ac.uk

West Lothian College
Almondvale Crescent, Livingstone, West Lothian, EH54 7EP
Tel: (01506) 418181 Fax: (01506) 409980
E-mail: enquiries@west-lothian.ac.uk
Web: www.west-lothian.ac.uk

HOUSING ASSOCIATIONS

Scottish Federation of Housing Associations
Fourth Floor, Pegasus House, 375 West George Street
Glasgow, G2 4LW
Tel: (0141) 332 8113 Fax: (0141) 332 9684
E-mail: sfha@sfha.co.uk
Web: www.sfha.co.uk

Chief Executive . . . . Miss Jacqui Watt

INFORMATION

Scottish Information Commissioner
Kinburn Castle
Doubledykes Road
St Andrews, KY16 9DS
Tel: (01334) 464610
Web: www.itspublicknowledge.info

LAND

Macaulay Land Use Research Institute
The Macaulay Institute, Craigiebuckler
Aberdeen, AB15 8QH
Tel: (01224) 498200 Fax: (01224) 311556
E-mail: enquiries@macaulay.ac.uk
Web: www.macaulay.ac.uk

Chairman . . . . .Mr Michael Gibson

Chief Executive . . . . .Mr Richard Aspinall

LAW

Supreme Courts of Scotland
Court of Session, Parliament Square
Edinburgh, EH1 1RQ
Tel: (0131) 225 2595 Fax: (0131) 240 6755
E-mail: supreme.courts@scotcourts.gov.uk
Web: www.scotcourts.gov.uk

Lord Justice General and
  Lord President of the Court
  of Session . . . . Rt Hon Lord Hamilton

LOCAL ENTERPRISE COMPANIES

SCOTTISH ENTERPRISE
Atrium Court, 50 Waterloo Street, Glasgow, G2 6HQ
Tel: (0141) 248 2700
E-mail: enquiries@scotent.co.uk
Web: www.scottish-enterprise.com

Chairman . . . . Mr Crawford Gillies

Chief Executive . . . . Ms Lena Wilson

Aberdeen
27 Albyn Place, Aberdeen, AB10 1DB
Tel: (01224) 252000 Fax: (01224) 213417

Bellshill
New Lanarkshire House, Dove Wynd
Strathclyde Business Park, Bellshill, ML4 3AD
Tel: (01698) 745454 Fax: (01698) 842211

Clydebank
Spectrum House, Clydebank Business Park
Clydebank, Glasgow, G81 2DR
Tel: (0141) 951 2121 Fax: (0141) 951 1907

Dumfries
Solway House, Dumfries Enterprise Park,
Tinwald Downs Road, Dumfries, DG1 3SJ
Tel: (01387) 245000 Fax: (01387) 246224

Dundee
Enterprise House, 3 Greenmarket, Dundee, DD1 4QB
Tel: (01382) 223100 Fax: (01382) 201319

Edinburgh
Apex House, 99 Haymarket Terrace, Edinburgh, EH12 5HD
Tel: (0131) 313 4000 Fax: (0131) 313 4231

Galashiels
Bridge Street, Galashiels, TD1 1SW
Tel: (01896) 758991 Fax: (01896) 758625

Glasgow
Atrium Court, 50 Waterloo Street, Glasgow, G2 6HQ
Tel: (0141) 204 1111 Fax: (0141) 248 1600

Glenrothes
Kingdom House, Saltire Centre, Glenrothes, Fife, KY6 2AQ
Tel: (01592) 623000 Fax: (01592) 623149

Kilmarnock
17/19 Hill Street, Kilmarnock, Ayrshire, KA3 1HA
Tel: (01563) 526623 Fax: (01563) 543636

Paisley
27 Causeyside Street, Paisley, PA1 1UL
Tel: (0141) 848 0101 Fax: (0141) 848 6930

Stirling
Laurel House, Laurelhill Business Park, Stirling, FK7 9JQ
Tel: (01786) 451919 Fax: (01786) 478123

HIGHLANDS AND ISLANDS ENTERPRISE

Highlands and Islands Enterprise
Cowan House, Inverness Retail and Business Park, Inverness, IV2 7GF
Tel: (01463) 234171 Fax: (01463) 244469
E-mail: info@hient.co.uk
Web: www.hie.co.uk

Chairman . . . . Mr William Roe

Chief Executive . . . . Mr Sandy Cumming CBE

Argyll and the Islands
The Enterprise Centre, Kilmory Industrial Estate
Lochgilphead, PA31 8SH
Tel: (01546) 602281 Fax: (01546) 603964
E-mail: lochgilphead@hient.co.uk

Area Manager . . . . Mr Douglas Cowan

Aviemore
Room 1/2, Aviemore Business Centre
Grampian Road, Aviemore, PH22 1RH
Tel: (01479) 810188 Fax: (01479) 811183
E-mail: inverness@hient.co.uk

Area Manager . . . . Mr Martin Johnson

Dingwall
Earl Thorfinn House, 6 Druimchat View,
Dingwall Business Park, Dingwall, IV15 9XL
Tel: (01349) 868360 Fax: (01349) 868361
E-mail: info@hient.co.uk

Area Manager . . . . Mr Martin Johnson

OTHER CONTACTS

Highlands and Islands Enterprise (Continued)

Fort William
St Mary's House, Gordon Square, Fort William, PH33 6DY
Tel: (01397) 704326 Fax: (01397) 705309
E-mail: fortwilliam@hient.co.uk

Area Manager . . . . Mr Robert Muir

Moray
Horizon Scotland, The Enterprise Park
Forres, Moray, IV36 2AB
Tel: (01309) 696000 Fax: (01309) 696001
E-mail: forres@hient.co.uk

Area Manager . . . . Mr Callum MacPhearson

Orkney
14 Queen Street, Kirkwall, Orkney, KW15 1JE
Tel: (01856) 874638 Fax: (01856) 872915
E-mail: kirkwall@hient.co.uk

Area Manager . . . . Mr Ken Grant

Shetland
3 North Ness Business Park
Lerwick, Shetland, ZE1 0LZ
Tel: (01595) 744940 Fax: (01595) 693208
E-mail: shetland@hient.co.uk

Area Manager . . . . Mr Stuart Robertson

Skye
Kings House, The Green, Portree, Isle of Skye, IV51 9BS
Tel: (01478) 612841 Fax: (01478) 612164
E-mail: portree@hient.co.uk

Area Manager . . . . Mr Robert Muir

Stornoway
9 James Street, Stornoway, Isle of Lewis, HS1 2QN
Tel: (01851) 703703 Fax: (01851) 704130
E-mail: stornoway@hient.co.uk

Area Manager . . . . Mr Archie Macdonald

Highlands and Islands Enterprise (Continued)

Sutherland
The Links, Golspie Business Park, Golspie, Sutherland, KW10 6SN
Tel: (01408) 633872 Fax: (01408) 633873
E-mail: thurso@hient.co.uk

Area Manager . . . . Mr Roy Kirk

Thurso
Tollemache House, High Street, Thurso, Caithness KW14 8AZ
Tel: (01847) 896115 Fax: (01847) 893383
E-mail: thurso@hient.co.uk

Area Manager . . . . Mr Roy Kirk

POLICE
Central Scotland Police
Randolphfield, Stirling, FK8 2HD
Tel: (01786) 456000 Fax: (01786) 451177
Web: www.centralscotland.police.uk

Chief Constable . . . . Mr Kevin Smith

Dumfries and Galloway Constabulary
Police Headquarters, Cornwall Mount, Dumfries, DG1 1PZ

Tel: (0845) 600 5701
Web: www.dg.police.uk

Chief Constable . . . . Mr Patrick Shearer

Fife Constabulary
Detroit Road, Glenrothes, Fife, KY6 2RJ
Tel: (0845) 600 5702 Fax: (01592) 418444
E-mail: force.executive@fife.pnn.police.uk

Chief Constable . . . . Mrs Norma Graham QPM

Grampian Police
Police HQ, Queen Street, Aberdeen, AB10 1ZA
Tel: (0845) 600 5700 Fax: (01224) 643366
E-mail: servicecentre@grampian.pnn.police.uk
Web: www.grampian.police.uk

Chief Constable . . . . Mr Colin W McKerracher CBE QPM

Police (Continued)

HM Chief Inspector of Constabulary
Ground Floor, Ashley House, 2 Monck Street, London, SW1P 2BQ
Tel: (020) 7035 2001 Fax: (020) 7035 2176
Web: www.inspectorates.homeoffice.gov.uk/hmic

HM Chief Inspector of
Constabulary . . . . Sir Ronnie Flannagan

Lothian and Borders Police
Fettes Avenue, Edinburgh, EH4 1RB
Tel: (0131) 311 3131 Fax: (0131) 311 3085
Web: www.lbp.police.uk

Chief Constable . . . . Mr David Strang

Northern Constabulary
Police Headquarters, Old Perth Road, Inverness, IV2 3SY
Tel: (08456) 033388 Fax: (01463) 230800
E-mail: mail@northern.pnn.police.uk

Chief Constable . . . . Mr Ian Latimer

Police Advisory Board for Scotland
Area 1WR, St Andrews House, Regent Road, Edinburgh, EH1 3DG
Tel: (0131) 244 5143 Fax: (0131) 244 2666
E-mail: scott.mcewen@scotland.gsi.gov.uk
Web: www.scotland.gsi.gov.uk

Chairman . . . . Cabinet Secretary for Justice

Secretary . . . . Mr Scott McEwen

Scottish Police College
Tulliallan Castle, Kincardine, Fife, FK10 4BE
Tel: (01259) 732000 Fax: (01259) 732100
E-mail: mail@spsa.pnn.police.uk
Web: www.tullialan.police.uk

Director . . . . Mr John Geates

Strathclyde Police
173 Pitt Street, Glasgow, G2 4JS
Tel: (0141) 532 2000 Fax: (0141) 532 2475
E-mail: contactus@strathclyde.pnn.police.uk
Web: www.strathclyde.police.uk

Chief Constable . . . . Mr Stephen House QPM

Police (Continued)

Tayside Police
PO Box 59, West Bell Street, Dundee, DD1 9JU
Tel: (01382) 223200 Fax: (01382) 200449
E-mail: executive@tayside.pnn.police.uk
Web: tayside.police.uk

Chief Constable . . . . Ms Justine Curran

PUBLIC APPOINTMENTS
Commissioner for Public Appointments in Scotland
MWB Business Exchange, 9-10 St Andrews Square
Edinburgh, EH2 2AF
E-mail: info@publicappointments.org
Tel: (0131) 718 6058

Commissioner . . . . Ms Karen Carlton

REGISTER OFFICE
General Register Office for Scotland
Ladywell House, Ladywell Road, Edinburgh, EH12 7TF
Tel: (0131) 334 0380 Fax: (0131) 314 4344
E-mail: records@gro-scotland.gsi.gov.uk
Web: www.gro-scotland.gov.uk

Registrar General . . . . Mr Duncan Macniven

RESEARCH
Moredun Research Institute
International Research Centre,
Pentlands Science Park, Bush Loan, Penicuik, EH26 0PZ
Tel: (0131) 445 5111 Fax: (0131) 445 6111
Web: www.moredun.ac.uk

Chairman . . . . .Mr John Jeffery

Director . . . . .Professor Julie Fitzpatrick

ROYAL SOCIETY
The Royal Society of Edinburgh
22-26 George Street, Edinburgh, EH2 2PQ
Tel: (0131) 240 5022 Fax: (0131) 240 5025
E-mail: rse@royalsoced.org.uk
Web: www.royalsoced.org.uk

Chief Executive.................. Dr William Duncan

SCOTTISH PRISONER COMLAINTS

Scottish Prisons Complaints Commission
Government Buildings, Broomhouse Drive, Edinburgh, EH11 3XD
Tel: (0131) 244 8423 Fax: (0131) 244 8430
E-mail: spcc@scotland.gsi.gov.uk
Web: www.scotland.gov.uk

Commissioner *(Acting)* .... Mr Richard Smith

SCOTTISH PUBLIC SERVICES

Scottish Public Services Ombudsman
4 Melville Street, Edinburgh, EH3 7NS
Tel: (0800) 377 7330 Fax: (0800) 377 7331
E-mail: ask@spso.org.uk
Web: spso.org.uk

Ombudsman .... Mr Jim Martin

SECRETARY OF COMMISSIONS

Secretary of Commissions
2J North, Victoria Quay, Edinburgh, EH6 6QQ
Tel: (0131) 244 5532
E-mail: tim.barraclough@scotland.gov.uk

Secretary of Commissions .... Mr Tim Barraclough

STATISTICS
UK Statistics Authority
Statistics House, Tredegar Park, Newport, NP10 8XG
Tel: (0845) 601 3034 Fax: (01633) 456179
E-mail: info@statistics.gov.uk
Web: www.statisticsauthority.gov.uk

Chairman........................ Sir Michael Scholar

TAXATION
HM Revenue and Customs
100 Parliament Street, London, SW1A 2BQ
Tel: (020) 7147 0000 Fax: (020) 7147 2186
Web: www.hmrc.gov.uk

Chairman . . . . Mr Mike Clasper CBE

National Insurance Contributions Office
Longbenton, NE98 1ZZ
Tel: (0191) 213 5005

Director . . . . Mr Alan Fisher

HM Revenue and Customs Adjudicator's Office
8th Floor, Euston Tower
286 Euston Road, London, NW1 3US
Tel: (0300) 057 1111 Fax (0300) 057 1212
E-mail: adjudicators@gtnet.gov.uk
Web: www.adjudicatorsoffice.gov.uk

Revenue Adjudicator . . . . Ms Judy Clements

HM Customs and Excise, Executive Unit, Scotland
44 York Place, Edinburgh, EH1 3JW
Tel: (0131) 469 2000 Fax: (0131) 469 7333

Collector . . . . Mr Ian Mackay

TRADE UNIONS
Scottish TUC
333 Woodlands Road, Glasgow, G3 6NG
Tel: (0141) 337 8100 Fax: (0141) 337 8101
Web: www.stuc.org.uk

General Secretary . . . . Mr Grahame Smith

TRANSPORT
Office of Rail Regulation
1 Kemble Street, London, WC2B 4AN
Tel: (020) 7282 2000 Fax: (020) 7282 2040
E-mail: [firstname.surname@orr.gsi.gov.uk
Web: www.rail-reg.gov.uk

Chairman . . . . Mrs Anna Walker

Chief Executive . . . . Mr Bill Emery

Transport (Continued)

Strathclyde Partnership for Transport
Consort House, 12 West George Street, Glasgow, G2 1HN
Tel: (0141) 333 3100 Fax: (0141) 333 3703
Web: www.spt.co.uk

Chairman . . . . Cllr Alistair Watson

Chief Executive . . . . Mr Ron Culley

UNIVERSITIES AND HIGHER EDUCATION COLLEGES
University of Aberdeen
King's College, Regent Walk, Aberdeen, AB24 3FX
Tel: (01224) 272000
E-mail: sras@abdn.ac.uk
Web: www.abdn.ac.uk

University of Abertay
40 Bell Street, Dundee, DD1 1HG
Tel: (01382) 308000
E-mail: sro@abertay.ac.uk
Web: www.abertay.ac.uk

University of Dundee
Nethergate, Dundee, DD1 4HN
Tel: (01382) 383000
E-mail: university@dundee.ac.uk
Web: www.dundee.ac.uk

Edinburgh College of Art
74 Lauriston Place, Edinburgh, EH3 9DF
Tel: (0131) 221 6000
E-mail: registry@eca.ac.uk
Web: www.eca.ac.uk

Edinburgh Napier University
Craiglockhart Campus, Edinburgh, EH14 1DJ
Tel: (0131) 444 2266
E-mail: info@napier.ac.uk
Web: www.napier.ac.uk

University of Edinburgh
Old College, South Bridge, Edinburgh, EH8 9YL
Tel: (0131) 650 1000 Fax: (0131) 650 2147
E-mail: communications.office@ed.ac.uk
Web: www.ed.ac.uk

Universities and Higher Education Colleges (Continued)

Glasgow Caledonian University
City Campus, 70 Cowcaddens Road, Glasgow, G4 0BA
Tel: (0141) 331 3000
E-mail: help@gcal.ac.uk
Web: www.gcal.ac.uk

Glasgow School of Art
167 Renfrew Street, Glasgow, G3 6RQ
Tel: (0141) 353 4500
E-mail: info@gsa.ac.uk
Web: www.gsa.ac.uk

University of Glasgow
Glasgow, G12 8QQ
Tel: (0141) 330 2000
E-mail: ugenquiries@gla.ac.uk
Web: www.gla.ac.uk

Heriot-Watt University
Riccarton, Edinburgh, EH14 4AS
Tel: (0131) 449 5111
E-mail: ugadmissions@hw.ac.uk
Web: www.hw.ac.uk

UHI Millennium Institute
Executive Office, Ness Walk, Inverness, IV3 5SQ
Tel: (01463) 279000
E-mail: eo@uhi.ac.uk
Web: www.uhi.ac.uk

The Open University in Scotland
10 Drumsheugh Gardens, Edinburgh, EH3 7QJ
Tel: (0131) 226 3851
E-mail: scotland@open.ac.uk
Web: www.open.ac.uk

Queen Margaret University
Queen Margaret University Drive, Edinburgh, EH21 6UU
Tel: (0131) 474 0000
E-mail: admissions@qmu.ac.uk
Web: www.qmu.ac.uk

Robert Gordon University
Schoolhill, Aberdeen, AB10 1FR
Tel: (01224) 262000
E-mail: admissions@rgu.ac.uk
Web: www.rgu.ac.uk

Universities and Higher Education Colleges (Continued)

Royal Scottish Academy of Music and Drama
100 Renfrew Street, Glasgow, G2 3BD
Tel: (0141) 332 4101
Web: www.rsamd.ac.uk

University of St Andrews
College Gate, St Andrews, Fife, KY16 9AJ
Tel: (01334) 476161
E-mail: admissions@st-andrews.ac.uk
Web: www.st-andrews.ac.uk

Scottish Agricultural College
King's Buildings, West Mains Road, Edinburgh, EH9 3JG
Tel: (0131) 535 4000
E-mail: recruitment@sac.ac.uk
Web: www.sac.ac.uk/learning

University of Stirling
Stirling, FK9 4LA
Tel: (01786) 473171
E-mail: recruitment@stir.ac.uk
Web: www.stir.ac.uk

University of Strathclyde
16 Richmond Street, Glasgow, G1 1XQ
Tel: (0141) 552 4400
Web: www.strath.ac.uk

University of the West Scotland
Ayr Campus, Beech Grove, Ayr, KA8 0SR
Tel: (01292) 886000
E-mail: info@uws.ac.uk
Web: www.uws.ac.uk

WATERWAYS

British Waterways Scotland
Canal House, Applecross Street, Glasgow, G4 9SP
Tel: (0141) 332 6936 Fax: (0141) 331 1688
Web: www.britishwaterways.co.uk/scotland

Director . . . . Mr Steve Dunlop

Caledonian Canal
Seaport Marina, Inverness, IV3 5LE
Tel: (01463) 725504 Fax: (01463) 710942

Highlands Canals Manager . . . . Mr Russell Thomson

Waterways (Continued)

Highland Canals
Canal Office, Seaport Marina
Muirtown Wharf, Inverness, IV3 5LE
Tel: (01463) 725500 Fax: (01463) 710942

Highlands Canals Manager . . . . Mr Russell Thomson

Lowlands Canals
Canal House, 1 Apple Cross Street, Glasgow, G4 9SP
Tel: (0141) 332 6936 Fax: (0141) 331 1688
Web: www.britishwaterways.co.uk

Lowland Canals Manager . . . . Ms Elaine Griffin

Waterways Ombudsman
PO Box 35, York, YO60 6WW
Tel: (01347) 879075
E-mail: enquiries@waterways-ombudsman.org
Web: www.waterways-ombudsman.org

Ombudsman . . . . Ms Hilary Bainbridge

WELSH ASSEMBLY

Welsh Assembly
Cardiff Bay, Cardiff, CF99 1NA
Tel: (0845) 010 5500
Web: www.assemblywales.org

Presiding Officer . . . . Rt Hon Lord Elis Thomas AM

First Minister . . . . Carwyn Jones AM

INDEX

INDEX

INDEX

INDEX

INDEX

INDEX

Page

Page

INDEX

INDEX

INDEX

INDEX

INDEX

INDEX

INDEX

INDEX

Page   Page

INDEX

INDEX

Page